GEORGE WASHINGTON'S
GREAT GAMBLE

AND THE SEA BATTLE THAT WON THE AMERICAN REVOLUTION

JAMES L. NELSON

New York   Chicago   San Francisco   Lisbon   London   Madrid   Mexico City
Milan   New Delhi   San Juan   Seoul   Singapore   Sydney   Toronto

Library of Congress Cataloging-in-Publication Data

Nelson, James L.
     George Washington's great gamble / James Nelson.
        p.   cm.
     Includes bibliographical references and index.
     ISBN 0-07-162679-4
       1. Yorktown (Va.)—History—Siege, 1781.   2. Washington, George, 1732–1799—
Military leadership.   3. United States—History—Revolution, 1775–1783—
Participation, French.   4. Southern States—History—Revolution, 1775–1783.
     I. Title.
     E241.Y6N45   2010
    973.3'37—dc22   2010009188

1 2 3 4 5 6 7 8 9 10 11 12 13 14 15   WFR/WFR   1 9 8 7 6 5 4 3 2 1 0

ISBN 978-0-07-162679-8
MHID   0-07-162679-4

McGraw-Hill books are available at special quantity discounts to use as premiums and
sales promotions or for use in corporate training programs. To contact a representative,
please e-mail us at bulksales@mcgraw-hill.com.

For Elizabeth, Nathaniel, Jonathan, and Abigail . . .
mes petits poulets

CONTENTS

In any operations, and under all circumstances, a decisive naval superiority is to be considered as a fundamental principle, and the basis upon which every hope of success must ultimately depend.
—GEORGE WASHINGTON *to the Comte de Rochambeau*
July 15, 1780

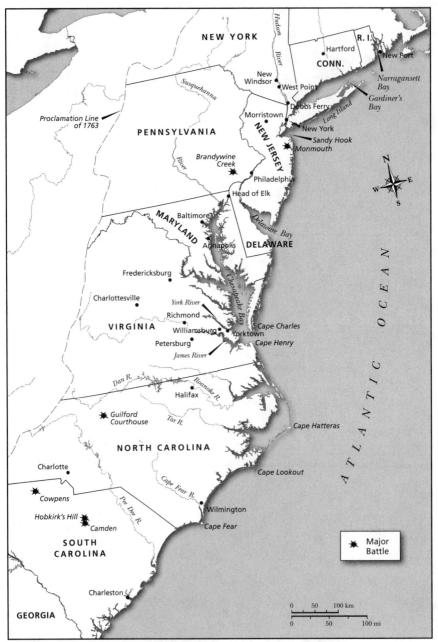

AMERICA'S ATLANTIC COAST

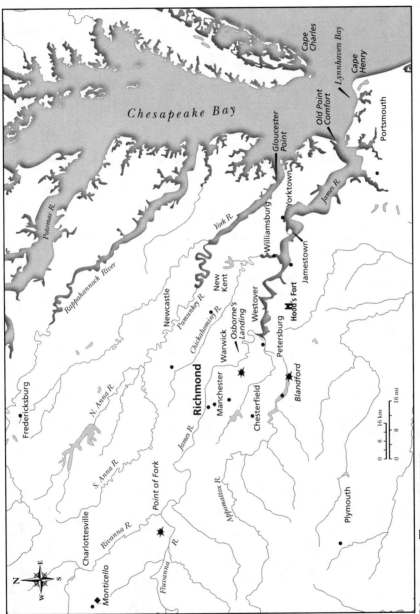

VIRGINIA TIDEWATER

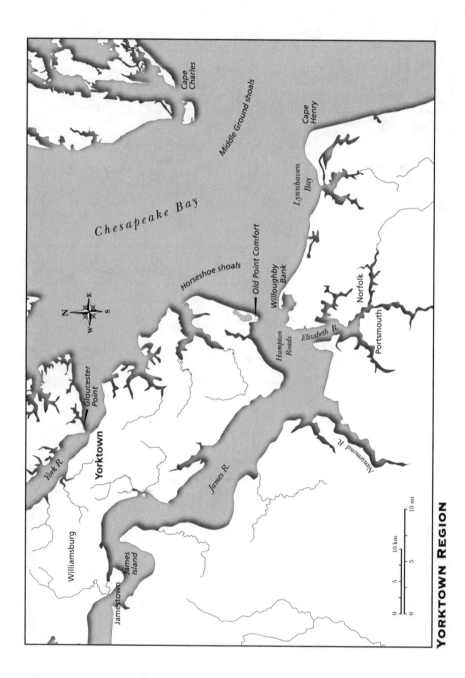

YORKTOWN REGION

Prologue

Yorktown, Virginia
October 14, 1781

THE EVENING IS cold, and the Marquis de Lafayette wraps himself tighter in his greatcoat and pushes his cocked hat down on his head. Around him, the freshly turned earth, the broken landscape, the town of York off to the north are washed golden by the last rays of the sun setting in a clear western sky. The dome of sky overhead is a great arch of variegated color—brilliant orange in the west fading to white, then deepening to pale blue, then navy blue like the cloth of his uniform coat, and finally night-black in the east. The wide York River is a great dark plain, and the ships riding at anchor there are lost in shadow.

General Lafayette is twenty-four, lean and hard. For three years, he has been at the forefront of the fighting in the American War for Independence. For the past half year, he and his ragged band of veteran troops have been marching around Virginia, dogging the army of Lord Charles Cornwallis. Lafayette has marched for days at a time through brutal heat and driving rain, has slept in the open, and has lived on salt rations—and little of that. He is in the most vigorous health of his life.

He and his army chased Cornwallis's superior force when able and made "retrograde motions"—retreats—when necessary. The armies tangled twice, in the battles of Spencer's Ordinary and Green Springs. Always, Lafayette tried to keep just out of Cornwallis's reach while never allowing the British general to see how weak he really was.

But all that is over. Cornwallis and his eighty-three hundred men are less than a mile away, hunkered down behind the earthworks surrounding Yorktown (as York is also called), and Lafayette has no fear of him now. More than seventeen thousand American and French troops surround his lordship, and a massive fleet of French ships of the line rides at anchor near the mouth of the Chesapeake Bay. The Americans have dug a trench parallel to Cornwallis's works and will soon dig another that is closer still, moving their heavy guns within 500 yards of the British defenses. After six years of war, so many lost chances, and so many bitter defeats, it is almost over.

The young Frenchman looks over the heaped earth that forms a low wall along the opposite face of the 3-foot-deep trench in front of him. Beyond, lit by the setting sun, is the piled earthwork of the British battery known as Redoubt Number 10. To the left, he can see Redoubt Number 9, larger than Number 10. These batteries, detached from the main defenses at Yorktown, guard the left side of the British line. As long as their cannons are in the hands of British troops, the Americans can advance their siege works no closer. Tonight, Lafayette intends to change that.

He is nervous, and, being young and French, he does not embrace the stoicism of his hero and mentor George Washington. He is pacing and drumming his fingers. The men who will be assaulting Number 10 are his men, the light infantry under his command. Many of them marched with him from New York in February. They were with him on the heights of Richmond in April, waiting for Major General William Phillips and the turncoat Benedict Arnold to attack. They stood with him in the great fusillade of shot at the Battle of Green Springs in July. They shadowed the British army with him through the long, hot summer until Cornwallis went to earth at Yorktown. Lafayette does not want to send these men into the British guns. He wants to lead them in.

Six weeks ago, he would have done just that, but six weeks ago the Virginia tidewater was not at the center of the American Revolution. At the end of August, the focus of the 1781 campaign season was still an attack on Sir Henry Clinton in New York City. Virginia and Cornwallis had been a sideshow. But that has all changed now, and with it Lafayette's status in the Continental Army. He is no longer commanding a motley force of twelve hundred troops. He is now one of three major-generals in the largest American force on the continent.

He has other reasons to be nervous. There are more than seven thousand French troops with the Americans outside Yorktown. Taking Redoubt Number 9 tonight will be the responsibility of the French infantry under the command of Baron de Vioménil. The two columns,

French and American, will be advancing at the same time, hitting their respective redoubts at the same moment. Lafayette wants the American light infantry to make a good show next to the professional soldiers of his native country. He will later write to a friend, "You will understand that my heart was beating rapidly for the reputation of my light infantry."

He looks to the west. The sun is half lost behind the ridgeline of the distant hills. Soon now.

In the American camp, Sergeant Joseph Plumb Martin is prepared for some sort of action, but he does not know what. His corps of miners and sappers has been ordered to the trenches, so he knows that "something extraordinary, serious or comical, [is] going forward."

Martin has been serving in the Continental Army since before the Declaration of Independence was signed more than five years ago. He fought at the battles of Brooklyn and Monmouth and suffered through winters of terrible cold and deprivation at Valley Forge and Morristown. And now, like the men around him, he senses that this long, long road may be reaching its end at last. Six weeks before, no one could imagine an end to the war. Now they are contemplating the very real possibility that American independence is at hand.

The lieutenant gives a guttural order, and Martin and four hundred others rise in the fading light and file out of camp. They head toward the trench, known in military parlance as a "parallel," that Sergeant Martin had a hand in digging just days ago. Some of the men are sappers and miners like him, others light infantry, their well-tended muskets unloaded and resting on their shoulders as they march. The ground around them is open, broken by small hills and ravines and steep defiles where streams run through. There are few trees to be seen.

The men hop down into the shallow trench—7 feet wide by 3 feet deep—and move east, toward the river. They move silently, hidden by the mound of earth between them and the British redoubt a few hundred yards away.

Near the eastern end of the parallel, they are ordered to hold up. Martin can see a few officers fixing bayonets on long wooden staves to fashion makeshift pikes. That means they'll be making an assault on the British works tonight. A veteran like Martin can tell that much from what the officers are up to.

Above and ahead of him, standing on the ground above the parallel, Martin sees a group of officers huddled in conversation. One is the Marquis de Lafayette, the French general, just a few years older than he is. Another is Lieutenant Colonel Alexander Hamilton. Martin grunts, shaking his head. Hamilton is a staff officer, more used to wielding a pen than a sword. Playing at soldiers, now?

The officers are talking in soft tones, and so is everyone else. No order has been passed. The men just know. Even the guns are silent along the line. Martin can hear crickets and the soft lap of water on the riverbank not far off. From time to time, a musket bangs out loud in the still evening—a nervous picket taking a shot at a moving shadow or someone in camp trying his skill on a goose flying overhead.

The meeting of the officers breaks up, and soon the sappers and miners are called forward. They move along the ditch as a body, past the grim-faced light infantry. The sun is well down now, the sky turning a uniformly deep gray, but they can still see well enough. At the end of the parallel, they are halted again, and axes are handed out. A young captain walks down the line, the legs of his white breeches gleaming unnaturally bright in the deepening twilight. *Redoubt Number 10,* he says. *That's for us. The one on the left there, you can still see it. Right hard against the bluff.* His accent is New York.

Martin nods. Of course. Those redoubts are smack in the middle of where the Americans need to extend their lines. They have to go before the works can advance any closer to Yorktown.

He hears someone mention New London, and a murmur goes through the men, a low growl as if from an angry beast. Over the past few days, they've heard that Benedict Arnold has been turned loose on Connecticut, just as he was turned loose on Virginia last spring. The mere mention of Arnold's name is enough to raise their ire, but there is more. The rumor is that troops in Fort Griswold who called for quarter were summarily butchered on Arnold's order. Now there is talk of taking revenge on the soldiers in Redoubt Number 10 for the sins of the traitor. To the men in the ditch, this seems like a just thing. Give no quarter.

The captain is still explaining the plan. *On the word, we'll move forward, sappers and miners first,* he explains. *The redoubts are near wrecked by the artillery, but there's still abatis there, and the sappers are to cut it away to clear*

the way for the light infantry. Then the light infantry will do their work with bay-
onets. Ain't even loading muskets at all.

Martin can see the abatis in his mind—saplings and the thin tops of
trees, cut to wicked points and mounted to jut like lances from the sides
of the redoubts. It is almost impossible to get through them, and the
enemy in his works will shoot you down like a bear in a pit while you try.

So the sappers and miners are sent in first to clear it away. And what
stops the sappers and miners from being shot down? Nothing. Luck,
maybe. God. Beyond that, nothing.

The watchword is "Rochambeau," the captain says. Rochambeau . . .
Sergeant Martin likes this. Say it quick and it sounds like "Rush on,
boys!" That will indeed be the watchword as the musket balls begin to
fly. "Rush on, boys!"

It is full dark now, and Joseph Plumb Martin and the rest are ordered
forward again, up and out of the trench, moving toward the redoubt
that is barely visible as a darker loom against a starry sky. After 50 feet
they halt, and the order goes down the line for the men to lie down and
wait for the signal to advance: three shells fired from a battery not far
from where the troops are hidden.

The grass is wet and cold with evening dew. Martin closes his eyes for
a moment. He can smell the grass, the fresh-turned earth of the parallel behind him, a slight salt tang from the brackish river. Wood smoke
from the cook fires in the camps. Sweat and damp wool from the men
huddled near him in the grass.

The waiting is the worst. Joseph Plumb Martin has done this many
times, and he knows. The waiting, with quiet all around broken only by
the breathing of the men, men clearing their throats, yawning. Fear lies
over you like a blanket while you wait for the fighting to begin, so oppres-
sive you want to kick it off, except that it feels better to remain absolutely
still. *Dear God, I've come this far,* he thinks. *It can't end for me tonight, it just
can't.* To be killed tonight would be so frightfully unfair. But if there's
one thing he knows from five years of soldiering, it's that fairness does
not exist in war.

He opens his eyes and there, burning in the night sky, are the shells
that say it's time to go. He pushes himself up, sees that no one else is
moving, and then realizes that the lights are Jupiter and Venus, bright
in the evening sky. He slumps to the ground again.

For long minutes, Martin and the rest lie in the cold grass. Far to the left, a mile or more, French artillery opens up on the British lines, and then, like a distant echo, Martin hears guns from across the river in Gloucester. *A feint*, he thinks. *Make 'em think we're coming at them from the left.* He has not been told this—a sergeant of the sappers and miners does not need to know these things—but he's seen it before, and he knows he's right. He hopes it fools the Redcoats.

Then suddenly, overhead, trailing their tails of light like comets, three shells arc across the western sky, and they are most certainly shells this time and not wayward planets. *Up! Up! Up!* The captain is running down the line of prone men, crouching low and moving fast, and there is just enough light for Martin to see him making an "up" gesture with his hands.

Martin is on his feet with no notion of how he got there, his ax held across his chest like a musket. The men in front are moving, and soon Martin is moving, too, one of a long column of men moving silently through the night, their pace a quick walk. Redoubt Number 10 is ahead, a black hump against the sky, no more. There are stars above them and spots of light scattered around the countryside—lanterns or small fires—but beyond that is blackness.

Lord Charles Cornwallis is standing on the rim of the earthworks that surround Yorktown. His sick and exhausted men have dug more than a mile of works, aided by hundreds of escaped slaves who have flocked to the British ensign.

Now he has had to turn the slaves out because he cannot feed them. What will become of them he does not know, but some may starve and others may be recaptured and punished. He had no choice. His own men will be starving soon. Food, medicine, and ammunition are running low. There is no fodder for the horses, and hundreds have been shot and tossed into the York River, where their bloated corpses float like so much flotsam in the wake of a storm.

He walks slowly toward the east, looking out at the American lines. The sky overhead is a dull gray in the dying light, but Cornwallis can see thin trails of smoke from the hundreds of cook fires in the American camp, well out of range of the 18-pounder cannons that make up most of the British artillery. To the west, he can see a few stars beginning to show, and low on the horizon and already brilliant, Jupiter and Venus.

Behind him, he hears General Charles O'Hara stumble and curse in a deep Irish tone, and then a few notes of concern from the cadre of aides following behind. The footing on the soft earthworks is difficult. Cornwallis's feet sink as he walks. The works are far too soft to stand up to the heavy siege guns of the French, and they are being torn apart.

Cornwallis pauses again, his eyes sweeping the landscape before him, now all but lost in darkness. It is eerily quiet out there, and that has his nerves on edge. The French and American guns have hardly stopped since approaching within range four days ago, and now they are silent. He is turning to comment on this to O'Hara when suddenly the darkness to the west is split with light and noise as the French artillery fires, a dozen huge guns blasting their wicked flames behind solid shot.

The earl watches the French battery for a moment, then looks east, but he sees nothing in the darkness in that direction. To the west, the siege guns are still hammering away. Then a flash of light above him catches his eye, and he looks up in time to see the dying trails of three shells dropping toward the horizon. It is a signal, but for what?

A feint off to the right there, m'Lord, O'Hara asks, *or do ya think the bastards are coming at last?*

Cornwallis is asking himself that very question. Is this a genuine attack? If so, will it be a general assault all along the line? General Washington and the Comte de Rochambeau must be eager to be done with this siege. Every day, Cornwallis lives in hope that Sir Henry Clinton—commander-in-chief of the British forces in North America—will lead the fleet from New York to the relief of his besieged army. The French and Americans must be living in fear of the same thing.

They'll want me in their pocket before Clinton shows up, Cornwallis thinks. He turns to O'Hara. *I think they are coming this time, General,* he says. *Let us have all the batteries firing. We'll sweep the field.*

O'Hara is bellowing orders almost before Cornwallis is done speaking. In mere minutes, the British guns all along the line are thundering out, spraying round shot and grape across the open ground before the earthworks. The sound envelops Cornwallis, pressing in on him, and muzzle flashes light up the night.

It has come to this, Cornwallis thinks. Not long ago, he and his army were the masters of Virginia and the Carolinas. Now he is backed into a corner, trying to hold on to the last few square miles he possesses.

It has been nearly a year since he and Clinton took Charleston, South Carolina, after a siege much like the one now before him, except that then it was the Americans who were trapped behind their works. He has spent much of the intervening year chasing Nathanael Greene's army all over the godforsaken Carolinas, enduring forced marches through driving rain and killing heat, struggling over rivers as wide as the Thames. When that game exhausted itself, he spent months flailing around in pursuit of some approach that would affect the outcome of this bloody war, meanwhile being dogged by Lafayette. And all that effort led to this, trapped in damnable Yorktown, and if the commander-in-chief whom he despises does not come soon, it will be over for him.

I am so tired, he thinks. *I am so dreadfully, bloody, damnably tired.*

They move onward, surprisingly calm and ordered for a night attack, and Joseph Plumb Martin feels his fear melt away. This is a phenomenon he has come to know, the moment when the gripping fear of waiting dissolves into the calm of action. The image in his mind is of a chunk of sugar dissolving in hot coffee. That is what he has always imagined. Sugar in coffee.

Martin can sense the redoubt looming ahead of him. He is maybe fifty men back from the front of the line, which means that those ahead must be nearly upon the abatis. And then the night seems to burst to life around them. Off to the left, clear as a gunshot over the distant sound of the French guns, he hears a voice, a German voice, and he can hear a note of panic in the shouted word *Werda?* A pause follows—a second or two, no more—and then he sees brilliant flashes of light from where he heard the voice, long thin columns of flame, the muzzle flashes of muskets, and the shouts of the men in Redoubt Number 9.

Joseph Plumb Martin, still quickly advancing, pulls his eyes from the fighting to the left just as the edge of the redoubt ahead of him bursts into flame, dozens of muskets firing at once, the familiar, rapid *pow* . . . *bang* of priming and charge going off, the whistle of musket balls, the festive sight of all those muzzle flashes in the dark. The redoubt is lit up for a second, as if in a flash of lightning, and Martin can see the brown earth, the line of men just visible from the chest up looking down the barrels of their muskets, and the wicked-looking abatis thrusting malevolently toward him.

The sound of heavy artillery suddenly doubles and then triples, and Martin sees that the British guns have begun firing all along the defensive works. The men in front of him are starting to spread out as they move forward, their pace quickening, the fire from the top of the redoubt uninterrupted. The British and German troops holed up in Yorktown are the cream of the army, the 23rd Brigade, the 71st, the Anspach Battalions, the light infantry. Whoever is in that redoubt knows how to load and fire fast and calmly, no matter how many rebels might be charging at them.

Men are disappearing. To his right and left, Martin can see men simply vanish, and he guesses that they are being shot down, falling behind as the rest rush on. Then his foot comes down ahead of him, but this time it meets no earth, just void, and he tumbles forward. The ax flies from his hands and his hands go out to break his fall, and then he hits the ground—soft, pungent earth under him—and grunts and rolls to a stop.

For an instant, he lies still, his senses knocked out of him. Then he realizes he's in a hole made by the relentless shelling from the American lines. The ground all around the redoubt must be pocked with holes big enough to swallow an ox. Realizing this, he actually smiles. At least some of the men he thought had been shot down must have fallen into holes like this one.

In the dark he feels for his ax, finds it, and grabs it again. There is an odd stillness in his hole as the battle swirls 4 feet above his head—as if he had found a small but sheltered lee in a hurricane—and he gets the momentary idea that he could lie in his sanctuary, maybe take a nap, and let the battle unfold without him. But it is not a serious idea, and in the next instant, he is on his feet and scrambling up the far side of his hole, back into the fight.

The entire edge of the redoubt, only a hundred feet away now, is rippling with musket fire that illuminates from inside the great pall of smoke hanging just above the works. The shouts of men, both attackers and defenders, threaten to drown out even the continuous crash of muskets and the roar of heavy guns, and Martin is sure he can hear the shouting of French troops off to the left, their tones oddly lilting and, to his ear, not at all military.

He reaches the abatis, halting just inches from the ragged point of a small oak trunk, and pulls back his ax and swings. The blade bites into wood, and he wriggles it free and swings again. Over the past decade and a half, on his grandfather's farm and in the army, he has spent more hours than he could ever count wielding an ax, and his muscles fall immediately into the rhythm—swing, strike, disengage, return—and chips fly from the trunk. Bullets make little dust clouds around his feet, but he does not pause.

All around him, he can feel men rushing past, and he hears shouts, *The fort's our own! Rush on, boys! Rush on!*

Swing, strike, wriggle the blade free. A bullet hits the abatis just inches from his ax, spraying splinters into the night. Martin flinches, feeling wood strike his face, then opens his eyes and draws the blade back again. His arms move in their practiced swing, and the abatis falls away, leaving a gap wide enough for a man. Even before the trunk has stopped rolling, one of the attacking troops rushes through. He is Rhode Island infantry, a black man in a white uniform, his eyes wide, the sweat on his dark skin shining in the flash of muskets. He races past Martin without a look, plunges through the gap the sapper has cut, then rushes down into the trench beyond and up the steep bank of the redoubt.

Rush on, boys! Rush on!

The shouting has grown like the thunder of an approaching storm. Martin looks around. There are gaps all along the abatis where the sappers and miners have done their work, and light infantry are pouring through and up the side of the redoubt. He can hear the clang of weapons hitting weapons in hand-to-hand fighting, and suddenly he feels that he, too, must rush into the redoubt. He pauses as another Rhode Islander charges through the gap he has made, then pushes on after.

Where are you going? Martin hears the peremptory challenge and turns. The commanding officer of his corps is there, his face vivid in the flash of muskets. *Sappers are ordered not to enter the fort!*

Martin knows this. Indeed, he was secretly relieved when the order came down. But now his blood is up. *We will go!* he shouts.

The officer pauses, looks around, then back at Martin. *Then go to the devil if you will!* he shouts back.

The gap that Martin cut is now jammed with men trying to get through. He sees a New Yorker, his blue coat looking black in the night, take a bullet in the chest, then fall back to lie on top of the abatis as if using it for a bed.

Twenty feet away is a gap in the spikes made by an American shell. Men are pouring through that opening, and Martin races for it as well, pushing through, dropping to the bottom of the 3-foot-deep trench beyond. Beside him is another of the Rhode Island light infantry, and they rush the breastwork side by side. Then the Rhode Islander shouts and jerks back, and Martin can see the shattered side of his head, the dark blood spilling on the white uniform. The man goes down, screaming. Martin pushes ahead.

Rush on, boys! Rush on!

Something sails by Martin's head, and, for a second, he thinks the British are throwing rocks, as the Americans did at Bunker Hill when their ammunition was gone. Then the thing bounces, sputtering, and Martin realizes that it is a hand grenade, and with that realization comes the first flash of panic he has felt since they began advancing. For a second, he does not know what to do, and then, with renewed energy, he pushes up the steep breastwork. He's halfway up the slope when the grenade explodes. He can feel the concussion against his back. Shards of metal pluck at his coat and breeches as they fly past, but he presses on, seemingly unhurt. He knows from past experience that he might be bleeding from a dozen wounds that he will not discover until the fighting is done, but none is bad enough to drop him here.

The top of the breastwork comes level with his eyes. Two more steps and suddenly a soldier is in front of him, a startled look on his face, an unlit grenade in his hand. Martin kicks him hard in the side of the head and he goes down, and Martin jumps the 4 feet down to the wooden platform that rings the inside of the redoubt. He is in a world of running men, awash in shouting, small arms fire, the clash of steel. Out of the dark, a soldier charges him, bayonet leveled, hat askew, screaming a wordless scream. Martin swings the ax in that familiar way, and it connects with the barrel of the musket and knocks it aside, the power of the blow throwing the soldier off balance. Martin brings the ax handle up into the soldier's face, meeting his forward momentum. The soldier's head skews to an unnatural angle, and he goes down.

Joseph Plumb Martin pulls his ax back for another strike and whirls around, searching out an enemy, but he can sense that the fight is fading, the shouting dying away. He can see muskets flung to the ground, hands raised, swords tossed away. Despite all the talk of revenge for Fort Griswold, the Americans accept the surrender. No bayonets are driven through those who call for quarter.

Off in the dark, he can hear the French shout, *Vive le Roi! Vive le Roi!*, and he knows Number 9 is in their hands. Then cheers go up around him as well, American voices joining the French. Number 10 is taken.

Rush on, boys! Rush on!

Joseph Plumb Martin is breathing hard, but once his breath subsides, he, too, joins in the shouting. They are victorious, and he is still alive. He will be shocked to learn later that the entire attack, from the moment they rose from the grass to the start of the cheering inside the redoubt, lasted just nine minutes.

George Washington keeps his horse at an easy walk, his eyes fixed on the guns along the British lines and the blaze of musket fire that mark the locations of Redoubts 9 and 10. *Looks like fireflies,* he thinks. There are fireflies in the northern states, where he has spent the past six years, but not like in Virginia.

It is a fine thing to be back in Virginia. It has been so very long.

Your Excellency, I think the French have carried their redoubt. The speaker is Henry Knox, riding beside him, his horse looking like a pony under his massive frame. Knox points a meaty finger, and Washington looks in that direction. Indeed, the gunfire at Redoubt 10 seems to have dropped off to nothing, and Washington thinks he can hear cheering, but it is faint and hard to detect beneath the great barrage of artillery, the balls whistling past, the dull boom of exploding shells.

They are on a small rise now, which gives as good a view of the field of battle as they are likely to get, so Washington reins his horse to a stop and dismounts, as do Knox and General Benjamin Lincoln and the various aides-de-camp who follow behind. The British guns are firing furiously, and Washington can feel the concussions in his feet when 18-pound round shot slams into the earth around him.

Sir? Washington turns. It is Colonel Cobb, one of his aides. *Sir, you are too much exposed here. Had you not better step back a little?*

This sort of solicitousness annoys Washington no end. He knows it comes from the sincerest of motives, yet it is irritating and it makes him feel old. *Colonel Cobb,* he replies, and he can hear the ice in his own voice, *if you are afraid, you have liberty to step back.*

His Excellency can hear Cobb begin to bluster in protest, but Knox saves them both. *Reckon Lafayette's men have their redoubt now, too, your Excellency.* The musket fire seems to have dropped off at Number 9 as well, and now Washington is certain he can hear cheering. Then a messenger comes running up as if he were an actor racing to make an entrance, his cartridge box and canteen thumping against his sides as he runs.

Your Excellency! Your Excellency! The young man is breathless from having run so far, and probably also from the embarrassment of having to stand before Washington, Knox, Lincoln, and sundry colonels and majors and say what he has been sent to say. But it doesn't matter. Washington knows already. He nods his head with a sense of profound satisfaction.

The taking of Redoubts 9 and 10 has been little more than a skirmish compared with the great battles of the American Revolution: Brandywine, Saratoga, Camden, Guilford Courthouse, and many others. But it will be the only significant combat to take place during the siege of Yorktown and the eventual capture of Cornwallis's army, and Washington already suspects as much. Even before the siege began, its final act—the capitulation of the British army—was as much a foregone conclusion as one could hope for in war. Only the sudden appearance, *in medias res,* of a miraculously reconstituted British fleet might—*might*—conceivably alter the outcome.

The reason for that is as clear to George Washington and the Comte de Rochambeau as it is to Lord Charles Cornwallis. The siege of Yorktown was won before it started, and it was won at sea, in a now all-but-forgotten fight called the Battle of the Capes.

PART ONE

AN OPPORTUNITY IN VIRGINIA

CHAPTER *I* *Washington and Rochambeau*

"FOR WANT OF a nail, a shoe was lost. . . ." So begins the old nursery rhyme that sets forth a chain of events progressing from the trivial to the loss of a kingdom. Like many nursery rhymes, this one captures a grain of historical truth—that seemingly innocuous or at least minor affairs can look like major turning points when viewed in hindsight. Never has this been more the case than during the American Revolution.

If the wind had not blown foul for British ships to sail into the East River in August 1776, General George Washington and his army almost certainly would have been crushed on Long Island, ending the war less than two months after Congress had declared independence from England. If Brigadier General Benedict Arnold had not fought so tenaciously against Sir Guy Carleton on Lake Champlain through the summer and fall of 1776, Carleton might have taken Fort Ticonderoga that summer and driven south to Albany, linking there with British forces moving up the Hudson River from New York. This would have isolated New England from the colonies to the south, again probably ending the war. The list of hairbreadth survivals for the American Revolution goes on and on. In hindsight, it seems incredible that the rebels won their independence in the end.

From the beginning, however, they had one dependable thing going for them, and that was America itself. The country (or group of colonies, from the British perspective) was huge, much too large to take *in toto* and hold by force. The British won battle after battle, but once the conquering army moved on, rebellion rose again in its wake. There was no center, no Paris or London, the capture of which would defeat the insurrection. Lord William Howe easily took the rebel capital of Philadelphia in 1777, forcing Congress to flee into the hinterland, but it made not the slightest difference. Nor did occupying New York for most of the war disrupt the rebellion (though it did provide the British with a comfortable base of operations). The vast American geography was tailor-made to support an indigenous army. It complicated every operation for a foreign invader and was arguably the only thing that allowed the Americans to keep fighting through the six long years that led to Yorktown.

Colonial America was not an easy place to get around. The roads were few and poor, the country cut up with rivers and mountains. British armies beat themselves to death chasing fast-moving Continental troops. Of course, that geography made life hard on American soldiers as well, particularly since, through the first five years of war, the British had a lock on the only rapid means of moving men and matériel—the sea. Once they lost that advantage, they lost the war.

The Americans on their own, however, could not have wrested control of the sea from the British. For that, they needed the French, and no one knew that better by 1780 than George Washington.

France in the War

In July 1780, two years almost to the day after declaring war on England, France disembarked its first significant land force on American soil. French soldiers had fought in the failed attempt to retake Savannah the previous October, but that had been an expeditionary force landed from ships. Now a French army would become a permanent part of an allied ground force, fighting shoulder to shoulder with Americans.

The division that clambered ashore in Rhode Island numbered fifty-one hundred soldiers, far fewer than Washington had expected. Still, the arrival of the French was the first good news the Americans had received in quite some time, and it was greeted with appropriate enthusiasm. Washington, in a general order, congratulated his men "on the Arrival of a large Land and Naval Armament at Rhode Island sent by his most Christian Majesty to Cooperate with the Troops of these States against the Common Enemy." He suggested that his officers, who wore black cockades on their hats, substitute cockades of intermixed black and white as a symbol of friendship with the French, who wore white. Even the general Sir Henry Clinton, who in May 1778 had replaced William Howe as commander of the British army in North America, would later admit that the arrival of the French "gave additional animation to the spirit of rebellion, whose almost expiring embers began to blaze up."

Such a lift was desperately needed. American morale was low and still ebbing. Since 1776, the British army had remained comfortably quartered in New York, with Washington powerless to do anything about it. No significant gains had been made since the Battle of Saratoga in the fall of 1777, when the surrender of British General John Burgoyne's fifty-seven-hundred-man army to Major General Horatio Gates had at last convinced France to sign treaties of commerce and alliance with America. That diplomatic coup, which a year's worth of Benjamin Franklin's most artful arguments to Louis XVI's ministry had failed to secure, had been a watershed event in the war.

Not since the summer of 1778 had Washington's forces in the North come to grips with the British army in any significant way. At that time, Clinton, the newly appointed British commander-in-chief, had been ensconced in the occupied city of Philadelphia. With France threatening to enter the war, King George III had decided to withdraw part of Clinton's army to protect the West Indies, and Clinton for the first time had faced the real possibility of an enemy superiority at sea. He deemed it time to consolidate forces by abandoning Philadelphia and marching his army back to New York. Washington sent a large portion of the Continental Army to dog the British forces across New Jersey, and the two armies fought to a draw at the Battle of Monmouth. As so often happened, the Americans came painfully close to victory, this time only to see it snatched away by the incompetence of Washington's subordinate, the British-born Major General Charles Lee.

Clinton had been happy to call Monmouth a victory, even though he knew it was something far less than that. He continued on to New York and, from that point forward, had mostly remained put, while Washington's forces deployed themselves in a loose cordon around the city. To Washington, this stasis must have been depressingly reminiscent of the siege of Boston in 1775–1776, with similarly corrosive results. Through the intervening two years of idleness, the Continental Army had suffered from neglect and shrunk from desertion. Recruitment had become nearly impossible, and the men who remained had grown increasingly

bitter by 1780, with some regiments turning to mutiny when their grievances became intolerable.

Expédition Particulière

The deployment of French forces to America was code-named Expédition Particulière. A total of seventy-five hundred men had been assembled in Brest, but the available transports could embark only fifty-one
hundred. A second division was therefore to follow the first when more
transports became available, but Brest was blockaded by Britain's channel fleet before the additional twenty-four hundred soldiers could put
to sea, and they were never deployed.

The thirty-six transports carrying the troops across the Atlantic sailed
under the protection of seven French ships of the line and three frigates.
Commanding the squadron was Admiral Charles-Henri-Louis d'Arsac,
Chevalier de Ternay, whom the Marquis de Lafayette described as "a very
rough and obstinate man, but firm, and clear in all his views." The expedition's land forces were under the able leadership of Jean-Baptiste
Donatien de Vimeur, Comte de Rochambeau.

Rochambeau was fifty-five years old when appointed to lead His Most
Christian Majesty's troops to America. He would prove an ideal choice.
A veteran of thirty-seven years of military service, Rochambeau was
skilled, experienced, and tactful, qualities that did not often combine
in the aristocratic upper echelons of the French military, and he maintained a genuine respect for Washington's authority. While some lesser
French officers in service to the American cause felt that they deserved
special privilege and consideration, Rochambeau, the highest French
authority in America, never forgot who was in charge.

At the same time, Rochambeau also understood that he was under
no obligation to waste the lives of his men on ill-considered American
adventures. Cooperation did not mean blind submission to Washington's strategic vision.

Rochambeau's men disembarked on July 11, 1780, sick and exhausted
from their ten-week voyage from France, which had included a brush
with the British navy in the Caribbean. They occupied the defensive
works in Newport abandoned by the British the previous year. This

ground, in fact, had been the object of the first combined Franco-American action two years before.

In July 1778, the French admiral Charles Henri Hector, Comte d'Estaing, had arrived off Sandy Hook with a fleet superior to that of Lord Richard Howe, then commanding the British fleet in North America. Washington, as ever, had hoped to take New York, but the large French ships were unable to get over the bar between Sandy Hook and Long Island and into New York Harbor. Instead, Washington and d'Estaing had agreed to launch an attack against the three thousand British troops who held Newport, Rhode Island. A successful action there would have captured a significant number of British soldiers and given the new allies possession of a strategically important harbor. In the end, mistrust between the French and Americans, the arrival of Richard Howe with a reinforced fleet, and a ship-killing gale doomed what might have been a successful joint effort. But the attempt gave Washington a glimpse of what French naval strength might accomplish.

Although the Americans were heartened by the French troops' arrival, the French were less impressed with their hosts. In fact, they were somewhat horrified to discover that their new allies, with whom they hoped to defeat their age-old enemy, were ill trained, ill equipped, and few in number. Just five days after arriving in America, Rochambeau wrote to his superiors in France saying, "Send us troops, ships and money, but do not count on these people nor their resources, they have neither money nor credit, their forces only exist momentarily."

Rochambeau and the Expédition Particulière, new to America, dull from their long voyage, and still expecting the second division that would never come, felt no need to rush into action. Washington was more eager to get to it. He wanted to attack New York.

Even before Rochambeau arrived, Washington had set up lookouts along the coast with letters for the French general suggesting that he sail directly to Sandy Hook, the anchorage in the outer reaches of New York Harbor, where he hoped they would outnumber the British fleet already there. Rochambeau received the message, but as the French squadron approached New York, de Ternay caught sight of a daunting number of ships that he took to be the enemy (they were not) and continued on to Newport.

Though disappointed, Washington was undeterred. He wrote to Lafayette that he would not "relinquish the idea of enterprizing against New York till it appears obviously impracticable from the want of force."

Perhaps the most trusted of Washington's aides—whom he called, collectively, his "family"—Marie-Joseph-Paul-Yves-Roch-Gilbert du Motier, Marquis de Lafayette, was twenty-two years old in the summer of 1780 and had been just nineteen upon his arrival in America in 1777. The young marquis was one of many young European aristocrats who had flocked to the rebellion for adventure, honor, and, in some cases, such as Lafayette's, a genuine passion for the cause. Washington despised most of these men, and with good reason, as they tended to be vain, arrogant, and certain of their own worth, qualities that would move the people of France to subject them to the guillotine a decade and a half later. (D'Estaing was among the aristocrats executed during the Reign of Terror. Just before being guillotined on April 28, 1794, he is said to have quipped, "After my head falls off, send it to the British; they will pay a good deal for it.")

Lafayette was different. He had some military experience, having served briefly in the French army (which he joined at age fourteen), but had been willing to accept any rank the Americans would offer, a rare concession. He served without pay. He had been wounded in the Battle of Brandywine, where he refused to stay out of danger, and he had suffered with the rank and file through the brutal winter of 1777–1778 at Valley Forge. What's more, Lafayette possessed a sharp wit and a lively sense of humor, and there was something about the insouciant young Frenchman that brought out the stoic commander-in-chief's human side. Soon, Lafayette became less a subordinate and more the son that Washington had never had.

The marquis, for his part, loved and admired Washington. (It is perhaps relevant that the marquis's own father had died before the boy's second birthday.) Lafayette proved to have a native genius for leadership and military affairs. He was one of those handful of men who rose to prominence during the Revolution, men such as Henry Knox, Nathanael Greene, Benedict Arnold, and John Glover, who had little or no prior military experience but an extraordinary aptitude for the work.

With the French army's arrival in Newport, Washington tapped Lafayette to serve as liaison with Rochambeau. This made good sense, especially since Lafayette had aggressively promoted and negotiated the French troop commitment during a temporary return to France from late 1778 through early 1780, but the arrangement did not work as well as Washington hoped. Many of the French officers were shocked to see how Americanized Lafayette had become, and they were unimpressed by a twenty-two-year-old general with little military experience. After Lafayette, perhaps with youthful intemperance, managed to irritate Rochambeau by pushing Washington's suggestion for an attack on New York with more force and less tact than the situation called for, Rochambeau opted to communicate directly with his American counterpart.

Initially, however, it was Lafayette who appeared in Newport to confer with Rochambeau. On July 15, while Rochambeau was still disembarking his men, Lafayette arrived with a letter from Washington outlining his ideas for an attack on the city. He proposed August 5 as the "day for the re-embarkation of the French efficient force . . ." in order that they might sail to New York.

Rochambeau agreed to act on Washington's ideas, or at least he told Lafayette as much. He felt that his men might be sufficiently recovered by August 15 to consider a landing on Long Island in preparation for a move against New York—thus reenacting, on a smaller scale, William Howe's massive landing of British troops on Long Island four years earlier. But before the combined French and American forces could make the first move, the British did.

War at Home and Abroad

While Washington's army had been encamped in Morristown, New Jersey, outside New York City, suffering with inadequate shelter and provisions through the harsh winter of 1779–1780, Clinton had rather enjoyed himself in town. New York was the most hospitable place a British officer was likely to find in America, and Clinton had taken full advantage. He occupied four different houses while his officers busied themselves staging theatrical productions and his commissaries and quartermasters made fortunes profiteering off the army. No one there was much inclined toward action against the rebels.

There were other reasons, of course. Clinton by nature was wont to consider and reconsider every move. In addition, the military priorities issuing from London were changing. The entrance of the French into the fight had assured that.

Lord George Germain, Secretary of State for the American Colonies and thus Clinton's civilian overseer and the chief architect of the war in America, had more on his mind than the fighting in the thirteen colonies, as did Prime Minister Frederick North, King George III, and all his cabinet. France's declaration of war, followed by Spain's, had turned a local rebellion into a war that engulfed the entire Atlantic world and beyond. The fighting in North America was one of the least important parts of this new world war.

Of foremost concern was the very real possibility that England would be invaded by the allied forces of Bourbon France and Spain. That very thing had nearly come to pass in August 1779, when a combined French and Spanish fleet of sixty-six ships of the line sailed up the English Channel with the intention of landing an army on English soil. The plan was to raze Portsmouth, Bristol, Liverpool, and the Isle of Wight and throw the British economy into chaos. Thirty-one thousand troops had gathered at St. Malo and Le Havre, ready to be transported across the channel once the combined fleet had secured the seas. The British Channel Fleet under Admiral Charles Hardy, half the strength of the enemy fleet, was far too weak to mount an offensive strike.

Meeting no resistance, the French admiral Comte d'Orvilliers headed for the English shore, where word of the approaching fleet had caused a near panic. On August 16, he wrote to his superiors in France that the "combined fleet is at this moment becalmed and anchored in sight of the Tower of Plymouth." Only an adverse wind, indecision in Paris, and sickness in the fleet prevented the French and Spanish from landing; after a fruitless search for Hardy's ships, the fleet returned to the Continent. It was a close call, and, but for French and Spanish ineptitude, it might have been a disaster for England. (D'Orvilliers was censured for the failure and resigned his command.) What had started as an insurgency in the thirteen American colonies had become an international conflict and a very real threat to the English people.

Of almost equal importance to the king and his ministry was the protection of British possessions in the West Indies. The Sugar Islands generated revenues far in excess of those from any other British colony. With the exception of tobacco, nothing of importance could be grown in North America that could not be grown in England. Those things that came from the West Indies, however—coffee, cotton, and, of course, sugar and its derivatives, molasses and rum—were unique to the subtropical climate. At the same time, West Indian planters with all their wealth constituted a much larger and more lucrative market for British goods than cash-starved North America. Simply put, the West Indies were far more valuable to England than her rebellious thirteen North American colonies.

Central as they were to the British economy, the Sugar Islands were too important to lose. France and Spain's entry into the war meant on the one hand that British possessions in the West Indies had to be defended, and on the other that a few more islands might be brought within the British sphere the old-fashioned way, by conquest.

Even before France officially declared war in July 1778, King George had been contemplating a withdrawal of most of his troops from North America to counter the looming threat in the Caribbean. When France did finally make its declaration, the king insisted that no more reinforcements be sent to America, and troops were subsequently withdrawn from there. As orders sent to Admiral Richard Howe in 1778 regarding the realignment of the fleet explained, "The object of the war being now changed, and the contest in America being a secondary consideration, our principal object must be distressing France and defending . . . His Majesty's possessions."

Germain wanted a quick victory in America so that he could turn his attention and resources to the West Indies. Five years of war had proven that the British army could take almost any part of America they wanted, but they could not take it all, and each local conquest lasted only as long as the troops remained. Once they moved on to the next theater of operations, the subdued territory reverted to rebellion. But still they tried, because there was little else they could do. The early strategy to cut off New England from the rest of the colonies by controlling the Hudson River and Lakes George and Champlain had failed, a failure highlighted by Burgoyne's disastrous loss at Saratoga. The perennial British fantasy of thousands of Loyalists in the northern colonies taking up arms in defense of the king had gone unrealized. It was time to look elsewhere for victory.

The latest thinking was that the colonies might be restored to the crown one at a time, with each success building on the last. In late December 1778, British forces had captured Savannah, Georgia. Reports of the success of that venture, and the assistance of Loyalists there, turned the attention of London's war planners toward the southern colonies. The following year, a joint venture of French forces under d'Estaing and American troops led by General Benjamin Lincoln was repulsed after a bloody attempt to retake the city. Georgia, the southernmost colony, had remained at least nominally in the king's possession, and it was thought that the other southern colonies were the most likely candidates to return to British rule.

Sir James Wright, Royal Governor of Georgia, summed up this strategy when he wrote to Clinton saying,

> And I am of the opinion that if South Carolina is thoroughly reduced it will give a mortal stab to the rebellion, and I am firmly persuaded it will in a great measure break the spirit of it. In short it is of the utmost consequence to Great Britain and without that is done it is much to be feared America will be lost. Hold Carolina and Georgia and America may yet be recovered.

This thinking, however, was based largely on the self-interested and ill-informed opinion of southern refugees. The existence of southern Loyalists willing to bear arms for the king in any meaningful way would prove as illusory as the existence of northern Loyalists had.

By late 1779, however, British successes in the South had convinced King George and his ministers of the wisdom of a southern strategy, and in late December, Clinton had sailed south from New York with eight thousand British soldiers. Second in command was Lord Charles Cornwallis, with the navy under the direction of Vice-Admiral Marriot Arbuthnot.

After a rough passage, the fleet arrived off South Carolina in January 1780, and by February, the troops were making a slow approach toward Charleston, the fourth largest city in America. Rather than a head-on assault, Clinton opted for a conventional siege, with sappers digging approaches closer and closer to the city. The process was slow, but the results were inevitable. On May 12, the city capitulated.

The capture of Charleston was one of the most significant blows delivered by British arms during the entire course of the war. Lincoln and five thousand American troops were captured, including more than twenty-five hundred irreplaceable Continental troops—the entire southern army. The Americans also lost thousands of muskets and hundreds of barrels of gunpowder. Most of what remained of the Continental navy was taken in Charleston Harbor.

At the onset of the siege, Cornwallis and Clinton had enjoyed an amicable relationship. Indeed, the two men had been close friends as young officers serving in the European theater during the Seven Years' War, a friendship that had continued at the onset of the American Revolution. But the friendship cooled as the siege of Charleston wore on. Clinton, frustrated by the increasing lack of attention from the ministry in London to the war in the former colonies, had attempted to resign his position as commander-in-chief, but his resignation had not been accepted. Cornwallis, who wanted to take Clinton's place as head of the British army in America, was as frustrated as Clinton by this development, and the two men turned their frustrations on each other. From that point, it would only get worse.

With the fall of Charleston, Cornwallis moved out into the country, the start of the proposed conquest of the Carolinas. Clinton had entertained hopes of carrying the fight into the Chesapeake as well, but around the time of Charleston's capitulation, word arrived from Germain that the French were on their way. Germain's intelligence with regard to the strength of the Expédition Particulière and its date of sailing was extremely accurate. He even knew about the proposed second division, but he did not know where de Ternay was going. "Their destination is still supposed to be Canada," he told Clinton.

As it happened, Clinton had a pretty good idea that the French were heading for Rhode Island. He had been told as much by his most highly placed informant, Benedict Arnold, who was still a general in the American army. Clinton conveyed this information to Arbuthnot, but the admiral was skeptical. Given Arbuthnot's doubts and Germain's suggestion that the French were heading for Canada, Clinton abandoned the plans he had been putting in place for the defense of Rhode Island. Later, he would claim that Arnold's intelligence regarding the French destination was the most important advice Arnold ever gave, though ultimately it did the British no good.

Knowing that the French destination was at least somewhere to the north, Clinton was eager to return to New York, particularly as nearly the entire British fleet in North America was then at Charleston. He abandoned for the moment his hope of moving on the Chesapeake, writing to Cornwallis, "I am apprehensive the information which the Admiral and I received, may make it necessary for him to assemble the fleet in New-York, in which case I shall go there likewise."

By June 17, 1780, Clinton was back in New York with half the troops that had sailed for Charleston, leaving Cornwallis to carry on the southern campaign with the other half. More important, Arbuthnot's fleet was also back in New York, though with much of the British navy protecting the valuable West Indies, that fleet amounted to only four ships of the line—that is, four vessels of more than sixty guns—the ships that formed the basis for all fleet actions of the eighteenth century. De Ternay had seven ships of the line, giving him, upon his arrival, naval superiority in the waters around New York.

Germain, however, had anticipated this and had dispatched Admiral Thomas Graves with six ships of the line immediately upon receiving word of de Ternay's sailing. Graves's squadron made a remarkably quick passage, arriving on July 13, just two days after de Ternay and while Rochambeau was still disembarking his men. Once again, the British controlled the sea.

"[R]ather too indecent to be suffered"

On July 18, Clinton received an express informing him that the French had come to anchor at Newport and the troops were all ashore, an unpleasant surprise. Clinton had hoped to catch them at sea or immediately upon their arrival. The longer the French were allowed to entrench and recoup from the voyage, the harder it would be to dislodge them. A coup de main, a swift attack before they were prepared, might solve the problem. If they waited, they were looking at a siege, for which Clinton felt ill prepared.

Any action against Rochambeau would require a joint effort between Clinton's land forces and Arbuthnot's fleet, but Clinton had begun feuding with the aging, irascible Arbuthnot in Charleston—even as his relations with Cornwallis had deteriorated—and things had only gotten worse since. It did not augur well for cooperation.

Even before Rochambeau arrived, Clinton had proposed three different plans of attack. But the admiral, according to Clinton, "seemed to look upon my proposals as premature . . ." and felt his fleet was sufficient to deal with the French.

Arbuthnot had set up a screen of cruisers that were supposed to alert him and Clinton to the arrival of the French fleet, but de Ternay's ships had slipped through unseen. Dismayed to learn that the French had already had a week to recover from their voyage and improve the works at Newport (which had proved formidable when the British had occupied them), Clinton proposed to Arbuthnot that they immediately put one of his plans into action. Arbuthnot, in turn, told Clinton that he should get his men aboard the transports in New York Harbor while the fleet cruised to Rhode Island to assess the enemy's strength.

Lafayette was still at Newport consulting with Rochambeau when word arrived that Clinton was preparing for an attack. At first, Lafayette dismissed the reports, but, as he wrote to Washington, "So many letters Came to hand that at lenght I was forc'd to take the general opinion about theyr intended expedition." Lafayette was pleased to report that Rochambeau "Can't hear of the idea of evacuating the island, and Says he will defend this post to the last man." Men and ships were put into a defensive position, and all thoughts of an attack on New York were deferred until the current crisis could be weathered.

Washington, too, was watching Clinton's moves and wrote to Rochambeau on July 21 that a fleet of fifty transports had moved up the Hudson River to take on troops: "[T]he object of it is said to be your fleet and army."

On the same day, Arbuthnot's fleet appeared off the coast of Rhode Island. Rochambeau, who was holding a council of officers, mounted his horse and rode for the shore to see for himself. He ordered artillery batteries to be established on the headlands, while de Ternay arranged his ships in a defensive line. There was nothing more they could do.

Clinton, for all his desire to fall on Rochambeau at the first possible moment, was plagued with problems. The transports Arbuthnot had promised were not ready, having been sent to carry drinking water to the fleet. Intelligence regarding the size of the French fleet was incomplete. By July 27, the British still had not moved, and Washington wrote to Rochambeau, "it is extraordinary that there should have been so much delay." Washington assured Rochambeau that the American army was under marching orders and would be ready to march in support of the French when and if it became necessary. To make Clinton nervous, Washington shifted "a very considerable force to the east side of the North [Hudson] River, and advanced with it to the Croton."

Communications and miscommunications flowed between Clinton and Arbuthnot. Meanwhile, the French continued to dig in and fortify, while Washington's troops inched closer to New York City. Finally, on August 13, Clinton received a message from Arbuthnot suggesting that they meet at Gardiner's Bay, at the eastern end of Long Island, to discuss a joint move against Newport. Clinton sent an express telling Arbuthnot he would be there, then rode "120 miles in the most inclement and sickly season of the year through the excessive heats of that climate," only to find that Arbuthnot had put to sea on the morning of the day Clinton had told him he would arrive.

"[T]his last extraordinary treatment of his colleague in commission was rather too indecent to be suffered to pass unnoticed," Clinton wrote. He fired off a letter to Arbuthnot complaining in no uncertain terms of the treatment he had received. He wrote to Germain that he would not be able to do his job as commander-in-chief without having "in the commander of the fleet a gentleman whose views with respect to the conduct of the war are similar to my own and whose cooperation with me as commissioner and commander in chief is cordial, uniform and animated." But for the time being, and for many months to come, Clinton and Arbuthnot were stuck with each other.

By the time Clinton realized he had been stood up by Arbuthnot, any hope for a coup de main against the French was over. Rochambeau had been ashore more than a month, and his defenses were far too formidable to be taken with a quick stroke. Washington was hanging on the outskirts of New York, ready to exploit any weakening of the British garrison. Clinton returned to New York, disembarked his men, and prepared to endure the French presence in Rhode Island.

It would be a long wait for both him and Washington before the French did anything at all.

CHAPTER **2** *Sea Power for the General*

By 1780, GENERAL George Washington believed absolutely in the need for sea power. It had been a steep, five-year learning curve.

Upon taking command of the Continental Army encamped around Boston in July 1775, Washington had known little about the sort of joint land and naval operations that were commonplace for the British military, the sort that Sir Henry Clinton would plan but fail to launch against Newport in the summer of 1780. Nearly all of Washington's prior military experience had been on the western frontier. He was an expert woodland fighter but had had virtually no exposure to the open-field European-style tactics that would characterize the warfare of the next six years, and he had never worked with naval forces.

The first maritime issue to confront Washington after taking command of the nascent American army in Cambridge was the need to stop or at least hinder the British in Boston from resupplying themselves by sea. At first, the objective had seemed unachievable. Luckily, the new commander-in-chief had in his officer corps men who had spent their lives at sea and understood sea power and shipping in a way he did not. Foremost among them was Colonel John Glover of Marblehead, Massachusetts.

Glover was one of those indispensible men without whom the American Revolution would have collapsed within two years. It was his regiment of Marbleheaders that ferried Washington's army across the East River after the disastrous Battle of Long Island in August 1776. On Christmas Eve of that year, it was Glover's regiment that carried Washington's bedraggled soldiers across the Delaware River for the attack on Trenton that did so much to revive the spirit of the rebellion. In 1775, it was likely Glover who pointed out to Washington that capturing unarmed merchant vessels required only small schooners armed with a few cannons. And it just so happened that Glover had a schooner for hire.

Once Washington understood the utility of small, nimble armed vessels, he embraced them wholeheartedly, ultimately sending seven of them out to prey on British shipping in Massachusetts Bay. Operating from Beverly and Plymouth—shoal-water ports that His Majesty's warships dared not enter—the schooners did their job, depriving the British garrison of much-needed food, firewood, and military stores and delivering those provisions to the rebel forces instead. Knowing that a vacillating Congress was not yet ready to endorse naval action—a move King George III, his ministers, and Parliament would interpret as an irrevocable declaration of war—yet knowing also that his ill-equipped, ill-trained army might not last the next winter without some positive development, Washington went so far as to withhold knowledge of his tiny navy from Congress for two critical months in the late summer and early autumn of 1775. It was an early indication of Washington's adaptability and a demonstration of why he was the only man in America who could have held the rebellion together over the next six years.

In October 1775, nearly half a year after adopting the army around Boston as the Continental Army, the Continental Congress at last created the Navy of the United Colonies. Washington, despite his newfound interest in naval power, was deeply skeptical. He had seen the benefits of small commerce raiders, but he saw no chance of the United Colonies matching the massive ships of the line that formed the backbone of the British and French navies. Anything smaller, he felt, would be a waste of money, resources, and manpower.

In the end, his assessment proved correct. The American navy managed to build a mere handful of frigates and only one ship of the line, the 76-gun *America*, launched in 1782 when the war was essentially over. Given to the government of France to replace a French seventy-four wrecked in Boston Harbor, the ship demonstrated sailing qualities that were, in polite terms, not all the French might have wished. It hardly mattered, however, because four years later, she was found to be so rotten she was broken up.

Still, Washington never stopped longing for a real naval force. For years, he could only watch his enemy disappear over the horizon and then reappear at any place of its choosing along the coast. He saw the British abandon Boston only to reappear in New York, and leave New York for the Chesapeake and a march on Philadelphia. British ships drove the Americans from Quebec, dominated the Hudson River, carried troops to Rhode Island, took command of the Delaware Bay, and landed the troops that captured Savannah in 1778.

In a February 1780 letter to one of his major generals, Washington said of the coming campaign season, "If a foreign aid of money and a fleet are to be depended upon, I should then recommend that all our dispositions should have reference to an offensive and decisive campaign. . . . But as I doubt whether these two preliminaries can be placed upon such a footing of certainty, as to justify our acting in consequence, I imagine we must necessarily adopt a defensive campaign." In other words, in the absence of a powerful French fleet, he had no hope of attacking the British and could only continue to play defense.

By the time the Comte de Rochambeau arrived in America, Washington entertained no trace of doubt that without a superior or at least neutralizing force at sea, the Continental Army could never win, and, further, he knew that his only hope of matching England's strength at sea lay with the French. To the Comte de Vergennes, the French Foreign Minister, Washington wrote, "Next to a loan of money, a constant naval superiority on these coasts is the object most interesting. This would instantly reduce the enemy to a difficult defensive and, by removing all prospects of extending their acquisitions, would take away their motives for prosecuting the war."

And so, when the Expédition Particulière arrived in American waters, Washington was at least as pleased with Chevalier de Ternay's ships as with Rochambeau's troops, if not more so. He made no secret of the importance he put on control of the sea. The very first article in his *Memorandum for Concerting a Plan of Operations*, which he had the Marquis de Lafayette deliver to Rochambeau and de Ternay, made the point forcefully: "In any operation, and under all circumstances, a decisive Naval superiority is to be considered a fundamental principle, and the basis upon which every hope of success must ultimately depend."

Unfortunately, the narrow window of French naval superiority slammed shut almost immediately with the arrival of Admiral Thomas

Graves's squadron to reinforce Vice-Admiral Marriot Arbuthnot. The British fleet cruised for a while off Rhode Island, then took up position in Gardiner's Bay, maintaining a loose blockade of Narragansett Bay.

Washington's assessment, however, was spot on. Naval superiority was the key. But when it did come, it would be at a place and under circumstances that Washington was not even contemplating in the summer and fall of 1780.

Stalemate and Treason

After the first tense weeks following the arrival of the Expédition Particulière, Rochambeau and his men settled into something like a routine. He and Washington agreed to meet in Hartford, Connecticut, in September to discuss joint operations, their apparent lack of urgency suggesting that neither man saw much hope of action in 1780. Even before speaking with Washington, Rochambeau began to send back to France the transports that would have been needed to position his troops for an assault on New York.

Washington and Rochambeau met for the first time in Hartford on September 20. Accompanying Washington were Lafayette and the chief of artillery, General Henry Knox. Two days later, the allies signed a joint memorandum outlining their mutual vision for prosecuting the war. New York would be their chief objective, but they would undertake no attack on the city until they had more men and ships at their disposal. Until such time, the French would remain in a defensive position in Newport.

On their way back to their New Windsor, New York, headquarters from Hartford, Washington, Lafayette, and Knox stopped at West Point, just south of New Windsor, to inspect the fort and to confer with the commanding officer there, Benedict Arnold. Arnold was one of Washington's most trusted and active generals, a hero to the Glorious Cause who had twice been wounded in battle.

"From the commencement of the American war," wrote Revolutionary War surgeon James Thacher, "General Arnold has been viewed in the light of a brave and heroic officer, having exhibited abundant proof of his military ardor and invincible temper." Arnold had been in the thick of the fighting since shortly after the battles of Lexington and Concord. He had joined Ethan Allen in taking Fort Ticonderoga and in the autumn of 1775 had led a heroic march through the wilds of Maine to attack Quebec.

His had been the most consistent leadership presence on the American side throughout the brutal fighting in Canada that winter and the following spring. Shot in the leg during the desperate December 30 nighttime assault on the walls of Quebec, he had recovered to help lead the American retreat to Lake Champlain in the summer of 1776 and there had taken command of a small fleet of ships. In October, he had engaged and fought a superior British fleet at Valcour Island, losing the battle and his fleet but stalling the British advance a full year and thus setting the stage for the American victory at Saratoga.

By 1777, having been unfairly passed over for promotion, Arnold was ready to resign his commission but was talked out of it on several occasions. When the northern front again heated up, Washington asked Arnold to return and lend his martial skills to the fight, and Arnold consented. Unfortunately, Arnold and commanding officer Horatio Gates, despite an earlier friendship, began to quarrel. Gates stripped Arnold of his command, but as the Battle of Saratoga reached its high point on October 7, Arnold rode onto the field and led the American troops in one final, heroic charge, turning what might have been a partial victory into a complete rout. In the course of that attack, Arnold took a bullet that shattered his leg, the same one that had been wounded at Quebec.

During months of agonizing recovery, Arnold had to endure the praise heaped on Gates (who never left his headquarters during the battle), while his own role was ignored and even vilified. By the time Washington gave him military command of Philadelphia—a post Arnold assumed after Clinton abandoned the city in June 1778—he was a bitter man and done with the Glorious Cause. In Philadelphia, Arnold met and married the beautiful eighteen-year-old Peggy Shippen (his first wife having died in 1775). The Shippen family had Loyalist tendencies, and during the British occupation Peggy had become close to a number of British officers, including Major John André of Clinton's staff. Peggy helped morph Arnold's discontent into treason, with André the go-between for Arnold and Clinton. When Washington, who thought highly of Arnold, offered the major general his choice of commands, Arnold chose West Point specifically so that he might turn over the fort to the British.

Two days before Washington arrived at West Point, André had been captured in civilian clothes trying to make his way back to New York after conferring with Arnold. In his stockings were incriminating letters in Arnold's handwriting. André's captors, not recognizing Arnold's part in the plot, sent news of the incident to Arnold. This note arrived the morning of Washington's expected visit; upon reading it, Arnold was "thrown into some degree of agitation." Realizing that his treason would soon be discovered, he escaped to a British man-of-war anchored downriver.

Washington arrived just a few hours after Arnold's desertion, unaware of what had happened. Failing to find Arnold at his quarters on the east shore of the Hudson, Washington crossed the river to the garrison at West Point only to find that Arnold had not been there all day. Returning to Arnold's quarters, Washington found that a packet had arrived from a Lieutenant Colonel Jamison containing news of André's capture and the incriminating letters in Arnold's own hand. Only then did Washington realize that one of his most esteemed senior officers had turned traitor.

Arnold's treason came at what was already a low point in American fortunes. The army in the North had accomplished nothing for more than two years, nor did it appear likely to anytime soon. The French, on whom so much hope had been pinned, were bottled up in Newport. Cornwallis was running rampant over the Carolinas, rolling over the southern army. Many, including Washington, wondered how long the fight could go on. Arnold's treachery was yet another terrible blow.

As late summer turned to autumn, and as the air grew chill and leaves turned their brilliant fall colors, activity in the northern theater slowed to a near standstill. By the end of November, Clinton could write to George Germain, Secretary of State for the American Colonies, "The French have not moved from Rhode Island, but are adding Fortifications to that Place. — Admiral Arbuthnot is Watching Monsr Ternay. — While we remain superior at Sea, and can Command the Sound of Long Island, I do not think the Enemy will attempt anything against us."

Indeed, wary of Arbuthnot's superior fleet, de Ternay refused to dispatch even a single frigate to patrol the area, to the disgust of his officers. Then, on December 15, an old man at fifty-seven, the admiral died after a few days' illness. One French officer wrote in his journal, "[De Ternay] was not popular, his death created very little stir. It was the last event of the year that might have interested us."

And Lafayette wrote to his wife, "The French squadron has remained constantly blockaded in Rhode Island, and I imagine that the Chevalier Ternay died of grief in consequence of this event."

"[A]nother Expedition into the Chesapeak"

With the French bottled up in Newport, Sir Henry Clinton began to look for other uses for his army, preferably ones that did not require him to leave the comforts of New York. His thoughts returned to the Chesapeake, where he had hoped to go after the fall of Charleston in May, before Rochambeau's impending arrival in America had sent him hurrying back north instead.

Once again, Arbuthnot was the sand in the gears. The vice-admiral enjoyed only a slim superiority over the French fleet and would not weaken his blockade by sending any of his ships to escort transports south. But in September, British Admiral George Brydges Rodney arrived unexpectedly at New York with ten sail of the line. Rodney was senior to Arbuthnot and thus took charge of naval affairs in North America. This caused considerable friction between him and Arbuthnot, but Rodney's arrival gave Clinton the ships he needed and an admiral with whom he could work.

On September 20, Clinton wrote to Cornwallis,

> I have always thought operation in the Chesapeak of the greatest importance, and have often mentioned to Admiral Arbuthnot the necessity of making a diversion in your Lordship's favour in that quarter; but have not been able until now to obtain a convoy for this purpose.

When he penned this letter, Clinton did not know with certainty what Cornwallis was doing. After the fall of Charleston, the two men had agreed that Cornwallis would correspond directly with George Germain, an arrangement that engendered nothing but misunderstanding and confusion. Still, Clinton was fairly certain that Cornwallis was in the process of subduing South and then North Carolina, as agreed. Men and supplies flowed from Virginia to the rebels in those colonies, and control of the Chesapeake and the Virginia tidewater could close that pipeline.

Germain, who could not resist trying to direct the war from London, likewise felt that the Chesapeake was vital to England's southern strategy. About the time Clinton was preparing to send men south, Germain wrote to Cornwallis that he was impatient to hear "that Sir Henry Clinton and Vice-Admiral Arbuthnot have found Means of sending a Force into the Chesapeak, to cooperate with you." Germain, exercising his usual baseless optimism, felt that if that were only done, "the whole Country South of the Delaware will be restored to the King's Obedience in the Course of the Campaign."

Clinton tapped General Alexander Leslie to lead twenty-five hundred men on this foray into Virginia, his instructions making it clear that the main purpose of the expedition was "to make a diversion in favour of Lieutenant-general Earl Cornwallis." Leslie was to "proceed up the James River as high as possible, in order to seize or destroy any magazines the enemy may have at Petersburg, Richmond, or any of the places adjacent; and finally to establish a post on Elizabeth River." Once in Virginia, he was to make contact with Cornwallis and consider himself under Cornwallis's authority.

Leslie sailed from New York on October 16, arriving in the Chesapeake a few days later. A considerable number of Virginia militia gathered to oppose the British threat, but Leslie never had a chance to meet them or, indeed, to do any of the things he had been sent to do, other than begin entrenchments at Portsmouth. Soon after his arrival, he received a letter written for the ailing Cornwallis by one of his officers, Lord Francis Rawdon. Cornwallis's northward advance had been shaken by the October 7 defeat of a thousand Loyalist militia at King's Mountain, on the border between North and South Carolina, by a near equal number of patriot militia. This battle, though not fought by regular troops, delivered a signal, much-needed victory to the Americans following the loss of Charleston and the rout in August of Major General Horatio Gates's army in the Battle of Camden, South Carolina. In consequence of King's Mountain, Cornwallis was falling back to Charleston from Charlotte, North Carolina, and now ordered Leslie's troops to join him. Leslie reboarded his transports and sailed south, arriving at Charleston on December 14.

News of this development displeased Clinton. "My Instructions to General Leslie," Clinton wrote to Cornwallis, "put that Corps entirely subject to Your Lordship's orders; I did not, I confess, however, suppose it would move to Cape Fear." Clinton still deemed it vital to disrupt the supply line from Virginia and choke off the southern army opposing Cornwallis, and he had orders from Germain to establish a naval base in the Chesapeake, one capable of harboring ships of the line. The twenty-five hundred men he had sent for those tasks had been swallowed up by Cornwallis. Now he would have to send even more.

"Wishing, however, to give your Lordship's operations in North Carolina, every Assistance in my power," he wrote, "tho' I can ill spare it, I have sent another Expedition into the Chesapeak."

This new force would be led by Clinton's most newly minted brigadier general, Benedict Arnold.

BENEDICT ARNOLD AND the fifteen hundred men under his command sailed for Virginia on the twenty-first of December, anchoring in Hampton Roads nine days later. Foul weather had scattered the fleet, and several of the transports failed to arrive until January 4. Half the cavalry horses died en route, the transports carrying them being "very bad, infamously provided, and totally unfit for service." It was only with great effort, apparently, that the quartermaster had convinced the captains of the ships to put to sea in the first place.

Sir Henry Clinton had several good reasons to select Arnold for this job. One was "the very high estimation in which he was held among the enemy for active intrepidity in the execution of military enterprises." Clinton believed that Arnold would be eager to prove to his new masters that he was still capable of such good work. In that, Arnold would not disappoint. In addition, by rewarding Arnold with trust and a high position, Clinton hoped to lure other high-ranking American officers to switch sides.

The hope for further defections drove another of Clinton's decisions as well. Before Major John André was hanged as a spy, General Washington let it be known that he would swap André for Arnold—spy for traitor. But Clinton refused. Though he would much rather have had André than Arnold, Clinton understood that a betrayal of Arnold's trust would have ended any chance of another American officer defecting. Instead, André died and Arnold was sent south.

Clinton informed Secretary George Germain that the "objects of this expedition are nearly the same as that of General Leslie but rather more positive as to establishing a post at Portsmouth on Elizabeth River." Arnold was also instructed to prepare material for building boats so that troops might be conveyed around the Virginia tidewater, which was dominated by rivers. It was a mission for which the onetime ship owner and captain was well suited. Five years earlier, he had fulfilled a similar mission for Washington, supervising the creation of a fleet of small vessels to transport troops and supplies on Lake Champlain.

The troops under Arnold's command were certainly the best that he had ever led. Among them were the Queen's Rangers, an American Loyalist regiment that had become, under the skilled command of Lieutenant Colonel John Simcoe, one of Clinton's most lauded units. Wearing distinctive short green jackets, white breeches, and tall, pointed leather caps with a crescent symbol on the face and feathers protruding from the crown, they would distinguish themselves in the coming action.

Also with Arnold were the Hessian Field Jaeger Corps, whose green coats were trimmed with red facings and cuffs. The Jaegers were commanded by Captain Johann Ewald, an excellent officer. Arnold himself was as active and energetic in the service of the king as he had been formerly in the service of the Continental Congress.

Arnold's instructions were to take post at Portsmouth and fortify the town as a safe haven for ships of the Royal Navy and a rallying point for Loyalists. The British army had a history in America of taking rebel-held territory, rallying Tories to the king, and then moving on, leaving their collaborators unprotected and twisting in the wind. It was one reason that they were encountering fewer Loyalists in the South than expected. Now Clinton instructed Arnold to "make known your intention of remaining there . . . and assemble and arm such of those people as you shall have reason to believe are well affected to His Majesty's government and are inclined to join you." Few were.

Arnold was also instructed to attack the American supply depot in Petersburg and to go after other rebel magazines if "it may be done without much risk." Never a risk-averse soldier, Arnold began his move up the James River to Petersburg and Richmond even before the last of his transports arrived in Hampton Roads. His troops were ferried up the wide river in boats borrowed from the British transports and men-of-war or requisitioned from their owners in Portsmouth. Accompanying the flotilla were the 24-gun sloop-of-war *Hope* and the 12-gun *Cornwallis*, which the Hessian captain Ewald referred to as a "privateer." Waiting to oppose them were more than a thousand Virginia militia commanded by the Prussian Friedrich Wilhelm Ludolf Gerhard Augustin de Steuben, known in republican America simply as Baron de Steuben.

Steuben had arrived in America two years earlier, a minor Prussian aristocrat who had no money but did have experience as an officer in the army of Frederick the Great, the finest army in the world at the time. He had carried with him a letter of introduction from Benjamin Franklin, whom he had met in Paris. Recognizing how beneficial Steuben could be to the struggling American army, Franklin had helped embellish the old soldier's credentials to ensure that he would be given a prominent role in Washington's camp. It worked. At Valley Forge, Steuben was assigned the task of standardizing the drill and training the men in battlefield maneuvers. He also rewrote the American manual of arms, creating a simpler version of the European practice. Ultimately, the baron brought to the Continental Army a professionalism it had not hitherto enjoyed and a discipline that showed itself on the battlefield in the following campaign season.

When Washington tapped Nathanael Greene for command of the southern army in the fall of 1780, he picked Steuben as Greene's second. That fall, Steuben and Greene traveled south together, stopping at Mount Vernon, where they were welcomed by the wife of their commander-in-chief.

Above all things, Steuben wanted to command troops in the field, but that desire had been thwarted, at least temporarily. Seeing how poorly organized the Continental troops and the militia in Virginia were—and what little help they could offer the southern army—Greene had decided to leave the baron in Richmond to gather men and supplies while he himself rode south to take command of the troops in South Carolina.

Steuben was still in Virginia organizing troops and matériel for Greene when Arnold made his appearance, and as senior Continental officer in Virginia, he became the de facto military commander there. He had already urged Governor Thomas Jefferson to strengthen a small fortification on the James River known as Hood's Fort, about 14 miles downstream of the Appomattox River confluence, to prevent just the sort of incursion Arnold was now making. Jefferson had dismissed the suggestion, in part because he knew he would never find militia willing to do it. Now, as Arnold's flotilla came to anchor half a mile downstream of Hood's, the few pieces of artillery there—three 18-pounders, one 24-pounder, and an 8-inch howitzer—opened up on them.

The Americans "kept up a brisk fire," killing one of Arnold's men, until Arnold landed 250 troops under Simcoe, at which point the Americans abandoned the fort to the advancing enemy. The British and Jaegers spiked the cannons, took the howitzer, and plundered nearby plantations.

Steuben continued to organize what defenses he could, sending local militia and Continentals to oppose the British and Hessians as they advanced up the James River, but Arnold's troops brushed them aside. A major and two captains of the Virginia volunteers were taken prisoner, "their pockets filled with orders from Baron Steuben for assembling the militia."

In another instance, an American militia unit mistook the Queen's Rangers, with their green coats rather than the usual British red, for Americans. They approached Simcoe, "who immediately reprimanded them for not coming sooner, held conversation with them, then sent them prisoners to General Arnold."

On January 4, Arnold landed his men at Westover, just below the Appomattox confluence, for the final overland push to Richmond and Westham. The following day, after a forced march of "33 miles in the heart of the enemy's country," part of it in a driving rain, Arnold reached Richmond. He had ordered his troops to "march as open and to make as great an appearance, as possible."

Around three hundred American troops waited to stop them on the high ground through which the road ran, and Arnold ordered Simcoe and Ewald to dislodge them (each would imply in his memoirs that the task was his alone). The Americans were "greatly superior in numbers, but made up of militia, spectators, some with and some without arms," and after firing a single volley they "galloped off."

In Richmond, Arnold found a wealth of goods, including "a large quantity of tobacco, West India goods, wines, sailcloth etc.," along with thirty or forty ships loaded with tobacco. He proposed to the merchants remaining in the city that those who delivered their goods to His Majesty's fleet in the James River would be paid half value, which was better than they would get if their merchandise were burned. Arnold, who was at this point as much concerned with himself as with any cause, likely envisioned some personal profit in this arrangement.

But the merchants needed permission from Governor Jefferson for such an arrangement, and an agent was dispatched to find him. When no word came back from Jefferson the following day, Arnold found himself "under the disagreeable necessity of ordering a large quantity of rum to be stove, several warehouses of salt to be destroyed; several public storehouses and smith's shops with their contents were consumed by the flames," as well as a ropewalk and a magazine with quartermaster's stores. "[A] printing press and types were also purified by the flames." The detail and gusto with which Arnold described the destruction to Clinton suggests a soldier taking an outsized pride in his work—and perhaps also trying to justify Clinton's faith in him.

Troops under Simcoe were dispatched to a cannon foundry and magazine at Westham, about 6 miles upriver from Richmond. There, cannons, small arms, and manufacturing equipment were destroyed. Rather than blow the magazine up, Simcoe's detachment laboriously carried barrels of powder—about 5 or 6 tons in all—down the nearby cliffs and dumped them in the river. Finally, the various buildings housing the foundry and magazine were put to the torch. Despite having been emptied of powder, they went up in a series of spectacular explosions.

A hard rain set in as Simcoe and Arnold finished their work. According to Ewald (who considered Arnold "detestable" for his treason, though Simcoe, at a later date, referred to Arnold's "daring courage"), the general set fire to all the magazines and workshops used in Richmond's vigorous shipbuilding industry, including all the partially built vessels still on the blocks. Forty-two vessels were then loaded with merchandise for the corps' booty and sailed down the James River.

Ewald reflected that "the expedition greatly resembled those of the freebooters, who sometimes at sea, sometimes ashore, ravaged and laid waste everything. Terrible things happened on the excursion; churches and holy places were plundered." As an officer in the Continental Army,

Arnold had always been an advocate of all-out warfare, but then he had been defending his homeland against an invading army. Now, after switching allegiance, he was waging war against his homeland—and doing so with a vigor that would further cement his reputation as the most reprehensible man in American history.

As Arnold plundered Richmond, Steuben and what few troops he could round up prepared to make a stand at Manchester, across the river on the south bank, but Arnold ignored them. Having largely destroyed Richmond's ability to aide Greene's army to the south, he began to move his troops back down toward Hampton Roads and Portsmouth, with Steuben following tentatively behind. Arnold's attack had been lightning quick. As Thomas Jefferson informed Washington, "Within less than 48 hours from the time of their landing and 19 from our knowing their destination they had penetrated 33 miles, done the whole injury and retired." The whole force, Jefferson wrote, was "commanded by the parricide Arnold."

British and American forces skirmished as the invaders moved back down the James River. On January 8, Simcoe led a surprise attack with forty-two mounted troops against two hundred American cavalry and infantry at Charles City Courthouse, 9 miles from Richmond. About twenty Americans were killed and eight taken prisoner, at a cost of one of Simcoe's men killed and three wounded.

On January 10, back at Westover, Arnold reembarked his men on board the boats and ships that had carried them upriver and fell back down toward Williamsburg. Learning that Steuben was waiting with six to eight hundred men at "Flour de Hundreds," the plantation on which Hood's Fort was located, he once again landed Simcoe with three hundred men to drive them off. After a sharp exchange of fire, the Americans fled, pursued by the British until deep night and heavy rain intervened.

For the next week, Arnold and his troops moved slowly down the James River, burning or confiscating anything they found that might be of benefit to the rebels. Finally, on the night of January 19, Simcoe and advance units of the Rangers and Jaegers crossed the Nansemond River on flatboats and entered Portsmouth just as the sun was coming up over Norfolk to the east. The following day, Arnold joined them with the rest of his men. It was time to begin building a British naval base on the Chesapeake.

"The Divine Providence manifests itself"

Washington kept himself well informed of comings and goings in New York. He was told when Arnold's troops were loading on board their transports, though his information was imperfect and he did not yet know that Arnold was in command.

As preparations continued, Washington's intelligence grew more thorough and accurate. On January 2, he wrote to Thomas Jefferson to report that the fleet had sailed. In his letter, he gave a detailed account of the ships in the convoy and the number of troops, including "Light Infantry and Grenadiers, with some other Corps." Washington even knew that Simcoe's regiment was among those embarked. "The whole under the command of Arnold, and still conjectured to be destined to the Southward," he wrote in conclusion.

Any number of points regarding the British embarkation must have galled Washington. Arnold was in command, the destination was unknown, and, with the French fleet still bottled up in Newport, there was not one thing he could do about it.

Clinton wanted to make sure it stayed that way. With the winter deepening and Gardiner's Bay becoming increasingly uncomfortable, Vice-Admiral Marriot Arbuthnot entertained notions of sending Admiral Thomas Graves's squadron of six ships of the line to the West Indies. Clinton argued against this because he, like Washington, understood that naval superiority was the key to the war. "If the advantages a superiority at sea gives were to be transferred from us to the enemy," he wrote Arbuthnot, "I should not only lose the hope of the success, but fear for the safety, of the forces that are and may be sent on different and distant expeditions."

He was thinking specifically about the Chesapeake, which was looming larger in his strategic thinking as well as Germain's. Even as Arnold's troops were disembarking in Virginia, Germain in England was writing to Clinton to reiterate the importance of "a secure port in the Chesapeake for our ships to resort to for supplies." Such a port would also deprive the French of that important strategic location.

Germain had learned that Leslie had been withdrawn from the Chesapeake, and he wondered if Clinton could not send another detachment in his place, which, of course, was exactly what Clinton had just done. For five years, the war had been concentrated between New York and Pennsylvania in the North and through the Carolinas and Georgia in the South. Virginia, in the middle, had been largely spared, but that was about to change.

The navy, of course, was central to British initiatives in the Chesapeake region, and to Clinton's undoubted relief, Arbuthnot agreed to keep his fleet intact. He assured Clinton that the "squadron shall remain in Gardiners Bay as long as the season will admit." The British navy would continue to keep the French at bay.

The French navy, however, was no longer quite as passive as it had been. With the death of de Ternay, the senior captain, Charles-René-Dominique Sochet, Chevalier Destouches, took command of the fleet. Destouches was a far more popular commander than de Ternay, in part because he was more willing to risk his ships in action rather than let them sit idle at anchor. Upon taking command, he had set his men to work getting the ships ready for sea, and at the request of the Connecticut state government, he sent a small vessel into Long Island Sound— right under Arbuthnot's nose—to protect merchant shipping around New London.

In early January, Destouches continued to poke the British bear by dispatching a couple of frigates to Boston to escort a small convoy of supply vessels to Newport. With them was the transport *Ile de France*, which had sailed with the Comte de Rochambeau's fleet the previous summer but had become separated. The frigates put to sea on January 10 and soon found themselves beaten by violent winter storms of the sort that periodically lash the coast of New England. They managed to make Boston and got underway again on the fourteenth with the merchant vessels under their guns. Again they were hammered by gales as they clawed their way around Cape Cod and the treacherous shoals to its south.

By January 20, Rochambeau and Destouches were growing concerned for the safety of the convoy. Showing more boldness than de Ternay would have done, Destouches sent two of his ships of the line to sea in search of it, despite the storms rolling through and the British fleet waiting and watching at Gardiner's Bay.

Arbuthnot was in New York, which left Thomas Graves in command of the British squadron. With the French sallying forth and storms threatening, Graves was not entirely sure what to do, but he, too, opted for the bold move. During a break in the weather he sent three ships of the line—*Bedford*, *Culloden*, and *America*—in pursuit of the French.

Culloden crossed the mouth of Long Island Sound and appeared off Newport Harbor, where the French at first mistook her for one of their own. The British man-of-war fired a gun, ran up her flag, and came about, standing out to sea again, her captain perhaps hoping to tempt one of the French ships to come out and fight.

As it happened, the sea would give him all the fight he needed. That night, with the French squadron struggling to get back to Newport and the English ships of the line cruising for them, another storm blew up, hitting the New England coast with hurricane conditions. The wind howled, and massive seas rolled out of the darkness to crash on the shores of Rhode Island and New York, driving everything before them.

In those conditions, the French and British ships had all they could do to stay in one piece as they battled the wind and seas in the narrow strip of water between Montauk Point (at the tip of Long Island), Block Island, and the entrance to Narragansett Bay. Finally, to the great relief of Rochambeau and Destouches, the two frigates with their charges, including the *Ile de France*, limped into Newport Harbor and came to anchor. They had survived three gales on the short run to Boston and back. Around that time, the two ships of the line also made it safely back to harbor.

With the success of the Boston mission, Destouches grew still bolder in his willingness to deploy ships. By way of the Chevalier de La Luzerne, the French minister to the Continental Congress, Thomas Jefferson had requested that two frigates and a ship of the line be spared to carry arms from Connecticut to the militia in Virginia and to cruise off the mouth of the Chesapeake Bay so as to disrupt British communications. Destouches now decided to honor the request. Though at first he felt that he could spare only the two frigates, Rochambeau convinced him to add the relatively shallow-draft, 64-gun ship of the line *Eveillé* to the little squadron.

Washington, meanwhile, had a lot on his mind. Foremost was the Pennsylvania line of Continental troops, under the command of Anthony Wayne, which had mutinied over the deplorable conditions they were forced to endure and their unfair and generally nonexistent pay. Nor had Washington forgotten about Arnold. Even as negotiations with the Pennsylvania troops were nearing a successful conclusion, he was writing to Rochambeau on various topics, the Chesapeake among them. "Recent letters from Virginia give me the particulars of Arnold's incursion to Richmond," Washington reported. "He burnt there some public and private stores and buildings, a foundry and some other public works in the vicinity." Washington added, perhaps by way of a hint, "Virginia intersected as it is with large navigable Rivers is greatly exposed to those kinds of predatory expeditions; nor is there any remedy against them but a naval superiority."

He would get his wish. On that same day, Rochambeau wrote a breathless letter to Washington with news that seemed like a gift from God.

"The Divine Providence manifests itself always for our cause," he began, and then went on to explain how the storm that had nearly wrecked Destouches's frigates had devastated the squadron that Graves had sent out to capture them. The 74-gun *Culloden* had been driven ashore on Long Island and was a total wreck, though her crew had gotten off safely. The *Bedford*, also a seventy-four, had ridden out the night at anchor and would have been driven ashore as well if her crew had not cut her masts away, saving the ship but totally disabling her. The *America*, a sixty-four, had been blown south clear to Virginia. (She returned weeks later in need of major repair.)

As the result of the January storm, the French and British fleets were now nearly equally matched, and Destouches was even more enthusiastic about sending his force to sea. Rochambeau felt that Destouches would certainly dispatch the *Eveillé* and two frigates, and to Washington he dangled the possibility of the admiral sending the entire fleet to the Chesapeake.

Though gratified to hear of the damage to the British fleet, Washington tempered his optimism with caution, replying that he hoped "the confirmation will have enabled Mr. Destouches to take advantage of the event, in a manner as advancive of his own glory as of the good of the service. I impatiently wait further advices." To Jefferson and Steuben, he wrote that he and Destouches were waiting for confirmation before sending ships to sea.

In Newport, the restless French troops began to wonder openly why the navy did not make use of its newfound equality with the British. "Why are we not ready to sail with troops for Virginia to destroy the English ships and Arnold's troops?" one officer asked his journal, claiming that "the same ideas has occurred to everyone."

The same ideas had, in fact, occurred to Rochambeau and Destouches. On February 3, Rochambeau went on board the admiral's flagship to confer with him and to ask whether he meant to send three ships or the entire squadron. After considering all factors, Destouches decided that the sixty-four and the two frigates would suffice.

Events were outpacing the express riders carrying letters over the broken, frozen roads between Newport and Washington's headquarters at New Windsor, New York, about 150 miles away. The correspondence between Washington and Rochambeau seemed always to be out of phase. On February 7, Washington wrote to Rochambeau with an update on Arnold's movements, suggesting for the first time that "If Mr Des touches should have acquired a superiority, which would make it prudent to act," then Arnold's division might be a proper object of attention. By the time Washington's letter reached Rochambeau, the first naval detachment of 1781 was already on its way to the Chesapeake.

CHAPTER *4* *Copper Bottoms*

IN 1761, ADMIRAL George Anson initiated an experiment that would lead to one of the most significant breakthroughs in the history of wooden shipbuilding. He fastened copper sheathing below the waterline of a ship's hull.

From the first ocean voyages in wooden ships thousands of years ago, two problems had plagued mariners and shipbuilders. One was the rapid buildup of weeds and other marine growth that clung like an inverted forest to the bottom of a ship and cut its speed in half or worse. The only cure by Anson's day was careening, which involved unloading everything from the ship's hull and rolling the vessel on her side by means of a block and tackle at the masthead. With the bottom thus exposed, the growth was loosened with flaming torches and scraped off, a process called breaming. The entire operation was hugely laborious and had to be done with tedious frequency.

The other problem was teredos, or shipworms, which look like worms but are actually mollusks that burrow into wood and can destroy a ship's bottom much the way termites can destroy a house. Teredos are a particular problem in tropical climates, though they exist in colder climates as well. As England's merchant marine and navy expanded their reach around the globe, teredos became an increasingly expensive threat.

For hundreds of years, various combinations of tallow, sulfur, pitch, and the like had been smeared on ships' bottoms to address these issues, but with little success. It was not uncommon to cover the bottom of a ship with an extra, outer layer of sacrificial fir planking that could easily be replaced, a partial cure for teredos that did nothing, however, to slow marine growth.

Then Anson tried sheathing the bottom of a frigate with rectangular copper plates about fourteen inches wide and a couple of feet long. It was an expensive proposition, and he encountered technical problems (such as galvanic corrosion caused by the use of dissimilar metals), but once those were addressed the sheathing proved remarkably effective. The copper repelled marine growth, and teredos could not bore through it. Falconer's *Universal Dictionary of the Marine* from 1780 called copper sheathing "a very late invention. . . . [I]t seems, however, to answer the purpose much better than the fir-planks."

The officers who sailed the ships certainly understood the value of this new technology. One captain wrote to the Controller of the Navy in 1779, begging, "For God's sake, and our country's, send out copper-bottomed ships to relieve the foul and crippled ones." Admiral George Rodney's flag captain wrote the Controller of the Navy in 1780, "It is impossible for me to describe the advantages attending it [coppering]." He went on to describe how, when forming a line of battle, the coppered vessels were able to quickly take their stations. Then, with sails adjusted to kill headway, they would wait upward of six hours for the uncoppered ships to get in line, which, in the end, they often failed to do.

Not long after Anson's initial experiment, the British navy began to sheath its men-of-war with copper, as did the navies of other nations, though the practice would not become universal until after the American Revolution.

By 1780, about half of the British fleet was copper sheathed. Indeed, the reason that Admiral Thomas Graves was able to make such a quick passage to Rhode Island, giving Chevalier de Ternay only a couple of days of naval superiority despite the Frenchman's head start from Europe, was that Graves's ships were all coppered and many of de Ternay's were not.

So advantageous was copper sheathing that naval personnel would regularly note when a ship was so equipped. Thus, Comte de Rochambeau wrote to General George Washington on February 8, 1781, to say that the "Chevalier Destouches waits only for a favorable wind to send a Line of battle ship, a 64 copperbottomed, with two frigates to go and warmly fall upon Arnold's convoy in the rivers of Virginia." Destouches did not dare send a 74-gun ship into the shallow bay and did not want to send an additional sixty-four, because only the *Eveillé* was coppered. This squadron, Destouches was certain, would suffice to handle the 44-gun *Charon*, the frigates *Guadeloupe* and *Fowey*, and the smattering of smaller vessels in the fleet under Commodore Thomas Symonds that had remained in support of Benedict Arnold.

Destouches's squadron, commanded by Captain Le Gardeur de Tilly, sailed undetected from Newport on the evening of February 9 with a fresh breeze to carry it off. The squadron was in the Chesapeake before Washington even knew they had left, but by that time, Washington was warming to the idea of trapping Arnold between land and sea forces. Before, he had felt that there was nothing he could do but read reports of Arnold's depredations in Virginia. Now, with what the Marquis de Lafayette called "divine naval superiority," it seemed possible to take positive action against the traitor.

On February 15, not having received Rochambeau's letter of February 8, Washington wrote to Rochambeau suggesting a coordinated land and sea attack on Arnold. He asked that Rochambeau send a thousand men and "as many pieces of siege artillery, with the necessary apparatus, as you will think proper to spare." Washington hoped that Destouches would send his entire fleet with the detachment.

Washington had no idea what level of cooperation he could expect from the French, who had shown little willingness to stir from Newport in more than half a year, but he was ready to gamble a major detachment from his own army that Rochambeau would move and that the French could control the waters of the Chesapeake. As Lafayette wrote to the Chevalier de La Luzerne, "The general must be very convinced of the importance of the expedition to weaken himself so much here."

Indeed he was. Washington wrote to Rochambeau,

> to give the enterprise all possible chance of success I have put under marching orders a detachment of twelve hundred men which will proceed in a few days towards the Head of Elk River there to embark and proceed to a cooperation. I did not delay the march of this detachment, 'till I could hear from Mr. Des touches and you, as there is not a moment to be lost, if the expedition is to be undertaken.

On February 19, still not having heard from Rochambeau, Washington wrote again to reiterate his determination. "The destruction of the detachmt. under the Comd. of Arnold, is of such immense importance to the welfare of the Southern States that I have resolved to attempt it with the detachment I now send in conjunction with the Militia." Washington assured Rochambeau that he would send troops even if Rochambeau decided not to send any French soldiers, "provided Mr. Des touches is able to protect our operations by such a disposition of his fleet as will give us the command of the bay."

At long last, Washington was sensing the possibility of naval superiority. He could not have guessed that what he was proposing in February— sending a detachment of his army south and hoping for French naval superiority—was essentially a dry run for the series of events that, later in the year, would bring about American victory in the War for Independence.

"Three french Ships of War"

On January 20, the day that the transport *Ile de France* and her naval escort fought their way through a winter gale and dropped anchor in Newport and that the *Culloden* piled up on the eastern end of Long Island, Benedict Arnold and his troops crossed the Nansemond River to the partially fortified town of Portsmouth. They had cut a swath through Richmond and surrounding towns, putting to the torch anything that might give aid to the American army to the south. Now it was time to begin securing the harbor town.

Portsmouth consisted of about one hundred fifty wood frame houses, most of them occupied by merchants and seamen, though all but three families had abandoned the town by the time Arnold arrived. The land was flat, wooded, marshy, and considered unhealthy, but Arnold immediately began work on his primary mission of raising the works around the place.

The lay of the land, however, rendered Portsmouth more difficult to secure than Arnold had been led to believe. The work was slow and hard going, and, despite the help of some three hundred local "Negroes," probably runaway slaves, the works were far from complete by mid-February. Arnold wrote to Sir Henry Clinton that "Repairing Barracks, foraging, and patrolling with large Parties, has engrossed the Time of a great part of the Troops."

On February 14, news reached Arnold that concerned him more than any action the Virginia militia might take. As Arnold reported to Clinton, "Three french Ships of War, one of 64 Guns and Two Frigates," had anchored in Lynnhaven Bay, about 20 miles east of Portsmouth. "[I]t remains a doubt where they are from, and whether they are King's Ships or Merchantmen, I believe the latter, tho' the Gentlemen of the Navy are of the opinion they are the former, & from Rhode Island."

The gentlemen of the navy, of course, were correct. The ships were de Tilly's squadron, the *Eveillé* and the two frigates that had sailed from Newport on February 9. The lurking presence of French men-of-war must have given Arnold pause. Captain Johann Ewald suggested that Arnold was in a near panic, breaking into a cold sweat as he frantically drove the men to improve the works before the enemy could attack. But Ewald's letters betrayed a dislike of Arnold that probably colored his assessments. Arnold undoubtedly ordered the men with greater urgency to build the defenses, but it seems unlikely that he was panicked. In his short and bloody career as a soldier, he had always shown extraordinary physical courage.

Still, Arnold must certainly have guessed at Washington's orders regarding his treatment if caught. He may not have feared death in battle, but a dishonorable death at the end of a noose was something else, which was why he kept a brace of loaded pistols in his pockets.

Back in New York, the British command was showing little sense of united purpose or coordinated effort. Mistrust and miscommunication between Clinton and Vice-Admiral Marriot Arbuthnot, together with uncertainty as to what the French were up to, had thrown their strategy into chaos. A few days before receiving Arnold's letter regarding de Tilly's squadron, Clinton received word from a Newport Loyalist named William Brenton that the French were preparing to embark thirteen hundred men, presumably to attack Arnold in Virginia.

Brenton was well informed. On February 12, Rochambeau had proposed to Destouches that the grenadiers and *chasseurs*, or light infantry, be made ready to march, though there is no indication that they actually were.

Upon hearing this, Clinton wrote to Arbuthnot asking what plans the old admiral had "to frustrate the designs and attempts of the rebels and their French friends." Clinton, for his part, ordered a division of men to be ready to move in an instant to cooperate with anything Arbuthnot might have in mind. In an acid dig at Arbuthnot's having earlier stood him up, Clinton added, "I should most cheerfully have gone to Gardiners bay to communicate with you . . . but I am fearful it might be possible I should not be so fortunate as to meet you there."

In response, Arbuthnot ordered transports prepared to take the division aboard. Once the troops were embarked, the ships were to drop down to Sandy Hook from the Hudson River anchorage so they could get underway quickly. He also ordered "a general press both afloat and ashore to raise seamen for the fleet." Soon press gangs were sweeping the city for merchant seamen and civilians with seagoing experience to fill out the ships' crews.

On February 19, Clinton received the report of the French squadron that Arnold had sent five days earlier. Though Clinton kept close tabs on the French, this was his first confirmation that de Tilly had slipped unseen from Narragansett Bay, and he did not hesitate to act. He had already expressed a belief that control of the Chesapeake region was a key in the war, and he had demonstrated a keen awareness that naval superiority in the Chesapeake was the key to its control. Now the French had that superiority. Worse, as Clinton now wrote Arnold, there was "reason to suppose," based on Brenton's information, "that the ships seen last Wednesday were the avant garde" from Newport, with more to follow.

Arnold assured Clinton that he was "under no Apprehensions at present" that Portsmouth might be overrun by the Virginia militia, and he was certain they could hold off up to two thousand French troops as well, "till a reinforcement can arrive from New York." Clinton believed that Arnold could, indeed, hold off an assault from the landward side, but he feared that if the French controlled the water and landed troops along the Elizabeth River, they could overrun Arnold's position from the rear.

The force that Clinton now gathered for embarkation to Virginia consisted of British and Hessian grenadiers and light infantry along with the 42nd and 76th Regiments, twenty-two hundred men in all, soldiers whom he called "the elite of my army." This new force would be led by Major General William Phillips, who, upon arrival, would assume command in Portsmouth from Benedict Arnold. Phillips was one of the "band of brothers" of British officers, having served with Clinton and Lord Cornwallis in Europe during the Seven Years' War. His relationship with both men was unmarred by the animosity that had developed between Cornwallis and Clinton. Indeed, Cornwallis considered Phillips a close friend.

Having organized this third embarkation to the Chesapeake, Sir Henry Clinton, commander-in-chief of the British army in North America, could do nothing more. The next move would be up to Washington and Rochambeau.

Lafayette

To lead the detachment of twelve hundred men south after Arnold, Washington selected Lafayette, who was then with Washington's main army in New York. On February 20, he sent the young Frenchman detailed instructions. Lafayette was to march his men to Head of Elk, at the northern end of the Chesapeake Bay, near the site of present-day Elkton, Maryland, a march of some 50 miles from Philadelphia. He was to communicate with the Continental Army's quartermaster general and the officer commanding the French squadron (Washington did not yet know de Tilly's name) to arrange water transport from Head of Elk to the most advantageous landing place from which to mount an assault against Arnold. He was to "open a correspondence with the Baron De Steuben who now commands in Virginia," letting him know that the detachment was en route and requesting that Steuben assemble enough militia to act in conjunction with the Continental troops.

Speed was crucial. "You are not to suffer the detachment to be delayed for want of either provision, forage, or waggons on the route," Washington wrote. If Lafayette could not get those things through purchase, hire, promissory notes, or donations, he had permission to use military impressment. Commandeering from civilians was anathema to Washington; that he gave Lafayette permission to do so in this instance indicates how eager he was to make the plan work.

Washington also gave explicit instructions for dealing with Arnold if the traitor should be taken prisoner:

> You are to do no act whatever with Arnold that directly or by implication may skreen him from the punishment due to his treason and desertion, which if he should fall into your hands, you will execute in the most summary way.

To disguise the destination of the troops, word was spread that the division was bound for Staten Island or Bergen Neck, positions in the cordon around New York.

By the last week of February, Lafayette's detachment was marching south, struggling over broken roads and through freezing, driving rain. "It is amusing to see us traveling," Lafayette wrote to Luzerne. "We haven't a sou, a horse, a cart or a wisp of hay. . . . We shall live by our wits and march at the expense of our neighbors as far as Head of Elk." Along with their wits, Lafayette's troops had a contingent of supply agents riding ahead of the column to make what arrangements they could before the main body caught up with them.

Lafayette maintained an unbroken correspondence as he marched south. He wrote to Steuben as ordered, relating his eagerness to join the baron in Virginia, as neither he, Washington, nor Steuben felt "that Consistent with prudence such operations May Be Undertaken By Militia Alone." If Arnold tried to negotiate, Lafayette wrote, nothing must be said that might lead him to expect the rights of a prisoner of war. "His Excellency's Instructions which I will Show you Are Very Positive on this Point."

Express riders raced between Lafayette and his commander-in-chief. Washington warned Lafayette that the British might well send a fleet after de Tilly once the destination of the French squadron was known, and for that reason, it was vital that things move quickly. Washington reiterated that Lafayette was to arrange for transports to move his men from Head of Elk down the bay, and for "fast sailing vessels (Pilot Boats would be best)" to communicate with the French squadron. Washington added, "As your march will be rapid to the Head of Elk, leave good officers to bring up the tired, lazy, & drunken Soldiers."

Through rain and over battered roads, Lafayette and his twelve hundred Continentals pushed south for Morristown, then Trenton and Philadelphia, then onward for Head of Elk.

On the same day Washington sent Lafayette his marching orders, he wrote to Steuben, saying that he was "Convinced that a naval operation alone will probably be ineffectual, and that Militia would be unequal to the reduction of Arnold in his works." Therefore, Washington told Steuben, he was sending the Frenchman with twelve hundred Continentals.

De Tilly's squadron had long since arrived by the time Steuben received Washington's letter, but the baron needed no orders from the commander-in-chief to understand what an opportunity the presence of the French ships represented. "On Monsr Tillys arrival in James River," he wrote Washington, "I began to prepare for an enterprize against Portsmouth."

General Thomas Nelson of the Virginia militia rowed out to *Eveillé* to confer with de Tilly. The Frenchman informed Nelson that the squadron could not remain long in the river. Nevertheless, Steuben began to move militia units into positions around Portsmouth and ordered more men called up. He arranged for "Seven or eight Merchant Vessells of 8, to 20 Guns" to prepare to move men and heavy cannon across the river. Every move was designed to tighten the noose around Arnold.

De Tilly's arrival gave the French control of the Chesapeake, but they soon found there was not much they could do with it. Washington, with his growing appreciation for naval tactics, had foreseen this problem. He had warned Rochambeau, "There are a variety of positions where Arnold by putting his vessels under protection of land batteries, may defy a naval attack . . . ," and that was exactly what happened. Arnold moved the *Charon* and the frigates and other ships far up the Elizabeth River, beyond the reach of de Tilly's squadron, and he anchored the larger ships broadside to the river so as to threaten any approaching ships with raking fire.

De Tilly did not give up easily. He sought out local pilots to help him work his ships upriver to attack the British, and although no pilot would attempt this with the sixty-four, they were willing to try it with the two smaller frigates. After the ships worked their way through the muddy, winding channels, however, one of them, the *Surveillante*, ran aground. Even after pumping her stores of fresh water overboard and removing her guns, her crew needed twenty-four hours to free her from the grip of the mud.

Realizing he could do nothing to Arnold's fleet, de Tilly shifted his squadron to Lynnhaven Bay, at the Chesapeake Bay entrance, where the ships anchored with British ensigns flying, hoping to lure unsuspecting enemy vessels into a trap. This *ruse de guerre* worked well, and de Tilly snatched up a number of privateers and smaller vessels standing in past

Cape Henry, the southern tip of the Chesapeake. While lying in wait, the Frenchmen also caught sight of a British man-of-war and a smaller vessel outside the cape. The squadron got underway, and the fast, copper-sheathed *Eveillé* quickly overhauled the English ship, which surrendered after firing a single shot. The ship proved to be the *Romulus*, a 50-gun ship of the line, though she was mounting only forty-four guns at the time. She had on board a large sum of money, the payroll for Arnold's troops.

After lying nearly a week in the Chesapeake and taking a number of prizes, de Tilly felt that he was pressing his luck by remaining where he was. If Arbuthnot's fleet should arrive, his squadron would be overwhelmed. So, with the French flag flying over the British at *Romulus*'s gaff, the squadron and its flock of prizes made its way north.

"On the 24ᵗʰ, during a very strong wind, we perceived four large vessels pretty near to shore," wrote a French officer in Newport. It was de Tilly returning with his prizes, just fifteen days after leaving. Lafayette, meanwhile, had been marching three days and was barely halfway to Head of Elk. It was one more demonstration of the advantages of naval operations along America's coast.

While de Tilly was carrying on his largely unsuccessful mission to Virginia, letters continued to flow between Washington and Rochambeau. Miscommunications mounted as the situation changed faster than letters could move between New Windsor and Newport, leading Rochambeau to complain that the post "marches but very slowly."

Washington's suggestion that Destouches send the entire squadron arrived after de Tilly had sailed. Had it arrived earlier, Rochambeau assured Washington, the admiral might well have decided to send the whole fleet, and Rochambeau would gladly have provided the thousand men Washington requested. Unfortunately, in that time, Arbuthnot had managed to remast the *Bedford*, and the *America*, which had been blown south to Virginia in the January storm, had since clawed her way back to Gardiner's Bay. With those ships returned to service and *Eveillé* gone, the British once again controlled the seas off Newport.

The return of de Tilly and the *Eveillé*, however, scrambled the strategic picture yet again. With the sixty-four back and the *Romulus* added to the French fleet, Destouches's force was nearly equal to Arbuthnot's. In a secret letter to Rochambeau, Destouches pointed out that *Romulus* drew less water than *Eveillé* and thus would be better able to get up the Elizabeth River and attack Arnold's fleet. The admiral immediately set to work returning the prize to her full armament of fifty guns.

Further inspiring this renewed effort were letters and prisoners captured aboard transports taken by de Tilly. The letters revealed a plan by the British to repopulate Portsmouth with the Tory families who had fled, thus strengthening the British hold on the Chesapeake. The prisoners taken aboard the transports had been the vanguard of that effort.

"The Letters, found on board the Vessels taken by Mr. De Tilly, have decided Mr. Destouches to follow at full the plan given by your Excellency," Rochambeau wrote to Washington, "and to risk every thing to hinder Arnold from establishing himself at Portsmouth in Virginia." This time, Destouches would lead his entire fleet to the Chesapeake. Rather than the 1,000 men Washington had requested, Rochambeau would send 1,120, including all the elite grenadiers and chasseurs. For artillery, he would send four 4-pounder and four 12-pounder guns. The navy would be able to supply 24-pounders if necessary, but Rochambeau "presumed that against earthen intrenchments, the 12 pounders will be Sufficient."

When Arnold had arrived in Virginia two months earlier, he had faced only local militia with no naval support. Now, that militia was numerically superior to his army and had him boxed in at Portsmouth. Twelve hundred Continental troops were hurrying overland to join the attack, and eleven hundred well-trained and well-equipped French troops would be sailing to the Chesapeake, their transports escorted by eight ships of the line. The net, it seemed, had encircled Arnold and needed only to be drawn tight.

CHAPTER 5 *Head of Elk*

GEORGE WASHINGTON NEVER had a chance to be disappointed by Captain Le Gardeur de Tilly's failure in the Chesapeake. The same letter from Comte de Rochambeau that carried news of the squadron's return also included the very welcome news of the decision to send the full fleet and French troops after Benedict Arnold.

Rochambeau's letter, long and detailed, reflected the lift the French forces were receiving from the prospect of action. He told Washington that his troops would be ready to embark in twenty-four hours, though the fleet would take longer. Chevalier Destouches was still struggling to get his ships ready for sea after the neglect they had suffered under Chevalier de Ternay, and it would be another eight days before they could get underway. Rochambeau intended to ask "the States of Boston [sic] and Rhode-island to send me . . . 2000, militia to stay here all the time this expedition may last," to protect Newport from British attack. He hoped Washington would "approve of my making use of your name in my demand."

Upon receiving Rochambeau's letter on March 1, Washington immediately sent word to the Marquis de Lafayette that the French intended "to operate in Chesapeak Bay with their whole fleet and a detachment of 1100 french troops grenadiers and Chasseurs included." Rochambeau had asked Washington to send an aide-de-camp to Baron de Steuben, the commanding officer in Virginia, to assemble the militia and have everything in readiness for the fleet's arrival. Washington was sure that such arrangements had already been made, "but to gratify the Count [Rochambeau]" he asked Lafayette to send Colonel Jean-Baptiste Gouvion, an engineer with Lafayette's detachment, to confer with Steuben.

Washington had earlier requested that Destouches send armed vessels to Head of Elk to escort Lafayette's transports down the Chesapeake

Bay, a distance of some 200 miles. Rochambeau informed Washington that Destouches would try, but "he says that he cannot answer for it by reason of the Length 1st. of the way by Land, 2d. of the Navigation thro' all the Length of the Bay." Washington told Lafayette that Destouches "seems to make a difficulty, which I do not comprehend about protecting the passage of your detachment down the bay." It was, in Washington's opinion, "entirely without foundation," and he had no doubt that, once in the bay, the French fleet would find no difficulty with the matter.

To reduce the likelihood that Lafayette's continued march south would raise British suspicions of the French fleet's return, Washington put out word that the division was heading to the aid of General Nathanael Greene in the Carolinas. At the same time, he ordered part of the formerly mutinous Pennsylvania line under the command of Anthony Wayne and Arthur St. Clair to move south and join Lafayette.

On March 1, Lafayette was in Philadelphia preparing for the final push to Head of Elk. Despite the "Depth of the Mud, and the Extreme Badness of the Roads," his division had made a rapid march south. He knew nothing of Rochambeau's new initiative, however, as Washington was writing the letter outlining the new French plans that very day (the letter apparently never reached him).

The marquis had, however, heard rumors that de Tilly had left the Chesapeake, removing half of the offensive pincer against Arnold. "My expectations are not Great," he wrote to Washington, "and I think we Have But few chances for us." He assured the commander-in-chief that he would continue to press on as rapidly as possible and would only turn back if he heard from Gouvion (whom he had sent to Steuben even before Washington asked) that de Tilly had definitely returned to Rhode Island.

By March 3, Lafayette and his men were at Head of Elk, arriving three days earlier than his most optimistic estimate. He still did not know Rochambeau's plans, though he had received a letter from his commander—written before Washington knew the full extent of the French expedition—telling him that Destouches intended to send *Romulus* and a couple of frigates back to Portsmouth.

That was enough for Lafayette. With renewed enthusiasm, he began to fire off letters to the principal actors in Virginia. Under the mistaken belief that Steuben had gone south to join Greene, he wrote to "The Commanding Officer in Virginia," whoever that might be, that "The Sailing of Mr. de Telly's squadron must have disappointed your expectations, and of course relaxed the preparations against Portsmouth." He then informed the officer (who was in fact Steuben) of the second squadron that would be sent to trap Arnold. He requested that as many militia as possible be collected. He also requested that the commanding officer "collect as much artillery, ammunition &c. as will be within your reach," as well as horses, boats, and pilots. Once again, he made it clear that no communication was to be held with Arnold "that may any way give him the least claim to the advantages of a prisoner of war."

And that was about all Lafayette could do, because, much to his disappointment, he found few of the boats and ships he had requested waiting for him at Head of Elk. "This delay may prove fatal to the Expedition," he wrote to Baltimore businessman and brigadier general Mordecai Gist, asking him to use his "whole Influence and your Most Strenuous Exertions to send immediately to this place Every Vessel fit for the Navigation of the Bay." He repeated the plea in letters sent off in every direction, and then he embarked on what was for him the most difficult activity of all: he waited.

Approximately 200 miles away by water from Head of Elk, Steuben was not waiting for anything. He had begun preparations for Arnold's capture as soon as de Tilly arrived in the bay, and he had continued even after de Tilly announced his departure. "I have it therefore in my Power to afford the necessary assistance to the affair now in agitation," he wrote to Washington, "much sooner than could be expected." He had collected over fifteen hundred militia, four 18-pounder cannon and mortars with 800 shells, mounted troops, riflemen, ships and boats, "and indeed every other article that may be necessary, if Working Day, & Night will procure them."

The baron had spent a good portion of his time in Virginia making requests—many said demands—of the government, and the new operations only increased that activity. He wrote to Governor Thomas Jefferson in French, their common language, asking that at least forty thousand rations for Lafayette's men to be sent to Williamsburg by March 7 and that at least the same amount be sent to the Virginia militia in Suffolk under the command of Peter Muhlenberg. He called for ships to be collected at Hood's Fort, 40 miles up the James River from Portsmouth, by March 6, and for carriages for the guns, vessels for transporting them, and all necessary supplies to be ready by March 7.

By the second week in March, even before the arrival of Lafayette's troops or the French army, Arnold was well hemmed in, surrounded by upward of two thousand militia with only one road out of Portsmouth. Steuben even had the order of battle worked out. He wrote to Washington, "You need not, my Dear General be under any apprehension that Arnold will escape by Land. Let the retreat by James River be cut off & I will answer for delivering him over to the Marquis."

Cutting off a retreat by way of the James River was, of course, the business of the French navy, upon which all else depended. It is hardly surprising, then, that everyone was eagerly looking out for the French ships. Even as he was organizing his troops and supplies, Steuben began to dispatch boats to intercept them, though in fact the fleet had not yet left Newport. Instead of the French, Steuben's people discovered that the British had "a number of Cruisers out up the Bay as well as down to the Capes on a Continual look out." Arnold and his naval commander, Commodore Thomas Symonds, wanted no more surprises like the one de Tilly had given them.

"[A] sufficient force to clear the Chesapeake Bay"

By early March, Benedict Arnold was sounding less sanguine about the security of his position. Sir Henry Clinton had informed him that the sixty-four and the two frigates might only be the first of a fleet from Newport. If a French fleet did sail from Rhode Island, Clinton wrote to Arnold that he could "rest assured every attention will be paid to your situation, and that our movements will be regulated by theirs."

Such an assurance may not have been too comforting. Arnold had intended to launch another foray up the James River under the command of Lieutenant Colonel Dundas, but in light of the rebel threat he countermanded that order. Instead, Dundas was sent against American troops at Williamsburg and Norfolk, where he skirmished with little result. For the first time since his arrival in Virginia, Arnold was not concentrating on offensive action. Lieutenant Colonel Simcoe recalled, "There being indications that a serious attack upon Portsmouth was in agitation, Gen. Arnold was very active in putting it into a respectable state of defense."

Arnold invited his senior officers to meet for a discussion of the manner in which they would defend themselves against the rebels. He believed that the Americans had "upwards of three Thousand Men" within 12 miles of Portsmouth and were ready to attack. "I have every reason to believe that they have collected this Force to cooperate with the French Ships and Troops which they hourly expect from Rhode Island," he wrote to Clinton.

Given their circumstances, there was nothing for Arnold and his men to do but dig in and hope that Clinton would send support before they were overwhelmed by the French and Americans. "We are however all in high Spirits," he wrote to Clinton, "not doubting but that our Wants and critical Situation will be properly attended to."

Both Clinton and Vice-Admiral Arbuthnot were well aware of French preparations. Word reached them that Rochambeau was embarking men and removing ordnance from batteries in preparation for a move against the Chesapeake. By early March, they were aware of Lafayette's division moving south to link up with Steuben and the Virginia militia.

Like Destouches, Arbuthnot was racing to get his fleet ready for sea. *Culloden* was a total loss, though all her crew had been saved, which was no doubt an enormous relief. Of all the things a ship needed to operate, seamen were the most difficult to obtain.

Culloden had gone ashore 18 miles from Gardiner's Bay, "in an uninhabited country, a few Indians," as Arbuthnot described it. Most of the guns and stores from the ship had been saved before the hull had broken up. Arbuthnot next set his men to salvaging the wreck for masts and yards to rerig the dismasted *Bedford*. Gales continued to lash the Long Island coast as the crews struggled to save the massive spars.

Once freed from the wreck, the masts and bowsprit were towed to Gardiner's Bay, where the 98-gun *London* had been prepared to assist in stepping them aboard *Bedford*. The huge and ponderous spars arrived on March 3 and were in place by the next day—an impressive accomplishment. But considerably more work remained, including constructing the huge tops, or platforms, on which marines were stationed in battle to snipe at the enemy's deck, before *Bedford* was ready to take her place in the fleet.

While seamen struggled to ready the men-of-war for sea, Arbuthnot and Clinton continued to wrangle about how best to relieve Arnold. Arbuthnot was in poor health. Around the time de Tilly's squadron had first been reported, he had written to Lord Sandwich, First Lord of the Admiralty, asking to be recalled. "I have lost almost totally the sight of one eye," he complained, "and the other is but a feeble helpmate." Further, he added, "I have lately been seized with very odd fits, resembling apoplexy, because almost instantly I faint, remain senseless and speechless sometimes four hours." Upon recovering, he would have no memory of fainting, but he remained sick for two or three days.

A lifetime at sea had taken its toll. Arbuthnot had been shipboard for the past nine months almost without break, and he had spent the previous fifty-four years in the naval service. The current crisis called for a younger and more vigorous officer, but for the time being it was all on the shoulders of Marriot Arbuthnot.

In early March, the troops intended for Virginia under the command of Major General William Phillips were embarked, and the transports dropped down to Sandy Hook, ready to sail to Arnold's relief. Clinton was waiting to learn Arbuthnot's intentions, but Arbuthnot was not very forthcoming. "I flatter myself, though you do not mention it," Clinton wrote to the admiral at the end of February, "that you have already detached a sufficient force to clear the Chesapeake Bay." In fact, Arbuthnot had not yet sent any ships south, nor had he bothered to tell the commander-in-chief what he had in mind.

Finally, as the French prepared to sail, Arbuthnot sent a series of seemingly contradictory letters to Clinton outlining his plans. Initially, he proposed to meet the transports at Sandy Hook and escort them with his fleet to the Chesapeake without waiting to see what the French would do. This idea did not sit well with Clinton. If Arbuthnot headed south with his fleet and the French did not sail, then the numerous supply ships and transports Clinton was expecting from England would be vulnerable to capture with no British naval force to defend them. On the other hand, if Arbuthnot sailed with Phillips's troops in company and met the French fleet at sea, the transports would interfere with Arbuthnot's ability to fight.

Soon after, Arbuthnot wrote to say once more that he would "proceed instantly with the squadron off Sandy Hook." But, in another letter, he said he would send a frigate to reconnoiter Newport and "regulate [his] measures by what was discovered there." Then he sent orders to one of his frigate captains instructing him "to take the *Orpheus* and *Savage* under your command" and escort Phillips's transports to the Chesapeake.

Clinton certainly did not want Phillips's division sailing south with no idea where the French navy was or who controlled the sea lanes. As he told Lord Cornwallis, "to send them under two frigates only, before the Chesapeake is our own, is to sacrifice the troops and their convoy." Ultimately, however, there was nothing that either Clinton or Arbuthnot— or, for that matter, Washington, Lafayette, Steuben, or Arnold—could do but wait for the French to make their move.

By March 9, the British fleet was ready for sea, and Arbuthnot began to move his ships out of Gardiner's Bay in preparation to sail. He sent two frigates across the mouth of Long Island Sound to see what was happening in Newport. The next day, the frigates came racing back with the news that the French fleet was gone.

The French Move

Rochambeau and Destouches were as eager as any American officer to launch an expedition against Arnold. They appreciated the significance of such a victory, even if it involved only the capture of Arnold's small, fifteen-hundred-man force. And they were embarrassed by the failure of the Expédition Particulière to accomplish anything in the eight months it had been on American soil. Their eagerness was shared by the rest of the French officer corps. As Captain Louis-Alexandre Berthier later recalled, "Everyone was vying with everyone else to take part in this expedition."

Although Rochambeau had made it clear to Washington that the French were organizing the expedition as quickly as they could, Washington decided to go to Newport to help move things along. He wrote to Lafayette on March 1, "I set out in the morning for Rhode Island where I hope to arrive before the fleet sails to level all difficulties and be in the way to improve circumstances." What difficulties he may have foreseen is unclear, but the pomp his presence would occasion in Newport was more likely to slow things up than to hasten them.

Washington arrived at Newport on March 6, having been ferried from the mainland in Destouches's barge (there being no bridge to Rhode Island at the time). Already a great hero to the French, the American commander-in-chief had recently been made a marshal of France after it was pointed out in the French court that only the king or a marshal could be considered senior to Rochambeau in command of the French troops in America. "I mark, as a fortunate day," wrote the commissary Claude Blanchard of Washington's arrival, "that in which I have been able to behold a man so truly great."

Washington was escorted directly aboard Destouches's flagship, the *Duc de Bourgogne*, where all the general officers had assembled. This may well have been the first time Washington ever set foot on a ship of the line. The guns of the fleet roared out the honor due a man of Washington's stature. An American eyewitness, Daniel Updike, later recalled, "The firing from the French ships that lined the harbor was tremendous; it was one continued roar and looked as though the very bay were on fire." According to Updike, Washington wore the Marshal of France insignia on his uniform.

Having met with the generals on board the flagship, Washington and Rochambeau repaired ashore to receive honors from the rest of the army. Many of the officers were French nobles, accustomed to the pomp of Versailles, and they were not about to take half measures in greeting the American commander-in-chief. The guns of the batteries boomed out their salutes. The troops in their brilliant white uniforms, all five thousand, mustered under arms, "forming a great parade and lining his route on both sides of the street from the quay to his lodgings."

As Washington proceeded along the great line of soldiers, each general stood at the head of his division to salute him. Rochambeau and his staff hurried ahead to take their places at the front of the Bourbonnais Regiment, the senior regiment in the Expédition Particulière. The reaction of Berthier was typical of the French officers. He wrote in his journal, "The nobility of his bearing and his countenance, which bore the stamp of all his virtues, inspired everyone with the devotion and respect due his character."

That afternoon, Washington dined with Rochambeau, and later he was escorted through the town of Newport, which was illuminated in his honor. A local Tory who chose not to illuminate his house had his windows broken by stone-throwing patriots until he relented and showed Washington the proper respect. Townspeople carried torches to light Washington's way to the quarters of the Baron de Vioménil, Rochambeau's second in command, where he had supper.

Washington spent the following week in Newport, fêted in the homes of the town's leading citizens, including, ironically, Metcalf Bowler. Bowler, a leader of the revolutionary movement in Rhode Island, had become a British informer to protect himself and his property, but his treachery would remain hidden until the 1920s, when his secret correspondence was found during a cataloguing of Sir Henry Clinton's papers.

The party ended the day following Washington's arrival for more than a thousand French troops, including de Vioménil, whom Rochambeau chose to lead the attack on Arnold. The fleet was at last ready to put to sea, and the men who had been chosen for the expedition boarded their assigned ships. But now it was the wind that proved an obstacle, blowing from the wrong quarter and holding the ships wind-bound in harbor. It was not unheard of for ships to spend days or weeks awaiting a fair wind, but luckily for the French, the breeze came around to "a light norther" the following day, fair to waft the ships south to the open ocean.

Around five o'clock on the afternoon of March 8, the ships of Destouches's squadron won their anchors and stood out to sea. There were eight ships of the line if the 50-gun *Romulus* were counted as such, though the French sometimes considered her a heavy frigate. The flagship was the 80-gun *Duc de Bourgogne*, followed in size by the seventy-fours *Conquérant* and *Neptune* and the sixty-fours *Jason*, *Ardent*, *Provence*, and *Eveillé*, the latter making her second foray to the Chesapeake.

Two frigates accompanied the fleet. One was the 32-gun *Hermione*, famous as the ship that had carried Lafayette back from France twelve months earlier after the marquis had convinced the king to send military aid to America. The other was the *Fantasque*, armed *en flute*—that is, with guns missing so her gunports were empty, like the holes of a flute. *Fantasque* was used as a supply ship, though she still mounted twenty-two guns on her lower deck. In all, the French squadron mounted 588 heavy guns. Only a portion of the fleet, however, was coppered.

While standing out of the harbor, *Fantasque* managed to run aground. Boats were sent to tow her off, and after a few hours she was freed with no damage to her bottom.

From the fortified high ground at the harbor entrance, George Washington watched the fleet put to sea. One can imagine the mixed emotions he must have felt, watching the eight big men-of-war standing south, bearing away on a mission to trap Benedict Arnold. Here was the fleet on which all his hope of victory against the British rested—and which had already disappointed him again and again.

He must have wondered if this time, perhaps, things would be different.

CHAPTER 6 *The Battle of Cape Henry*

CHEVALIER DESTOUCHES'S FLEET made its way south into fluky winds that backed from north to southwest, driving the ships eastward of their destination. Laboriously, they worked their way toward Cape Henry, marking the entrance to the Chesapeake Bay. Their progress was further hampered by an absence of copper sheathing on a number of the ships, which created great disparities in speed throughout the squadron.

On March 11, three days out of Newport, the fleet was well offshore and still 70 leagues, or 210 miles, from Cape Henry, having completed scarcely half the passage. A few hours after midnight on March 12, wrapped in darkness and fog, the ships were suddenly headed, the wind swinging around their bows. Captain Berthier wrote that "part of the squadron was caught in irons with sails aback [i.e., with the wind hitting the wrong side of the sails, pressing them back against the masts], and at daybreak the *Duc de Bourgogne*, the *Neptune*, the *Eveillé*, and the *Surveillante* found themselves isolated from the rest of the squadron." (Several participants mentioned the frigate *Surveillante* in their letters and journals, though she is not listed as one of the ships that sailed with the squadron. She might have joined the fleet at sea.)

A ship "caught in irons" loses steerageway with its bow pointing directly into the wind and is temporarily unable to move. In high winds, the ship might easily be dismasted, but in this case, the wind was light and the danger was from a different quarter. The scattering of the ships exposed them to the possibility of being picked off by a superior English force. "This separation was alarming," wrote Claude Blanchard, who was on board the flagship, "for thus each of our divisions was very inferior to the English." In fleet tactics, there was safety in numbers.

The rest of the fleet was nowhere in sight in the thickening fog. Destouches tacked his flagship and the three vessels still in company with her back and forth, firing volleys as a signal to the others, but it did no good. The wind had swung into the southwest and was building, so the admiral shaped a course for the Chesapeake in hope of meeting the remainder of his fleet there. His biggest unknown was also his biggest worry—where was Vice-Admiral Arbuthnot?

The British Fleet

The British fleet had already cleared Gardiner's Bay, Long Island, on March 10 when the frigates sent to reconnoiter Newport returned with news that the French fleet was out. Arbuthnot immediately set out in pursuit, certain from the intelligence he had received that they were bound for the Chesapeake. He believed that the Marquis de Lafayette was marching south at the head of twenty-five hundred men and that Baron de Steuben had assembled six thousand militia under his command, enough to capture Benedict Arnold and then threaten Lord Cornwallis from the north while Nathanael Greene's forces closed in from the south. British ships were sorely needed in the Chesapeake.

Arbuthnot's fleet, all copper-bottomed, made good time, though the hurried manner in which the ships had been readied for sea had consequences. "The *Bedford* was rather in confusion," Arbuthnot reported, "and soon after sprung [broke] her maintopmast." A broken topmast was routine, but it was still a big problem. The topgallant mast and sail had to be sent down to the deck, then the topmast itself—over a hundred feet long and several feet in diameter—had to be lowered down and a new one sent up, then everything rerigged as before.

Such problems aside, Arbuthnot enjoyed significant advantages over Destouches. Not only were his ships coppered, they were more powerful, starting with the *London*, a three-decker of ninety-eight guns, far bigger than anything in the French fleet. The flagship *Royal Oak* was a seventy-four, as were *Robust* and *Bedford*, compared with just two French seventy-fours. The *Europe, America,* and *Prudent* were sixty-fours, and the *Adamant* was a fifty, like *Romulus*. Arbuthnot also had three frigates, including the 44-gun *Roebuck*, the 32-gun *Iris*, and the 22-gun *Medea*. In all, the British fleet mounted 660 guns to the French fleet's 588—a big advantage in any last-ship-standing battle of attrition like those that characterized naval actions of the time.

By March 12, as Destouches was struggling to reunite his fleet, Arbuthnot was just south of Delaware Bay. There, he crossed paths with a British merchant ship nine weeks out of Cork, bound for New York. The captain of the merchantman told Arbuthnot that the day before he had seen a French fleet "consisting of ten sail of large ships" about 75 miles south of their present location. The merchantman had been chased by one of the ships but had managed to get away.

Soon after, a brisk wind sprung up from the north northeast, driving the ships south toward the Chesapeake. Arbuthnot's sense of urgency had been further heightened by the merchantman's news. He did not expect to beat the French to Virginia, but he hoped to arrive close enough on their heels to prevent them from landing troops or maneuvering to trap Arnold. He knew that Destouches would not attempt either action with a superior enemy fleet in the offing. In fact, however, the British had managed to overtake and pass the French and, without knowing it, were now closer to the Chesapeake than the enemy fleet.

The British were 60 miles from Cape Henry when the wind tapered and veered into the south, temporarily preventing further progress toward their destination. The same wind that had driven Arbuthnot south had also helped the French fleet, so that Arbuthnot's complete squadron and the two halves of Destouches's force were all within 60 miles of one another, though they remained unaware of this in fog and occasional heavy weather.

On March 14, at eight bells in the morning watch (8:00 A.M.), Cape Henry was spotted from the deck of the *Duc de Bourgogne*, a little too close for comfort. The flagship put about to stand to sea with its three companions. As they worked their way offshore, the frigate *Surveillante* signaled sails on the horizon. The flagship's drummers beat to quarters, and sailors scrambled over the decks to clear for action. Gun tackles were cast off, sand was spread on the decks, fires in the galley were doused. Gunners prepared their cartridges, and surgeons laid out their instruments. The bulkheads that walled off the officers' cabins were struck, opening the decks from one end of the ship to the other. While the crew prepared for battle, however, the signal officer raised the recognition signal aloft, and to the relief of everyone on board, it was answered correctly. The distant vessels were the second half of the French fleet, which had become separated. Soon all eight ships of the line were reunited "to the great satisfaction of all."

The wind out of the south kept strengthening, driving both the French and the British north of the capes. For days, the ponderous ships of the line tacked against the contrary wind, making little headway. Destouches dispatched the more weatherly *Surveillante* to close with Cape Henry and keep a lookout for the British fleet, as each side struggled to beat the other into the sheltered waters of the Chesapeake Bay. Both fleets were in the same area of the sea, making for the same destination, and neither knew that the other was there.

"[A] more pleasing prospect"

The morning of March 16 began foggy with the wind blowing from the north northeast, but the breeze dropped and shifted into the west southwest as the sun rose. Visibility was a mile or two as the men-of-war in Destouches's fleet sailed on port tack, meaning that the wind was blowing over the port, or left, sides of the vessels. In the nautical parlance of the day, they were sailing "with their larboard tacks aboard," larboard being then the more common term for a ship's left side.

The French squadron, according to its logbooks, was on a northeasterly heading in light air when a frigate suddenly appeared to the south, which was now to windward, about a mile off. "At first the Admiral gave the signal to chase her," the official report recorded. The copper-bottomed *Eveillé* and the frigate *Surveillante*, which had rejoined the fleet, were sent after the stranger, "but soon afterward several vessels loomed out of the fog." The French and British fleets had found one another.

The French fleet was several miles to the north and downwind of the British, sailing in a loose formation. Destouches "signaled the squadron to form in line of battle on the port tack." The heavy ships began to wheel into line, with the *Conquérant* leading the way and the flagship *Duc de Bourgogne* in the middle, the customary position for the admiral in command. Once again, the drummers beat to quarters and the ships cleared for action. This time, however, there was no doubting the identity of the ships emerging from the mist.

Destouches did not particularly want this fight. According to Berthier, he "neither avoided nor sought battle. He thought only of upholding the honor of the King's arms." Arbuthnot's arrival convinced Destouches that his mission could no longer be accomplished. "He realized the impossibility of disembarking troops under fire," the official report read, "even from his warships, while opposed by a superior squadron." And if he could no longer assist in trapping Arnold, Destouches saw no benefit in engaging the more powerful British fleet.

But neither could he withdraw and "give the boastful English any opportunity for claiming that he had been chased away by a fleet of comparable strength to his own." Instead, he maneuvered his ships to seek the most advantageous position, while allowing Arbuthnot to decide whether there would be a fight. Having only recently been elevated from senior captain after de Ternay's death, Destouches was not an experienced fleet commander. The possibility that he could beat the British so thoroughly as to drive them off does not seem to have occurred to him.

Arbuthnot, for his part, entertained no doubt that engaging the enemy was the advantageous thing to do. "[I]t favoured our operations," he wrote to the Earl of Sandwich, First Lord of the Admiralty, "to bring them to action." The most he had hoped for upon leaving Long Island was to arrive in the Chesapeake before the French troops could disembark. He had been playing catch-up, and it must have been a great relief to find Destouches still on open water.

Unfortunately for Arbuthnot, the wind soon hauled around again, this time into the northeast, giving the French the favored windward position. Arbuthnot's fleet fell off on port tack, sailing line ahead, that is, with one ship directly astern of another. *Robust* was in the lead, with the flagship, *Royal Oak*, like *Duc de Bourgogne*, in her proper place in the middle of the line, and the three frigates out to windward.

No sailing vessel can sail directly into the wind. To get to windward, or to "weather," any ship must sail a zigzag pattern upwind, called tacking. Modern boats can sail within 45 degrees of the wind, but ponderous eighteenth-century men-of-war could do little better than 70 degrees, often losing to leeway what little windward progress their courses might otherwise have conferred. Thus, the downwind ships might not be able to get up to the enemy, and if they tried they would likely be shot to pieces trying to tack in the face of the enemy's broadsides. The fleet that held the windward position, known as the "weather gauge," had the choice of whether and when to sail downwind and engage.

By eight o'clock on the morning of March 16, the weather gauge belonged to Destouches. Arbuthnot began to work his ships to windward as best he could, trying to sail higher on the wind than the French in order to reel them in to the range of his big guns. Destouches, however, chose not to close with the British. Instead, for the next hour, the two fleets maintained an easterly heading, sailing in two roughly parallel lines a mile or more apart, with their larboard tacks aboard and their rows of black guns leering at each other through a thickening haze. As the visibility deteriorated, Arbuthnot sent one of his nimble frigates to weather to maintain contact with the French feet.

At nine o'clock, Destouches made the signal for his fleet to tack, and one by one the big ships turned into the wind, their sails flogging in the growing breeze and showering the decks with moisture that had condensed on the canvas. With a squeal of bosun's pipes and the slap of bare feet on wooden decks, the sailors hauled away on braces and the ships swung through the wind from port tack to starboard, standing off toward the northwest.

Arbuthnot maintained his port tack for another half hour, perhaps hoping for a wind shift that would give him the weather gauge, then he too made the signal for the fleet to tack in succession. Once again, the two fleets were sailing in roughly parallel lines, the distance between them closing. The coppered bottoms of the British ships allowed them to sail higher—closer to the direction from which the wind was blowing—than the French ships with their growth-encrusted bottoms could sail.

As the two fleets settled on their new courses, Destouches discovered another reason to postpone battle. In tacking, both the *Eveillé* and the *Ardent* had broken a topsail yard, the long, horizontal spar supporting the topsail, the second highest sail on a mast and the most crucial sail for maneuvering. Each ship had three topsails, one on each mast, the fore, main, and mizzen. The broken yards on the two French ships must have been critical fore or main topsail yards, as Destouches felt the need to maneuver "so as to allow the *Eveillé* and *Ardent* time to repair their topsail-yards."

This was no easy task. Like the topmasts, the topsail yards of a ship of the line were huge and unwieldy, upwards of 80 feet long and 20 inches

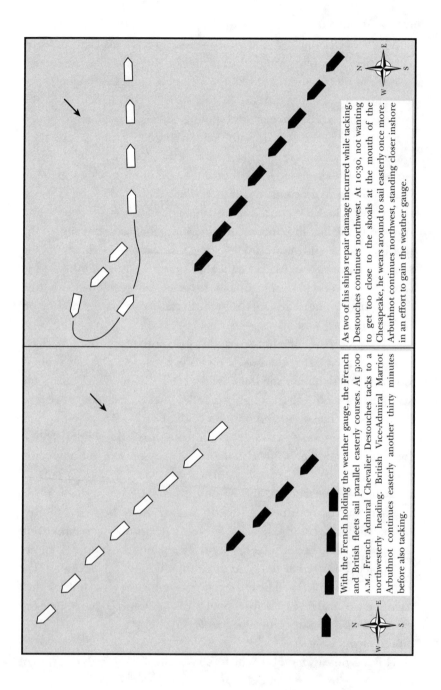

With the French holding the weather gauge, the French and British fleets sail parallel easterly courses. At 9:00 A.M., French Admiral Chevalier Destouches tacks to a northwesterly heading. British Vice-Admiral Marriot Arbuthnot continues easterly another thirty minutes before also tacking.

As two of his ships repair damage incurred while tacking, Destouches continues northwest. At 10:30, not wanting to get too close to the shoals at the mouth of the Chesapeake, he wears around to sail easterly once more. Arbuthnot continues northwest, standing closer inshore in an effort to gain the weather gauge.

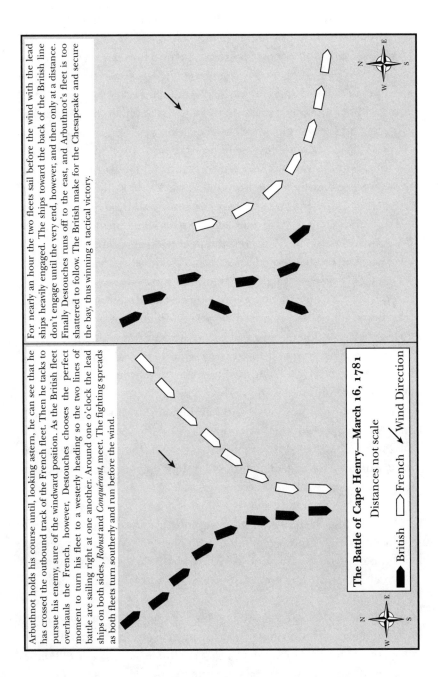

Arbuthnot holds his course until, looking astern, he can see that he has crossed the outbound track of the French fleet. Then he tacks to pursue his enemy, sure of the windward position. As the British fleet overhauls the French, however, Destouches chooses the perfect moment to turn his fleet to a westerly heading so the two lines of battle are sailing right at one another. Around one o'clock the lead ships on both sides, *Robust* and *Conquérant*, meet. The fighting spreads as both fleets turn southerly and run before the wind.

For nearly an hour the two fleets sail before the wind with the lead ships heavily engaged. The ships toward the back of the British line don't engage until the very end, however, and then only at a distance. Finally Destouches runs off to the east, and Arbuthnot's fleet is too shattered to follow. The British make for the Chesapeake and secure the bay, thus winning a tactical victory.

The Battle of Cape Henry—March 16, 1781
Distances not scale

◆ British   ▷ French   ↙ Wind Direction

in diameter in the center. Along with the massive topsail that was lashed along its length, each of these behemoths was rigged with lifts, braces, halyards, studdingsail booms, footropes, flemish horses, reef tackle, and various other pieces of gear. It is a testament to the size and expertise of an eighteenth-century man-of-war's crew that they could get those huge spars and their attendant sails and rigging down, repaired or replaced, rerigged, and set again in a few hours or less.

Destouches continued his northwesterly course, his ships in their line of battle, as the wind and seas continued to build. To his south, the British were following a roughly parallel track, but sailing higher and faster, closing the gap. Around half past ten, "finding that the present tack was carrying his ships too close to the reefs along the northern coast of Virginia," Destouches ordered the fleet to wear around, back onto port tack. The French settled once again onto an easterly course as the two damaged vessels struggled to get things squared away aloft.

Arbuthnot, meanwhile, chose to continue northwest on a starboard tack, despite the nearness of the Virginia shoreline, passing to leeward of Destouches on the opposite tack. "The enemy was taking full advantage of their greater speed," Berthier recounted, "and, encouraged by their superior strength, continued to come on to windward, setting all their sails and running on the starboard tack."

The British fleet was faster and handier, and by noon, Arbuthnot, looking astern, could see that he had crossed the wake of the French squadron and achieved the weather gauge. "[T]he enemy," he wrote, "having their larboard tacks, and we standing on contrary one to fetch their wake, being so far advanced to weather of them, I made the signal to tack."

Now the English ships swung through the wind, yards groaning and canvas booming as the sails filled on the port tack. When they settled onto the new course, Arbuthnot's line of battle was directly astern of Destouches's and a few points to windward, and he quickly began to overhaul the French fleet.

"Nothing could bear a more pleasing prospect than my situation," Arbuthnot wrote. Destouches could no longer avoid a fight, and Arbuthnot enjoyed superior firepower. There were, however, a couple of points of concern. The British line had become too spread out, so Arbuthnot ordered the signal to be made for *Robust*, in the lead, to shorten sail. In addition, the weather continued to deteriorate. Visibility was poor in a spitting rain, with the wind rising and a big sea running.

Holding the weather gauge meant that Arbuthnot could bring Destouches to battle, but in the rising wind and sea he did not want to be upwind of the French when the fighting began. A sailing ship heels to leeward in a blow, and the farther a man-of-war heeled, the more difficult it became to elevate the guns high enough to hit the enemy. In high winds and big seas, a ship's lower gunports could not even be opened for fear of flooding.

Arbuthnot later reported that he "hailed Captain Cosby [captain of *Robust*] to inform him I meant to engage them to leeward, as the weather was very disagreeable, hazy, and a large sea." Before Arbuthnot could make his move, however, Destouches made his. With the British overtaking the end of his line, the French admiral realized that it was time to turn and fight. Just before one o'clock, Destouches's fleet wore around onto the starboard tack, turning 180 degrees to sail straight at the oncoming English and a little to leeward so as "to give his ships a better chance to use their lower batteries in the heavy sea then running."

Now the two fleets were converging quickly. It was too late for Arbuthnot to claim the leeward position, so he decided instead to keep his fleet on their current heading and pass the French to windward, each ship firing broadsides as the fleet moved down the line. But before he could make that signal, Cosby in *Robust* reacted to Destouches's maneuver on his own accord. He turned to intercept *Conquérant*, the lead ship of the French line, as she passed to leeward, wearing around so that *Robust* and *Conquérant* were both on starboard tack, sailing side by side. "At one o'clock," Berthier wrote, "the lead ship of the French came within range of the lead ship of the English, and several moments later both sides opened fire." The maneuvering was over, and the battle had begun.

Fleet Action

When Cosby wore *Robust* around to engage *Conquérant*, Arbuthnot was forced to order the rest of the fleet to follow suit, "which obliged me to form under the fire of the enemy's line." As the two seventy-fours hammered away at one another, Destouches's ships fell off, away from the wind. Arbuthnot's order for his fleet to wear ship was not only unexpected by the British captains but had to be done under the barrage of the French broadsides, and "the van was by this means soon put into confusion." This gave the next ships in the French line, the sixty-fours *Jason* and *Ardent*, the chance to rake British ships as they passed.

Arbuthnot, aboard *Royal Oak*, charged down into the fray and took a terrific beating for it. The French flagship *Duc de Bourgogne*, aided by *Ardent* and *Neptune*, concentrated her fire on the British flagship as she ranged alongside. The foresail aboard *Royal Oak* "was so torn with shot that it hung to the yard by four cloths and the earrings only." The flagship's rigging was shredded, and the "maintopsail halliards, braces, ties, also the foretopsail and fore braces and bowlines" were all shot away so that for a brief period the ship was adrift and out of control.

With *Royal Oak* momentarily knocked out, Destouches's flagship and two others, likely *Ardent* and *Neptune*, charged ahead to engage the three lead ships of the British line, the *Europe*, *Prudent*, and *Robust*. *Europe* and *Prudent* had already taken a severe beating from the lead French ships as they passed, and they were drifting out of control while their officers and men struggled to sort out the damage and get their ships underway again.

That left *Robust*, and *Duc de Bourgogne* and her consorts ran up alongside the seventy-four and poured fire into her. "[N]othing can exceed the gallant behaviour of Captain Cosby and his ship's company in general," Arbuthnot wrote, but gallantry was not enough against heavy broadsides. *Royal Oak*, now once again under control, came to *Robust*'s aid, drawing the French off, but not before the French gunners had "entirely cut up his masts, sails, and rigging." *Robust* drifted out of the line, turning stern to the passing French ships and receiving in her vulnerable stern "the fire from the French vanguard and, in addition, two broadsides from *Neptune*, which passed within pistol range."

Claude Blanchard, aboard *Duc de Bourgogne*, was likely writing of *Royal Oak* when he later recalled, "One of their ships was so disabled that it fell to the leeward and made a signal of distress; it had encountered our ship and two others at the same time." Blanchard speculated that *Neptune* "might have captured it or compelled it to run ashore" if she had wished. The 64-gun *Prudent* was similarly knocked out of action.

For nearly an hour, the two fleets kept up their running battle, sailing with the wind astern, the lead ships nearly side by side as they exchanged broadsides. The air was filled with choking gray smoke that swirled away in the growing wind. Flashes of gunfire punctuated the smoke and haze, and the flat, heavy, nearly continuous roar of the huge guns—18-, 24-, and 32-pounders—blanketed the ships and the sea. Sails jerked and flapped like wounded men as they were torn by flying metal. Thick lines and heavy blocks crashed to the decks below. Round shot smashed gaping holes though oak planks and frames and sent showers of deadly splinters through the close-packed men on deck.

While the lead ships of both fleets fought it out, the rear guard of the British line failed to engage. Possibly by oversight, Arbuthnot had kept the signal for line of battle flying and had never signaled for close action, which would have directed his ships to engage as best they could. This failure made him the target of considerable criticism in the aftermath of the fight. His captains, at least those at the end of the line, might have shown more zeal and initiative, but the Royal Navy valued strict adherence to command over initiative; there could be career-ending penalties for initiative, but not for scrupulous obedience. In these same waters half a year later, the situation would repeat itself. Once again, confusion over the line-of-battle signal and the signal for close action would result in a failure of the British rear guard to engage. In this future instance, however, the consequence of that confusion would be the loss of the war.

The ships at the head of the fleet, both British and French, bore the brunt of the fighting. Blanchard wrote that *Conquérant,* at the head of the French line, "had, for its part, to sustain the attack of three of the enemy's ships, and fought hand to hand with the ship of three decks." Her decks were a bloodbath, "the boatswains, the captain at arms and seven steersmen among the dead." Her wheel and tiller were shot away, and her rudder had been damaged. Unable to steer, she drifted out of the line and was subjected to the broadsides of each passing ship. *London*, with her three decks of heavy guns, threatened to crush the French seventy-four under her broadsides before *Neptune* came to her aid.

Realizing that he could not bring the last of the British ships into the fight if he continued to run downwind, Destouches swung his fleet to the east, coming up on a port tack, each ship firing at the van, or the lead, of the British fleet as it passed. *Robust* was completely disabled and drifted off downwind until Arbuthnot dispatched a frigate to take her in tow.

As the French fleet moved off to the east, the British afterguard finally engaged, firing at long range and doing little damage. *Romulus* found herself some distance from the rest of the French fleet, and "the English three-decker *London* appeared to cut her off" from the French rear guard. With less than half of *London*'s firepower, *Romulus* was no match for the ship of the line. Undaunted, *Romulus* "delivered her a timely broadside that broke her [*London*'s] principal topsail-yard." The smashed main topsail yard, hanging like a broken wing, "obliged her to bear away and retire from the line, while keeping up a withering fire to little avail."

Arbuthnot continued to pursue Destouches's fleet, but not for long. His own fleet was in no shape to continue the action. "After a very short show of pursuing the enemy, who was now pretty far advanced ahead," he wrote to Sandwich, "I returned to the assistance of the *Robust, Prudent* and *Europe*. The two former it was necessary to cause to be towed." Those battered ships and the loss of *London*'s main topsail yard, Arbuthnot wrote, "put it out of my power to pursue the enemy far."

The French fleet was in considerably better shape as they stood off to the eastward on a port tack before falling off to the southeast. Destouches ordered the ships "to close up the battle line on the port tack, without regard to the ship's regular position in line." All the fleet fell in line save for *Conquérant*, which was still without use of her rudder and largely unmanageable. Night was falling and the British had the weather gauge, and though the enemy had four ships disabled to Destouches's one, the French admiral chose not to resume the fight.

From the site of the battle, Cape Henry bore west by south, around 40 miles away, an easy downwind run in the northeast winds of March 16. Why Destouches, with his less-damaged fleet, did not make for the Chesapeake is unclear, except that the French commander had been convinced since first sighting Arbuthnot that his mission was over and there was no point in going on. As the sun sank into a gray, heaving ocean, the French fleet "sailed to the south under shortened sail, with all our lamps lighted."

The following day, the weather had cleared and the British were nowhere in sight. Destouches ordered the fleet hove to and the captains to repair on board the flagship. Each captain reported the condition of his ship, and all save *Conquérant* were found to be fit to resume battle.

But they did not. "A council of war was held," Berthier wrote, "and despite our slight advantage M. Destouches decided to proceed to Newport to repair his squadron."

By any reasonable analysis, the Battle of Cape Henry was a victory for the French. Destouches had outmaneuvered Arbuthnot in nearly every instance, most notably with his near perfect timing in turning to fight, snatching the leeward position just as the British were coming up on his rear guard. Arbuthnot's squadron was copper bottomed and more powerful, but they had had four ships knocked out of action, some quite severely, compared with only one of Destouches's fleet. Two British ships of the line would be absent from the Battle of the Capes six months later in part because they were still undergoing repairs from the Battle of Cape Henry. And yet, Destouches was the one who sailed home.

His decision lay partly with his understanding of orders. He was to bottle up Arnold and his fleet and land French troops, neither of which he now deemed possible. His instructions did not involve seeking out and destroying Arbuthnot's fleet. The French military philosophy of the day also played a part in his thinking. The French considered it a principle of war that much should be risked in defending a position, but little should be risked in attacking one.

Admiral de Barras, who would soon relieve Destouches, wrote of Destouches's decision to return to Newport, "M. des Touches, whose object was purely offensive, could and should, when the enemy opposed him with superior forces, renounce a project which could no longer succeed unless, contrary to all probability, it ended not only in beating but in destroying entirely that superior squadron."

Had he resumed the fight, Destouches might well have entirely destroyed Arbuthnot's fleet. But he had done enough to bring honor to king and country, and so the next day, in continued good weather, the fleet repaired their damaged rigging and shaped a course for Rhode Island. Ultimately, Destouches would receive less criticism from his superiors and fellow officers for abandoning the attack on Arnold than Arbuthnot would for staving it off.

CHAPTER 7 *"An attempt to conquer Virginia"*

"WE ARRIVED HERE on the 18th," Vice-Admiral Arbuthnot wrote from Lynnhaven Bay, Virginia, "in time, I am bold to say, to save both Mr Arnold's forces here and also Lord Cornwallis." Arbuthnot was clearly pleased with the outcome of what would be the last significant action in his largely undistinguished career.

Others felt differently. Reactions ranged from outright criticism to the king's damning of Arbuthnot's accomplishment with faint praise. George III wrote to the Earl of Sandwich, First Lord of the Admiralty, "I was much hurt that the action had ended without any other advantage in our favour but the retreat of the French squadron. . . . [But] though it has not proved decisive as a naval engagement, yet it has saved the troops under the command of Arnold."

Brigadier General Benedict Arnold had no idea what was taking place at sea. Since the arrival of Captain de Tilly's fleet a month before, he had been driving his men to strengthen the defenses around Portsmouth in preparation for an anticipated attack. On the morning of the day Arbuthnot arrived in the bay, he "gave orders for every person to work on the lines, and the town people, who should refuse, to quit it."

The following day he received news of "a squadron with French colours being at anchor, on the 19th, at Lynnhaven bay." Sir Henry Clinton, however, had earlier warned Arnold that if "a fleet should appear under French colours, do not be alarmed, as I shall advise the admiral to send it in that manner, to deceive the enemy." Thus, Arnold knew that the ships could be either British under false colors or French under true colors, and he sent Lieutenant Colonel Simcoe to find out which it was.

Simcoe took a mounted patrol overland to Lynnhaven Bay, a distance of some 20 miles, where "he had the pleasure to find it was Admiral Arbuthnot's fleet." Arbuthnot had even had the good fortune to capture a ship deceived by his false colors, just as de Tilly had done three weeks earlier.

That same day, Arbuthnot sent a note to Arnold informing the general that he would "put to sea immediately" to bring Chevalier Destouches's squadron to action again, but he did nothing of the sort. Rather, he moved his fleet into the James River to oversee the disembarking of the reinforcements at Portsmouth when they arrived.

"The troops under Phillips," Clinton had written to Cornwallis before Arbuthnot sailed for Virginia, "have been embarked for some Time, and are now at the Hook waiting for the Admiral or a Message from him." That message arrived in New York soon after the Battle of Cape Henry, and on March 20, Major General Phillips's transports, escorted by the frigates *Orpheus* and *Savage*, weighed anchor from Sandy Hook and set sail for the South.

The addition of Phillips's two thousand men to the fifteen hundred under Arnold would make Virginia a rapidly evolving center of the British war effort, though not by any choice or plan of Clinton's. Clinton, like Cornwallis and George Germain, was a proponent of the southern strategy, which involved taking the Carolinas and stabilizing them under the king's rule, then moving north from that secure base. The only reasons Clinton could see to send troops to Virginia were to cut off the pipeline of rebel supplies and to pin down American troops that could otherwise march to the aid of Nathanael Greene's army in the Carolinas. "I will frankly own," Clinton wrote, "that I ever disapproved of an attempt to conquer Virginia before the Carolinas were absolutely restored."

By the spring of 1781, however, the Carolinas were far from restored. British troops found something akin to local support in each new area they occupied, but that support evaporated once they moved on. The hard truth was that the British lacked sufficient force to take and hold the Carolinas and maintain the king's peace throughout the region. Had every British and German soldier in America been in the Carolinas, it still might not have been enough.

It was equally pointless, however, to take an area and then move on. Time and again, the British army had told Loyalists who declared their allegiance to the king that troops would remain to protect them, but time and again, the army had then shifted to another area and left the Loyalists in the hands of the rebels. There was, in fact, no good solution.

Clinton wanted to stick to the plan. He did not want to involve himself in Virginia until the Carolinas were stabilized, and he had no intention of leaving a large force in Portsmouth. His instructions to Phillips, before the major general left New York for Virginia, read, "It is probable, whenever the objects of this expedition are fulfilled, and that you have strengthened the present works . . . that you may return to this place." He was to bring with him Arnold and most of the troops, leaving only one or two regiments to garrison Portsmouth or whatever alternative harbor they ultimately decided to fortify.

Germain did not share this view. At the conclusion of the Battle of Cape Henry, Arbuthnot sent a vessel express to London with a report to the American secretary of his "victory." (Admirals and generals were always eager to see that their version of events was the first to reach the king and ministry.) Germain wrote to Clinton upon hearing "the very agreeable and important intelligence of [Arbuthnot's] having defeated the French admiral's project of carrying his squadron and a detachment of French troops to attack General Arnold." Reading between the lines of Arbuthnot's account, Germain could see that the victory was far from complete. "I greatly regret that all the French ships escaped," he wrote.

That said, Germain addressed the question of Virginia, failing entirely to appreciate Clinton's position:

> Conceiving, therefore, as highly as I do of the importance of the southern provinces, and of the vast advantages which must attend the prosecution of the war upon the present plan of extending our conquests from south to north, it was a great mortification to me to find by your instructions to Major-General Phillips that it appeared to be your intention that only a part of the troops he carried with him should remain in the Chesapeak.

Germain "thought it proper to ask the advice of His Majesty's other servants," who, not surprisingly, agreed with him, and their proposals were laid before the king. The king had commanded Germain to remind Clinton that "the recovery of the southern provinces and the prosecution of the war by pushing our conquests from south to north is to be considered as the chief and principal object for the employment of all the forces under your command."

Clinton did not disagree with any of that. He simply felt that there was no point in putting large numbers of troops into Virginia while the Carolinas remained as rebellious as ever. And he also had to consider what the Americans and French were up to. General Washington's army was still the main rebel force, and it was still threatening New York. Destouches's return to Newport had reunited all of Comte de Rochambeau's troops in Rhode Island, just a day's sail from Sandy Hook.

Germain assured Clinton that it was not the king's intention to "restrain you from availing yourself of any favourable event or change of circumstance which may happen at any other time in the northern provinces . . . ," a not-so-tacit reminder that he was expected to operate on offense, not defense. The South, however, was to be the strategic focus. And that, Germain told Clinton, would most certainly include Virginia.

Best-Laid Plans

On March 8, the day Destouches's squadron left Newport, the Marquis de Lafayette had been at Head of Elk five days, wind-bound and fretting. The day before, he had sent Washington a list of his woes: "Contrary Winds, Heavy Rains, disappointments of vessels, And Every Inconvenience to which we Had No Remedy Have Been from the day of My Arrival Combined Against our Embarkation."

High among his concerns were the motives of his countrymen, Rochambeau and Baron de Vioménil, in coming to Virginia. "Comte de Rochambeau thinks His troops Equal to the Business, and wishes that they Alone May display their zeal, and shed their Blood, for an expedition which All America Has so Much at Heart," he wrote to Washington. The marquis felt that de Vioménil, too, would "want to do Every thing Alone," and that this would be detrimental to the honor of American arms. More than anything, Lafayette feared being stuck at Head of Elk while the Jacques-come-lately got the glory of taking Arnold.

By the second week of March, Lafayette had assembled enough vessels to move his troops down the Elk River and into the upper Chesapeake, if not comfortably. For escort, he had one vessel of twelve guns and another aboard which he had mounted some field pieces. Two more armed ships would meet them in Baltimore and escort them as far as Annapolis.

Lafayette himself preceded the fleet south in a boat with thirty soldiers and some swivel guns for protection. He intended to reach Annapolis ahead of his men, where he hoped to gain intelligence of enemy movements and decide the next move. Convinced that the French admiral would not of his own accord send a frigate to escort the Continentals down the bay, Lafayette planned to seek out the French fleet and make the request in person. Summoning proper nautical jargon, he informed Washington that "in order to add Weight to My application I Have Clapp'd on Board My Boat the only Son of the Minister of the french Navy," the Comte de Charlus, who was traveling with him.

As Lafayette was making his way through the upper reaches of the Chesapeake Bay, Baron de Steuben arrived at Williamsburg to be closer to the action and to eagerly await the arrival of the French fleet. From this vantage point on the north shore of the James River, some 35 miles upriver from Portsmouth, he continued to fire off letters complaining of his lack of everything from militia to boats. Governor Jefferson, tiring of Steuben's insinuation that he was not doing all he could, wrote to the baron, underlining the words for emphasis, "We can only be answerable for the orders we give, and not for their execution. If they are disobeyed from obstinacy of spirit or want of coercion in the laws it is not our fault." He ended the letter with, "I have the honor to be with very great respect Sir your most obedt. humble servt." Florid even by eighteenth-century standards, the salutation was likely dipped in irony.

On March 14, the day that the *Duc de Bourgogne* spied Cape Henry close aboard, Lafayette arrived at Yorktown. He had managed to safely transport his division from Head of Elk to Annapolis, but "The Number of Small frigats and Privateers that Are in the Bay" made it impossible to move his troops any farther by water. Instead, he left them at Annapolis and took a boat to Yorktown, "and very Luckily Escaped the dangers that were in the Way." There to greet him was Steuben.

Steuben had worked furiously to prepare for an assault on Portsmouth, particularly as he had expected Lafayette and his men to arrive eight days earlier. Since then, the militia had been waiting with little to do, and idleness was never healthy for militia. Steuben was worried. "[I]t is to be feared," he wrote Washington, "that if the blow is not soon struck the Militia will get tired & leave us."

Steuben worried, too, about "the amazing tranquility of the Enemy." Arnold had to be aware of the troops arrayed against him, nearly five thousand militia at that point, and the baron wondered why the British did not try to break out and escape. He could only attribute it to "their expecting some Assistance unknown to us."

Steuben had been mulling the plan of operation for some time, and now the two discussed how to proceed. Lafayette still wanted to mask the plan of attacking Arnold by spreading word that his detachment was heading for the Carolinas, but Steuben warned against this. Lafayette's true destination was already well known, and if the militia became convinced that the Continentals would not be there to lead the attack on Portsmouth, Steuben was certain they would all desert. He wanted Lafayette to take command immediately, but Lafayette "thought it More polite not to do it" until his men arrived from Annapolis or the attack began. Preparations for land operations were in place, and Arnold was trapped. Lafayette felt that they had enough men for the fight even without Rochambeau's interlopers. All they needed was the French fleet.

On March 16, while the Battle of Cape Henry was taking place 50 miles away, Lafayette wrote to Jefferson, "To My Great disappointment we Have not yet Seen the french fleet, But they Must Be Hourly Expected." A few days later, he traveled from Yorktown to General Peter Muhlenberg's camp at Suffolk. Muhlenberg was a former clergyman who had commanded the Virginia line of Continental troops at the battles of Brandywine, Germantown, and Monmouth. He had since returned to his native Virginia to head the defenses there, primarily militia. He was junior in rank to Steuben, but the two men enjoyed a good professional relationship. From Suffolk, Lafayette and a small force reconnoitered Arnold's works at Portsmouth, even skirmishing with British troops. But still no fleet had appeared.

Finally, on March 20, word filtered in of a fleet in the bay. Colonel Everard Meade wrote to Steuben, "From the information we have just received from the Bay The French Fleet got into Lynhaven the night before last. The appearance has worked a great change in the minds of the Tories in Princess Ann—they now want to engage on our side." It was Arbuthnot's fleet, of course, but flying the French flag per Clinton's orders, and no one ashore was certain who they were.

"We are full of anxiety here," John Walker wrote to Steuben from Williamsburg, "in consequence of having a certainty at the arrival of a Fleet in our Bay, without being able to ascertain whether it is friendly or hostile."

As the days passed, the truth of the matter came out. "Nothing Could Equal My Surprise in Hearing from Mjr. McPherson the fleet Announced By a former letter was Certainly Belonging to the Ennemy," Lafayette wrote to Washington with even more than his usual amount of capitalization. Whether the French fleet had been beaten, gone someplace else, or were still on their way, the plan to trap Arnold was finished. "Upon this Intelligence the Militia were Removed to their former position and I requested Baron de Steubens to take such measures as would put out of the Ennemy's Reach the Several Articles that Had Been prepared."

It was a bitter disappointment for Steuben and Lafayette, who had put enormous effort into trapping Arnold and had organized what would certainly have been a major American victory, and for whom the capture of the traitor would have been a personal triumph. Instead, all they could do was ensure that the newly reinforced Arnold would not capture the state's military stores. Lafayette sent word to his men in Annapolis to prepare themselves for the march back to New York.

No one, of course, felt the disappointment more keenly than Washington. For weeks after Destouches sailed, he had waited for some word from Virginia. On March 29, he wrote to Rochambeau that he had heard nothing since a letter sent from Lafayette on March 15, in which the marquis informed him that the fleet had not yet arrived. Washington did not know that Destouches's fleet had returned to Newport on March 26 and that even as he was writing to Rochambeau, a detailed account of the Battle of Cape Henry was on its way to him.

On reading the account, Washington wrote to Destouches expressing his thanks for the effort and his regret for "A circumstance in which the Winds and Weather had more influence than valour or skill. Had it depended upon the latter, I should have had perfect confidence." The language was graceful and diplomatic but also inaccurate. A lack of copper sheathing was more to blame than the wind for Destouches's failure to beat the British fleet to the Chesapeake, and the weather had played no part in Destouches's failure to capitalize on the thrashing he had given Arbuthnot.

Though Washington kept his frustration to himself, he was disappointed on many levels. Arnold's treason had cut him deeply, and he wanted the man hanged both for personal reasons and as an example of what became of traitors. He wanted to strike a blow against the British after so many months of inactivity, during which enthusiasm for the Glorious Cause had been fading. He wanted to make use of America's French ally to advance this endless war toward a propitious conclusion. And he wanted to exploit the sea power that had so long been denied him.

To view the event with the great advantage of hindsight, however, it is clear that if Arnold had been defeated, Phillips would not have gone to the Chesapeake. Clinton was awaiting word that the bay was secure before sending Phillips off. Had neither Phillips nor Arnold been in Virginia, Cornwallis certainly would not have moved his army there in the summer of 1781. The capture of Arnold and his small force would have been a satisfying victory but not nearly significant enough to change the course of the war. The loss of the army ultimately assembled under Cornwallis would be a different matter.

As so often happened during the Revolution, an apparent American loss would, in the end, prove to be a major gain. The events that played out around the attempt to capture Arnold would play out again half a year later, almost exactly the same way but with very different results. Piece by piece, a puzzle was coming together in the Virginia tidewater region, and its completion would bring about America's victory in the War for Independence.

And even as Washington waited for word of the expedition against Arnold, the balance of power and the entire strategic situation in the South was blown apart at a place called Guilford Courthouse.

PART TWO

GREENE AND CORNWALLIS: LOOKING NORTH

CHAPTER *8* *The Beginning of the End*

THE TWO ARMIES, American and British, were battered, exhausted, threadbare, and starving when they met on March 15, 1781—the day before Chevalier Destouches and Vice-Admiral Marriot Arbuthnot would fight the Battle of Cape Henry—for what would be the last major set-piece land battle of the American Revolution.

The British march began at four o'clock that morning. The troops advanced in two columns, east along the New Garden Road, through country described as "a Wilderness, with a few cleared fields interspersed here and there." Their destination was the town of Guilford, North Carolina, a cluster of buildings surrounding the Guilford Courthouse.

The army, which numbered fewer than two thousand officers and men, included the 33rd Regiment; the 23rd Regiment, or Royal Welsh Fusiliers; and the 71st, a Scottish regiment known as Fraser's Highlanders, jauntily uniformed with "green plaid pants, close fitting red vests and high caps." The force also included royal artillery, a Brigade of Guards, and cavalry. There were German troops as well: a Hessian infantry regiment called the Regiment of Von Bose and a battalion of Jaegers, troops trained in woodland tactics, wearing their distinctive green uniforms with red trim. These troops were hardened professionals, some of the finest in the world, but even soldiers like these could be pushed only so far, and they were near the end of their endurance.

The commander of the British force was forty-four-year-old Lord Charles Cornwallis. Cornwallis's pedigree was as good as they came. His father had been the fifth Baron of Eye and the first Earl and Viscount Brome, and his mother was the daughter of the second Viscount Townsend. Like most of his peers, Cornwallis had been educated at Eton. At age seventeen, he had purchased his first commission as an ensign in the 1st Regiment of Foot Guard and sought further training at a military academy in Italy.

In 1758, with the outbreak of the Seven Years' War, Cornwallis had finally had the chance to put his training to use on the battlefields of Germany. In later years, British officers who had served in Germany would feel a kinship with each other and a slight superiority over those who had not. Cornwallis was a member in good standing of that band of brothers, having won honors at the bloody Battle of Minden and in other fighting during the war. In 1766, he had become colonel of the 33rd Regiment, which now, fifteen years later, he again led into battle.

Cornwallis possessed every attribute that an officer in the eighteenth-century British army needed to achieve high command: wealth, connections, and genuine skill, the last being useful but perhaps least important. The Cornwallis family certainly had wealth, the result of hundreds of years as peers of the realm and a number of fortuitous marriages. Charles Cornwallis's connections in court were impeccable. He had served as aide-de-camp to King George III, lord of the bedchamber, and later constable of the Tower of London.

In the 1760s, following the death of his father, Charles had become Lord Cornwallis and had been seated in the House of Lords. Known as a liberal even within the liberal Whig party to which he belonged, he had opposed the harsh measures imposed on the American colonies, including the Townsend Acts implemented by Charles Townsend, to whom Cornwallis was related through his mother. Ironically, Cornwallis had been a staunch opponent of nearly every government policy that led to the American Revolution.

When war finally came, however, Cornwallis did not hesitate to join the fighting. Though he harbored sympathy for American grievances, that sympathy did not extend to condoning open rebellion. In 1776, he had joined Sir Henry Clinton in the first siege of Charleston, South Carolina. When that attempt failed, he had come under the command of Lord William Howe and had taken a lead role in the Battle of Long Island, which nearly ended the Revolution a month after the signing of the Declaration of Independence. Since then, Cornwallis had taken part in nearly every major action in the northern theater, including the battles of Brandywine, Germantown, and Monmouth.

In 1778, Cornwallis had sailed for England to be at the side of his beloved Jemima, to whom he had been married for ten years. Jemima's health had never been robust, and she died a few months after Cornwallis's return home.

In July of 1779, a heartbroken Lord Cornwallis arrived back in America to rejoin the fight. In October of that year, a failed attempt by American and French troops to recapture Savannah, Georgia, revealed the weakness of patriot forces in the South. Clinton, who was by then commander-in-chief of His Majesty's armed forces in America, decided to try another assault on Charleston. This time, in May 1780, the British were successful.

After the fall of the city, Clinton returned to New York with four thousand of the men he had taken to Charleston, leaving the rest under Cornwallis's command to carry the new southern strategy to its conclusion. The war in the South had begun in earnest.

The Battle of New Garden

About noon on March 15, Cornwallis's lines drew within sight of the enemy arrayed before Guilford Courthouse. "Immediately between the head of the Column, and the Enemy's Line, was a considerable Plantation," Cornwallis later wrote, "one large Field of which, was on our left of the Road, and two others, with a Wood of about two hundred yards broad between them, on our right of it." Stretched out from left to right before him was a long line of American troops, its center hunkered down behind split rail fences and the flanks extending into the woods to the north and south. On a small hill near the middle of the road sat two American 6-pounder field pieces.

The cavalry, the Brigade of Guards, and the Jaegers comprised the advance units of the British line. "As the front of the British column approached the open ground facing the American position," wrote Lieutenant Colonel Banastre Tarleton, "the enemy's six pounders opened up."

Tarleton was the commander of the British light cavalry, twenty-six years old, redheaded and stocky. He was either a talented and active officer or a brutal murderer, depending upon one's point of view. The Americans called him "Bloody Tarleton" and accused him of numerous war crimes, including killing men who had surrendered. The alleged bayoneting of captives became known as "Tarleton's Quarter." But Cornwallis relied on him and never failed to praise him in his reports, even when Tarleton was beaten.

Tarleton was certainly an able, ambitious, and motivated leader. But for all his considerable skill as a cavalry officer, he and his men had often been roughly handled by their American counterparts, most recently earlier that morning.

Opposing Tarleton earlier in the day had been thirty-five-year-old Lieutenant Colonel Henry "Light Horse Harry" Lee, a scion of the Virginia aristocracy and the future father of Civil War general Robert E. Lee. Lee commanded a regiment known as Lee's Legion, which consisted of cavalry, infantry, and a contingent of tough frontier riflemen under the command of Colonel William Campbell.

As the two armies maneuvered within 20 miles of each other and battle grew increasingly imminent, Lee sent out a patrol to keep an eye on Cornwallis's movements. Hearing from his scouts that a large body of cavalry, and perhaps Cornwallis's entire army, was on the move, Lee ordered his troops "to arms at four in the morning, and to take breakfast with all practicable haste." Lee and his weary men mounted up and headed off through the predawn darkness to investigate the British movement, with infantry and rifle companies ordered to follow behind.

The American horse soldiers had covered only 2 miles when they met their own advance party riding in just ahead of advancing British cavalry. It was unclear to Lee whether the British cavalry was a patrol or the vanguard of the entire army, but, in either event, he hoped to lure them closer to the American army and the infantry currently marching toward them. He ordered "the column to retire by troops, taking the proper distance for open evolution." The rearmost horsemen spun around and galloped off, followed by the next rank and then the next, each rank following at a somewhat slower pace to avoid bunching up.

Tarleton, seeing this retreat, felt he could convert the Americans' orderly retirement into a frightened rout. He ordered his troopers ahead with the kind of impetuousness that sometimes won him accolades and sometimes precipitated disaster. As the British closed with the rear of the American line, they found the horse soldiers not fleeing at all, but rather "still in a walk," letting the ground open up between themselves and the next rank ahead. Lee was with the last rank, "attentively watching the British progress."

The British troops pushed hard against the American rear but could not induce Lee's cavalry to run or even quicken their pace. Tarleton's men drew pistols and fired on the Americans, then charged again.

Lee chose that moment to spring his trap. He ordered his horsemen to wheel around, and "the dragoons came instantly to the right about, and, in close columns, rushed upon the foe."

The Americans pounded down the narrow lane, which was lined by high fences on either side. The American horses were greatly superior to the British, the Continental cavalry having access to fine mounts from all over the South while the British had to take whatever they could get, and Lee felt "he should trample his enemy under foot, if he dared to meet the shock."

Tarleton admitted that "the fire of the Americans was heavy, and the charge of their cavalry spirited." Lee's troops crashed into Tarleton's. The leading British riders were dismounted and their horses knocked to the ground, but the narrowness of the road prevented any but the front ranks from coming to grips. Tarleton sounded the retreat, and the British cavalry—those not killed, wounded, or captured—whirled about and charged back toward the head of the marching British column.

Tarleton led his men directly back toward the British camp, but Lee, who knew the area well from weeks of patrolling, took his men by another route in hopes of cutting Tarleton off from the main body of Cornwallis's army. The sky had lightened and the sun was just peeking above the trees when the American mounted troops broke onto open ground around the New Garden Meeting House and ran right into the light infantry of Cornwallis's Brigade of Guards, who were advancing in support of Tarleton. The flash of sunlight on British muskets "frightened Lee's horse so as to compel him to throw himself off." Lee grabbed another horse, pulled himself into the saddle, and ordered a retreat.

As the cavalry charged off, the American infantry and rifle companies that had been following behind "came running up with trailed arms, and opened a well-aimed fire upon the guards." For a short time, this small, fierce fight, a precursor of bigger things to come, continued between the Guards and the American light infantry and riflemen. Cornwallis, no doubt hearing the sounds of sharp fighting and seeing smoke rising in the early light, sent the 23rd Regiment, the Royal Welsh Fusiliers, in support of his troops. Sergeant Roger Lamb of the 23rd recalled later that "Lee . . . behaved himself with the most undaunted bravery and maintained himself against the most formidable opposition, until the 23rd Regiment advancing to the support of Tarleton, compelled him to give way."

Lee now had no doubt that Cornwallis's entire army was close behind the 23rd, and he knew it was time to retire. Tarleton said that Lee "retreated with precipitation," though Lee himself characterized it as an orderly withdrawal, with the cavalry covering the retreat of the foot soldiers. Just as Lee did not want to stick around knowing Cornwallis's main body was coming up, Tarleton did not care to chase Lee into the arms of the American army, so he did not pursue.

The British lost "between twenty and thirty of the guards, dragoons and yagers . . . killed or wounded." Among the wounded was Tarleton, who took a musket ball through the hand, though the wound does not seem to have slowed him in the least. American losses are unknown but were certainly much less than the British. Nonetheless, Cornwallis would later report that Tarleton "attacked with his usual good conduct and spirit, and defeated" the Americans.

Both sides understood that the Battle of New Garden was merely a prologue to much bigger things to come. "An engagement was now become inevitable," Tarleton recalled, while Lee wrote that "the long avoided, now wished-for, hour was at hand."

This was the moment that month upon dreary month of crippling marches, bloody skirmishes, and desperate retreats had been building toward. And though neither side knew it, the outcome of that day would add one more link, a crucial link, to the chain of events that would decide the fate of the American continent.

CHAPTER *9* *The American Command*

LORD CORNWALLIS BELIEVED that the American troop strength he was facing at Guilford Courthouse amounted to "9 or 10,000 men," or so he wrote to George Germain. This seems to have been the generally accepted estimate on the British side, with the "Journal of the Von Bose Regiment" reporting that the Americans were "standing drawn up in perfect battle order, 9,000 men strong, behind the defenses and brushwood." The British and Germans, with around nineteen hundred officers and men, marched into battle under the impression that they were outnumbered five to one.

In fact, Cornwallis's estimate was more than double the true number of roughly 4,440 men in the American lines. Though the odds were better than Cornwallis believed, the Americans still enjoyed a two-to-one advantage.

But troop numbers were only part of the story. According to Lieutenant Colonel Henry Lee, the only veteran troops facing Cornwallis were the first regiment of Maryland, the Delaware Regiment of the Continental line, two Virginia regiments, and Lee's Legion. In total, these amounted to around fifteen hundred combat-hardened men. Of the rest, most were militia who had never been in battle, never fired a musket at an enemy, nor ever tried to hold their ground in the face of a bayonet charge.

The American army was under the command of thirty-eight-year-old General Nathanael Greene. Greene was one of those rare few soldiers who, with virtually no training but with an inherent genius for military command, became, in the course of the American Revolution, as brilliant an officer as any of the professionals in the British army. Nothing in Greene's background suggested a military future. He had been born near Warwick, Rhode Island, into a family of Quakers who discouraged formal education. As a result, Greene's schooling was limited, but he continued to educate himself throughout his lifetime, reading and collecting books with great enthusiasm.

In 1770, Greene, who had been trained in blacksmithing, moved to Coventry, Rhode Island, to manage a family-owned forge. He was active in Rhode Island politics and served in the colony's general assembly. As the rift between England and the American colonies grew irreparable, Greene helped organize a local militia, dubbed the Kentish Guards, with whom he drilled despite a permanent limp. He also began to immerse himself in the study of military theory. His growing patriotic fervor and his marriage to a non-Quaker in 1774 precipitated a gradual parting from his pacifist upbringing.

Soon after the fighting began, Greene was made a major general in command of Rhode Island's forces in recognition of his early leadership. When various colonial militias became the Continental Army under control of Congress, Greene's rank was lowered to brigadier general, a demotion that would have caused many in the officer corps to resign, but he accepted it with equanimity (he would end the war as a major general). General George Washington recognized Greene's native ability; before long, the young Rhode Islander was one of Washington's most trusted officers. Greene, in turn, worshiped his commander-in-chief.

Like Cornwallis, whom he now faced, Greene had served as a general officer in most of the major campaigns of the northern theater, fighting at New York, Trenton, Princeton, Brandywine, Germantown, and countless smaller skirmishes. In 1778, he had agreed to assume the thankless position of quartermaster general, charged with supplying the army's many needs but given no resources to do so. Despite the Sisyphean nature of the assignment, he did an outstanding job, eventually resigning when his struggles with Congress wore him down.

When the British took Charleston in May 1780, General Benjamin Lincoln was captured, and Congress faced the need to choose a new commander of the southern army, particularly as the British seemed to be shifting their attention in that direction. Washington favored Greene for the post, but Congress was still enthralled by the nominal hero of the Battle of Saratoga, Horatio Gates. On June 13, 1780, ignoring Washington's suggestion, Congress resolved unanimously that "Major General Gates immediately repair to and take command in the southern department."

Gates arrived in North Carolina on July 25 and took leadership of the ragged fourteen hundred Continental troops, whom he dubbed the "Grand Army." With his ranks swelled by militia, Gates marched into South Carolina, where, on August 16, he led his army into a disastrous fight with Cornwallis at the Battle of Camden. Around nine hundred Americans were killed or wounded, and another thousand were captured.

As the southern militia fell back in panic and Cornwallis's troops over-ran American lines, Gates and some of his officers fled the field. Not content just to leave the ongoing fight, they kept riding until they arrived that evening at Charlotte, North Carolina, some 60 miles north. From there, Gates continued another 120 miles to Hillsborough, ostensibly to rally troops. This headlong flight from the scene of action put the coup de grâce on a reputation already badly wounded by the series of mistakes that had led to the disaster at Camden. Alexander Hamilton expressed the views of many when he wrote,

> Was there ever an instance of a General running away as Gates has done from his whole army, and was there ever so precipitous a flight? One hundred and eighty miles in three days and a half. It does admirable credit to the activity of a man at his time of life. But it disgraces the General and the soldiers.

Despite the devastating defeat at Camden and Gates's subsequent behavior, it was not until October that mounting criticism of the general convinced Congress to suspend him from command until a court of inquiry could look into his conduct. Congress then turned to Washington to suggest a new leader in the South, and Washington tapped Greene for the post. William Moultrie, the brigadier general from South Carolina, recalled that Greene's appointment "gave great satisfaction to every one" and that his experience and qualities "rendered him a proper officer to collect and organize an army that was broken up and dispersed."

Five years of war had transformed Greene from an inexperienced Quaker militia officer to a veteran field commander, and five years with the ragged Continental Army and his experience as quartermaster general had taught him what genuine deprivation could look like. But even he was unprepared for what greeted him when he arrived on December 2 to take up his new command.

Five days after arriving in Charlotte, Greene wrote to Washington with an account of the state of his army, "if it deserves the name of one," as he put it. "Nothing can be more wretched and distressing than the condition of the troops, starving with cold and hunger, without tents and camp equipage. Those of the Virginia line are literally naked, and a great part totally unfit for duty." Conditions must indeed have been extreme to so move a man who had lived through the winter encampments at Valley Forge and Morristown.

Greene may have found himself short of clothing, food, and equipment, much of it lost at Camden, but he had a good supply of excellent officers, including Henry Lee, Otho Williams, William Washington, and, foremost, Daniel Morgan.

Morgan was a rough backwoods fighter and a former teamster turned leader of Virginia riflemen. During the French and Indian War, he had hired out as a wagoner to the British army, during which service he received five hundred lashes for fighting with an officer. This punishment would have been a death sentence for a lesser man, but Morgan survived the flogging, though he did not forgive or forget the affront he had suffered.

Unlike Gates, Morgan had been a genuine hero of Saratoga, as well as the attack on Quebec under Benedict Arnold, during which Morgan had been taken prisoner. Like Arnold, Morgan was no politician and found himself repeatedly passed over for command. Unlike Arnold, he successfully resigned his commission and left the army until he was persuaded, after the debacle at Camden, to return. His leadership would be a major factor in reversing American fortunes in the South.

The Road to Guilford Courthouse

Soon after taking command, Greene made two important and controversial decisions. Realizing he could not remain in the Charlotte area, which had long been stripped of the resources needed to support an army, the new commander marched his men southeast to the Pee Dee

River, straddling the border between North and South Carolina, to what he called a "camp of repose." There he hoped he might begin "improving the discipline and spirits" of the weary, battered troops. Prior to that move, Greene's army had stood between Cornwallis and any attempt he might make to invade North Carolina. Now the British path was clear for a march north.

The second and perhaps more important decision was to split the army in two, sending a corps of light infantry, militia, and Lieutenant Colonel William Washington's dragoons, about six hundred men in total, into the backcountry west of Charlotte where they were to link up with other militia units. This was contrary to the standard military practice of the time, which held that forces should never be divided in the face of an enemy. The purpose of this risky move was to "give protection to that part of the country and spirit up the people, to annoy the enemy in that quarter," and to snatch up valuable provisions before Cornwallis could get his hands on them. Greene put Daniel Morgan in command of this flying column.

Greene felt certain that Cornwallis would not move north with Morgan in his rear, but rather would split his own force in the hope of destroying Morgan before undertaking any other operations. And he was right. In early January 1781, Cornwallis dispatched Banastre Tarleton with around eleven hundred men, slightly more than Morgan's force, to destroy or drive off that part of Greene's army. The two leaders, Morgan and Tarleton, played cat and mouse through the cold, rain-soaked countryside. Finally, on January 16, Morgan, who had just crossed into South Carolina, decided to make a stand at a place called Hannah's Cowpens, 55 miles west and a little south of Charlotte.

British officers often dismissed the fighting qualities of American troops, and Tarleton was particularly contemptuous of his enemy. That contempt was not entirely without basis, particularly as it related to militia, who made up a big part of the American force and who were notoriously unreliable. Moultrie had correctly observed that militia, in line of battle, rarely "could be brought to stand and reserve their fire until the enemy came near enough. The charge of the bayonet they never could stand."

But Moultrie also understood that militia "are brave men, and will fight if you let them come to action in their own way." The Battles of Lexington and Bunker Hill had demonstrated that sort of bravery, which Morgan now used to best advantage. Preparing the lines to meet Tarleton's attack, he put his militia in front, behind a screen of riflemen, and asked only that they get off two good volleys, aiming primarily at the officers, before falling back to the next line of regular troops. Even this was asking a lot, and most of the militia got off no more than one shot. But rather than giving in to a panicked rout, the part-time soldiers gave a decent volley and retired in good order.

Advancing beyond the positions abandoned by the retreating militia, Tarleton's men ran smack into the line of Continental troops, who were not about to yield as easily as the citizen-soldiers had. A stubborn fight ensued, with both sides refusing to give ground. Tarleton then moved up the 71st, whom he had held in reserve, and also ordered the cavalry to make a flanking attack. As Tarleton later recalled, the "continentals and backwoodsmen gave ground: the British rushed forwards: An order was dispatched to the cavalry to charge: A unexpected fire at this instance from the Americans, who came about as they were retreating, stopped the British, and threw them into confusion."

The Americans, who were falling back but not running in panic, turned and delivered a volley to the surprise of their enemy. Just as the British ranks were falling apart, William Washington's cavalry charged out from behind a small hill and hit the frightened men on the flank. An "unaccountable panic extended itself along the whole line," Tarleton recalled. The Battle of Cowpens was over. The British, soundly beaten, lost one hundred dead and more than eight hundred captured, a significant portion of Cornwallis's command. Tarleton himself escaped.

Cornwallis admitted that it was "impossible to forsee all the consequences that this unexpected, & extraordinary event may produce." Despite the blow, however, the British force remained greatly superior to Greene's haggard troops. Morgan began to fall back into North Carolina with Cornwallis and the remnants of Tarleton's command on his heels.

It had long been Cornwallis's intention to move into North Carolina. Now, disgusted with a lack of local Loyalist support despite the victory at Camden and with Morgan on the loose, he headed north in pursuit of the troops that had so mauled Tarleton. To facilitate his quick march, Cornwallis "employed a halt of two day in collecting some Flour, and in destroying superfluous Baggage, and all my Waggons, except those loaded with Hospital Stores, salt and Ammunition." This deprived the men of considerable quantities of stores, along with "a great deal of Officer's Baggage, and of all prospect in future of Rum." Despite the loss, Cornwallis reported "there was the most general and chearfull acquiescence."

By the beginning of February, Morgan had rejoined Greene at Guilford Courthouse, 100 miles northeast of Charlotte on the northern outskirts of present-day Greensboro. Greene was ready to stand and fight, but his officers did not agree. The returns of the army indicated that it consisted of "1426 Infantry Men, many of whom are badly armed and distressed for the Want of Clothing." With Cornwallis at their heels, the southern army raced north for the Dan River, pushing hard through bitter cold and driving rain, often shoeless, leaving bloody tracks in their wake. The British kept up a relentless pursuit, hoping to get between the outnumbered Americans and the Dan River and force them to fight. On February 13, Greene crossed the Dan a day ahead of Cornwallis.

With no boats to take them across the river and little desire to march north in search of a fordable place, the British pursued no further. Cornwallis's men were scarcely better off than Greene's, short of supplies and battered from exposure. The "Journal of the Von Bose Regiment" recorded on February 12: "The Corps had now a great number of sick and exhausted men owing to the frequent wettings and the forced marches and also the lack of provisions."

Cornwallis, despite his wealth and title, shared his men's suffering. "In this campaign," wrote Sergeant Roger Lamb of the Royal Welsh Fusiliers, "Lord Cornwallis fared like a common soldier." Cornwallis ate what his troops ate, which consisted of whatever they could find: turnips, Indian corn, occasionally lean beef. "In all this hardship his lordship participated, nor did he indulge himself even in the distinction of a tent; but in all things partook our sufferings, and seemed much more to feel for us than for himself." The troops loved and respected Cornwallis for this. Now, with the Americans inaccessible on the other side of the Dan River, Cornwallis headed east to Hillsborough, where he hoped to raise additional troops among the Loyalist population.

He met with little success. Greene, on the other hand, was finally experiencing a change of fortune as men began to pour into his camp.

Virginia sent more than seven hundred Continental troops to join his army and 1,693 militia who had pledged to serve for six weeks. North Carolina sent two brigades of militia numbering 1,060 men. Greene wrote that his "force was much more respectable than it had been," but he also knew the militia would not stay forever, nor could he long provide for them "in the field in this exhausted country." Both he and Cornwallis were eager for battle, and now Greene could choose the time and place. On March 14, he recrossed the Dan, marched 20 miles south, and took up his position at Guilford Courthouse.

"We waited the approach of the Enemy"

Greene had more troops than Cornwallis, but he no longer had Daniel Morgan. On January 24, Morgan had submitted his resignation. A chronic "ciatick pain" in the hip had become so debilitating that he could not go on. Morgan explained to Greene that the disorder "has ceazed me more violently, which gives me great pain when I ride, and at times when I am walking or standing am oblig^d to set down in the place it takes me, as quick as if I were shot."

Despite the pain, Morgan had continued to lead his troops as Cornwallis chased them northeast from Cowpens through 200 miles of near wilderness, over rivers and roads choked with winter mud, until they were able to link up with Greene. Only then did Morgan leave for his home in Virginia. The former teamster, around forty-five years old, had been overtaken not by years but by mileage.

Though Greene was deprived of Morgan's presence, he did enjoy the continued benefit of Morgan's wisdom. On February 20, Morgan wrote to Greene from Virginia with advice on how to deploy troops based on his experience at Cowpens. Morgan suggested that any veteran soldiers among the militia be put in the ranks of the regulars, with riflemen on the flanks. "[P]ut the remainder of the Militia in the centre with some picked troops in their rear with orders to shoot down the first man that runs," Morgan advised, adding that "if anything will succeed a disposition of this kind will."

In deploying his troops at Guilford Courthouse, Greene borrowed freely from Morgan's tactics at Cowpens but also employed much of his own thinking. Like Morgan, Greene arrayed his men in three lines to make things successively hotter for the enemy as they advanced. Morgan's first line had consisted of seasoned riflemen, but Greene's was made up of two brigades of North Carolina militia, one to the north of the New Garden Road under the command of General Thomas Eaton, and the other, commanded by General John Butler, to the south of the road. All told, the North Carolina militia amounted to more than a thousand men, but they were militia, many of them newly recruited at that, making them the most unreliable troops Greene had.

Despite that weakness, the first line of Greene's defense enjoyed a few advantages. Most of the North Carolina militia were arrayed behind a zigzag split rail fence that ran north to south across the field; any such protection, no matter how feeble, greatly improved the ability of untrained soldiers to stand and fight. From behind the fence, the North Carolina men looked out over an open field to the narrow defile where the New Garden Road disappeared around a curve, 300 yards of open ground that Cornwallis's men would have to cross under fire just to get into the fight.

The left and right flanks of the first line seemed to terminate in the woods at the edge of the field and be otherwise unsupported, but that was not the case. Positioned in the woods to the north and south of the first line were some of Greene's most seasoned and trusted troops. On the right flank, to the north, under the command of Lieutenant Colonel Washington, were dragoons of the 1st and 3rd Regiments; a detachment of light infantry that included Captain Robert Kirkwood's Delaware Continentals, some of the hardest-fighting troops in the Continental Army; and a regiment of riflemen under Colonel Charles Lynch. On the left flank, in the woods to the south, were Light Horse Harry Lee and his legion, along with Colonel William Campbell's riflemen, who had fought that morning at New Garden, and another detachment of light infantry. These troops, which Greene called a "Corps of observation," were positioned to watch the enemy's movements and to move in quickly in support of their own lines or to exploit a weakness in the enemy's.

On the New Garden Road itself, in the middle of the two battalions of militia, were stationed two 6-pounder cannons under the command of Captain Anthony Singleton of Virginia. Singleton's orders were to move his artillery with the flow of the battle and to avoid being isolated and captured.

From where the first line was arrayed, the land rose gently to the high ground at Guilford Courthouse. It was not open country, however, but rather hilly ground broken by gullies and thick woods. "The greater part of the County is a Wilderness," Greene wrote, "with a few cleared fields interspersed here and there." The area in front of the first line consisted of those cleared fields, but right behind them were thick woods of oak and other hardwoods and tangled underbrush. Those woods extended for about a mile before yielding to open fields surrounding Guilford Courthouse. It was difficult terrain for fighting, but it favored Greene, whose men were less accustomed to slugging it out in open country.

The second American line was positioned about 300 yards behind the first, on top of a slight rise in the thick of the woods. This line, too, consisted of militia—in this case, two brigades from Virginia commanded by Generals Edward Stevens and Robert Lawson. Stevens had seen his men routed in panic at Camden, and he was not going to let that happen again. As he later wrote to Henry Lee, "I posted in my rear a number of riflemen, behind trees, as you know we were formed in a skirt of woods. I informed my men that they were placed there to shoot the first man who might run," and then, in case that message was too harsh, added, "and at the same time they would serve to cover their retreat in case of necessity."

The second line did not have the same support on the flanks that the first line enjoyed. It was Greene's intention that the corps of observation should fall back with the first line and join the second, forming flanks even as the need for them developed.

Greene's third line, 300 to 500 yards behind the second, was not really a line at all but rather a crescent-shaped formation around the top of the high ground near Guilford Courthouse. Rather than straddling the road, this line was all to the north of it. Like the first line, the third was in an open field with the woods at its back and two 6-pounders positioned at the center of the crescent. Unlike the first line, the third was made up of Greene's best troops, "two Brigades, one of Virginia and one of Maryland continental Troops, commanded by General [Isaac] Huger and Col° [Otho] Williams." This was the anchor of the entire formation, the line to which, ideally, the first two lines would fall back in orderly withdrawal, pulling the enemy along to be crushed.

With his troops in place, Greene rode along the lines, giving final orders and trying to bolster the men's spirits. Henry Lee added his own brand of encouragement, riding the length of the front line and exhorting them to stand firm, and, in reference to the Battle of New Garden, to "not be afraid of the British; for he had whipped them three times that morning and would do it again."

Greene's message to the North Carolina militia was a little more practical. Taking another page from Morgan's playbook at Cowpens, he assured the men that if they would only stand their ground long enough to give the British two volleys, "they should obtain his free permission to retire from the field."

With that, Greene rode back to the third line, back to his fellow Continental troops, and as he later reported, "In this position we waited the approach of the Enemy."

CHAPTER *10* *The Battle of Guilford Courthouse*

THE NOON HOUR of March 15 was "calm, and illuminated with a cloud-less sun; the season rather cold than cool . . . ," when Lord Cornwallis's column, with the general in the lead, emerged from the defile on the New Garden Road and came face to face with Nathanael Greene's line of North Carolina militia. The militia stood poised behind a rail fence, 300 yards away across an open field.

The second American line, hunkered down in the band of woods between the first line and Guilford Courthouse, was invisible to Cornwallis. The third line may have been visible more than a thousand yards away on the raised, open ground by the village.

As Cornwallis called a halt to his army's advance, Virginia captain Anthony Singleton opened up with his two 6-pounders. Cornwallis called up the Royal Artillery under the command of Lieutenant John McLeod to "bring forward the Guns and cannonade their Center." Three British 6-pounders opened up on the American lines, and the artillery prelude to the Battle of Guilford Courthouse was underway.

Cornwallis was not sure what he was up against. "The Prisoners taken by Lieut Colonel Tarleton, having been several days with the advance Corps, could give me no account of the Enemy's Order or position," Cornwallis wrote, "and the Country people were extremely inaccurate in their description of the Ground." As the American and British guns boomed away at each other, the general consulted with guides attached to his column and studied as much of the enemy lines as he was able to see.

The guides informed Cornwallis that the woods to which the American line was anchored were "impracticable for cannon," but from what he could see the woods on the American left wing, south of the New Garden Road, were less dense. Though Cornwallis's men would be hitting the entire length of the American line, he resolved to throw the bulk of his force against the enemy's left. He began to arrange his troops for battle.

The west end of the field, where the British formed up, was bordered by woods, and the troops found some shelter there from Singleton's guns as they formed their line of battle. On his far right, south of the road, Cornwallis positioned the Hessians of the Von Bose Regiment, and next to them the 71st, Fraser's Highlanders. Behind them, in reserve, was the 1st Battalion of Guards. In command of this right wing was General Alexander Leslie, whom Sir Henry Clinton had sent to Virginia the previous October to fortify Portsmouth.

On the left flank, to the north of the road, Cornwallis placed his old regiment, the 33rd. Next to them was the 23rd Regiment, the Royal Welsh Fusiliers, while the Jaegers and the Light Infantry of the Guards were deployed behind them in the woods near the guns. This left wing was commanded by Lieutenant Colonel James Webster. Brigadier General Charles O'Hara commanded a reserve force comprising the 2nd Battalion of Guards and a company of grenadiers, some three hundred men in all. This force was deployed behind the Jaegers and light infantry, while Tarleton's cavalry held its position on the road, ready to move up where they could be most effective.

For about half an hour, as Cornwallis prepared his attack, the British and American artillery fired away. The guns were neither large nor numerous, but they managed to do some damage. Tarleton recorded that "Lieutenant O'Hara, a spirited young officer, was unfortunately killed, whilst directing the three pounders before the line was ready to move."

On the American side, some reports suggested that all of Singleton's horses were killed in the exchange. Major St. George Tucker of the Virginia militia described it as "a most tremendous fire," though it is unlikely that citizen-soldier Tucker had ever experienced a genuinely tremendous cannonade. He added, "Major Hubbard, of Colonel Mumford's regiment, had the skirt of his surtout [overcoat] shot away by a Cannon ball, and his horse slightly wounded by the same. There were not, however, above ten men killed and wounded during the whole cannonade."

Around one o'clock, with the smoke from the artillery still hanging in the afternoon air, Cornwallis sent his troops forward. Here was the opportunity toward which Cornwallis and his men had suffered and struggled for so long, the moment when they could advance under arms for a decisive battle against Greene's entire army, and they advanced like the professionals they were. "The order and coolness of that part of Webster's brigade, which advanced across the open ground, exposed to the enemy's fire," wrote Tarleton of the left wing's movement, "cannot be sufficiently extolled."

The British and Germans advanced across the open field, trudging through wet, muddy, uneven ground toward the split rail fence and the muskets of nearly a thousand American troops. The North Carolina militia had been in position for hours, waiting for the British army to appear, watching the artillery duel, watching the British form their line of battle, and now watching the enemy's relentless advance, and the wait had worked on their nerves. When the British were about 150 yards away, still too far for effective musket fire, the North Carolinians opened up on them. The long-range volley had some effect, but not enough to deter Cornwallis's veterans, and they continued their advance without wavering.

South of the road, Leslie could see that the American left was far longer than his right and threatened to flank him, so he brought up the 1st Battalion of Guards, whom he had been holding in reserve, to take up the line to the right of the Von Bose Regiment. Now all of Leslie's men were committed, strung out in one long line opposite the Americans.

As Leslie's troops advanced toward the split rail fence, Lieutenant Colonel Henry Lee's men, including his cavalry and Colonel William Campbell's riflemen, watched them unseen from the woods on the flanks of the American left wing. Lee's men "raked by their fire the right of the British wing, entirely uncovered . . . ," and the British began to take casualties as they approached the fence. Lee and many of his officers saw a prime opportunity as they watched the British right flank march toward them. If they could slam into the flank with cavalry and infantry, they could rout the British even before they hit the first of Greene's three lines. But that was not going to happen. Fifty yards from where the line of North Carolina militia were carrying on their sporadic fire, the British lines stopped and fired their first volley, then charged with their bayonets, so mortally terrifying to untrained militia.

To the north of the road, Webster's left wing was also advancing. Webster had ridden to the front of the troops and led the way with a shout as the red line rolled forward. Sergeant Roger Lamb of the Royal Welsh Fusiliers recalled that "the movement was made, in excellent order, in a smart run, with arms charged." As the British advanced, Singleton withdrew his guns, knowing that the North Carolina militia would be gone after two volleys.

With the Fusiliers toward the center and the 33rd on the left, the left wing moved forward, and like Leslie's men on the right advanced in good order to within 40 or 50 yards, through a sporadic but deadly fire, before firing their first volley. Before them was the long American line, "arms presented, and resting on a rail fence, the common partitions in America. They were taking aim with the nicest precision," Lamb later recalled.

For a moment, the British line wavered in the face of those American muskets. Sensing a do-or-die moment, Colonel Webster charged to the front of the line and shouted

> with more than even his usual commanding voice (which was well known to his Brigade,) *"Come on my brave Fuzileers."* This operated like an inspiring voice, they rushed forward amidst the enemy's fire; dreadful was the havoc on both sides.

The havoc may have been dreadful, but it was short-lived. In the face of the long scarlet line advancing with steel bayonets, the line of North Carolina militia folded. "To our infinite distress and mortification," wrote Lee, "the North Carolina militia took to flight." Generals John Butler and Thomas Eaton struggled to keep their men in position, but it was hopeless. Panic swept them away.

Greene had asked very little of the North Carolinians, and, for the most part, that is what he got. Many of the militia fled while the enemy was still 150 yards away. According to Greene's own account, they ran "without firing at all; some fired once, and some twice, and none more, except a part of a Battalion of General Eaton's Brigade." Many of the men threw away their knapsacks, canteens, and even their muskets as they ran.

The center of Greene's first line had folded at the sight of the 20-inch steel bayonets advancing on them, but on the flanks, the corps of observation held. These were some of Greene's best and most tested men, and they had the added advantage of being in the woods, which made it impossible for the British to launch a coordinated bayonet charge.

On the British right, Leslie's troops were taking a beating from Campbell's riflemen and Lee's Legion, which were close on their flank. Leslie wheeled the Von Bose Regiment and the 1st Battalion of Guards until they were facing Lee's men, then pressed his attack forward. An evolution of that kind, realigning two regiments under heavy fire, could be executed only by seasoned and professional soldiers, and it was yet another example of the disparity in training and discipline between Cornwallis's troops and Greene's.

Now it was Lee who was in trouble. Rather than forming the left flank of the first line, Lee and Campbell's men had been cut off by the "base desertion" (as Lee called it) of the North Carolina militia and were left fighting on their own. The Americans gave ground grudgingly, falling back toward the second line, as the battle began to devolve into a handful of small and bloody fights.

As the 1st Battalion of Guards and the Von Bose Regiment advanced, they had passed right by a portion of Lee's corps of observation, allowing the Americans to circle around behind until the British found themselves "warmly engaged, in front, rank and rear." The "Journal of the Von Bose Regiment" recorded that "the regiments became somewhat more separated, the v. Bose Regiment was attacked not only in the front but also in the rear, which necessitated the rear rank wheeling round to the right and firing backwards." A less disciplined regiment would have collapsed under such pressure on three sides.

To the north, Webster's left wing of the British line was in much the same situation as the right, with Captain Robert Kirkwood's Delaware Continentals, the riflemen under Colonel Charles Lynch, and Lieutenant Colonel William Washington's cavalry inflicting casualties from their flank with enfilading fire. Like Leslie, Webster realigned his men and brought up the Jaegers and Light Infantry of the Guards, who had been held in reserve. Cornwallis would later report, "[O]n finding that the left of the 33rd was exposed to a heavy fire from the right Wing of the Enemy, he [Webster] changed his front to the Left, & being supported by the Jagers & Light Infantry of the Guards, attacked & routed it."

Despite Cornwallis's claim, the American left wing was not routed, but rather, like Lee's men to the south, fought stubbornly and made the British pay a high price for their slow advance. While the left and right flanks of the British line were locked in their battles with the tough American troops of the corps of observation, the center of Cornwallis's line pressed on, and the fight surged east toward Guilford Courthouse.

The Second Line

The Royal Artillery rolled forward down the New Garden Road toward the next front, hard on the heels of the fleeing North Carolina militia. South of them, the Highlanders of the 71st continued their advance, clambering over and knocking down the rail fence that had briefly shielded the North Carolina men. North of the road, the 23rd Regiment, the Royal Welsh Fusiliers, also advanced quickly over ground briefly held by the militia.

Webster's realignment of the 33rd to go after Kirkwood's Delaware Continentals, Lynch's riflemen, and William Washington's troops on the American right had left a gap in the British line, and this was filled by the grenadiers and the 2nd Battalion of Guards, who had been held in reserve. These were the last of Cornwallis's reserves; now every man in his army was committed.

Following behind these troops was Tarleton's cavalry. Cornwallis had given the hotheaded Tarleton orders to "keep his Cavalry compact, and not to charge without positive orders, except to protect any of the Corps from the most evident danger of being defeated."

Just beyond the rail fence where the North Carolina militia had stood, there commenced a skirt of woods like a barrier between the open fields that the British had just crossed and the open ground around Guilford Courthouse. The center of the British line now plunged into those woods in pursuit of the fleeing enemy and ran into the Virginia militia, Nathanael Greene's second line.

Unlike the North Carolina men, the Virginians held their ground. They did, of course, have several advantages that the first line had not enjoyed. Rather than sheltering behind the dubious protection of a rail fence, they were hunkered behind trees. Samuel Houston, a soldier in the Rockbridge County, Virginia, militia recalled, "our brigade major came, ordering [us] to take trees as we pleased. The men chose their trees, but with difficulty, many crowding to one, some far behind others."

As the British line moved through the woods, their perfect order naturally began to break down, and they could not present the Virginia militia with the frightening spectacle of an unbroken line of bayonets. Nor was that weapon particularly effective in such terrain. As Cornwallis wrote, "The excessive thickness of the woods rendered our bayonets of little use."

Then, too, the militiamen of General Stevens's brigade, posted south of the New Garden Road, had the added incentive of knowing that riflemen had been positioned behind them, ready to shoot down anyone who ran. Encouraged by all those factors, the second line put up a much more spirited and deadly resistance than the first. Unlike the North Carolina militia, Greene wrote, the Virginians "stood their ground for a considerable time, and fought with great resolution."

The fight was no longer a single, cohesive battle, but rather a series of sharp encounters in the thick woods. Lamb, advancing with the Royal Welsh Fusiliers, found as he hit the second line that "the conflict became still more fierce." Bullets buzzed past his head as he stopped to replenish his ammunition from the cartridge box of a fellow redcoat who had been shot down. Lamb had apparently become separated from his regiment. When he looked up, he saw a company of Guards advancing on the Americans who were shooting at him, but Lamb was unable to join the company, "as several American parties lay between me and it."

Suddenly, into this confused, broken fight rode Lord Cornwallis on a dragoon's horse, his own having been shot out from under him. Apparently failing to realize that this was no single battle front, but rather a cluster of skirmishes, he was charging right toward a band of Americans when Lamb managed to grab the horse's bridle and stop him, explaining that "if his lordship had pursued the same direction, he would in a few moments have been surrounded by the enemy, and, perhaps, cut to pieces or captured." Lamb accompanied Cornwallis back to the 23rd Regiment, which was "drawn up in the skirt of the woods."

It is unclear how long this brutal fighting lasted. Greene would write that the "Virginia Militia gave the Enemy a warm reception and kept up a heavy fire for a long time." Some troops recalled firing a dozen or more rounds.

Not all the Virginia militia, however, stood so boldly against the British advance. Tucker, on the American right, wrote to his wife that while they were advancing, they found that the enemy had turned their flank and were now in their rear. It was the same situation that the Von Bose Regiment had found themselves in earlier. While the Germans had wheeled part of their line around to meet the new threat, the inexperienced Americans were unable to do the same. "This threw the militia into such confusion," Tucker wrote, "that Holcombe's regiment and ours instantly broke off without firing a single gun and dispersed like a flock of sheep frightened by dogs."

The Virginia militia, Tucker observed, came in for a great deal of praise after the battle. While some were entitled to it, he felt that "others ought to blush that they were undeservedly included in the number of those who were supposed to have behaved well."

Tucker managed to rally some of his men to make a stand. At one point, they came across a British officer who lay dying. One of Tucker's men "gave him a dram as he was expiring and bade him die like a brave man."

On the British right, the Von Bose Regiment and the 1st Battalion of Guards continued to fight their isolated battle with Lee's Legion and Campbell's riflemen, along with a few companies of North Carolina militia who had joined them. On the left, William Washington's cavalry, Lynch's riflemen, and Kirkwood's Delaware Continentals were doing as Greene had intended, falling slowly back to join the second line and then, as the fighting continued to move east, linking with the third line. They were pressed hard throughout by Webster with the 33rd, the Jaegers, and the Light Infantry.

Slowly, Greene's second line of Virginia militia, ably led by Generals Edward Stevens and Robert Lawson, fell back toward the third line by Guilford Courthouse. Lawson's brigade broke first, in what was likely neither an orderly retreat nor a general rout, but rather one pocket after another of militia falling back and melting away or joining the Continentals in the third line.

Stevens's line held a bit longer before it, too, began to dissolve, a movement no doubt accelerated when Stevens took a bullet in the thigh and his men were deprived of his command. Like Lawson's line, Stevens's brigade likely broke up piecemeal, the fighting having devolved into a number of small skirmishes. Many of Stevens's men followed the edge of the woods around to the courthouse, where they watched the remainder of the battle.

Cornwallis wrote that the thick woods allowed "the broken enemy to make frequent stands, with an irregular fire, which occasioned some loss." In Cornwallis's manner of understatement, "some loss" can be construed to mean "significant casualties." In fact, nearly a quarter of the men of the 23rd and the 71st were killed, wounded, or missing after running up against Stevens and Lawson's lines.

Because the American retreat was uneven, so was the British advance. Tarleton recalled, "Some corps meeting with less opposition and embarrassment than others, arrived sooner in presence of the continentals [the third line] who received them with resolution and firmness."

Perhaps the first of the British troops to break from the skirt of woods onto the open ground around Guilford Courthouse were the 33rd, the Jaegers, and the Light Infantry under Webster's command, but they were too far ahead of the rest of the British line for safety. With "more ardour than prudence," according to Lee, Webster led his men down into a ravine and up the other side and onto the open ground west of the courthouse. Here, Kirkwood and Lynch's men had linked up with the regulars of the third line, and they were done falling back. What's more, Webster was unsupported, as the British units to his right were still struggling in the skirt of woods.

Climbing out of the ravine, Webster's men found themselves confronting the right wing of Greene's third line, including Virginia regulars and the 1st Maryland Regiment, though in that broken, scrubby ground it is unlikely that Webster was able to see the enemy line in its entirety. The Americans let the redcoats approach before they delivered a disciplined and devastating fire. Lieutenant Colonel Howard of the 1st Maryland wrote, "When Webster advanced upon our third line, his left and centre engaged, and were worsted by Kirkwood and Lynch, while his right attacked the first Maryland regiment."

The Marylanders charged Webster's men with the bayonet, a taste of British medicine, and Webster's advance was flung back. His men recrossed the ravine and retreated to the high ground on the opposite slope, where they could wait for the rest of Cornwallis's line to advance. It was perhaps during this assault that Webster received a wound in his knee that would ultimately prove fatal.

More British troops began to reach the eastern edge of the skirt of woods, not as a coordinated line but in isolated units. They had driven back two lines of militia, but now they were facing a line of seasoned regulars, including some of the men who had whipped them at Cowpens two months before. What's more, the British had been locked in desperate fighting for an hour at least, while the Continentals were fresh. As Tarleton put it, "At this period the event of the action was doubtful, and victory alternately presided over each army."

CHAPTER *II* *A Pyrrhic Victory*

SHORTLY AFTER THE failure of Lieutenant Colonel James Webster's attack from the British left against Nathanael Greene's third line, the 2nd Battalion of Guards, numbering about two hundred fifty men, emerged from the woods to press the British advance. These soldiers had moved into the middle of the British line to fill the gap that had opened there, and, having been held in reserve at the start of the battle, they were still relatively fresh.

The 2nd faced a formidable-looking line across the open ground, with two regiments of Virginia regulars on the American right and the 1st and 2nd Maryland regiments on the American left. Captain Robert Kirkwood's tough Delaware Continentals, having fallen back all the way from the first line, had joined the third, and Lieutenant Colonel William Washington's cavalry, which had fallen back with Kirkwood, had taken a position south of the New Garden Road on high ground overlooking the field of battle. In the center of the line were two 6-pounders, and to the American left, by the 2nd Maryland, were Captain Anthony Singleton's two guns that had opened the fight.

Without hesitation, the 2nd Battalion advanced across 300 yards of open ground toward the 2nd Maryland and Singleton's guns. "Glowing with impatience to signalize themselves," Lord Cornwallis wrote, "they instantly attacked and defeated them, taking two six pounders." The left flank, as it happened, was the weakest section of the American third line. The 2nd Maryland soldiers were regulars, but they were new and as untried in battle as the North Carolina militia. Like the North Carolinians, the 2nd Maryland gave a "premature, confused and scattering fire," then turned and ran.

Their blood up from having driven off the Marylanders with so little effort or cost, the 2nd Battalion continued their pursuit headlong into the brush and woods. But their quick advance did not last long. Watching the action unseen was William Washington, who now led his cavalry forward to meet the onrushing redcoats. Suddenly, the 2nd Battalion's easy victory turned into a bloody fight against mounted troops. A dragoon fighting with Washington later recalled, "Leaping a ravine, the swords of the horsemen were upon the heads of the enemy, who were rejoicing in victory and safety; and before they suspected danger, multitudes lay dead."

Also hidden from the 2nd Battalion of Guards' view by woods and brush was the 1st Maryland, the veteran regiment that had just driven off Webster's advance. Now the Marylanders turned on the Guards, hitting them on their left flank with a vicious bayonet charge. This fight, the battle's first real combat on open ground, quickly turned into a bloody affair, the fighting hand to hand. William Washington drove his horsemen right through the Guards, then wheeled and turned back, slashing again through the ranks. The Marylanders pressed their charge home and, as Lieutenant Colonel Banastre Tarleton put it, "retook the cannon and repulsed the guards with great slaughter."

As the British lines advanced, Lieutenant John McLeod's artillery had followed. Now the guns were positioned on a rise overlooking the fight, where Cornwallis had also positioned himself. The general had been riding toward the lines to observe close-up the progress of the battle.

One recounting, perhaps apocryphal, holds that William Washington, seeing Cornwallis approach the lines with several aides-de-camp, led his cavalry in a charge to capture the British commander. In the middle of the charge, Washington's hat fell from his head, and he dismounted to retrieve it. At that moment, a ball struck the officer at the head of the column, who then lost control of his horse. The horse turned and raced back the way it had come, and the rest of the cavalrymen, thinking this was an ordered retreat, followed behind, thus saving Cornwallis from capture.

True or not, Cornwallis managed to get a sense for how things were going, and he was not pleased. Like Tarleton, the general understood that the outcome of the battle was an open question. The hard advance of the American cavalry and the Marylanders and the slaughter of the 2nd Battalion of Guards were turning the fight in Greene's favor.

Cornwallis ordered the artillery to pour grapeshot into the enemy and stop the American advance. According to Cornwallis, William Washington's cavalry was driven off "by a well-directed fire from two three pounders, just brought up by Lieu^t Macleod . . . ," and the Guards, badly beaten, stumbled back toward the British lines to regroup.

It has become a standard anecdote in the Battle of Guilford Courthouse storyline that Cornwallis ordered McLeod to fire directly into the mass of fighting men, British and American, knowing that the grapeshot would kill indiscriminately. Certainly Lieutenant Colonel Henry Lee believed this to be the case, writing in his memoir that "Cornwallis, seeing the vigorous advance . . . determined to arrest their progress, though every ball leveled at them must pass through the flying guards." But Lee was not on that part of the field, and, though Cornwallis undoubtedly used his artillery to fling the Americans back, the evidence that he fired deliberately into his own men is scant and inconclusive.

Just as William Washington's horsemen and the 1st Maryland were being driven back by Cornwallis's guns, the grenadiers and the 71st Regiment struggled out of the woods. A series of deep ravines had impeded their progress, but now they broke onto the open ground to the right of the 2nd Battalion of Guards. At nearly the same time, the 23rd, the Royal Welsh Fusiliers, emerged from the woods and formed to the Guards' left.

Meanwhile, Webster had continued to observe the battle from the high slope to which he had led his men after being driven back. Seeing the 2nd Maryland turn and run from the Guards, he chose that moment to lead his men back over the ravine and fall on the Virginia regiments on the American right.

Brigadier General Charles O'Hara, who had been leading the 2nd Battalion of Guards and had been wounded in the Americans' counterattack, now rallied the remainder of the Guards and led them forward with the other regiments. Behind them, Tarleton's cavalry advanced for their first chance to come to grips with the enemy since the Battle of New Garden nearly twelve hours earlier. After their broken and disjointed attack through the woods, the British were now essentially reformed into a line of battle as they advanced upon the Continentals over open ground.

Greene could see clearly now how things would turn out. Some of his best troops, Lee's Legion and Colonel William Campbell's riflemen, were still engaged in a private battle far to the southwest. The left of his line, the 2nd Maryland, had scattered, and attempts to rally them had failed. The enemy had turned the left flank "and got into the rear of the Virginia Brigade and appeared to be gaining our right, which would have encircled the whole of the Continental Troops."

It had always been Greene's understanding that he could not risk the loss of his entire army, the only significant American force left in the South, and he was not going to do so now. He peeled off one of the Virginia regiments under the command of Colonel John Green and ordered them to fall back toward the Guilford Courthouse and prepare to cover the army's retreat. Green was "much dissatisfied with the general's selection of his regiment for this service," since they had not yet participated in the battle. That it was deemed a great honor to be selected for that duty did little to mollify him.

As it happened, there was little fight left. The North Carolina militia had dissolved, Lee and his men were fighting off to the southwest, and with Green's regiment and the 1st Maryland gone, the Americans were badly outnumbered by their re-formed enemy. There was nothing for Nathanael Greene to do but pull his troops back to where Green's Virginians could cover their retreat.

"[A] well-contested action"

Cornwallis later informed George Germain, Secretary of State for the American Colonies, that the 23rd Regiment and Tarleton's cavalry advanced and "the enemy were soon put to flight," leaving behind their four cannon and two ammunition wagons. At the same time, Cornwallis reported, Webster and "the 33rd Regiment and Light Infantry of the Guards, after overcoming many difficulties, completely routed the Corps, which was opposed to them."

The general's report was accurate, but only to a point. Nearly all the Americans' horses had been killed, and Greene did not want to order the guns and wagons drawn off by hand at the risk of those men being captured or killed. But Cornwallis's implication that Greene's army had been driven off in a panicked rout was misleading. Most of the militia had already abandoned the field, and the regulars who were left in the third line made an orderly, fighting retreat. Greene wrote, "General Huger [in command of the Virginia regulars] was the last that was engaged and gave the enemy a check. We retreated in good order to the Reedy Fork River." Even Tarleton wrote that the Americans "were retreating in good order."

Cornwallis ordered the 23rd, the 71st, and part of Tarleton's cavalry to pursue the retreating Americans, but the pursuit was desultory at best. Lee wrote that the British "followed our army with the show of falling upon it; but the British general soon recalled them, and General Greene, undisturbed, was left to pursue his retreat."

Cornwallis was in no position to push Greene's army. As the general explained to Germain, the American cavalry "had suffered but little; our troops were excessively fatigued." British wounded were spread all over the battlefield and needed attending. And Cornwallis had other concerns as well.

Off to the southwest, he could still hear the guns of Lee's Legion and Campbell's riflemen engaged with the Von Bose Regiment and the 1st Battalion of Guards. For the full duration of the battle, as the rest of the British had pushed through three lines of American troops, those units had fought it out in broken, wooded country. That fight had continued to move east as both sides attempted to link with the flanks of their respective armies.

Eventually, as the fighting there began to wane, the 1st Battalion of Guards broke off and made to link with the British right flank. Seeing this, Lee sent his cavalry, which had been kept in the rear to cover an American retreat, back to "close with the left of the Continental line, and there to act until it should receive further orders." With the cavalry gone to bolster Greene's third line, only Campbell's riflemen and the Light Infantry of Lee's Legion were left to engage the Von Bose Regiment. Still, the Americans pressed the Germans hard, driving them back over the rough ground.

As the Von Bose fell back, Lee detached the infantry of his legion to join the cavalry on the American left. They again encountered the 1st Battalion of Guards on the high ground where General Robert Lawson's Virginia militia had stood earlier, and again the two regiments clashed, with Lee's men pushing the Guards back toward the Von Bose Regiment before continuing on toward Guilford Courthouse. By the time they arrived there, Greene's army had already retreated from the field.

The fighting that Cornwallis heard was Campbell's riflemen still engaged with the Von Bose Regiment. "[T]he Remainder of the Cavalry," Cornwallis wrote, "was detached with Lieu^t - Colonel Tarleton to our right, where a heavy fire still continued."

Tarleton and his horsemen charged off toward the sound of fighting, where the last act of the battle was playing out. When they arrived, "the guards and the Hessians were directed to fire a volley at the largest party of the militia." That done, Tarleton and his men charged the riflemen, sabers drawn, through the cover of the smoke. With Lee's cavalry gone, the Americans had no defense against the mounted troops. As one of Campbell's men, Samuel Houston, recalled, "their light horse came on us, and not being defended by our own light horse . . . we were obliged to run, and many were sore chased and some cut down." Campbell's men, the last of the Americans to be engaged, retreated east with the rest of Greene's army.

"Thus ended," Tarleton wrote, "a general, and in the main, a well-contested action, which had lasted upwards of two hours."

"[A] signal Victory"

Greene marched his men east. Three miles from the battlefield, they crossed the Reedy Fork River and halted there long enough to collect most of their stragglers. Night came on, and with it a driving rain and bitter cold. The defeated Americans continued to their former camp at the Speedwell Iron Works, about 10 miles from the battlefield, and there they stopped.

Cornwallis was left in possession of the field, the traditional mark of victory, a victory he was quick to claim. "My Lord," he wrote to Germain, "I have the satisfaction to inform Your Lordship, that His Majesty's Troops under my command, obtained a signal Victory on the 15th Ins^t over the Rebel Army."

As night came on, the British troops found what cover they could. They had no tents to shelter them from the torrential rain. They had very little food. The wounded and dead were scattered over the broad expanse of the battlefield. Major Charles Stedman, Commissary of the British army, wrote,

> The night . . . was remarkable for its darkness, accompanied by rain, which fell in torrents. . . . The cries of the wounded and dying who remained on the field of action during the night exceeded all description. Such a complicated scene of horror and distress, it is hoped, for the sake of humanity, rarely occurs, even in a military life.

In short, it did not feel much like a victory.

Cornwallis had 93 men killed, 413 wounded, and 26 missing, for a total of 532 troops put out of action, more than a quarter of his force. Greene's army had suffered 79 killed and 185 wounded. There were also 996 Americans missing, but that number is deceptive. Whereas Cornwallis's missing were likely dead and lost on the field or deserted, Greene's missing were mostly militia who had gone home, in Greene's words, "leaving us in great numbers, to return home to kiss their wives and sweet hearts." Greene's missing could be called upon again; Cornwallis's could not.

The American forces suffered fewer than half as many casualties as the British, and there were several reasons why. The Americans were generally fighting from cover, while the British, who were advancing toward their lines, had to expose themselves to enemy fire. The Americans had a number of riflemen in their ranks whose accurate weapons could inflict damage at distances considerably longer than a musket shot. Also, as Lee would later point out, the Americans "were acquainted with wood and tree fighting; he [the British soldier] ignorant of both. And lastly, we were trained to aim and fire low, he was not so trained." While neither side was in a good position to sustain casualties, the loss was much worse for Cornwallis, for whom replacements had to come from New York, the West Indies, or Europe.

In *The Parallel Lives*, Plutarch quotes King Pyrrhus as saying after two costly victories in Italy, "If we are victorious in one more battle with the Romans, we shall be utterly ruined." What Cornwallis had won was just such a Pyrrhic victory, and there would be repercussions in England as reports filtered back in the months to come. The colorful Whig leader Charles James Fox, an outspoken supporter of the American cause who often wore buff and blue (the American regimental colors) and rarely missed a chance to accuse King George III and Lord North of warmon-gering, is said to have thundered in the House of Commons, "Another such victory would ruin the British Army!"

As night and rain fell, the British army suffered on the ground they had taken. For the ostensibly defeated Americans, however, things looked better than they had in some time. Though Greene's men were suffering the same physical discomforts as the British, their morale was notably higher. "Our army is in good spirits," Greene wrote to Joseph Reed, the president of the Pennsylvania Council and Washington's for-mer aide-de-camp. He went on to say that, for months, he had been torn with anxiety over the fate of his army, "until since the defeat of the 15th; but now I am perfectly easy, being perswaded it is out of the enemies power to do us any great injury."

Despite his optimistic outlook, Greene did not entirely dismiss the possibility of Cornwallis renewing the attack. He allowed his men to rest, but at the same time, he prepared for a second fight with the British. The troops, Greene reported, were "wishing for an opportunity of engaging the enemy."

Still, the army could not remain long where they were. The sparsely populated area around Guilford Courthouse had never been abundant with supplies, and after having supported two armies totaling around seven thousand men, it was more barren still. "We have little to eat," Greene wrote, "less to drink, and lodge in the woods in the midst of smoke."

Cornwallis found his store of supplies untenable. The countryside was, in his words, "so totally destitute of subsistence, that forage is not nearer than nine miles, and the soldiers have been two days without bread." Seventy of his men were too badly wounded to move. In the after-math of the battle, Cornwallis had attended to the American wounded as well as his own. Now he would leave his own severely wounded at the New Garden Meeting House under flag of truce to be cared for by the Americans.

Three days after the battle, Cornwallis once again put his army in motion. He was not looking to renew his fight with Greene, but rather for a place where supplies might be found more easily. Before leaving Guilford, he issued a proclamation announcing the "compleat victory obtained over the Rebel forces" and promising that anyone currently fighting on the American side, "murderers excepted," who surrendered himself and his arms before April 20 would be allowed to return to his home on parole. This was likely a pro forma gesture. After more than a year in the southern theater, Cornwallis could not have entertained high expectations of American cooperation.

On March 18, the day that Vice-Admiral Marriot Arbuthnot was anchoring in Lynnhaven Bay, Cornwallis moved his army south to Bell's Mill on the Deep River, a place where "the greatest number of our friends were supposed to reside." Once again, the general found that loyalty to the king did not necessarily translate into a desire to fight for him. "Many of the Inhabitants rode into Camp," he wrote to Clinton, "shook me by the hand, said they were glad to see us, and to hear that we had beat Greene, and then rode home again." Despite the area's reputation as a seat of Loyalist sentiment, Cornwallis could not get a hundred men to join him, even as short-term militia.

The British army remained a few days in Bell's Mill, where they were able to collect some flour and meal but not much else. Cornwallis knew that his army was spent, a third of them sick or wounded and unable to march, "the remainder without Shoes, and worn down with fatigue." He knew that he had to pause somewhere to allow his men to rest and refit and that that place had to have a strong Loyalist population and ample supplies, which was a tall order. Soon after reaching Bell's Mill, Cornwallis continued south to the town of Cross Creek, near present-day Fayetteville, which he believed would fit his needs.

Greene had not thought that Cornwallis would abandon North Carolina "without being soundly beaten," or so he wrote to General George Washington three days after the Battle of Guilford Courthouse. When Cornwallis began his march toward Bell's Mill, however, Greene came to realize just how badly the British had been mauled, and he saw an opportunity to finish Cornwallis once and for all.

Greene hoped to strike out after Cornwallis as soon as the British began to move, but a lack of ammunition and provisions held him in camp. Unable to mobilize his entire army, Greene sent his veterans, Lee's Legion and Campbell's riflemen, along with William Washington's cavalry, to harass Cornwallis's army. Lee later recalled Greene telling him that "Lord Cornwallis don't wish to fight us, but you may depend upon it, he will not refuse to fight if we push him." Lee's instructions were to "push their rear all you can." Meanwhile, Greene would march his army hard, with the intention of cutting off the British before they could stop and make a stand. Now Greene was chasing Cornwallis. The military situation of the past four months had been inverted.

The American horse troops and light infantry caught up with Cornwallis's rear guard, consisting of the Jaegers, the Guards' light infantry, and Tarleton's cavalry, as the British were moving by easy march from Bell's Mill to a place called Ramsey's Mill. The Americans were able to annoy the enemy ("the Americans insulted the yagers in their encampment" is how Tarleton worded it) but were unable to bring on a full-scale battle; nor did they wish to, with Greene's main army still trying to catch up.

The British paused at Ramsey's Mill to build a bridge over the Deep River. On March 27, Cornwallis moved his army across the bridge and continued on to Cross Creek, where, as usual, he hoped to find supplies and Loyalist support. Greene arrived at Ramsey's Mill the next day to find that he had barely missed the chance to bring Cornwallis to battle.

Though Greene was now the aggressor, he was wrestling with many of the same issues that hounded Cornwallis plus some specifically his own. Provisions were no more available to him than to the British. The country between Ramsey's Mill and Cross Creek was, in Lee's words, "so barren and thinly settled as to forbid any hope of obtaining the requisite supplies," and anything that was there would be snatched up by Cornwallis, who had a day's march on Greene. What's more, the time for those militiamen still with the army would soon be out, and once again Greene's numbers would be inferior to Cornwallis's.

Greene was undecided what to do next, not least because he did not know what Cornwallis intended. He feared that Cornwallis would continue on to Wilmington, then in British hands, and once there would be in so strong a position that Greene could not hope to defeat him.

The day after missing Cornwallis at Ramsey's Mill, Greene made his decision. He wrote to George Washington, informing the commander-in-chief that he was "determined to carry the War immediately into South Carolina." There he would link up with American forces still in that state and attack the remaining British posts. Cornwallis would be forced either to leave his troops in South Carolina to their fate or to follow Greene and abandon North Carolina, neither a terribly good option.

With that decision reached, Greene wrote to General Thomas Sumter to begin gathering the South Carolina militia while he himself prepared to march south, leaving North Carolina and Charles, Lord Cornwallis behind.

CHAPTER *12* *Reinforcing the Chesapeake*

EVEN BEFORE VICE-ADMIRAL Marriot Arbuthnot had sailed from Gardiner's Bay in pursuit of Chevalier Destouches and the French fleet, two thousand men under the command of Major General William Phillips had boarded transports and were anchored off Sandy Hook, awaiting their chance to go south and link up with Benedict Arnold.

Sir Henry Clinton had long had his eye on the Chesapeake. "The very numerous important advantages, military, political, and commercial, which were likely to result to Great Britain from the possession of this very valuable district are too obvious to require detail," he wrote. Taking and holding Virginia, he thought, would require "a reinforcement of 6000 men and security against a superior fleet and a foreign army." Until those things could be provided, and to help facilitate them, he hoped to "secure a small naval post in the Chesapeake, to cover the King's cruisers and to supply a fit rendezvous for more serious operations."

In Clinton's mind, the immediate object was simply to lay the groundwork for future operations. Until the Carolinas were secured, until he received a major reinforcement from England, and until the Royal Navy held absolute control of the seas between New York and Virginia, he had no interest in sustained operations in the Chesapeake. The elite troops under Arnold and Phillips were to return to New York once the immediate job was done.

Clinton's orders to Phillips instructed the major general to join Arnold and take command of the combined forces. The "principal object" of Phillips's mission, as Phillips understood it, was to see that Arnold's troops and the posts he had established were secure. Having done so, he was to continue acting in support of Cornwallis by destroying military stores and magazines and cutting off supplies that might otherwise flow south to Greene.

Arnold had, under Clinton's orders, begun to fortify Portsmouth as a base for naval operations, although Arbuthnot, who was actually in charge of naval operations, had never indicated whether Portsmouth would be suitable for that purpose. "If the Admiral, disapproving of Portsmouth, and requiring a fortified station for large ships in the Chesapeak, should propose York Town or Old Point Comfort," Clinton wrote in his orders to Phillips, "you are at liberty to take possession thereof," as long as doing so would not put his troops at risk. Indeed, Clinton had earlier written, "With regard to a station for the King's ships I know of no place so proper as Yorktown." Arbuthnot was not seriously consulted in any of this. (Old Point Comfort, site of the present-day Fort Monroe Military Reservation, is about 18 miles southeast of Yorktown as the crow flies and juts south into the James River mouth from the north shore, facing Norfolk and Portsmouth across the waters of Hampton Roads.)

The fleet that carried Phillips and the men under his command weighed anchor and departed Sandy Hook, New Jersey, on March 20, as soon as Clinton received word of the outcome of the Battle of Cape Henry. After an easy passage, during which they were fortunate not to meet Destouches's returning squadron, the ships arrived at Portsmouth on March 31, anchoring among Arbuthnot's fleet. On the first of April, the men began to disembark.

Phillips was an efficient and well-liked commander. Captain Johann Ewald "recognized in him the skillful and industrious officer . . . ," though the discipline he imposed caused considerable grumbling among "the lazy and worthless element of the men. . . . In short," Ewald concluded, Phillips "was a man just as a man should be."

Phillips's first order of business, he thought, was to see to the defense of Portsmouth, and he began to strengthen those parts of the works that seemed inadequate. But he did not find Portsmouth a particularly good choice for a post. A week after arriving there, he wrote to Clinton, "I think the present situation not calculated for a post of force, or for one for a small number of troops." It would be better, Phillips thought, to fortify three points along the Elizabeth River, which could more efficiently protect ships anchored within their arcs of fire and offer mutual support in the event of an assault. But until he received word to the contrary from New York, his orders as he understood them were to continue strengthening Portsmouth.

Clinton, however, was surprised and displeased to learn, upon reading Phillips's report, that Phillips considered establishing a base at Portsmouth his prime objective. That had not been Clinton's intention at all. His orders had, in fact, instructed Phillips that "the principal object of your expedition is the security of [Arnold], the troops at present under his orders, and the posts he occupies on Elizabeth River." What he actually meant, Clinton explained, was that the security of the troops and bases had been a priority while Arnold had been threatened by the Marquis de Lafayette and the French fleet (though he had not allowed Phillips to sail until the French fleet had been neutralized), which was no longer the case.

The true primary object of Phillips's mission to Virginia, Clinton now emphasized, was an "operation in favor of Lord Cornwallis." Establishing a naval base was secondary. Clinton did not care if that base was at Portsmouth or any other spot, as long as it was "a station to protect the King's ships, which is capable of being maintained by a garrison of about five or six hundred men." It was yet another in a long list of instances in which Clinton's vague and ambiguous orders were misinterpreted—much to his dismay.

Part of the difficulty in establishing a strategy for supporting Cornwallis was that no one actually knew what Cornwallis was up to. Upon leaving Lord Charles in South Carolina ten months earlier, Clinton had agreed to let him correspond directly with George Germain in England. This odd abdication of responsibility produced predictable results. Clinton and Cornwallis were both writing to Germain, and Germain was directing each of them from London, but neither general had much idea what the other was up to.

Cornwallis sent Germain a detailed report of the Battle of Guilford Courthouse just days after the action, but he did not write Clinton of the affair until almost a month later—ten days after Phillips, unbeknownst to Cornwallis, had landed at Portsmouth. Thus, by the first week in April, Phillips and Cornwallis were within 200 miles of one another, with Clinton intending that their armies should cooperate, but Cornwallis did not know that Phillips was there and Phillips did not know what Cornwallis was doing. "It is unlucky for us," Phillips wrote to Clinton, "that we know so little of Lord Cornwallis, in favor of whom, and his operations we are directed by your Excellency to direct our utmost attention."

Phillips was a sufficiently experienced campaigner to realize from the reports trickling in that Cornwallis's victory at Guilford Courthouse might not have been quite so uniformly successful as his lordship suggested. He wrote to Clinton that he was certain Cornwallis's victory was complete, but that "he may have bought it dear, and that his Lordship remained a little crippled after the Action." But still no word from Cornwallis was forthcoming.

The Next Move

Two weeks after the Battle of Guilford Courthouse, with Greene no longer hounding his retreat, Cornwallis continued by easy marches to Cross Creek, taking care to pass through only those settlements that were "described to me as most friendly." Once again, he hoped that his new destination would prove at least adequately rich in supplies and would be populated by people sympathetic to the Crown.

Even if resources were not to be found in Cross Creek, the general believed that they might be shipped 150 miles up the Cape Fear River from Wilmington, which had been occupied specifically to serve as a supply base for the operations in North Carolina. As far back as February, Cornwallis had written to Major James Craig, the commanding officer there, instructing him to establish water communications with the North Carolina interior for resupply purposes.

Arriving at Cross Creek, Cornwallis found a letter from Craig explaining why he could not, in fact, send supplies from Wilmington. The distance, Craig explained, was too far, the river too narrow, the banks too high, and "the Inhabitants on each side, almost universally hostile."

Writing some years later, Banastre Tarleton pointed out that these issues should have been discovered before the British army entered North Carolina, since even the most fortunate campaigns could be ruined "by blindly trusting to a communication that cannot be opened." Now, despite having once again been told of an abundance of supplies ahead, Cornwallis found himself in a part of the country where "it was impossible to procure any considerable quantity of provisions."

At least the inhabitants of Cross Creek "retained great zeal for the interest of the royal army," according to Tarleton. But zeal alone could not feed Cornwallis's men, nor did Cornwallis feel that Cross Creek's enthusiasm was all it might be. Given that the army could not remain there, Tarleton felt they should march 100 miles southwest back to Camden, South Carolina, since Camden was an important crossroads for control of the Carolina backcountry and since the troops left there under Lord Francis Rawdon were spread out and vulnerable to Greene's army. What's more, one of the objects of the campaign from its inception a year earlier had been to secure the ground won in battle.

Tarleton's arguments were sound. Whether he mentioned them to Cornwallis is unclear, but it wouldn't have mattered. Cornwallis had no intention of returning to South Carolina. Instead, he followed the Cape Fear River south to the relative safety and comfort of Wilmington, North Carolina.

Several wounded officers died during the march to Wilmington, among them Lieutenant Colonel James Webster, perhaps Cornwallis's finest officer, who had been wounded leading his men in the first assault on Nathanael Greene's third line of veteran troops at Guilford Courthouse. Webster, Tarleton recalled, "united all the virtues of civil life to the gallantry and professional knowledge of a soldier."

On April 7, as Phillips and Arnold to the north were waiting out the weather to launch an attack on Williamsburg, Cornwallis's battered army arrived in camp near Wilmington. A few days later, Cornwallis finally wrote to Clinton, his commander-in-chief, in New York, giving him a perfunctory overview of the past half year of campaigning. Clinton had been under the impression that Cornwallis had three thousand men under his command, and he would be surprised to learn from this report that the true number was less than half that.

By the time he received Cornwallis's letter, Clinton had heard something of the battle of Guilford Courthouse from the American press, but if he was looking for a thorough report from his subordinate general, he was disappointed. Cornwallis said merely that "our military operations were uniformly successful" and promised to enclose copies of his reports to Germain in his next dispatch. What Cornwallis claimed to want from Clinton was direction, a thing he had conspicuously neglected to seek over the previous ten months. "I am very anxious to receive your Excellency's command," he wrote, "being yet totally in the dark, as to the intended operations of the Summer."

Three options were open to Cornwallis. One was to lead his army back into the Carolinas in pursuit of Greene. Cornwallis was concerned that the troops under Rawdon would be taken apart piecemeal by the

Americans. He sent several warnings by express to Rawdon from Cross Creek, but all were intercepted. As it happened, several of Rawdon's outposts were in fact picked off by American troops and partisans, though Greene himself was defeated by the brilliant Rawdon at Hobkirk's Hill while trying to take Camden.

Cornwallis's other options were to move his men by sea back to Charleston or to move north into Virginia. Despite his pro forma turn to Clinton for leadership, Cornwallis already had a pretty good idea which of the three he preferred, and he said so in the very next line: "I cannot help expressing my wishes, that the Chesapeak may become the Seat of War, even (if necessary) at the expense of abandoning New York."

After half a year of chasing Greene around the Carolinas, Cornwallis was done. Time and again, he had been told that one pocket of Americans or another was solidly loyal to the Crown, only to find that not to be the case at all, and the Loyalists he did meet were largely unwilling to do anything in support of their professed convictions. Nor did Cornwallis believe he could reach Camden in time to aide Rawdon against Greene. Among the dangers he enumerated were "the great rivers I should have to pass, the exhausted state of the Country, the numerous Militia, the almost universal spirit of revolt which prevails in South Carolina and the strength of Greene's Army."

He could see no advantage in returning to Charleston. That left Virginia.

On April 22, Cornwallis received an express from Charleston, carried aboard a small vessel, informing him that a frigate with dispatches from Clinton was at Charleston and would make its way to Wilmington once it could cross the bar. The express also notified Cornwallis for the first time that Phillips had been dispatched to Virginia "with a considerable force, with instructions to co-operate with this Army."

For Cornwallis, word that his old friend Phillips was in Virginia with a substantial force of men who, unlike his own troops, were not worn to the bone by half a year of forced marching must have seemed like a gift from God. In the first line of the letter Cornwallis wrote the next day to Phillips, he said, "My situation here is very distressing," and he went on to enumerate the many perils that awaited him in the Carolinas and his absolute inability to do any further good in that theater.

Phillips's presence further strengthened Cornwallis's resolve to march north and begin serious operations in Virginia. His affection for

Phillips showed clearly when he wrote, "Now, my dear friend, what is our plan? Without one we cannot succeed, and I assure you I am quite tired of marching around the country in quest of adventures." Cornwallis went on to suggest again, as he had to Clinton, that the British should abandon New York and focus on Virginia.

Cornwallis understood that Greene was still a threat in the Carolinas, but he was done chasing the Rhode Islander and his elusive army. Instead, Cornwallis wished for Greene to chase him, and he informed Phillips that he would immediately begin a march north "in hopes to withdraw Greene . . ." and presumably bring the Americans to battle once more. But Cornwallis's heart was not in that plan. His eyes were on Virginia, as he had already made clear in his correspondence with Clinton, and he told Phillips that if Greene could not be lured north, "I should be much tempted to form a junction with you."

In fact, Cornwallis was more than just tempted, he was decided. He sent Phillips a cipher by which they could carry on a secret correspondence and told him, on the one hand, not to "expose your Army to any danger of being ruined," while at the same time to "make every Movement in your power to facilitate our Meeting which must be somewhere near Petersburgh."

Why the small vessel from Charleston could carry word of Clinton's dispatches to Cornwallis but not the dispatches themselves is unclear; indeed, Clinton would raise that very question years later. Perhaps there was fear of the smaller vessel falling prey to an American privateer. In any event, there was little in Clinton's letters by way of specific orders, just the rather vague "it is my wish that you should continue to conduct operations as they advance northerly," whatever that meant, and a request that Cornwallis not ask for any more troops than Clinton could possibly spare.

Although Cornwallis knew that Clinton's dispatches were in Charleston and would be sent on to Wilmington, he decided he could wait no longer. The day after receiving the express, Cornwallis wrote a letter to Germain explaining in detail his decision to march north. Virginia was the key to the South, he wrote: "I take the liberty of giving it as my opinion, that a serious attempt upon Virginia would be the most solid plan, because successful operations might not only be attended with important consequences there, but would tend to the security of South Carolina, and ultimately to the submission of North Carolina."

Cornwallis's thoughts made a certain amount of sense, but they also reflected the desperation shared by most of the British leadership to try something new, because what they had done so far wasn't working. He did not convey to Germain what was perhaps the most compelling reason to march for Virginia, which was simply that he did not have enough men left to be effective against Greene in the Carolinas.

He also wrote to Clinton that day, telling the commander-in-chief that he was enclosing copies of all his letters and reports to Germain, that Clinton could read those to find out what was going on, and that he, Cornwallis, had "nothing to add to it for your Excellency's satisfaction." The enclosed reports to Germain would be Clinton's first detailed notice of the Battle of Guilford Courthouse, more than a month after the event.

Cornwallis also wrote, "I have reflected very seriously on the subject of my attempt to march into Virginia," and enclosed a copy of his letter to Phillips by way of informing Clinton of his intentions. In his letter to Phillips, Cornwallis concluded with "I am, dear Phillips Most faithfully y^{rs}. . . ." To Clinton, he wrote, "I have the honour to be, &c. . . ."

He did inform Clinton that it was "very disagreeable to me to decide upon measures so very important, and of such consequence to the general conduct of the war, without an opportunity of procuring your Excellency's directions or approbation." This was certainly Cornwallis at his most disingenuous. If he had been desperate for word from Clinton, he had only to await the dispatches being routed from Charleston.

The feuding between the two generals would continue long after the Treaty of Paris ended the American War for Independence, and in later years, Clinton would claim that he had explicitly ordered Cornwallis not to go to Virginia. It is true that Clinton considered the security of North and South Carolina to be of the utmost importance, but it is also true that Clinton was no more able to give an unambiguous order to Cornwallis than he was to stir himself to decisive action.

To his request for direction on how the summer campaign should proceed, Cornwallis received nothing but equivocation. Clinton's reply pointed out that Cornwallis's next move must depend on "your Lordship's success in Carolina, the certainty and numbers of the expected reinforcement from Europe, and, likewise, on your Lordship's sending back to me the corps I had spared to you."

Clinton did go so far as to express concerns about major operations in the Chesapeake going forward before "those to the southward of it are totally at an end . . . ," and he reminded Cornwallis of the thoughts he had expressed the previous November with regard to operations in Virginia. But the essence of his reply was that, absent further information regarding the state of things in the southern theater, "it must obviously be impossible for me to determine finally upon a plan of operations for the campaign."

Not that Clinton's reply mattered much. Cornwallis had come to believe that the entire southern strategy would never work until Virginia was subdued and the American pipeline of supplies and communications from the North shut off. By the time Cornwallis received instructions, such as they were, from his commander-in-chief, he and his army were marching on the road that would lead them to Yorktown.

CHAPTER *13* *"[T]he Enemy have turned so much of their attention to the Southern States"*

By late March, Baron de Steuben was thoroughly disgusted— disgusted by the lack of cooperation he had been receiving from the government of Virginia; disgusted by the failure of the seemingly perfect trap he, the Marquis de Lafayette, and General Peter Muhlenberg had constructed to catch Benedict Arnold and his troops; and disgusted by the failure of the French fleet to fulfill their role in that trap. He was ready to be done with Virginia, even if it meant also being done with his independent command. He wanted to head south and join Nathanael Greene, taking an army with him if possible.

What's more, Virginia was about done with the baron. His constant badgering of Governor Thomas Jefferson and other state officials for men and supplies had finally driven them over the edge. As Greene informed General George Washington, "Baron Stuben will join this Army, he having so offended the Legislature of Virginia cannot be as useful there as he has been."

"As soon as we were assured that our Expedition against the Portsmouth had failed," the baron wrote to Muhlenberg—who commanded the militia units defending Virginia and was reporting to Steuben as ranking Continental officer in the state—"I proposed to Government to carry the whole of our force immediately to Carolina and fall on Cornwallis." Steuben was certain—and likely right—that his army combined with Greene's could destroy Lord Cornwallis's. He also believed, incorrectly, that the French fleet had not returned to Rhode Island after the Battle of Cape Henry but rather had continued south to Cape Fear and was anchored just 20 miles from Wilmington, where they would be in a position to cooperate with the Americans.

The troops under Steuben's command were mostly Virginia militia who could not be taken out of the state without the approval of the governor and the legislature. Steuben's plan was approved by Lafayette and informally by General George Weedon, who commanded the principal brigade of Virginia militia and reported to Muhlenberg, but it was soundly rejected by the government of Virginia—a decision the military officers found frustrating but unsurprising. Steuben and Weedon, in particular, had been unimpressed with the efforts made by Virginia's government and citizens in defense of their state. Steuben had failed to rouse the state to garrison Hood's Fort, and his repeated requests for men and supplies had gone largely unanswered. In the months to come, Lafayette would not even be able to convince plantation owners to move their horses out of the path of the British army, thus allowing Lieutenant Colonels John Simcoe and Banastre Tarleton to equip themselves with some of the finest mounts in the country. To officers and men who had been fighting for years in New York, New Jersey, and Pennsylvania, it often seemed as if the people of Virginia could not be bothered with their own defense.

Jefferson, the governor, came in for particular criticism from military men, though he himself blamed the problems on a lack of cooperation from the legislature and leading citizens. As Weedon put it to Steuben, "I was fearful our Scheme would be rejected by the Executive who has not an Idea beyond local security."

For the moment, however, Virginia seemed secure enough that Weedon asked permission to go to Fredericksburg on personal business provided "no Extraordinary Movement of the Enemy . . ." made it necessary that he stay with his brigade in Williamsburg.

Steuben did not think Virginia was in much danger. Rather, he thought that Major General William Phillips and Arnold would "carry the greatest part of their force around [by sea] to the support of Cornwallis," even, perhaps, abandoning Portsmouth altogether. He intended, therefore, to march south and join Greene at last. That had been his reason for journeying south with Greene the previous year, and the time had come to fulfill that mission with or without the militia troops then under his command.

He did not want to go empty-handed, however. Greene had made it clear on more than one occasion that he was desperate for troops and hoped that Steuben, left in Virginia for the express purpose of supplying the southern army, would find more men. So, with "nothing left to do," and unable to take the troops he currently had south, Steuben set about recruiting more. His headquarters were at Chesterfield Courthouse, halfway between Richmond and Petersburg. From there, he wrote to Greene that he would, if possible, bring with him the first detachment of troops raised in Virginia, hopefully as many as five hundred infantry and sixty or eighty cavalry.

It was soon clear to the baron that this would not be easy. "The beginning of this month [April]," he wrote to Weedon, "was fixed for the departure of the first detachment of 500 Men and only Seven have yet come in, two of whom have already deserted." Steuben began to fire off letters to the various rendezvous established for new recruits to see why things were not moving forward and how long the recruitment was likely to take. Once again, however, events would quickly overrun even the short-term plans the Prussian devised.

Like Steuben, the Marquis de Lafayette was done with Virginia. He rejoined his troops in Annapolis to prepare for the march north to link up with Washington in New Windsor, New York. Greene, not wanting to see any troops leave the southern theater, opposed this move. "I cannot think this will be advisable for you to return," he wrote to Lafayette on April 3, just three weeks after the Battle of Guilford Courthouse, "as the enemy are greatly reinforced in Virginia, and superior by far to the Southward." He felt that Washington would be better able to reinforce the northern army than Greene could the southern, and that success in the North depended upon success in the South. He suggested that Lafayette march instead to Richmond, from where he could either continue south to the Carolinas or fight in Virginia as circumstances dictated.

Washington, still contemplating an attack on New York City, was bitterly disappointed that Arnold had slipped through his fingers, though he tried to console Lafayette (and doubtless himself) that they had done everything humanly possible to capture Arnold and his army. Now he was eager to get Lafayette back. "I wish the detachment may move as quickly as they can without injury to the troops," he wrote to the marquis on April 5, two days after Greene had written ordering him to Richmond. Brigadier General Anthony Wayne and his Pennsylvania line of

Continental troops were still on their way to Greene, and Washington thought that would be reinforcement enough. He instructed Lafayette to leave his artillery for Wayne "at some safe and proper place" so that the Pennsylvanians could carry it southward.

Lafayette was as eager to get back to New York as Washington was to receive him, and he was wasting no time despite the logistical difficulties he faced. There were few wagons or horses and fewer boats to be had in Annapolis. By far, the easiest route was by water up the Chesapeake Bay to Head of Elk, but two British men-of-war, the *Hope* of eighteen guns and the *General Monk* with sixteen, were blockading Annapolis Harbor.

Rather than make the time-consuming march by land, Lafayette ordered two 18-pounder cannon mounted on a sloop in the harbor, enormous guns for so small a vessel, which "Appeared Ridiculous to Some, But Proved to Be of A Great Service." Another vessel was crammed with armed men, and, on the morning of April 6, the tiny squadron sallied forth under the command of Captain James Nicholson, commodore of the Maryland navy, with their oversized guns blazing. This little display of sound and fury worked better than Lafayette had dared hope, and the British ships, after a few maneuvers, retreated far enough from the harbor to allow him and his men to sail away, finally giving the Americans a naval victory in the Chesapeake. "Wether the Sound of the 18 pounders or the fear of Being Boarded Operated Upon the ennemy I am not able to Say," Lafayette wrote.

Even as Lafayette was moving his troops north, however, Washington began rethinking his orders. The commander-in-chief had long understood the importance of the southern theater, writing to Steuben months before that, "Since the Enemy have turned so much of their attention to the Southern States, the situation of our affairs in them has become extremely interesting and important." Washington was still focused on attacking Sir Henry Clinton in New York, but he could hardly be indifferent to the fact that the British were turning more and more of their attention to the South. Three times in the past half year, Clinton had sent troops to the Chesapeake. While the northern theater had devolved into a stalemate, the situation in Virginia and the Carolinas remained fluid. Though Washington may have been disinclined to focus on the South of his own accord, the enemy was forcing him to do so.

The day after asking Lafayette to return to New York as quickly as possible, Washington wrote again, saying, "Since my letter of yesterday I have attentively considered of what vast importance it will be to reinforce Genl. Greene as speedily as possible," in particular because it was clear that the reinforcements under Phillips would be used in some manner to bolster Cornwallis. Washington had consulted with his general officers as to the wisdom of turning Lafayette around and sending him south again, and the officers were unanimous: Greene needed reinforcements, and since the marquis and the thousand or so men under his command were already 300 miles closer than any other division, they should go.

Lafayette had made it to the Elk River at the head of the Chesapeake, intending to be back with Washington in just a few days, when he received Washington's orders to "turn the detachment to the southward." Though unhappy about the change of plan, he was always ready to comply with any orders from his beloved commander-in-chief. He assured Washington that were he able, he would begin marching his men south the following day, but that was not going to be possible. He had intended to march to Philadelphia, where supplies would be waiting, but now he would need to organize supplies and transport for moving in the opposite direction.

He had other concerns as well, which, as he put it, "I would Have Been allowed to present, Had I Been at the Meeting of the General officers," where the decision had necessarily been made without his input. The most immediate problem was a lack of adequate clothing, in particular, shoes to replace those that had been worn out from considerable forced marching. Lafayette's move to the Chesapeake had been conceived as a quick strike against Arnold, not a protracted stay in the South. The officers and men "thought at first they were Sent out for a few days And provided themselves Accordingly." Now the officers "Had no Monney, No Baggage of Any Sort, No Summer Cloathes and Hardly a Shirt to Shift. To these Common Miseries the Soldiers Added their Shocking Naked[ness and] a want of Shoes &c. &c." The men were all from northern states and looked to their home governments to provide clothes and money, both of which would be much harder to receive at such a distant remove.

Lafayette knew as well that his northern troops would object to being attached to the southern army, particularly as they had marched with the understanding that this would not be the case. "They will Certainly obey," he assured Washington, "But they will be Unhappy and Some will desert." Lafayette admitted that he, too, "would Most Certainly Like Better to Be in a situation to Attak Newyork."

Having stated his reservations, Lafayette dutifully prepared his troops to move south again. There was no chance of moving by water this time, since the British naval presence on the Chesapeake was now too strong and Lafayette did not think they would be fooled again by a sloop with a pair of 18-pounders. As a late spring storm rose up and lashed the men, destitute of shoes and with their clothes in tatters, Lafayette marched them southwest toward Baltimore. The army crossed the Susquehanna by ferry, but the wind was too strong for the wagons to get across, so the men hunkered down on the south side of the river and waited for the storm to blow itself out.

Lafayette was glad at least to have the men across the river, as the water formed something of a barrier against desertion, which, as he had predicted, had already begun. Even while writing to Washington, he had received news that nine men from a Rhode Island company, veterans of many bloody fights and among his best soldiers, had deserted, claiming "they like Better Hundred Lashes than a journey to the Southward." They had been willing to venture south on a mission to capture Arnold, but they were less than happy about remaining there.

The British on Offense

On the day that Washington was writing to Lafayette directing him to march south, Muhlenberg's Virginia troops, still watching Phillips and Arnold, realized that something was in the offing. Muhlenberg had about a thousand men under his command, and they were arrayed along the Nansemond River with their left flank anchored on the Chuckatuck—two small tributaries emptying into the James River from the south—facing the enemy in Portsmouth. On April 6, he wrote to Weedon, who was stationed on the north side of the James River with about six hundred men, saying, "This Much is certain They are preparing, &

nearly ready for a Move; & from the best intelligence I can get, a Junction with Cornwallis is the Main Object."

What they did not know was what direction the British would take, whether overland, up the James River, or by sea to Wilmington. But a few days later, Steuben reported to Washington that the enemy was "busied strengthening their works and in Building Boats." The baron knew they had been purchasing boats as well, a clear indication that they meant to move upriver.

A few days after that, the transports that had carried Phillips and his men from New York set sail without the army, which meant that the British would not be going anywhere by sea and that the Americans would soon have a fight on their hands. Weedon asked that all the militia that had been dispersed after the failure of the expedition to capture Arnold be sent back to the Williamsburg area, but Steuben refused. He did not want to leave the area around Richmond unprotected when he did not know where the British were heading. "In endeavoring to guard the whole we shall guard nothing," he warned. Until they could be certain what Phillips and Arnold would do, they would watch and wait.

What Steuben and Muhlenberg did not know was that Phillips and Arnold were also unsure what to do. Clinton had made it clear that their primary mission was to act in support of Cornwallis, but the generals had not heard from Cornwallis, did not know where he was or what he required, and so did not know how to help him.

The generals wrote a joint letter to Clinton offering two possibilities. One was that they should advance on Lafayette, whom Phillips understood to be in Baltimore, and take possession of Baltimore, Annapolis, and perhaps all of Maryland. The other was that they should move on Petersburg, where "a Post of force" might be established "from whence Detachments might be made in such Strength as to break up entirely Mr Greens Communication with Virginia." Either of these options, the generals wrote, would require more troops in the Chesapeake, news that must not have pleased Clinton.

Both Phillips and Arnold were bold and active officers, not given to waiting patiently for communications from headquarters. By the second week in April, Phillips regarded his defenses in Portsmouth "so tolerably complete as to enable me without any probable Risk to move with

2,000 Troops." His object was to hit the American troops quartered in Williamsburg under Weedon's command. Arnold, who, five years earlier, had overseen the construction of a diminutive American fleet on Lake Champlain, had been building boats in Norfolk since his troops had arrived in the area and was still doing so. Now those boats were prepared for their amphibious purpose.

By April 11, a mere ten days after Phillips's men had landed at Portsmouth, the preparations Muhlenberg had been watching were finished and the men ready to embark. Unfortunately for Phillips, "the Winds blew directly contrary, & very strong," keeping the boats pinned down in harbor. Even a march by the light infantry and Queen's Rangers to Norfolk was postponed by the "most violent Storm of Wind and Rain."

This was the same storm that was keeping Lafayette hunkered down at the Susquehanna, and it held Phillips's troops on the south side of Hampton Roads (the mouth of the James River) for eight days. Not until April 18 did the weather allow "the light infantry, part of the 76th and 80th regiments, the Queen's Rangers, yagers and American Legion" to board their disparate craft in the Elizabeth River and fall down to Hampton Roads.

The following day, Phillips boarded a ship and made his way downriver to where his men and transports were assembling, but, before he could reach them, the ship in which he was sailing went aground. As Phillips and the rest waited for the tide to lift them off, an express boat drew alongside with a letter, at last, from Lord Cornwallis.

Phillips found in the letter "a plain Tale of many Difficulties and Distresses, great Perseverance and Resolution, and Honour." He had been right, he realized, with regard to the damage done to Cornwallis's forces. "The Action of the 15th was glorious," he wrote to Clinton, "but as I feared, that Sort of Victory which ruins an Army." (Like the Whig leader Charles James Fox in the House of Commons, Phillips was channeling Plutarch.)

"The Face of Affairs seems changed," Phillips continued. He now understood that Cornwallis would not be bringing many troops to Virginia and that he and Arnold had to provide Cornwallis with some degree of relief—and quickly. He wrote to Clinton, "The operation I had proposed against Williamsburg shall take place to Morrow Morning. But

I think it my Duty to call a Council of War, circumstanced as Lord Cornwallis is, to judge whether an attempt on Petersburg may now be proper." For Phillips, the question of what to do was settled.

By April 19, the expedition was underway. "Gen. Phillips informed the officers commanding the corps," Simcoe wrote, "that the first object of the expedition was to surprise, if possible, a body of the enemy stationed in Williamsburgh, at any rate to attack them."

The movements of Phillips and Arnold were closely watched by the Americans. Command of the six hundred militia on the north shore of the James River had devolved to Colonel James Innes, Weedon having left to attend to his personal business in Fredericksburg and the second in command, Thomas Nelson, being too ill to take over. At midnight on the eighteenth, Innes wrote to Muhlenberg, "I have recd Intelligence that fourteen sail of the Enemy's vessells - two of which carry Cavalry are ascending the James River and were this evening several miles advanced up - at the stern of the vessells there are a number of flat bottomed boats."

In all, there were five vessels carrying horses, an armed sloop, two brigs, three gunboats, two transports, and twenty-five flat-bottomed boats carrying seventy-six men each, a formidable armada of small craft. Innes ordered all the public stores to be packed and made ready to move at a moment's notice, then braced for the attack.

It came on the twentieth, and from four different directions. Wind and tide held the fleet downriver most of the day, but by seven o'clock that evening, they were ready to move ashore. Taking advantage of his army's numbers and mobility, Phillips opted to land men at four points along the north shore of the James. One division went upriver past Williamsburg to land at the mouth of the Chickahominy River, while another pushed farther up the Chickahominy in boats. Phillips and Arnold maneuvered the bulk of the army to land near Williamsburg, while Simcoe was to land a detachment at Burrell's Ferry, southeast of town.

Simcoe assembled his flotilla about 2 miles from the designated landing spot and got underway as the sun was setting. Opposing them was a fully manned entrenchment thrown up by the Americans, which a gunboat leading Simcoe's flotilla hammered with its 6-pounder. The other boats appeared to follow in the gunboat's wake, but at a signal, they peeled away and landed below Burrell's Ferry. The Queen's Rangers and the Jaegers under Simcoe's command clambered out of the boats and formed up. Marching to the ferry landing, they met no opposition, the militia having abandoned their entrenchments as the British advanced.

The bulk of the army with Phillips and Arnold was opposed by what Arnold guessed were some five hundred militia, which was about right, though the number must have been hard to estimate given how fast the Americans fled from the advancing British regulars and Hessians.

Phillips ordered Simcoe to ride to Yorktown. It was full night, "uncommonly dark and tempestuous," as he and forty of his green-clad cavalrymen of the Queen's Rangers pounded up the road. They stopped at a farmhouse to let the storm blow past, and in the morning, continued on, "galloped into the town, surprised and secured a few of the artillerymen, the others made off in a boat." Simcoe burned the rebels' barracks, spiked the guns, and ran the British colors up the flagpole on the battery. In the distance, they could hear cannon fire at Williamsburg, so they saddled up and rode to the sound of the guns. Writing to Jefferson that same day, Steuben paid Simcoe an unintended compliment, saying, "Colo. Simcoe has his Corps of 140 Cavalry in good order. This is the terror of our Militia."

Phillips and Arnold had meanwhile encountered more opposition than Simcoe had, but not much. A party of militia drove in a British picket near the College of William and Mary, but after a brief skirmish the Americans fled, "Quartermaster M'Gill, with some of the huzzars of the Queen's Rangers, having charged and dispersed the only patrol of the enemy who had appeared in the front." With Williamsburg in their possession, they set about destroying stores, but there was little left, Innes having spirited away everything of value. As David Jameson, writing to James Madison, put it, "they destroyed the few articles of public Stores that were left there—mere trifles—did no damage to the inhabitants." Jameson, reflecting the now general understanding that the key to victory in the Chesapeake was naval superiority, concluded his letter with the wish, "O! for a French Fleet."

Having driven off the militia and destroyed what military infrastructure they could find, Phillips marched his troops to Barret's Ferry, near the Chickahominy, to link with the other divisions.

Lieutenant Colonel Robert Abercrombie, who had taken the light infantry 10 or 12 miles up the Chickahominy River in boats, found more targets than Phillips had and left behind a swath of destruction. Innes reported that "they possessed themselves of the Shipyard about 4 o'Clock," and, seeing flames later that day, feared they had put it to the torch. Indeed they had. Arnold reported that Abercrombie "destroyed several armed ships, the state shipyards, warehouses, etc." Among those was the Virginia navy vessel *Thetis*.

By April 23, all the disparate units of Phillips's force were reassembled and embarked on their vessels once again, with the Queen's Rangers staying ashore for the night to form a rear guard. The following morning, the Rangers joined the other troops, and the massive convoy of boats continued upriver, stopping that night at Westover, where Arnold had landed his overland assault on Richmond some three and a half months earlier. In the course of the day, they had passed Hood's Fort, one of the only places on the river where the militia might have halted their progress, but they found no opposition there. Governor Jefferson had tried a unique tactic to get men to fortify the battery, offering credit for six weeks' militia duty to every man who contributed twelve days' work there himself or through a surrogate laborer. Phillips and Arnold made their move before that plan could be put into action, however, and Hood's Fort lay unfinished and abandoned.

The Americans on Defense

At the first sign of the British move from Portsmouth, Steuben had written to Innes with instructions that, "should the enemy Land a party Superior to any resistance you Can make you will always Retreat toward Richmond." If they moved upriver, Innes was always to keep ahead of them and keep Steuben constantly informed. Muhlenberg, likewise, was to keep ahead of the enemy on the south side of the river, always retreating toward Petersburg.

Muhlenburg's men had so far been left alone, but by the time Phillips's men reembarked from Williamsburg, Innes's troops had been pushed 24 miles north and had taken up a position at Frank's Ferry, across the Pamunkey River. Innes reported to Governor Jefferson that his men "by intense Fatigues & vigilances & a Scarcity of Provisions are much worn down." He determined to pause there "until the men are comfortably recreated," though one wonders how comfortable they could be with hardly any food. Innes ended his note to the governor by saying, "When I get an hours Sleep which I have not enjoyed for upwards of sixty Hours I will write you more fully."

A few days before Phillips and Arnold began their advance, Lafayette and his men had arrived in Baltimore, where they would "Halt one Day to Refresh and Clean themselves." Lafayette's troops had been nearly destitute of clothing and supplies, particularly shoes. The marquis informed Greene that he had pledged his own credit to the amount of 2,000 pounds to the merchants in Baltimore in order to outfit his troops with "a few Hatts, Some Shoes, Some Blanketts, and a pair of Linnen over alls, and a Shirt to Each Man." At a ball given in his honor, the dashing young French aristocrat managed to recruit a number of women with a strong interest in, among other things, the patriot cause. It was his plan, he wrote Greene, to "Sett the Baltimore Ladies At work for the Shirts."

Desertion was still a problem, as Lafayette had predicted it would be. "I then Made an Address to the Detachement," he wrote to Greene, "which Enforced By the difficulty of Crossing [back over the Susque-hanna] and the Shame I Endeavoured to throw upon Desertion Has Almost Entirely Stopped it." Lafayette's hanging of a few deserters probably helped as well.

A few days later, with the men better outfitted and more resigned to serving with the southern army, Lafayette was ready to march. He was not yet certain *where* to march, but he knew he had to get there fast. The standard eighteenth-century approach to moving an army, with great trains of artillery and baggage, he felt, was "So dilatory that I would Be upon the Roads or at the ferries for An Eternity." Instead, he intended to leave behind the tents, the sick, and the artillery and make forced marches to Fredericksburg, impressing every horse and wagon along the way to help move things even faster. Once in Fredericksburg, he hoped to receive orders from Greene, and if he did not, he would push on to Richmond, the likely target for Phillips and Arnold.

Washington had made it clear to Lafayette that he and Greene both considered Phillips's army to be the marquis's primary objective, a point Lafayette well understood. "My conduct to the time when I'll Hear from You Are pointed toward Phillips . . . ," Lafayette assured Greene, ". . . and if General Phillips appeared to Intend Such Motions as would Be of disservice to You I will Make it My Business to Be Ready to Check Him as far as it Can Be done with Such an inferiority of forces."

Lafayette had made it as far south as Alexandria, Virginia, on April 21, when he received word from Steuben that the enemy was on the move and that the Virginia government was preparing to abandon Richmond. "The Battery at Hoods is not half finished," Steuben informed Lafayette. "Every thing is in the same confusion as when Arnold came up the River. There is not a single Company of Regular troops in the State & the Militia are too unexperienced to hope the least resistance from them." The prospects of mounting a solid defense against the British looked dim. By the time Lafayette received Steuben's letter, they looked even worse.

The baron had left his headquarters at Chesterfield and ridden 13 miles south to Petersburg, making what preparations he could "to oppose the Enemy should they advance on this side of the James River." But, in fact, he did not think they would. Writing to Innes, Steuben suggested that Phillips and Arnold were merely interested in occupying the neck of land between the York and James rivers. But by the time Innes received Steuben's letter, the British had already left that neck in their push toward Petersburg and a union with Cornwallis.

Innes had been driven far north of the James River, over the Pamunkey River, keeping his men between the British and Richmond. On April 23, as Steuben was writing that he did not think Phillips would advance up the river, Innes wrote to him saying that the British army had once again embarked and was "now Standing up James River." Innes was too far away to offer any resistance. Only Steuben and Muhlenberg, on the south side of the James, stood between Phillips, Arnold, and whatever their destination might be.

The British spent the night of April 24 aboard the transports a few miles from Westover. As the ships and boats swung at their anchors, Baron de Steuben rode down to the river to have a look. He guessed their numbers to be about twenty-five hundred men, and he knew that some of the best troops in America were among them. To oppose them were only the thousand or so militia under Muhlenberg's command, which, per Steuben's order, had been retreating along the banks of the

James ahead of the British. The Americans were not just untried in battle, they were barely trained.

At eleven o'clock the next morning, the British weighed anchor and made their way to City Point, at the confluence of the James River, leading to the north and Richmond, and the Appomattox River, leading to the south and Petersburg. It was early evening when they anchored again and the thousands of troops in their uniform coats—red, or green, or the blue of the artillery and the navy—swarmed ashore, a well-disciplined, well-supplied army.

The next morning, they marched for Petersburg.

CHAPTER *14* *The Battle of Blandford*

MAJOR GENERAL WILLIAM Phillips and Brigadier General Benedict Arnold met no opposition in the first 8 miles of their 10-mile march to Petersburg on April 26, despite passing through country that, according to Lieutenant Colonel John Simcoe, presented the Americans excellent opportunities for ambush. "[I]t was apparent," Simcoe wrote, "that they rather distrusted their own strength, or were miserably commanded."

The Americans did distrust their strength, and rightly so, given the great disparities in numbers, equipment, training, and experience between the two armies. But the American command—in particular, Baron de Steuben and General Peter Muhlenberg, both excellent soldiers—was hardly miserable. Steuben, on seeing the British fleet standing upriver, had "ordered General Muhlenberg to move up as high as the Vicinity of Blandford." It was there they would make their stand.

Steuben had no hope of defeating the British with Muhlenberg's thousand untrained, untested militia, but he felt that he must put up a fight even so. "[T]o retire without some show of Resistance," he wrote to Greene, "would have intimidated the Inhabitants and encouraged the Enemy to further incursions," though the British—Arnold, in particular—gave every indication of having all the encouragement they needed.

Two miles from Petersburg, on the outskirts of the town of Blandford, the road the British troops were following emerged from woods onto open ground. There the vanguard halted, waiting for the rear to close up before pushing on. The houses of Blandford with small, fenced-in yards lined the road. The ground was hilly and dotted with woods.

Around noon, their lines formed up again, the troops resumed their advance, right into musket range for American skirmishers concealed in a gully beyond the cluster of houses. The Americans peppered the enemy with gunfire, killing one man, but this didn't last long. A party of

Jaegers, concealing themselves in an orchard, worked their way around the skirmishers' flank and drove them back.

Phillips and Simcoe rode forward to observe the American lines. Neither man had much regard for American troops, militia in particular, but they also understood that the British occasionally paid a heavy price for underestimating their enemy. Phillips had spent three years as a prisoner of war after being captured with General John Burgoyne's army at Saratoga, and he was not going to dismiss out of hand the threat confronting him now. He ordered Lieutenant Colonel Robert Abercrombie to make a frontal assault while Simcoe and his Rangers moved unseen through a wooded area to fall on the Americans' right flank.

At around three o'clock in the afternoon, the British lines advanced. "Lieut. Col. Abercrombie pushing forward his battalion," Simcoe recalled, "the enemy's first line quitted their station in confusion." Simcoe's Rangers worked their way around the American right along a high wooded ridge, hoping to cut off the American retreat across the bridge over the Appomattox River.

Simcoe wrote that the Americans "fled so rapidly that the Queen's Rangers had no opportunity of closing with them . . . ," and Arnold as well suggested that the British brushed the Americans aside, but Steuben reported it differently. Immediately after the fight, he wrote to Greene, "I have the pleasure to say that our Troops disputed the ground with the Enemy Inch by Inch & executed their Manauvers with great exactness."

Steuben was not given to doling out undeserved praise. For more than two hours, the Americans stubbornly resisted the British advance. Twice, the British line was flung back by well-coordinated American musketry, advancing again only after more troops were brought up. For as long as they were able, until overwhelmed by superior British and Hessian numbers, arms, and discipline, the Americans stood their ground. At last, they made an orderly retreat from one post to the next, holding their positions until ordered to fall back and then doing so with professional calm.

As the Americans fell back through the streets of Petersburg to the bridge over the Appomattox, pressed hard by the troops Phillips committed to the fight, their cannon on the opposite side of the river began to blast away with grapeshot, but to little effect. Low on ammunition and greatly outnumbered, the militia fought a rear-guard action as they filed over the bridge "in the greatest Order notwithstanding the fire of the Enemy Cannon & Musketry." The rebels tore up the bridge as they retreated over it, preventing any further pursuit but abandoning Petersburg to the enemy.

At the Battle of Blandford, Steuben and Muhlenberg had done what they could; they put up a respectable fight without incurring significant losses of men or arms. "Indeed," Steuben wrote, "the gallant conduct of all the Officers & the particular good behaviour of the Men I am persuaded attracted the admiration of the Enemy." If so, the enemy kept it to themselves.

Having made their stand, Steuben and Muhlenberg retreated north to Chesterfield, thankful that the Appomattox River now ran between them and the British. Steuben intended to link with Colonel James Innes's troops north of the James River, and then with the Marquis de Lafayette, who was in Fredericksburg, about 60 miles north of Richmond, and closing the distance fast with forced marches. Once united, the three disparate forces would find a place to make a more concerted stand and harry, if not stop, the British push.

"[A] scene of singular confusion ensued"

With Steuben and Muhlenberg pushed across the Appomattox River, no force remained south of the river to offer the least resistance to Phillips and Arnold. The British troops that had been held in reserve marched into Petersburg in the early evening, and the next morning the destruction began.

Benedict Arnold was by now an old hand at inflicting scorched-earth tactics on Virginia, and he demonstrated his talent for the work once again. The Americans had long since removed anything of any value to Greene's army, as they had at Williamsburg, but the British managed to burn four thousand hogsheads of tobacco, one ship, and a number of smaller craft, some in the river and some still on the stocks.

The next day, Phillips divided his forces, a mark of his confidence and the knowledge that he had more than a two-to-one advantage in men. Phillips "with the light infantry, part of the cavalry of the Queen's Rangers and part of the jagers" crossed the Appomattox, likely by repairing the bridge, and followed in pursuit of Steuben and Muhlenberg, marching north to Chesterfield and Steuben's former headquarters. Steuben was by then at Falling Creek Church, a few miles to the west, and Phillips found little in Chesterfield except empty huts, the barracks for two thousand recruits that Steuben had ordered his men to build. These were burned, along with three hundred barrels of flour and similar supplies. With some pride, Steuben wrote to Greene that "of all the stores collected at Chesterfield Ct. Hs. [Court House] and Petersburg for the equipment of the Virginia Troops, not the least article fell into the Enemy's hands."

Meanwhile Arnold, in command of the second division, marched northeast to Coxen Dale, known locally as Osborne's Landing, which was some 15 miles up the James River from its confluence with the Appomattox at City Point. Four miles upriver from Osborne's Landing, Arnold found something he had not previously encountered in Virginia—"a very considerable force of ships" belonging to the Americans. This was the remains of the Virginia navy, under the command of Captain James Maxwell, and a few privateers and merchantmen that had been at Richmond. Three days earlier, on April 25, Steuben had "expressed a desire" to the Virginia Board of War that any armed vessel at Richmond be "sent down to attack the enemy's shipping at City Point." Displaying the Virginia government's characteristic risk-aversity, the board had insisted that Captain Maxwell first reconnoiter the enemy fleet and report its strength to the board and Steuben.

By the time this was done, Phillips and Arnold had landed their troops, marched toward Petersburg, and met the Americans at Blandford. There was little point in attacking the empty flotilla of boats that remained at City Point—and probably little desire to do so. Instead, Maxwell moved the ships from Richmond downriver to Osborne's Landing, where he arranged them in a semicircle across the river between a marsh on the south shore and open land to the north, both of which could be commanded by the ships' broadsides. Spring lines were rigged to the anchor cables to allow the vessels to be swung in an arc, bringing their great guns to bear where need be. In this manner, Maxwell hoped to fend off the British advance upriver and save both his fleet and the Virginia capital from capture or destruction.

Thus deployed across the upper James River, the ships and guns looked impressive. The largest of the vessels were the Virginia navy ships

Apollo, of eighteen guns, and *Tempest* and *Renown*, both of sixteen guns. The brigantine *Jefferson* carried fourteen guns. All told, the fleet mounted ninety-six cannon, certainly far more artillery than Arnold's division was carrying.

Unfortunately, the potentially powerful fleet was crippled by a stunning manpower deficiency. The *Apollo* had just 5 of its intended complement of 120 men. The *Tempest* had 6. *Renown* was only a little better off with 23 men out of an intended complement of 120. All told, the fleet should have had 512 men, whereas in actuality it had just 78. The crew numbers were likely augmented somewhat by untrained militia assigned temporarily to the ships, since all that impressive ordnance would do no good with no one to load and fire it, but the ships were much less potent in fact than appearance. Arnold wasn't fooled.

Benedict Arnold had already shown a willingness bordering on eagerness to burn rebel stores, but the thought of sending these ships and their possibly valuable cargoes up in flames gave him pause. As in his raid on the Richmond waterfront more than three months earlier, perhaps he envisioned some personal gain from the capture of the ships, similar to the prize money earned by naval officers. (He would, in fact, later refer to the ships as "prizes.") In any event, under flag of truce he sent the fleet a proposal for a negotiated surrender. According to Simcoe, Arnold told the Americans they might keep half the cargo if they did not destroy any of it. The only response to this offer, however, was a promise that the Americans would defend their fleet "to the last extremity."

Arnold was perfectly willing to give them that chance. He sent two brass 3-pounder field guns down to the edge of the river with orders to fire on *Tempest*. The guns were no more than 100 yards away, point-blank range, when they opened up on the *Tempest*'s stern. Round shot blasting straight through the fragile after end of the ship and flying her full length aft to forward would have been devastating, but the *Tempest* had a spring rigged to her cable. Her tiny crew threw themselves on the capstan and heaved around, and "With difficulty she brought her broadsides to bear, and returned a smart fire."

As *Tempest* swung around, another British battery of two brass 6-pounders "opened from an unexpected quarter, with great effect." Now the rest of the fleet—the *Apollo*, the *Renown*, the brigantine *Jeffer*-

son, and the other vessels—opened up as well, pitting the heavily armed but badly undermanned ships in an artillery duel with Arnold's crack troops and a smattering of small cannon.

Rebel militia began to gather on the far shore—around two or three hundred men by Arnold's count—and "kept up a heavy fire of musketry . . ." on the British and German troops. Simcoe ordered one of his lieutenants to lead a party of Jaegers to a spot within 30 yards of *Tempest*'s stern, where they might pick off some of her crew with their deadly accurate rifles. Part of the route was hidden by ditches, but in places the Jaegers were exposed to the ship's broadsides. Luckily for the Germans, the ships were loaded with round shot, having expected an attack over the water, as "grape shot must inevitably have killed or driven the artillery from their guns" and wreaked havoc on troops moving through the field of fire.

A hail of lead—round shot, musket balls, and rifle bullets—flew over the river north of Osborne's Landing, and gray smoke whipped around as the wind built in strength, but neither side could gain an advantage in the firefight. Arnold ordered Simcoe and the Queen's Rangers down to the shore to add their musket fire to the battering the *Tempest* was enduring. As Simcoe was organizing his men, a lucky shot parted the spring on the *Tempest*'s cable. The big ship swung away from the shore so that her broadside would no longer bear on the enemy, and her stern was once again exposed to the raking fire of the field artillery. Any American who showed his head above the ship's rails risked being cut down by the Jaegers lining the riverbank.

With no possibility of rigging another spring under rifle and field artillery fire, and with no way to defend the ship, the *Tempest*'s crew abandoned the vessel. As they pulled for shore in the ship's boat, the Jaegers unleashed on them, prompting some of the ship's crew to leap overboard and take their chances in the river. At last, the lieutenant commanding the detachment of Germans ordered a cease-fire and, "parlying with the boat's crew," convinced them to row ashore and surrender themselves. This the Americans did, rather than endure any more German rifle fire.

A dozen of the Queen's Rangers, under the command of a Lieutenant Fitzpatrick, clambered into the Americans' abandoned boat and pulled for the *Tempest.* Once there, Fitzpatrick sent another of the ship's boats back to the British lines for more men and then proceeded on to another of the American fleet. The boat Fitzpatrick sent back was manned by Highland troops, who returned to *Tempest* to take possession.

As Simcoe recalled, "a scene of singular confusion ensued." The crews of the ships, seeing *Tempest* taken and British troops in boats, apparently deemed it only a matter of time before they, too, were taken prisoner. They began to abandon their ships, scuttling some and setting others on fire. "Want of boats and the wind blowing hard prevented our capturing many of the seamen, who took to their boats and escaped on shore," Arnold wrote in his dry official report to Clinton.

According to Simcoe's more detailed and breathless account, Fitzpatrick continued to pull through a hail of musket fire from the militia on the far shore, cutting the anchor cable of one ship and setting men on board others as their crews abandoned them. The British crews then turned the ships' guns on the Americans.

Near the *Tempest,* one of the other ships was burning out of control. The Highlanders aboard *Tempest* cut the ship's cable in the hope that she would drift clear of the danger, but before she did, the flames on the neighboring vessel reached its magazine. The ship exploded in a fury of splintered wood and shattered spars. Flaming bits flew high enough to ignite the *Tempest*'s fore topgallant, close to 100 feet above the water. The ship drifted ashore near where Arnold's troops were arrayed, and the Highlanders, "whom their many sea voyages had made active and experienced in such dangers," managed to put out the flames and secure the prize.

On board another of the ships, the Queen's Rangers found themselves trapped as the flames mounted beyond the point where they might have been extinguished. A volunteer named Armstrong leaped into the river and swam ashore, where he took charge of the only boat left and returned to the burning vessel. The Rangers managed to get off just before the ship exploded.

The James River, more than 500 feet wide where the battle took place, was spread bank to bank with destruction and chaos. Ships were burning, some listing as they sank. Smoldering hulks lay low in the water, while other ships canted at odd angles where they had drifted against the shore. Arnold's report gave a sense of the number of vessels involved:

Two ships, three brigs, five sloops and two schooners, loaded with tobacco, cordage, flour etc., fell into our hands. Four ships, five brigs, and a number of small vessels were sunk or burnt. On board the whole fleet (none of which escaped) were taken and destroyed about 2000 hogsheads of tobacco etc.

The presence of the tobacco, and the fact that the number of ships as listed by Arnold far exceeded the number first enumerated by Maxwell, suggests that many of the vessels were merchantmen trying to get to sea ahead of the plundering British. They didn't make it.

Around five o'clock, Phillips and the light infantry rejoined Arnold, and the army made camp at Osborne's Landing. Steuben, Muhlenberg, and the remains of their army, having linked with Innes, were camped at New Kent Courthouse, about 16 miles north of Richmond on the other side of the Chickahominy River. There was nothing they could do to stop the enemy's depredations.

Phillips and Arnold's plan had been, in part, to break up the flow of supplies heading south to Greene and to act in support of Cornwallis. But mostly they had hoped to form a juncture with Cornwallis at Petersburg. So far, that had not happened. They had heard that the earl was making his labored way north to Virginia, but they had received no word of his progress.

Likewise, Steuben was anxiously awaiting the arrival of Lafayette, who was moving south by forced marches from Fredericksburg. The Frenchman's arrival would mean an end to Steuben's independent command, which, at that point, he may have been happy to relinquish. More important, however, it would mean the addition of nearly a thousand veteran Continental troops to the American forces in Virginia. All of the puzzle pieces that would precipitate the epoch-making events of 1781 were beginning to assemble in the Virginia tidewater. And in the race to get more troops into that theater, Lafayette proved the winner.

Lafayette and Phillips

On April 29, the Marquis de Lafayette and around nine hundred Continental troops arrived in Richmond without baggage or artillery, having covered 140 miles in eleven days, an impressive pace for an eighteenth-century army. Lafayette bragged to General George Weedon that even the British "Have Spoke with Surprise of the Rapidity of our March."

Phillips may have been surprised by the speed of Lafayette's army, but not by the fact that he was on his way. The British seemed fully apprised of every move the Americans made. Indeed, Phillips began addressing letters of complaint to Lafayette on the very day of the marquis' arrival in Richmond.

April 29 was also the day after Arnold's battle with the vessels of the Virginia navy, and Phillips wrote two letters to Lafayette. His foremost complaint was that one of the ships taken by Arnold, a brig named *Alert*, had fired on the king's troops despite flying a flag of truce. Phillips reminded Lafayette that he was "authorized to inflict the severest punishments in return for this bad Conduct," and, unless the men responsible for the act were delivered to the British, Lafayette himself would be "answerable for any desolation which may follow in Consequence."

But Phillips was also angling to continue the prize-taking so ably begun by Arnold. He informed Lafayette that the ships of war and other vessels bottled up in Richmond "beyond a possibility of escaping" were in the same condition as a blockaded town and that the rules of war dictated that no public stores should be destroyed. Therefore, Phillips demanded from Lafayette a full accounting of anything that might be destroyed in Richmond before it could fall into British hands. The letter was delivered by a Mr. Steel, an officer captured in the action at Osborne's Landing and released on parole.

In fact, the rules of war as commonly understood in the eighteenth century said nothing against the destruction of public property in a besieged town. The British in America routinely rewrote the rules to suit their objective of putting down an insurrection among an indigenous population, and Phillips apparently expected Lafayette to abide by whatever rules he might choose to dictate.

Phillips's second letter addressed his concern that people to whom he had given protection had subsequently been detained and sent to Lafayette's headquarters, "where preparations are making for their being ill treated." If any such detainees did receive ill treatment, Phillips warned Lafayette, he would "be under the necessity of sending to Petersburg & giving that chastisement to the illiberal persecutors of innocent People." If Lafayette put to death anyone found to be a spy or a friend of the British government, Phillips would "make the Shores of the James River an example of terror to the rest of Virginia."

Lafayette was unimpressed with Phillips's letters, which he called "Bombastic," and his response was calculated to needle the general as only a French nobleman could. After pointing out that, despite Phillips's claims, the actions of British troops had been anything but benevolent in the course of the war, Lafayette suggested that "your long absence for the Scene of action is the only way I have to account for your penegeries [panegyrics]," thus reminding Phillips of the three years he had spent as a prisoner of war.

Lafayette took seriously the charge against the *Alert*, assuring Phillips that he would look into the matter. He had heard from American sources that the master of the brig had acted properly, but if the truth were otherwise, Phillips would "obtain every redress, in my power that you have any right to expect," which, of course, was likely to mean something quite different from the redress Phillips was demanding. But the marquis dismissed Phillips's other demands. "Such articles as the requiring that the Persons of Spies be heald sacred," he wrote, "can not certainly be serious." He informed Phillips that the tone of his letters was unacceptable and "wanting in that regard due to the Civil and military authority of the United States," which Lafayette "construed into a want of respect to the american Nation." If future correspondence continued in that same vein, "I shall not think it consistent with the dignity of an american officer to continue the Correspondence."

As it happened, there was little opportunity for further correspondence. Lafayette wrote to Phillips a few days later with the results of his inquiry into the *Alert* affair. Witness depositions confirmed that the captain of the brig had acted properly, and Lafayette forwarded copies of the depositions to Phillips as proof that "there has on our side been no violation of Flags." And not long after that, Phillips was dead.

On April 30—the day that Lafayette was penning his epistolary chastisement—the British secured their prizes, moved them downriver to Osborne's Landing, and waited for boats from their fleet to move upriver from City Point. Once their water transport arrived, they headed the remaining few miles upriver toward Richmond, Phillips marching the main body of troops on the riverbank while Arnold "proceeded up the river with a detachment in boats."

There was not a whole lot left to sack in Richmond, but Phillips's warning about the ships still there had given Lafayette ample reason to think that the city was the target, and he was "determined to defend that Capital where a quantity of Public Stores and Tobacco was contained." His force of nine hundred Continentals had been augmented by militia under the command of their brigadier general, Thomas Nelson, now sufficiently recovered from illness to resume command from Innes. Lafayette arranged his troops on the heights of the city overlooking the James and penned a note to Steuben—whose forces must have been nearby—instructing him to secure any boats in the river, detail observers to keep an eye on the British, and to guard or remove any stores before joining the main army at Richmond. Then, with Phillips drawing closer, he added as a postscript, "The Ennemy are advancing and I Request you to Hasten Your March."

Phillips and Arnold rejoined their forces at Warwick, only a short distance upstream of Osborne's Landing on the south side of the James River, and continued on. Their target was not Richmond but Manchester, south of Richmond and across the river. There they burned warehouses with 1,200 hogsheads of tobacco. Lafayette and his troops on the heights of Richmond were clearly visible from Manchester. They were, according to Arnold, "spectators of the conflagration without attempting to molest us."

Phillips sent a small force of some six hundred men across the river to Richmond, but these were soon recalled. Lafayette reported to Greene that the troops, "being charged by a few Dragoons of Major Nelsons[,] flew into their boats with precipitation." Leaving the warehouses at Manchester in flames, the British marched back the way they had come.

Lafayette chose to believe that the presence of his troops on the Richmond heights had forced Phillips to retreat. "[W]hen he [Phillips] was going to give the Signal to attak He Recconnoitred our position," Lafayette wrote to George Washington. "Mr. Osburn who was with Him Says the He flew into a Violent passion and Swore Vengeance Against me and the Corps I Had Brought with me."

Osborne, likely a member of the family for whom the landing was named, might well have said that, and he might well have been trying to ingratiate himself with the new commanding officer of the American troops. (Having been in the company of both Phillips and Lafayette over the previous day or two, Osborne had apparently adopted a studied neutrality.) But it is unlikely that Phillips was much concerned by Lafayette's nine hundred ragged troops. As Lafayette himself acknowledged, the Americans were outnumbered nearly three to one, and Phillips's troops were among the elite of the British and German regiments. If Phillips did not advance on Richmond, it was because he chose not to, not because he was intimidated by Lafayette's forces. As things stood, the Frenchman could deliver a mightier blow with his pen than with his sword.

Arriving in America just before the Battle of Bunker Hill in 1775, Sir Henry Clinton became commander-in-chief of the British army in North America in 1778, though his indecisive nature and a fondness for the comforts of New York City made him less than effective. He and Charles, Lord Cornwallis had been friends before the war, but their friendship cooled during their successful siege of Charleston in the spring of 1780, after which a growing enmity hampered communications between the two senior officers. (Courtesy Bridgeman Art Library International)

The Marquis de Lafayette was only nineteen, with minimal military experience, when he was made a major-general by the Continental Congress and sent to George Washington. Though disillusioned with foreign officers looking for adventure, Washington took to Lafayette, and the Frenchman proved his worth many times in battle. Lafayette was sent to Virginia in the spring of 1781 and helped engineer the surrender of Lord Cornwallis. This painting by Jean-Baptiste Le Paon is entitled *General Lafayette at Yorktown*. (Courtesy Lafayette College Art Collection, Easton, PA)

Baron de Steuben had served as an officer in the renowned army of Frederick the Great, King of Prussia. At Valley Forge he was given the task of training Continental troops in standard battlefield maneuvers. Speaking no English, he resorted to barking orders in French, then waiting while they were translated by another officer, often either Alexander Hamilton or Nathanael Greene. The troops came to love the hot-tempered Prussian, and Steuben was largely responsible for introducing a degree of professionalism that the army had previously lacked. Steuben was trying to raise troops in Virginia when the fighting moved there in early 1781, and he found himself the senior Continental officer in that theater until Lafayette arrived. (Courtesy Bridgeman Art Library International)

Banastre Tarleton was young, flashy, and hotheaded but ruthlessly effective as a British cavalry officer in the southern theater. He ably served General Cornwallis, though Daniel Morgan defeated him soundly at the Battle of Cowpens, South Carolina, in January 1781 while Tarleton was operating on an independent command. To the British he was a hero; to the Americans, who accused him of atrocities, he was a monster. Killing troops who had surrendered came to be known as "Tarleton's quarter." (Courtesy Bridgeman Art Library International)

BATTLE OF GUILDFORD,

Fought on the 15th of March 1781.

A. *The Advance of Part of the Continentals who broke the British Center, and afterwards fell back to their original position.*

One English Mile.

British
Americans

Court House

Greene's Last Position

Second Position with the American Field Artillery

ORDER OF BATTLE

Fought on March 15, 1781, the Battle of Guilford Courthouse, North Carolina, ended with Cornwallis in possession of the field, but he paid a heavy price in dead and wounded soldiers. This battlefield sketch by a British engineer appeared in Tarleton's memoir. The British army approached from the southwest (bottom) to come face to face across 300 yards of open ground with a line of American militia that stretched across the road behind a rail fence (solid black bar). After overrunning that line the British encountered a second, stiffer American line (solid gray bar) hidden in the trees beyond. The third American line, comprised of battle-hardened troops, occupied the high open ground in front of the courthouse (top). "[N]ow I am perfectly easy," Nathanael Greene wrote after the battle, "being perswaded it is out of the enemies power to do us any great injury." The pyrrhic victory propelled Cornwallis northward to Yorktown. (Courtesy National Park Service)

John Graves Simcoe, seen here in a portrait done later in life, was in his late twenties when he led a light infantry unit called the Queen's Rangers during the raids in Virginia under Benedict Arnold and William Phillips in early 1781. Simcoe was an effective leader and a terror to the militia in Virginia, even more so when he hooked up with Banastre Tarleton in April of that year. He and Tarleton were both taken prisoner six months later at the surrender of Yorktown. (Courtesy Bridgeman Art Library International)

Major General William Phillips, whom one German officer called "a man just as a man should be," was well respected by his men and a friend to both Henry Clinton and Charles Cornwallis. Captured at the Battle of Saratoga, he spent three years as a prisoner of war before being exchanged. In 1781 he joined Benedict Arnold in ravaging Virginia, though his primary focus was on helping his friend Cornwallis in the Carolinas. He became ill and died shortly before Cornwallis's arrival in Virginia. (Courtesy Bridgeman Art Library International)

Fifty-nine years old when he commanded the French fleet that defeated the British in the Battle of the Capes, Francois Joseph Paul de Grasse was a physically imposing man, bigger even than George Washington, whom he is supposed to have addressed as "*mon cher petit général!*" at their first meeting. It was the Comte de Grasse who ultimately made the decision not only to sail to the Chesapeake but to take his entire fleet with him from the West Indies, giving Washington the decisive naval superiority he had longed for throughout the war. (Courtesy Bridgeman Art Library International)

Admiral Thomas Graves was second in command to Mariot Arbuthnot at the Battle of Cape Henry in March 1781 when the British fleet managed to drive off the French and save General Benedict Arnold from capture. Six months later, commanding a British fleet that was three times larger than Arbuthnot's had been, Graves was defeated in the Battle of the Capes by de Grasse's French fleet, and the result was the surrender of Cornwallis's army at Yorktown. Graves would eventually distinguish himself during the French Revolution at the Battle of the Glorious First of June. (Courtesy National Maritime Museum, Greenwich, England)

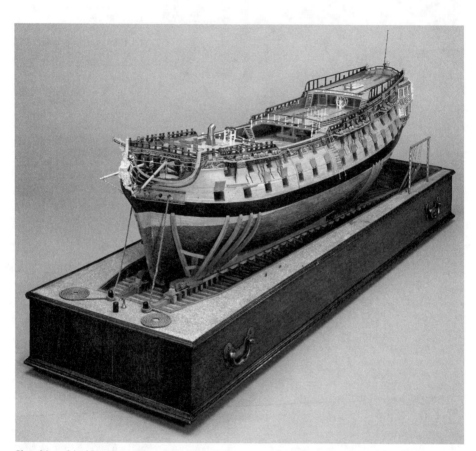

Sheathing ships' bottoms with copper plates was a new technology at the time of the American Revolution, one that proved enormously effective in preventing rot, borers, and the buildup of marine growth. Copper sheathing was such an advantage that it could make the difference between victory and defeat in naval combat. This model of a 74-gun ship of the line is believed to have been built to demonstrate the technique to King George III in order to gain his support for this expensive process. The bluff bow and deep draft (depth of hull below the waterline) of an eighteenth-century ship of the line are evident in this model. (Courtesy National Maritime Museum, Greenwich, England)

This painting from about 1788 by Dominic Serres, the Elder, shows three views of a 74-gun ship of the line getting underway in the Solent, on England's south coast. In two of the views, just her topsails are set. The massive "best bower" anchor is in the last stages of being hauled up below the foremast. Retrieving an anchor of that size could take an hour or more, which is why captains chose just to let the anchor cable go when they had to get underway in a hurry. The size of the men on deck gives a sense for the massiveness of the masts and yards. Seventy-fours were the backbones of the British and French fleets. (Courtesy National Maritime Museum, Greenwich, England)

This 1809 painting by Robert Pollard of a Revolutionary War–era 90-gun ship of the line with its three rows of heavy guns gives a sense for the power of these big men-of-war. The wide work platforms halfway up the masts were known as "tops" and served as stations for sharpshooters in battle. Nineties were designed as flagships, with two elaborate great cabins aft, one for the captain and one for the admiral. In the Battle of the Capes, both Graves's *London* and Hood's *Barfleur* were nineties, but large as they were, they were still "second-rates." The only first-rate in the battle was de Grasse's huge 110-gun flagship *Ville de Paris*. (Courtesy National Maritime Museum, Greenwich, England)

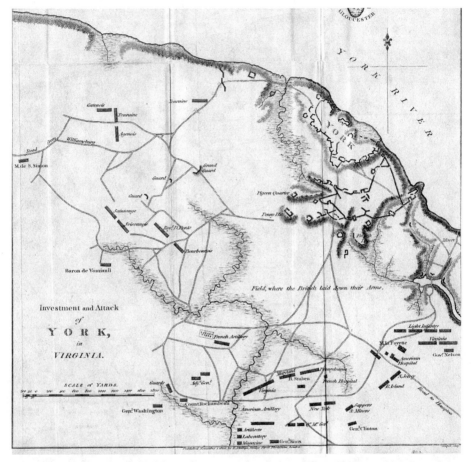

A map showing the disposition of troops during the Siege of Yorktown. The ragged line surrounding the town represents Cornwallis's inner defenses. Scattered redoubts (small squares, rectangles, and pentagons) anchored the loose outer perimeter of works that the British abandoned on the first approach of the French and American troops. The two roughly parallel curved lines running northwest to southeast to the south of York show the first and second parallel approaches dug by the American army. Off the left end of the more easterly parallel can be seen Redoubts 9 and 10, perfectly positioned to enfilade the parallel. These redoubts had to be taken before work could begin in the nearer approach. (Courtesy Archiving Early America)

This painting, though somewhat romanticized, shows the desperate fighting at Redoubt 9 when American troops led by Alexander Hamilton cut through the British and Hessian defenses at Yorktown and stormed the works using bayonets in hand-to-hand fighting. French troops overran Redoubt 10 at the same time. The fighting took place after dark (contrary to this depiction) and represented the only significant combat during the Siege of Yorktown. The redoubts were the last significant obstacles to an American and French victory, and Cornwallis surrendered soon after. (Courtesy Library of Virginia)

PART THREE

THE FIGHT ON LAND AND SEA

CHAPTER *15* *The British War at Sea*

BY THE TIME Lord Cornwallis was chasing Nathanael Greene across the Carolinas and Benedict Arnold, in red regimental coat, was laying waste to Virginia, the war in the rebellious colonies had been reduced, for England, to one detail on a larger canvas of trouble. While those events so familiar to students of American history were unfolding—the fall of Charleston, the Battle of Monmouth, Arnold's treason—England found itself in a wider war being waged across much of the rest of the world. This conflict played out in Europe, the Mediterranean, the East Indies, and the West Indies, and it was contested chiefly at sea.

Though the French in 1779 had come within a few miles of landing troops on British soil and were scheming to do so again in 1781, they had no intention of taking and occupying England. Their object, rather, was to inflict massive damage and instill fear in the British homeland. This was not a war of grand armies contesting the control of European soil, nor of nations seeking to subjugate nations. It was a war not for power but for colonies, which is to say, for wealth. England and France fought for territorial control in Africa and India, for rich plantation islands in the West Indies, and—almost incidentally—to determine whether the British colonies in North America would gain independence.

It had taken General George Washington long years to fully appreciate the role of sea power in the war he was fighting, but by 1781 he had learned the lesson well. It was in the summer of 1780 that he had written to the Comte de Rochambeau concerning "a decisive naval superiority" being "a fundamental principle, and the basis upon which every hope of success must ultimately depend."

The British and French ministries needed no ghost come from the grave to tell them that, of course. They had been maneuvering their big fleets around the oceans even before the French had officially weighed in on the side of the Americans. In the English Channel, off the coasts of France and Spain, in the West Indies, and even, occasionally, off the coast of America, the fleets had been contesting for mastery of the sea and the potential conquests that would come with it.

Just as the land war saw ongoing changes in command and strategy, so too did the war at sea evolve as the conflict dragged on. By 1780, England stood alone. All of maritime Europe was either actively at war with Great Britain or part of an Armed Neutrality that jealously guarded its countries' shipping against British incursion. France was focused on protecting her possessions in the West Indies and taking any of England's territories she could, while Spain was primarily concerned with taking back Gibraltar and Minorca.

With so much depending on naval superiority, the British Parliament in the autumn of 1779 voted to spend 21 million pounds on the navy—a princely sum in the day—and authorized the recruitment of eighty-five thousand sailors and marines. The Earl of Sandwich, First Lord of the Admiralty, suggested for the command of the Leeward Islands Admiral Sir George Brydges Rodney. Rodney was a temperamental sixty-one-year-old veteran of the Seven Years' War, during which he had distinguished himself in action even if he did show a more than proper interest in acquiring prize money. Prior to the war in America, he had been hiding in Paris from creditors, having run up gambling debts he could not pay. He was eager to get into the war and equally eager to find a means of climbing out of debt.

In December 1779, Rodney sailed with a small fleet under his command and a larger contingent of ships from the Channel Fleet. He was bound for the West Indies, but first he was ordered to lift the Spanish siege of Gibraltar. After decimating an inferior Spanish fleet, he landed troops and badly needed supplies for the beleaguered garrison there. Rodney credited his victory in part to the fact that his ships were copper-bottomed, which allowed him to catch the fleeing Spaniards. Without that not-so-secret weapon, he wrote, "we should not have taken one Spanish ship."

He then sailed with his five ships of the line to the West Indies, arriving at St. Lucia on March 27, 1780. There he took command of a fleet of twenty-one ships of the line, though many of them were in poor shape, having suffered the ravages of hurricanes and the rot that so quickly set in to wooden ships in the tropics. Throughout the summer of 1780, Rodney and the French fleet maneuvered against one another, meeting in a series of desultory battles that left the strategic situation largely unchanged.

In August, Rodney received word of Chevalier de Ternay's arrival at Newport with seven ships of the line and the Comte de Rochambeau's troops. Believing that "His Majesty's Territories, Fleet and Army in America were in imminent Danger of being overpower'd by the Superior force of the public Enemy . . . I flew with all dispatch possible . . ." to New York with ten ships of the line. There he found that although Vice-Admiral Arbuthnot had for a brief time been inferior in strength to the French fleet, the timely arrival of Admiral Thomas Graves's squadron, of which Rodney was unaware, had since given him a slight advantage over de Ternay.

Arbuthnot was extremely resentful of Rodney's assumption of command in New York, but there was little he could do about it, Rodney being senior in rank. Arbuthnot contented himself with sulking with his squadron at the east end of Long Island and making life difficult for Rodney in a hundred petty ways, just the behavior that had been driving Sir Henry Clinton to distraction for months. In any event, Rodney's tenure in North America was only long enough to convoy General Alexander Leslie and his twenty-five-hundred-man contingent from New York to Virginia, and by December and the end of the hurricane season he was back in the West Indies.

The situation that greeted him on his return was not good. A hurricane on October 10 had destroyed many of the ships stationed there as well as the naval stores needed to repair them. His own squadron had suffered damage in a gale during the passage from New York, and now his entire fleet was reduced to nine ships of the line, not one of them with spare rigging or sails. Early in the new year, however, he was reinforced by a squadron of eight ships of the line under the command of Rear-Admiral Sir Samuel Hood.

Hood had recently celebrated his fifty-sixth birthday when he joined Rodney in Barbados. He had entered the navy as a "captain's servant," and in 1744 he and Rodney had served together as midshipmen aboard the *Ludlow Castle*. By 1780, Hood had had a long and honorable, if not overly distinguished, career. He also had considerable experience on the North American station, having commanded several vessels there and served as commodore and commander-in-chief from 1767 to 1771.

In 1778, Hood had been appointed commissioner of Portsmouth Dockyard, a post that was generally the last before an admiral was ushered out of active service. As it happened, however, the Earl of Sandwich was having a hard time finding flag officers to command England's various squadrons at sea. Many did not want to serve under Sandwich's corrupt administration. Others did not care to find themselves second to the irascible Rodney. But Hood was willing. He received a special promotion to Rear Admiral of the Blue in September of 1780 and was sent with a squadron to join Rodney.

Despite this inauspicious entry to flag rank, Hood would prove an able commander in a career that would last another fourteen years and include heroic service during the French Revolution. When he retired from the sea in 1794, Horatio Nelson called him "the best officer, take him altogether, that England has to boast of; great in all situations which an admiral can be placed in."

In December of 1780, England declared war on Holland, that country having secretly supported the Americans since the early days of the Revolution. In January 1781, Rodney received orders to take the Dutch territory of St. Eustatius, a tiny, undefended volcanic island in the Caribbean. Though only 8 square miles, St. Eustatius had become a major depot in the Caribbean where French, Spanish, and even, quite illegally, British merchants traded, often with American merchants and often for the supplies that were vital to the American war effort. It was a fabulously lucrative trade, and one that had long galled the British. Now they could put a stop to it.

Rodney's fleet arrived off the island on February 3, before word had even arrived that England and Holland were at war. The governor wrote that on finding the British invading his island, his "surprise and astonishment was scarce to be conceived." St. Eustatius would have been in no position to defend itself in any event.

The capture of the island sent Rodney and the British military commander in the West Indies, General Sir John Vaughan, into a feeding frenzy. For three months, amid howls of protest throughout the Caribbean and in London, they inventoried and sold off loot calculated in the many millions of pounds, which they considered their spoils of war. Eventually the two would be censured for their actions, but in the meantime naval and military activity in the West Indies ground to a halt while the two leaders counted their money.

"I cannot venture to pass the Roanoke"

On April 24, 1781, as Major General William Phillips and Benedict Arnold were leading their twenty-five hundred men up the James River, having laid waste to Williamsburg, Cornwallis began moving his men out of Wilmington and toward Virginia. Ostensibly, Cornwallis hoped that Greene would pursue and the two armies might meet again, but he did not really believe that would happen.

Greene was 150 miles to the west, heading for Camden, South Carolina, by the time Cornwallis's troops moved out. This left Cornwallis in a difficult spot. He knew that Clinton would have preferred him to march after Greene in support of the troops under Lord Rawdon. Lieutenant Colonel Banastre Tarleton, and likely other officers under Cornwallis, felt they should concentrate on securing the Carolinas, and Cornwallis himself understood that Greene might well pick off the widely separated British outposts in the Carolinas one by one.

On the other hand, Cornwallis had come to realize that chasing Greene around the Carolinas was a losing proposition. He did not feel he had enough troops to take on Greene and the militia that would rally to him. Supplies were not to be had, and the many rivers presented a terrible obstacle to his movements. What was more, Cornwallis was just plain weary of marching after the elusive Americans. Rawdon and his garrisons would have to fend for themselves without the help of the earl's sixteen hundred footsore men.

Cornwallis sent several express letters to Rawdon, who was then at Camden, warning him of Greene's approach, but they were all intercepted by the rebels. Luckily for Rawdon, word reached him by other means, and he evacuated Camden before Greene could catch him there.

In preparation for marching north, Cornwallis sent Tarleton with an advance guard to "seize as many boats as possible on the north-east branch of the Cape-fear river" and bring them to a place about 15 miles above Wilmington. More boats were supplied by the Royal Navy. Cornwallis gave orders for the troops "to be in readiness to march as soon as the quarter-master-general's wagons were loaded with an ample supply of rum, salt and flour." When they were, the survivors of the Battle of Guilford Courthouse, the 23rd and the 33rd Regiments, the Von Bose Regiment, the Brigade of Guards, the artillery, and the rest began their march toward Virginia.

Tarleton moved his advance guard across the Cape Fear River first, to cover the crossing of the rest. They took post until the "stores, wagons, cannon, and troops were brought over." Cornwallis, who was now quite experienced with southern rivers, ordered two boats mounted on wagons to accompany the army.

The British troops once again marched through a country barren of provisions, and while they met no opposition, neither did they meet with any help. It was exactly the situation that Cornwallis had been encountering with the civilian population for the past year, the paucity of supplies and the prevailing lack of support for the king having led him to despair of ever effecting anything in the Carolinas. The troops lived off what they carried in the wagons, as provisions "could not be taken or bought from the inhabitants." Cornwallis ordered local mills to grind for the army "under pain of military execution."

Cornwallis moved cautiously. Letters were sent between him and Phillips, but like those to Rawdon, they were generally intercepted, so that neither officer knew what the other was doing. This created great anxiety for Cornwallis. He was well aware of his own weakness and the potential strength of the American forces under the Marquis de Lafayette in Virginia, both Continentals and militia. If he crossed the Roanoke River and found himself alone, unable to link with Phillips, his army might well be destroyed.

Soon after crossing the Wilmington River, Cornwallis sent Tarleton ahead with 180 dragoons and the light companies of two regiments, all mounted. It was Tarleton's job to see that the way was clear for the army. No less than Cornwallis's "honour and future happiness" was riding on his ability to do so, according to the earl himself. Cornwallis depended on Tarleton to determine the feasibility of crossing the Roanoke and meeting up with Phillips. He instructed the lieutenant colonel to "Send as many messages and notes as you can." In deference to the danger of interception, they were all to be written in cipher.

Tarleton's division moved out ahead of the army, and as they rode through the countryside they gave orders to civilians they encountered to collect provisions for Cornwallis's troops, who would follow. Tarleton exaggerated the number of men who were coming behind in order to frighten the militia.

Soon after detaching from the main force, Tarleton's horsemen passed the Tar River and continued north. The country was growing "more fruitful" as they approached the Roanoke, a relief for men who had been scrounging so long for supplies. Cornwallis sent word to Tarleton that he might move on to Halifax, a town on the Roanoke River less than 20 miles south of the Virginia border, "if it appears by your information that General Phillips is certainly within reach of joining."

In fact, Tarleton had received no intelligence concerning Phillips, only the various rumors that had reached Cornwallis, but, as was his wont, he chose to interpret Cornwallis's cautious suggestion as a positive order to make a bold move. His mounted troops advanced north toward Halifax by the most direct route. Local militia turned out to stop them, making stands at Aswift Creek and Fishing Creek, but "their efforts were baffled, and they were dispersed with some loss."

Tarleton pushed hard for Halifax, hoping to capitalize on any panic spread by the militia's rout at the creeks. The British troops galloped to the outskirts of town before the local militia had a chance to organize any real defense or take advantage of a naturally strong position about half a mile south of town. Once again, Tarleton and his men sent the militia running for safety, "routed with confusion and loss." Tarleton's casualties included three men wounded and a few horses wounded or killed.

The only useful thing the militia managed to do was secure most of the boats in town on the north side of the river. There, a number of militia began to entrench and take potshots at any of Tarleton's men who came near the south bank.

Tarleton immediately arrayed his men for the defense of Halifax. He sent spies across the river to keep an eye on the militia and to seek information about Phillips. He sent word to Cornwallis about the recent action and requested that Cornwallis send the light company of the guards to assist in the defense of the town.

Cornwallis, however, was unwilling to part with any of his men, and since he did not have enough horses to mount the light company, he did not see how they would be of any use to Tarleton. "I cannot venture to pass the Roanoke without some certain information of Phillips, or of the state of things in Virginia," he wrote Tarleton. He gave the lieutenant colonel two or three days to remain in Halifax, if he thought it was safe. If in that time Tarleton received no news of Phillips, he was to rejoin the main army, which was still well to the south.

At the same time, Cornwallis once again wrote to Phillips in cipher. "I can learn no satisfactory accounts of you: some say you are embarked; others that you have passed the James river." Once again, he begged Phillips for word of where he was and what he intended.

Cornwallis did have some good news to impart to his old friend. He had received word that Rawdon and Greene had fought outside Camden and that the British had routed the Americans. This fight, later known as the Battle of Hobkirk's Hill, was indeed a brilliant victory for the outnumbered British and an enormous relief for Cornwallis. He would later write to Rawdon, "I cannot describe my feelings on your most glorious victory, by far the most splendid of this war. My terrors for you had almost distracted me."

Any British victory would have been greeted as good news by Cornwallis, but this one was a particular relief. Cornwallis had likely guessed that Clinton would disapprove of his breaking off the fight with Greene and leaving North Carolina for Virginia. If Greene had beaten Rawdon, Cornwallis would have been blamed for abandoning his subordinates to their fate, which, in fact, he had. It was fortunate for Cornwallis that Rawdon had come out on top, but Rawdon was too weak to capitalize on his success. Soon after the battle, he withdrew his forces to Charleston, and Greene and his partisans began to systematically undo all of Cornwallis's earlier victories in South Carolina and Georgia.

As Cornwallis inched his weary way toward Virginia, Phillips and Arnold continued their depredations around Richmond. On the last day of April, with Lafayette watching from the heights of Richmond, the British troops put the tobacco stores of Manchester to the torch. The next day, retracing their steps downriver to Warwick, they burned five hundred barrels of flour and the mill the flour had been ground in. They also torched "several warehouses with 150 hogsheads of tobacco, a large ship and a brigantine afloat, and three vessels on the stocks, a large range of public ropewalks and storehouses, and some tan- and bark-houses full of hides and bark." The purpose of all this destruction was ostensibly to prevent supplies from reaching Greene, but there was still no word of Cornwallis.

For almost two weeks, Phillips and Arnold's troops had been moving through the James River basin, burning and taking American matériel and skirmishing with American militia. But their primary mission had been to form a junction with Cornwallis, and that had not happened. As April turned to May and no word arrived from the earl, they began to pull back toward Portsmouth, marching their troops from Warwick to Osborne's Landing and sending off the ships, boats, and considerable loot they had taken during their raid.

For the next few days, Phillips and Arnold continued downriver, finally arriving at Hog Island, near Jamestown, on May 6. Phillips was beginning to feel the effects of a fever that had come over him and was likely looking forward to getting back to Portsmouth, but that was not to be. On May 7, word finally arrived from Lord Cornwallis that he was marching for Virginia and hoped to rendezvous with Phillips at Petersburg. Phillips, who had been sleeping, awoke when the letter arrived and was informed of its contents. He ordered the troops to reembark for Petersburg and told Lieutenant Colonel John Simcoe and his men to ride cross-country to City Point and order the British troops still there to proceed to Petersburg as well. It was, according to Simcoe, "the last material order he gave."

With the troops back on board, the fleet once again sailed up the wide, brown James River. The next day, as the wind whipped the river into a short, steep chop and rocked the ships at their anchors, the men went ashore at Brandon, on the south bank not far from Hood's Fort. By this time, Phillips was too sick to sit a horse, so a post-chaise was located in which he could ride. From Brandon, the army moved unopposed to Petersburg, arriving on May 9 after a march of 30 miles in one day.

They still did not know where Cornwallis was.

Wethersfield

The opening of the 1781 campaign season in the North did not look terribly promising for the Americans. The Continental Army was in as poor a state as it had been at any time in the five and a half years of its existence. Washington, who had discontinued his diary in 1775, resumed it in May 1781, setting the stage in the preface:

> [I]nstead of having everything in readiness to take the Field, we have nothing and instead of having the prospect of a glorious offensive campaign before us, we have a bewildered and gloomy defensive one - unless we should receive a powerful aid of Ships - Land Troops - and Money from our generous allies and these, at present, are too contingent to build upon.

The failure of Chevalier Destouches to capitalize on his advantage over the British fleet at the Battle of Cape Henry, and the consequent collapse of the expedition against Arnold, had left Washington without a strategy for the spring of 1781.

Rochambeau tried to put the best face on the French failure at sea. "The Last engagement of the Chevalier Destouches has shewn to your Excellency the uncertainty of Success in naval fights and of combined operations upon that element," he wrote soon after the fleet returned to Newport. "We must not flatter ourselves that our successes will be greater, as long as we have not a decided Superiority."

The French general had more experience with combined army-navy operations and could likely accept their uncertain outcome with more equanimity than Washington. Nor had Rochambeau been suffering the stress and deprivations of six years of warfare, so it was hardly a surprise that such fatalism came easier to him.

But Washington was learning. Since France had joined forces with the Americans, he had seen his hopes for a dominant French fleet dashed again and again. He had finally come to understand that he could not win the war without naval superiority, and the French had the ability to provide that superiority, but every time they promised it they came up short. It was enormously frustrating.

The commander-in-chief once again put on a good show of public understanding, but he gave vent to his irritation in private. Even before the Battle of Cape Henry had played out, he wrote to Lund Washington, his cousin and the Mount Vernon overseer, "It is unfortunate; but this I mention in confidence, that the French Fleet and detachment did not undertake the enterprize they are now upon, when I first proposed it to them." Had they done so, Washington felt, Arnold's capture would have been "inevitable."

Unfortunately, this letter was intercepted by the British and published in the April 4 edition of the Rivington *Gazette*, a copy of which made it to Rochambeau's hands. Rochambeau wrote Washington asking if he was in fact the author of the letter and including a polite but firm reminder of the sequence of events and the fact that the first small squadron under Captain de Tilly had been sent on the request of the Congress and the State of Virginia. He pointed out that the deployment of the larger squadron had taken place about as swiftly as it could have considering the weather, the shortage of supplies in Newport, and the presence of the British fleet.

Polite as Rochambeau's letter was, Washington must have burned with humiliation when he read it. "I assure your Excellency," he wrote to Rochambeau, "that I feel extreme pain on the occasion of that part of your letter . . ." that touched on his comments regarding the fleet. While acknowledging authorship, the commander-in-chief averred that it was a private letter written before he knew all the facts of the case, both of which were true.

In truth, Rochambeau privately agreed that Destouches had not moved as expeditiously as he might have. He replied to Washington that he "wrote only to have the means of smothering up that trifle, at its birth." He assured Washington that Destouches knew nothing of the letter and that he would try to keep it that way.

Word of the Battle of Guilford Courthouse first reached Washington's headquarters at the end of March. Details were initially scant, but like most military people reading between the lines of Cornwallis's "victory," Washington divined the truth of the matter. Though Cornwallis had held the field, it was clear that the number of killed and wounded his army had suffered would "retard and injure essentially all his future movements and operations." It was not yet clear, however, what impact that would have on the strategic picture in North America. Only hindsight would reveal that Guilford Courthouse was the beginning of the end of the American Revolution.

The correspondence between Washington's headquarters at New Windsor and Rochambeau's at Newport continued to flow unabated, and the chief subject was, of course, what the combined armies might do next. Washington still had his sights on Clinton and New York City. To prepare for such an offensive, Rochambeau suggested moving his troops to the Hudson River, but Washington demurred, not feeling they were ready to begin such an undertaking. If Rochambeau left Newport, three thousand militiamen would have to be mobilized to protect the fleet at anchor there. Feeding, housing, and paying militia was expensive, and deploying them tended to hurt recruitment efforts for the Continental forces. As Washington, first among equals in the Virginia aristocracy, explained to the French count, "the Militia service is preferred by the peasantry to the Continental." Washington did suggest that Rochambeau make it *seem* as if he was going to march toward New York, which would likely prevent Clinton from sending any more troops to Virginia.

Other possibilities were raised. John Hancock and the Massachusetts legislature called on Rochambeau and Destouches to send an expedition to Penobscot Bay in the district of Maine (then part of Massachusetts). In 1779, the British had established a fort in Castine as a secure harbor in New England and a place for Loyalist refugees to resettle. An American expedition that summer to dislodge the British had met with disaster, thanks mostly to a lack of cooperation between the commanders of the army and navy. Three Continental navy men-of-war and sixteen armed vessels from Massachusetts, New Hampshire, and the privateer ranks—344 guns in all—had hovered ineffectually off Castine until a superior British squadron sailed up the bay, cutting off all hope of retreat and annihilating the fleet. Though the fort had never posed a great threat, it was a thorn in Boston's side that Hancock would have liked removed.

The French supported the idea, but Washington was lukewarm, suggesting that it was too risky to divide the French fleet by sending ships of the line and that frigates should be deployed instead. He also pointed out that militia were not to be found in great numbers in the wilds of Maine and that Rochambeau should use "such a force from your army as you deem completely adequate for the speedy reduction of the post."

Destouches did not think the attack could be carried out without employing ships of the line, but, rather than disagree with Washington, he canceled the expedition. The French Admiralty had ordered Destouches to send his transports to the West Indies, and they were supposed to have sailed in February. The acting admiral dragged his feet until mid-April, not wanting to deprive Washington and Rochambeau of the ability to move troops by sea, but finally he could hold out no longer, and on April 18 he sent the ships south.

When Washington wrote in his diary that French aid was "too contingent to build upon," he was touching on one of the chief problems both he and Rochambeau faced when considering strategy. Neither of them knew what the French government would be sending to North America in the way of troops, ships, and money, and, until they did know, it was hard to plan. On May 7, as an ailing Major General Phillips was receiving word at last that Cornwallis was on his way to Virginia, the answer came.

A storm was lashing New England with high winds and driving rain that day when the frigate *Concorde* plunged her way into Boston Harbor with topsails close reefed. Forty-two days out of France, she turned up into the wind and let her anchor go.

Concorde was the ship for which Rochambeau had been so eagerly waiting. She had on board one million livres in hard currency, together with letters and dispatches from the ministry in Paris, and she carried Jacques-Melchoir Saint-Laurent, Comte de Barras, the sixty-year-old admiral sent out to take command of the fleet at Newport after the death of de Ternay. Also on board was the Vicomte de Rochambeau, the general's son. The previous autumn he had been sent to Versailles to report on the situation in North America and to bring back orders, and now he had returned.

It was not until ten o'clock the following day that a courier rode up to Rochambeau's headquarters at Newport with word from the French consul of the arrival of *Concorde* with Barras and Rochambeau's son. The general immediately penned a note informing Washington of the arrival and indicating that he expected Barras and his son to be in Newport the following day, adding, "your Excellency may well think that I wait for them with great impatience." Rochambeau knew that his son and Barras would have with them the information the generals needed to plan the summer's campaign. "I believe it will be necessary as soon as we have received our Dispatches that we should have a conference with your Excellency," he wrote. "[Y]our Excellency may, however fix upon the place for our meeting."

Washington chose Wethersfield, Connecticut, just south of Hartford and nearly equidistant from both headquarters. The date would be Monday, May 21. Washington would bring with him General Henry Knox and General Louis Duportail, a French engineer serving with the American army.

When Barras and Rochambeau's son arrived at Newport, Rochambeau found that the young vicomte had some good news and some not so good. A convoy of about fifteen ships was following in the wake of the *Concorde*, carrying with it even more hard currency as well as six hundred replacements for the infantry. Those six hundred, however, were all that Rochambeau would be getting. The second division that had been promised him when he had sailed for America the previous year would not be coming. Instead, the French effort that year would be focused on the Caribbean. Like the British, the French viewed the West Indies as vastly more important than the thirteen newly minted states.

There was one other bit of news, however, which Rochambeau likely greeted most enthusiastically of all. The Comte de Grasse was sailing for the West Indies with a fleet of twenty-six ships of the line, and sometime in July or August he would be available to operate off the coast of North America.

On May 21, the heads of the American and French forces in the United States of America met in Wethersfield at the home of Joseph Webb, which Washington was using as his temporary headquarters. Rochambeau brought Major General Jean Chastellux, with whom Washington had struck up a friendship. Barras had also intended to go, but the appearance of British ships of the line off Newport had convinced him that he had better stay behind.

There were several questions to consider. One was whether the French fleet should remain at Newport or move to Boston, as Versailles instructed. It was decided that the fleet would move. The heavy artillery, too difficult to transport, would be stored at Providence. If the army moved against New York and the fleet was in Boston, Clinton would no longer have the means or motivation to move against Rhode Island, and five hundred militia would suffice to guard Newport.

But the primary question on the table was where the combined American and French armies should go—to the Chesapeake to fight Cornwallis, or to the Hudson River with an eye toward taking New York?

There was no question in Washington's mind. Like a dog beside the dinner table, for two years he had been camped outside New York, looking longingly and hungrily at the city. He had been chased out of there, badly beaten, five years before, and now he had a chance to take it back. What's more, with the French transports having sailed, there would be no moving of troops by sea. If the armies were to go to Virginia they would have to march there. In summing up the decisions made at Wethersfield, Washington wrote,

> The great waste of Men (which we have found from experience) in the long Marches to the Southern States; the advanced season now, to commence these in, and the difficulties and expense of Land transportation thither . . . point out the preference which an operation against New York seems to have, in present circumstances, to attempt sending a force to the Southward.

Rochambeau offered the possibility that a large French fleet might arrive off the American coast and asked how that might change the equation. Rochambeau, of course, knew about de Grasse's sailing with twenty-six of the line, but for the sake of secrecy he had been forbidden to share that information, even with Washington. Washington, however, was fully aware of de Grasse's sailing and the size of his fleet, Chastellux having leaked the information to him. Now he and Rochambeau spoke in hypotheticals, neither able to admit what both knew.

But the possibility of French naval superiority did not change Washington's mind. If a French fleet arrived off the coast, he felt they should go to New York, though he would agree that they might be "directed against the enemy in some other quarter as circumstances shall dictate."

Rochambeau's mind was not changed either. He still preferred the Chesapeake. But Washington called the shots, and one of Rochambeau's finest qualities was that he never forgot that. New York it would be. Unless he could help it.

CHAPTER *16* *Juncture*

THERE WERE FEW military secrets in the Virginia tidewater. Just as the British had known of the Marquis de Lafayette's march south, the size of his force, and his estimated date of arrival in Richmond, Lafayette was well aware of every move Major General William Phillips and Brigadier General Benedict Arnold made.

Lafayette and his Continentals and the militia that had joined them were still in Richmond when the British began their move back toward Portsmouth. He sent three hundred men around Phillips's army to Hood's Fort, where he, like Baron de Steuben, had visions of creating a battery. Another contingent of militia was "Sent to Annoy the Ennemies Boats . . . ," and a column under the command of Colonel Innes marched off for Williamsburg, shadowing the British but keeping their distance. Lafayette was in no position to let his army be forced into a battle not of his choosing.

The rest of the troops moved about 15 miles east of Richmond to Bottom's Bridge on the Chickahominy, where they would be well positioned to move in whatever direction they were needed.

Lafayette was still considering what had happened to the ill-fated attempt to capture Arnold and the extent to which a French fleet could change the entire balance of power in the Chesapeake. "It is not only on account of My own Situation that I wish the french fleet May Come into the Bay," he wrote to George Washington. "Should they Come Even without troops it is ten to one that they will Block up Phillips in Some Rivers and then I answer He is Ruined. Had I But Ships my Situation would Be the Most Agreeable in the world."

When Phillips reversed the direction of his march and once again headed up the James River, landing in Brandon, Lafayette was informed within twenty-four hours. He returned to Richmond and ordered his troops to move toward Brandon, with a detachment of Continental troops leading the way and militia following. He sent a handful of men, including two aides-de-camp, to Petersburg to collect boats for use by the Americans and to deny them to the enemy. The men arrived a mere two hours before Arnold and Phillips's troops, however, and were subsequently surprised and captured by the British.

What Lafayette did not know was why Phillips had turned around, but the day after sending his men to dog Phillips, he found out. "By letters from North Carolina," he wrote to Washington, "I find that Lord Cornwallis who I Had Been assured Had sailed for Charlestown is advancing toward Halifax." Lafayette's formerly desperate circumstance now seemed untenable. "Each of these armies is More than the double Superior to me. We Have no Boats, few Militia and less arms."

Boats were a big issue. In the Virginia tidewater with its wide rivers, nearly everything was reachable by boat, but moving troops over the region's ill-tended roads was something else again. To counter Phillips's latest move, Lafayette ordered Steuben to find "Every thing that Can do for Crossing a River, Boats, Canoes, Scows . . . ," but that would not be enough to counter the ships and boats Phillips now had at his disposal. "His Command of the water Enabled Him to Land where I Could not Reach Him," Lafayette told Washington. The Frenchman was enormously frustrated by the ease with which the British were moving troops up and down the rivers. He ordered all the bridges between Petersburg and Halifax destroyed, but he knew that would only slow the enemy down, and not by much at that. Lafayette reiterated to Washington the lesson learned from their failure to trap Arnold: "There is no fighting Here Unless you Have a Naval Superiority."

The young general at least maintained a sense of humor about the overwhelming odds he faced. Moving his army to Osborne's Landing, Lafayette took up residence in the house Phillips had used as a headquarters when he had been there a week earlier. Lafayette wrote to the Chevalier de La Luzerne, "Here I am in the enemy's former camp, in possession of General Phillips's quarters and bed but too polite not to give it back to him as soon as he needs it."

Phillips would have no need of the bed. He was at that moment at Petersburg, in what would be his deathbed, as he and Arnold awaited word from Cornwallis. Lafayette's troops moved down from Osborne's Landing and took position on the north side of the Appomattox River, with the British on the south side and nearly all the bridges between them destroyed. From the heights, the Americans cannonaded the British camps to no effect.

Lieutenant Colonel Simcoe approached Arnold for permission to take a patrol of the Queen's Rangers toward Halifax—some 70 miles away—to find out what Cornwallis was up to. At first Arnold refused, not wanting to weaken his force with Lafayette so close, but the following day he relented. Simcoe and his mounted troops rode off south to the Nottoway River, 27 miles from Petersburg, which he reached the next day.

The following day, the Rangers pressed on to Hicks' Ford on the Meherrin River, just north of the North Carolina border, where they managed to capture Colonel Hicks himself, a militia colonel who mistook the Queen's Rangers for an advance guard of Lafayette's army. From Hicks, Simcoe learned that Cornwallis was in Halifax and that troops from his army had already crossed the Roanoke. Simcoe was disappointed to learn this, since it meant that his "hopes of being in time to facilitate his Lordship's passage were at an end." With Hicks in tow, the Queen's Rangers pressed on.

As they drew closer to Cornwallis's army, Simcoe feared blundering into the advance party in the night and precipitating a friendly-fire incident. He feared, too, that there might be militia units between him and Cornwallis whom he would be unable by darkness to distinguish from their friends. To prevent this, after leaving Hicks' Ford he left the main road and took his men around to the west and then south. Unbeknownst to him, Lieutenant Colonel Banastre Tarleton was leading his men north on the east of the main road, pushing for Hicks' Ford. The two patrols passed one another a few miles apart.

A few days after leaving Petersburg, Simcoe's patrol arrived at the Roanoke to find, to his pleasure, that Lord Cornwallis and most of his army were still on the other side. The day after Tarleton had taken Halifax, positive word had finally arrived from Virginia that Phillips "had not quitted James river . . ." but was waiting to link up with Cornwallis. Tarleton had immediately relayed this news to Cornwallis, who replied, "I have just received yours of this date with much more satisfaction than that of yesterday. The light company of the guards shall proceed immediately; I will follow as fast as possible." Cornwallis reached Halifax around May 10 and ordered Tarleton to push on with two companies of mounted infantry to find the fords on the Meherrin and Nottoway rivers, exactly the information Simcoe had been hoping to provide.

Tarleton's patrol had not gone 4 miles beyond the Roanoke, however, when Cornwallis himself, accompanied by six dragoons of his guard, rode up and ordered a halt. He had Tarleton's companies dismount and form into ranks. The night before, some of the company had committed robbery and rape, and now Cornwallis wanted the victims to identify the guilty parties. That was done, and the sergeant and the private thus identified were taken back to Halifax, tried, found guilty, and immediately hanged.

"The immediate infliction of the sentence," Tarleton wrote in his memoirs, "exhibited to the army and manifested to the country the discipline and justice of the British general." The telling of the story, in a memoir meant for publication, might well have been an attempt to illustrate the impartial fairness of the British army by the very officer who stood most accused of barbarism in America.

When Simcoe crossed the Roanoke and reported to Cornwallis, the first face-to-face contact between the two armies, he informed the general of the disposition of the army in Virginia, and Cornwallis sent orders to Arnold to march for the Nottoway River to link up there. Simcoe also related the unhappy news of "the irrecoverable state of health in which Gen. Phillips lay."

Simcoe and his weary men rested a short while and then began the return trip to Virginia as Cornwallis's army labored across the Roanoke. This time, Simcoe and his men rode by the main road to Hicks' Ford on the Meherrin River, where they met Tarleton's patrol. Simcoe and Tarleton were the mounted officers most feared by the Americans, and together they constituted a frightening threat. Indeed, around the same day the two men met, Lafayette was lamenting about how his dragoons "will look without pistol, sword, saddle, bridle, or boots against the Simcoes and Tarletons."

The two mounted divisions having linked, the way was clear for Cornwallis's march into Virginia. Simcoe and a few dragoons rode back to Petersburg to report to Arnold, who, concerned that Lafayette might yet attack, had elected not to continue his march toward Cornwallis. He now had orders to meet Cornwallis at the Nottoway River, but with the way clear he deemed such a move unnecessary, as his men would just have to march back again. Instead, he went by himself to meet his new commanding officer, riding beyond the Nottoway to Hick's Ford on the Meherrin further south.

The next day, May 19, Arnold and Simcoe met Cornwallis at Hicks' Ford. Phillips was dead. He had died on May 13 of fever at the age of fifty, and Cornwallis grieved his passing. "You will conceive my distress at the loss of my poor friend Phillips," he wrote to Lord Rawdon. To Sir Henry Clinton, he wrote that it was a "loss I cannot sufficiently lament from personal or public considerations."

On May 20, Cornwallis's army marched the last miles to Petersburg and linked up with the army of Benedict Arnold. Lord Charles Cornwallis was now the commanding officer in Virginia, at the head of an army of over five thousand men. "I cannot immediately say what measures I shall pursue," he wrote to Rawdon. Cornwallis had no orders from Clinton and no real idea what he would do next, but at least he was free of the Carolinas.

New Theaters and Old

As Cornwallis was marching north and Phillips lay dying, as General Washington and the Comte de Rochambeau were settling on a strategy, Clinton in New York was making plans and issuing orders. But he was doing so with no understanding of what was happening in the southern theater, thanks to Cornwallis's reticence. Clinton was like a puppeteer, still pulling strings, unaware that the puppets had long since gone their own way.

Cornwallis had just left Wilmington on his march to Virginia when Clinton wrote to Phillips stressing the importance of the Carolinas. "The security of the two Carolinas," he wrote, "is certainly an object of the greatest importance, and should in all events be first attended to."

At the same time, Clinton was toying with yet another strategy, "which, if successful, would be most solidly decisive in its consequences." He reiterated that taking and holding territory in the Carolinas was crucial, but admitted it had not worked out as well as hoped. Virginia, Clinton understood, was universally hostile to the king. "But the inhabitants of

Pennsylvania," he explained to Phillips, "are represented to me to being friendly."

Clinton's new idea, which he called an "experiment," was for Phillips to move north and take and hold Philadelphia and the surrounding area. "I think this experiment should now be tried," he wrote. It was an extraordinary about-face and indicative of the degree to which Clinton was flailing in the dark, trying to locate a place where the king's authority might gain a foothold. The British had already held Philadelphia once, from the summer of 1777 to the summer of 1778, with no discernible benefit. It was Clinton himself who had been forced to abandon Philadelphia and retreat to New York after France entered the war and the king and ministry shifted their focus to protecting the West Indies. And now he wanted to go back.

Phillips would need more troops if he were to advance on Philadelphia and establish a deepwater port in the Chesapeake for the British navy, which was still a priority, so Clinton embarked another reinforcement of British and German troops, about seventeen hundred men in all. He wasn't just proposing his new "experiment" to see how Cornwallis and the others might react; he was setting it into motion. Phillips was to retain command of the army in Virginia unless and until things improved for Cornwallis in the South, "For, until they do," Clinton wrote Phillips, "I should imagine he [Cornwallis] will not leave the Carolinas."

By the time Cornwallis entered Virginia, the transports carrying the latest reinforcements were at sea. Their arrival in Virginia would increase the number of men under the earl's command to around seven thousand, leaving Clinton with slightly fewer than ten thousand fit for duty. The Siege of Yorktown was less than five months away, but still Cornwallis was the only high-ranking officer on either side who considered Virginia a major area of operations.

Clinton was focused on the Carolinas, New York, and now Philadelphia. He had sent troops to Virginia not to take and hold the state but to disrupt supplies flowing south to the Carolinas and to establish a naval base. He had always planned for the Virginia detachments to return north, and he still hoped to get most of them back. The crux of the contest, he continued to believe, would be between himself and Washington in a fight for New York.

Washington, too, was still focused on New York, as he had been since Clinton had marched there from Philadelphia three years earlier. He had sent Lafayette to Virginia for the sole purpose of trapping Arnold. When that did not work, he had initially ordered Lafayette to return to New York before changing his mind and instead sending his brigadier general farther south to reinforce General Nathanael Greene. Lafayette was merely interrupting his march through Virginia long enough to counter the offensive moves of Phillips and Arnold. He was, theoretically, still on his way to the Carolinas.

Despite the intense cat-and-mouse games Lafayette had already played with Phillips and was about to begin with Cornwallis, the marquis, too, considered his presence in Virginia a temporary distraction from the fighting in the Carolinas. "Nothing Can attract My Sight from the Supplies and Reinforcements destined to General Greene's Army," he wrote to Washington in the same letter in which he informed Washington that Cornwallis was on his way to Virginia. Lafayette assured the commander-in-chief that he and Steuben were still working hard to raise recruits for Greene, and that he had "forbidden every department to give me Any thing that May Be thought useful to General Greene." Lafayette was still awaiting the arrival of Anthony Wayne and his Pennsylvania regiment of Continental troops, and he intended to send them south to Greene "Unless I am Very hard pushed."

Ironically, it was Cornwallis, the man for whom Virginia would represent the greatest failure of his career, who was pushing hard for that state to become the central theater of the war. In his letter of April 11 to Clinton, he had suggested that Virginia was where they should concentrate their efforts even if it meant giving up New York. Clinton, for his part, agreed that such a move might end the conflict, though not in the way Cornwallis had in mind. "If the Chesapeake had become the seat of war," he commented later, "and New York evacuated to enable us to carry it there, it would certainly be the speediest way to finish the war. For the whole [British] army could probably have been annihilated in one campaign, commencing in July." In light of later events, it is hard to think him wrong.

After assuming command of the British forces in Virginia, Cornwallis read the official correspondence that had passed between Clinton and Phillips. He was not impressed with the idea of taking Philadelphia. The belief that friends of the Crown would rally to the support of British troops there was a tune he had heard before. Such assurances, he felt, "bear too great a resemblance to those of the emissaries of North Carolina to give me much confidence." If they were to take Philadelphia, he felt, they would either have to keep it or burn it, "neither of which appear to be advisable."

Once again, Cornwallis expressed the opinion that "Virginia appears to me to be the only province in which [offensive war] can be carried on, and in which there is a stake." In this, he had the backing of the most important if least informed decision makers in England: Lord Frederick North, the prime minister; Lord George Germain, Secretary of State for the American department in North's cabinet; and King George III.

Thanks to his direct correspondence with Cornwallis and Clinton's dithering, Germain now had more confidence in his second-in-command in the former colonies than in his commander-in-chief. The secretary made this perfectly clear on several occasions, writing once to Clinton, "I shall therefore only observe, in addition to all I have hitherto written upon the subject, that I am well pleased to find Lord Cornwallis's opinion entirely coincides with mine on the great importance of pushing the war on the side of Virginia with all the force that can be spared."

Germain also wrote a letter to Cornwallis that would have infuriated Clinton if he had read it at the time and no doubt did infuriate him when he read it years later. He assured Cornwallis that the king's intention was "to push the war from south to north, securing what is conquered as we go, and not by desultory enterprises taking possession of places one time and abandoning them another, and I have signified His Majesty's pleasure to Sir Henry Clinton to this effect." This, of course, was exactly Clinton's point in arguing that Cornwallis should secure the Carolinas before moving to Virginia. But what Clinton said no longer seemed to matter. Virginia was going to become the third seat of war whether Clinton liked it or not.

Clinton, in fact, did not like it, and he told Cornwallis as much. On receiving the unwelcome news that Cornwallis and his army were heading for Virginia, a move Clinton had known nothing about prior to its execution, he wrote Cornwallis that, had he known of the plan, "I should certainly have endeavored to have stopped you - as I did then, as well as now, consider such a move as likely to be dangerous to our interests in the southern colonies."

Still, Clinton was constitutionally incapable of giving a direct order. This might have been an expression of his personality, a means of covering himself, or both. He would spend years after the war parsing his words to demonstrate how none of it had been his fault, an attempt to write history that would have been even harder than it was had he given direct and unambiguous orders at the time. And so to Cornwallis he wrote,

> But what is done cannot now be altered. And, as Your Lordship has thought proper to make this decision, I shall most gladly avail myself of your very able assistance in carrying out such operations as you shall judge best in Virginia.

While stating for the record his opposition to Cornwallis's decision, Clinton still declined to give his second-in-command a direct order. Cornwallis's opinions, he wrote, "will have the advantage of being formed on the spot and upon circumstances which at this distance I cannot, of course, judge of." Once again, in wording that posterity could construe either way, Clinton toed the narrow line between issuing instructions and letting his subordinate have his head.

On two points, Clinton was unambiguous. One was that Cornwallis should not ask him for any more troops. Phillips and Arnold had both considered the number of men they had sufficient for their mission, and, in fact, Clinton still hoped that Cornwallis might send some troops back to New York.

The second point was that everything in the Chesapeake depended on naval superiority, a fact that Clinton had consistently understood better than most. He reminded Cornwallis that operations there "can be no longer secure than while we are superior at sea." Clinton suggested that Cornwallis find a base for his army that could be defended even if the French achieved a temporary superiority at sea. "For, should it become permanent," he added, "I need not say what our prospects in this country are likely to be."

Clinton had another reason for not issuing explicit orders. He did not know how much longer he would be commander-in-chief. He had first asked to be relieved of command in America more than a year earlier, during the siege of Charleston, and though his request had been denied at the time, his badgering had eventually secured from the king permission to resign his command if he so chose. Clinton had since raised that possibility repeatedly, like a petulant child threatening to hold his breath until he turns blue. In April, he had written to Germain, "I shall be constrained - though reluctantly - to avail myself of the permission His Majesty had graciously pleased to give me to resign this command," unless two requests were met. One was for a reinforcement of ten thousand men. The other was that Vice-Admiral Marriot Arbuthnot be replaced.

He and Arbuthnot had been at one another's throats for more than a year, and by the spring of 1781, Clinton could take no more. Nor were Clinton's concerns unreasonable. As he explained to Germain, operations in North America absolutely depended on naval support and transport, and if he could not count on the cooperation of the navy, he could not plan campaigns. In response, Germain assured Clinton that Arbuthnot would be transferred to Jamaica and another flag officer sent in his place.

Many months passed, however, and still Arbuthnot remained in New York. Finally, "in the civilest manner I was capable of," Clinton asked Arbuthnot what his orders were, and Arbuthnot replied that he had received no word of a transfer to the West Indies.

That was too much for Clinton. He again wrote to Germain, informing the American secretary that he was willing to wait for the arrival of one more packet from London, but if "Admiral Arbuthnot is not recalled, I trust that His Majesty from his gracious goodness will pardon me if I avail myself of the permission he has been pleased to give me to resign this command to Lord Cornwallis." Arbuthnot, "from age, temper, and inconsistency of conduct is really so little to be depended on" that Clinton feared the admiral would make a hash of any plans they laid.

Knowing he might soon resign his command and that Cornwallis would then become commander-in-chief, Clinton did not feel he should give Cornwallis any directions for the overall conduct of the war. At least that was what he wrote years later, when blame for the final outcome was being assigned.

Arbuthnot had, in fact, been asking since March to be relieved of command, though he assured the First Lord of the Admiralty, the Earl of Sandwich, that he would go to Jamaica if needed. However, his numerous requests for relief did not reach London until May. Upon reading Arbuthnot's complaints about his health and infirmity, Sandwich replied that "it would be cruelty to take you at your word by forcing you into the danger of a hot climate." Instead, Arbuthnot was given permission "to return to England without waiting for a successor from hence."

Clinton would have been much more at ease had he known of that exchange, but thanks to the speed of transatlantic travel at the time, nearly half a year elapsed between Arbuthnot's request to resign and his receipt of an answer. In the meantime, it probably amused Arbuthnot to get Clinton's goat with deliberate vagueness. And so, as the campaigning season of 1781 accelerated into full swing, Clinton could only stew and complain, with Arbuthnot close by and Cornwallis in Virginia—neither man where Clinton would have preferred.

CHAPTER *17* *"I am inclined to think well of York"*

A FEW DAYS after linking with Benedict Arnold, Lord Cornwallis began to prepare for the new fight he had bought himself. He "proceeded to learn the state of the enemy and the country" and sent out spies and light troops to report on the Marquis de Lafayette's strength and position. Lieutenant Colonel Tarleton and his dragoons were dispatched on the first of what would be many lightning cavalry raids through the Virginia countryside.

In a blinding, driving rain, the mounted troops, around three hundred strong, crossed the bridge at Petersburg and rode north toward Warwick. Near Chesterfield, southwest of the James River, with their movements shielded by the rain, they surprised a party of around four hundred militia. The British horsemen plunged into the enemy with sabers slashing. It would have been difficult even for the best troops to load and fire muskets in the rain, and the task was utterly beyond the capabilities of the militia. Rendered defenseless, the Americans fled, with six killed and around fifty taken prisoner.

Tarleton escorted these prisoners back to Petersburg, and Cornwallis was able to learn from them and from spies he had deployed that "about one thousand continental troops were posted between Wiltown [Wilton, on the northeast bank of the James River across from Warwick] and Richmond, waiting the juncture of General Wayne and the Pennsylvania line, and the expected reinforcements of militia."

Thus informed, Cornwallis wrote to Sir Henry Clinton that "I will now proceed to dislodge LaFayette from Richmond and with my light troops to destroy any magazines or stores in the neighborhood . . . ," though after Benedict Arnold and Major General William Phillips's serial sackings of the area, and American efforts to move things to safety, there could not have been much left to destroy. After beating up Lafayette,

Cornwallis intended to move to Williamsburg, which he understood was "healthy"—that is, less given to diseases such as malaria and yellow fever—and where provisions might be found. He would continue to look for a proper harbor, having been assured by Arnold that Portsmouth was not it. "I am inclined to think well of York," he wrote.

While Cornwallis was working out his strategy, the reinforcements sent by Clinton arrived in the James River under the command of General Alexander Leslie, who had fought with Cornwallis at Guilford Courthouse. Leslie had been too ill to continue in the Carolinas and had returned to New York, but, according to Tarleton, his "health had benefitted by the sea air of the late voyage, and [he] was always zealous for the public service." Cornwallis sent most of the new troops to reinforce Portsmouth until he could decide upon a more permanent base of operations.

Arnold's tenure in Virginia now drew to an end, and he was slated to return to New York by the next man-of-war bound north. Why he was leaving is unclear, though there is no suggestion of dissatisfaction with his performance. Tarleton recorded simply, "Brigadier General Arnold obtained leave to return to New York, where business of consequence demanded his attention."

Had Arnold remained in Virginia and been with the army during the capitulation of Yorktown, it would have set up an interesting conundrum. The Americans would certainly have insisted that Arnold not receive the privileges of a prisoner of war, while the British would likely have felt honor-bound to insist that he did. His presence might have thus created an insurmountable impasse in the surrender negotiations. Instead, with his return to the North, he once again ducked the hangman's noose.

On May 24, Cornwallis left a garrison to hold Petersburg, burned the bridge that the British had constructed over the Appomattox River to hinder any attack from the north, and marched his men along the south bank of the James River to a place just opposite Byrd's Plantation in Westover. There, the boats that Arnold had constructed were put to use moving the army across the river. Tarleton gave a sense for how big a job this was:

> The channel of the ferry, at which the infantry, the cavalry, the artillery, the bat horses [horses that carry the officers' baggage], the baggage, and

the wagons were to cross, exceeded two miles; but such was the exertions of the detachment of sailors . . . that the passage was completed in less than three days.

Cornwallis had stripped down his army in North Carolina, burning the baggage train and extraneous gear, but in the ensuing months it had swelled again. Now, joined with Arnold and Phillips's army, which had been plundering Virginia for nearly half a year, the baggage train had grown out of hand. "The army appears similar to a wandering Arabian or Tartar horde," wrote the German Captain Johann Ewald, who had rejoined the army after recovering from a wound and was always ready to express his disgust.

One problem was the ease with which horses were scooped up by the British. Another was the number of freed slaves who attached themselves to the army. Neither the officers nor the men could resist the temptation of this essentially free labor. Each subaltern, or junior officer, according to Ewald, was allowed two horses and one freed slave as a servant, each captain four horses and two servants, and so on up the ranks. But those limits were ignored, and each officer was traveling with four to six horses and three or four freed slaves along with a cook and a maid. Eighteenth-century soldiers often took wives or mistresses with them on campaign, and such was the case with Cornwallis's army, except that in this case each woman also had a freed slave and a couple of horses.

Nor were the officers the only ones who were able to obtain free servants. "I can testify that every soldier had his Negro," Ewald wrote in his diary, "who carried his provisions and bundles. This multitude always hunted at a gallop, and behind the baggage followed over four thousand Negroes of both sexes and all ages. Any place this horde approached was eaten clean, like an acre invaded by a swarm of locusts."

Upon rejoining his troops, Ewald found that "almost every jäger had his Negro." By the following day, he had put an end to that.

The Byrd plantation, where the British troops landed after crossing the river at Westover, was considered one of the finest in Virginia. It was owned by lovely forty-two-year-old Mary Byrd, widow of wealthy Loyalist William Byrd III, who had committed suicide in 1777. She was also, by coincidence, a first cousin of Peggy Shippen, the young wife of Benedict Arnold and the woman generally credited with having transformed Arnold from a disgruntled American officer into a full-fledged traitor.

When Cornwallis landed at Byrd's Plantation, it was the third time the British had done so during the Virginia campaign, and speculation began to grow that Mrs. Byrd was more than just unlucky, that perhaps she was in league with the enemy. To be sure, Arnold had plundered the plantation of slaves, boats, and horses, just as he had many others, but some speculated that that was just a cover. Mary Byrd was slated to be tried for these allegations, but the trial never took place, and it remains unknown to this day just where her loyalties lay.

While Phillips and Arnold had been in Petersburg waiting for Cornwallis, the Marquis de Lafayette and Baron de Steuben had been anxiously collecting militia, arms, supplies, wagons, and boats—all the matériel they would need to oppose the army gathering in the tidewater. Lafayette was still waiting for Anthony Wayne, and he was determined to attack Phillips if Wayne's troops arrived before Cornwallis, but they did not. "I cannot understand what has become of the Pennsylvania detachment," he wrote to a friend. He did not know that Wayne was still dealing with the aftermath of the mutiny, which included a forty-day furlough for the men and a reorganization of the regiments, and had not even set out for Virginia.

As commanding officers of their respective armies in Virginia, Phillips and Lafayette had exchanged letters with regard to prisoner exchange and the proper conduct of war, and after Phillips's death, Arnold had taken up the task. If Lafayette had had a hard time dealing with what he perceived as Phillips's haughty style, he found Arnold's intolerable. "A Correspondence With Arnold is So very Repugnant to My feelings that I Can Never Conquer them So far as to Answer His Letters," the marquis complained to Nathanael Greene. "I am the More Adverse to it as Arnold is A Very proud Correspondent, and I Can Not Submit to Such a Stile from the Rascal."

Perhaps it was a function of his youth or being French, but Lafayette, of all the officers in the American army, was the most forthright about his hatred of Arnold. He even returned letters from Arnold unopened. Cornwallis's arrival and Arnold's departure relieved him of having to suffer Arnold's "Stile."

After moving his troops across the James River to Westover, Cornwallis pushed north after Lafayette, and Lafayette, as he told General

George Weedon, "Moved Back in the Same proportion." All the public stores at Richmond had been removed, as well as any private property that people chose to send out of the city. There being nothing left in the former capital worth risking an army to defend, Lafayette retreated north, crossing the South Anna River and then the North Anna into Hanover County. His plan was to keep his army between Cornwallis and Fredericksburg, which he still believed was Cornwallis's target.

Lafayette had under his command about three thousand troops, Continentals and militia, against Cornwallis's more than seven thousand professional soldiers. The Americans suffered from their usual lack of arms, clothes, shoes, and other military necessities, but even more dire to Lafayette was their lack of horses for mounted troops. Though Virginia had the finest horse country in America, the American army was all but bereft of mounts. To Lafayette and Steuben's ongoing frustration, the locals were unwilling to sell horses to the army or to move them out of reach of the enemy, with the result that most horses fell into British hands.

Cavalry was critical to eighteenth-century warfare, and a significant imbalance could make all the difference when two armies contested the field. Even gathering intelligence became impossible without horses. Lafayette complained to Governor Thomas Jefferson that his men could not even reconnoiter the enemy as the British had so many dragoons to screen the movements of their army.

Jefferson and the Virginia General Assembly went to the extreme of giving Lafayette permission to impress horses from the enemy's line of march, a thing Lafayette hated to do. But even that did little to solve the problem. In a letter to Greene, the marquis expressed his concern:

> It is Said Clel. Tarleton Has Mounted a Large Body of His Infantry. Simcoe Has piked up every Horse He Could Come Across. Under these Circumstances We Have Every thing to fear from their Cavalry. They Will over Run the Country and our flanks; our Stores, our Very Camp will Be Unsecured. Major Nelson Had Some State Horses But they are So much Broke down that ten only are fitt for Duty. . . . The Men are Good But Nacked, Unarmed, Dismounted and fatigued to death. Cavalry is So Necessary that I Gave them Every Encouragement, Recommendation, and order that Could Recruit this Corps.

Lafayette's fears about Lieutenant Colonels Banastre Tarleton and John Simcoe were well founded. While the Frenchman was quite certain he could keep out of reach of Cornwallis's massive and slow-moving army, mounted troops were another matter. Likewise, as Lafayette's troops retreated ahead of him, Cornwallis must have seen shades of Nathanael Greene in North Carolina. It became increasingly clear that he could not bring Lafayette to battle unless Lafayette chose to fight, and, with the odds stacked against him, there was little chance he would.

Instead, Cornwallis sent Tarleton and Simcoe, the fast-moving bêtes noires of the Virginia militia, against the cavalry-challenged Americans. Unlike the full army, their flying columns could strike hard and fast, before the Americans even knew they were coming.

Charlottesville and Point of Fork

Lafayette's army was in Hanover County where, he informed Weedon, "if it pleases Lord Cornwallis I intend Remaining Some time." The Baron de Steuben was near Charlottesville, the new seat of the Virginia government, about 40 miles northwest of Lafayette. Steuben, who had been making himself obnoxious to the state government since the previous autumn, was still badgering them to raise and equip a significant force of militia and Continentals. He was also raising men for Greene and had intended to march south with them, but once again events were overwhelming his plans.

By the end of May, Steuben had "500 men under arms, tolerably armed, but Neither Cloathed nor Equipped, at Least very Badly." He had recently received a letter from Greene, dated May 11, ordering him to join Greene's army immediately with as many troops and cavalry as he could bring. "It is probable," Steuben wrote to Lafayette, "that at the time he was ignorant of Cornwallis moving this way." As eager as Steuben was to join Greene (and as eager as the Virginia government was to have him gone), it was becoming clear to the baron that the war was coming his way. He felt it prudent to wait for another letter from Greene before leaving Virginia. In any event, his troops would not be ready to march south for several more days.

Most of the military stores and artillery in Virginia had been moved to a place called Point of Fork, some 42 miles west and a little north of Richmond, where the Rivanna River running southeast from Charlottesville and the Fluvanna River flowing east combined to form the James. The only military advantage Point of Fork enjoyed was that it was about 50 miles from Cornwallis. Other than that, the stores were "By no means safe," Steuben wrote, "Considering the Decided superiority of the Ennemy."

Steuben informed Lafayette that he intended to march his men from his encampment near Charlottesville to Point of Fork. "There I Can Cover the Removal of the stores and keep open the Communications," he wrote. Point of Fork would also be a good position from which to march south if Greene reiterated his order to do so.

Lafayette continued to fall back from Cornwallis's advance, still believing that Cornwallis was marching for Fredericksburg and the Hunter Iron Works. He wrote to Weedon to "prevail upon the Gentlemen [of the surrounding counties] to mount & equip themselves as volunteer Dragoons." By his estimate, he had forty mounted troops to Cornwallis's five hundred.

On the last day of May, Anthony Wayne wrote to Lafayette informing him that he and his troops were in Maryland and would be in Virginia the following day. This was great news to Lafayette, who was sure he could not prevent Cornwallis from sacking Fredericksburg or from turning his own army's flank without Wayne's reinforcements. Even with them, the British would retain an overwhelming superiority.

Steuben was at Point of Fork as May turned to June. Having heard that Cornwallis was moving his way, he had removed most of the stores that were of any value. Now he remained in camp with his small force, awaiting orders. "Here I am with 550 men in this desert," he wrote to Lafayette, "with no shoes, no shirts, and what is worse no cartridge pouches. I write everywhere, I send express messengers everywhere and I get nothing." For lack of supplies, men were falling ill and beginning to desert. For Steuben, it was just more of what he had been enduring for months.

The baron's intention was to "cross the [Fluvanna] river with as much noise as possible," hoping that diversion would force Cornwallis to send a part of his army toward Point of Fork and thus weaken the force facing Lafayette. But Steuben had not heard from the marquis for nearly a week and did not know what was going on. "I beg you to send me news," he wrote. "It is as though I were in Kamchatka here. I don't know where you are, nor what has become of Cornwallis."

Cornwallis, as it happened, was about 60 miles to the east in Hanover County, south of Fredericksburg, pondering his next move. The size of his army, in particular the number of mounted troops at his disposal, allowed him to go anywhere he pleased, "without apprehension or difficulty," as Tarleton put it. As Lafayette suspected, Cornwallis was considering a march on Fredericksburg, but in the end decided against it. He wrote to Clinton, "From what I could learn of the present state of Hunter's iron manufactory, it did not appear of so much importance as the stores on the other side of the country."

Cornwallis had also hoped to prevent a juncture between Lafayette and Wayne, but Lafayette had withdrawn to the north shore of the Rappahannock River and Wayne was approaching fast, and it was clear now that their union was inevitable. Lafayette's decision to put the Rappahannock between his troops and Cornwallis, however, afforded his lordship even greater carte blanche to throw his weight around Virginia, and he was ready to take advantage.

Cornwallis was aware of Steuben's small force at Point of Fork and the military supplies there, and he also knew that Governor Jefferson and the General Assembly were meeting in Charlottesville, less than 30 miles northwest of Point of Fork. Here were two tasks tailor-made for the fast-moving Tarleton and Simcoe.

Tarleton's column consisted entirely of mounted troops, so Cornwallis sent him off to Charlottesville, "as most distant, and on that account more within the reach of cavalry." Simcoe, "with the yagers, the infantry, and the hussars of the rangers" as well as dragoons, was sent against Point of Fork. "It was designed that these blows should . . . be struck at the same moment; [and] that Tarleton, after completing his business, should retire down the Rivanna, to give assistance to Simcoe." Meanwhile, Cornwallis's main force would move west, closer to Point of Fork.

In the brutal early June tidewater heat, Tarleton rode out of camp with 180 troops from the British Legion, the 17th Light Dragoons, and

70 mounted infantry, keeping between the North and South Anna rivers as they made west for Charlottesville. The following morning, in the predawn hours, the mounted troops fell in with a lightly guarded wagon train filled with arms and clothing for Greene's southern army, supplies the Americans could ill afford to lose. Tarleton's men set the wagons on fire before continuing on. Reaching the homes of rebel leaders, they crashed through the doors of the still-sleeping households. "Soon after daybreak," Tarleton wrote, "some of the principal gentlemen of Virginia, who had fled to the borders of the mountains for security, were taken out of their beds." Some were paroled, some taken as prisoners.

The light troops pressed on toward Charlottesville, questioning any-one they met along the way as to what forces the Americans had mustered on the road ahead. They could get no straight answers, but Tarleton was unconcerned. The mounted troops had advanced 70 miles in just twenty-four hours, and the lieutenant colonel was confident that their speed had preserved the element of surprise. He rode hard, sending some of the dragoons ahead of the column to scout the approach to the town.

The scouts returned with word that the ford across the Rivanna River was lightly guarded by militia who could offer little resistance to Tarleton's shock troops. He drove his men forward, and when they reached the river, the mounted soldiers charged through the shallow water, sabers flashing and carbines firing, "and routed the detachment posted at the place."

Once Tarleton had one hundred men and horses across the river, he ordered them to "charge into the town, to continue the confusion of the Americans, and to apprehend, if possible, the governor and assembly." A short, sharp fight broke out as the few startled troops in town rushed to the defense of the acting capital. "A Brigadier-general Scott, and several officers and men, were killed, wounded or taken," Tarleton wrote. Seven members of the Virginia General Assembly were scooped up.

Thomas Jefferson escaped, but just barely. He was at nearby Monti-cello, a short distance south of the ford, when Tarleton's men made their fast approach. Monticello sits at the summit of a low mountain with a commanding view, and from there Jefferson saw the mounted troops coming. The governor "provided for his personal liberty," Tarleton recalled, "by a precipitate retreat." The governor got out ten minutes before the British troops arrived.

In Charlottesville, Tarleton and his men found a significant quantity of military stores, including one thousand muskets that had been manufactured in Fredericksburg. Lafayette had given repeated orders that no arms were to be kept at Charlottesville for just this reason, but the General Assembly considered the guns state property and had ordered them to the new capital for the defense of that place. The guns were abandoned in the face of Tarleton's raid, quite possibly without having fired a shot.

Along with the invaluable muskets, the British found tobacco, clothing, and various accoutrements, all of which they destroyed. Four hundred barrels of gunpowder (in Cornwallis's report to Clinton it became five hundred) were also destroyed. These were all things the Americans desperately needed. They had been moved to a place Virginia's leaders thought to be safe, but Cornwallis's great superiority in mounted troops was as advantageous in the backcountry as England's naval superiority had long been along the coast, allowing his men to move and strike at will.

Tarleton remained less than a day in Charlottesville. With flames consuming the captured stores and his prisoners mounted up, he headed out of town, down the Rivanna River toward Steuben, Simcoe, and Point of Fork.

"[M]y situation became critical"

Simcoe's men, both mounted and infantry, were covering 30 miles a day as they closed on Point of Fork, an impressive pace for a column that was mostly on foot, marching through killing heat with battered shoes, full packs, 10-pound Brown Bess muskets, and wool regimental coats. They had been on the road two days when they took some prisoners who could provide intelligence about the Americans. From them, Simcoe learned that Steuben was unaware of Tarleton's column to the north and did not know about the second column marching directly for him.

Hoping like Tarleton to retain the advantage of surprise, Simcoe sent a lieutenant named Spencer with a small detachment ahead of the main body to gain intelligence on Steuben's forces. Spencer made his way to

Napier's Ford, near the home of Colonel Napier, which was guarded by two members of the Virginia militia. Leaving most of his men on the road, Spencer and three of his company approached the guards, pretending to be American troops. "Lt. Spencer completely imposed on their credulity," Simcoe wrote. The militia gladly told him everything they knew about Steuben's disposition and strength. They even allowed Spencer to relieve them with two of his own men and accompanied Spencer to Napier's house, where the British officer made prisoners of them all.

As amusing as this must have been for Spencer and Simcoe, the news gleaned from the guards was not. Steuben, they learned, had been informed of Simcoe's approach and had already begun to evacuate Point of Fork. Simcoe was too late.

The baron had received word two days before. "I recev'd intelligence that the Enemy were at Goochland Co. [Court] Ho. [House]" to the east, he wrote to Lafayette, and confirmation came the next day when a militia colonel reported seeing the cavalry at Goochland as well as another column of "at least one thousand men" at Louisa Court House. That was Tarleton, on his way to Charlottesville. "[B]oth parties," Steuben wrote to Lafayette, "seemed to be directing their March this way."

That was all Steuben needed to hear. "[M]y situation became critical," he wrote, "and I therefore determined to change my position." He had with him five hundred fifty new recruits as well as three hundred militia under the command of General Robert Lawson, who had joined him a few days before. The two generals were expecting about four hundred more men, but even twice that number of militia would be no match for the well-armed and well-led veterans hurrying toward them. Nor was the Rivanna River, which the baron described as being fordable in several places, any sort of defense. It was time to go.

The only practical defense, in the baron's judgment, was to put the unfordable Fluvanna and James rivers (the Fluvanna being the main stem of the James above the Rivanna confluence) between himself and the advancing troops. "This I executed immediately . . . ," he told Lafayette, "having first crossed over all the baggage, and a quantity of State stores which were at the Point of Fork." Steuben capitalized on the one advantage the Americans had often held over the British during the Carolina and Virginia campaigns—he had all the boats.

Simcoe and his column approached Point of Fork on June 5. While still 2 miles away they encountered a patrol of American dragoons, whom they chased and took prisoner. The dragoons were part of the rear guard that had not yet crossed the river with the main body of troops. They told Simcoe that they had orders to patrol out 20 miles, from which Simcoe gleaned that Steuben was not yet aware of his enemy's arrival.

Spencer's ruse de guerre having worked so well, Simcoe decided to continue the theatrics. "The advanced men of the huzzars changed clothes with the prisoners," he later wrote, "and dispositions were now made for the attack. The huzzars in the enemy's clothing were directed to gallop to the only house on the point," where Simcoe believed Steuben must be. There, Simcoe hoped, the hussars would capture the Prussian. That done, the house would serve as headquarters for the coming attack.

As the disguised hussars were preparing to move out, however, Simcoe's advance guard returned with a new prisoner, Major James Fairlie, Steuben's aide-de-camp. Fairlie had seen Simcoe's advance party, whom he mistook for the now-captured dragoons, and had ridden out to see why they were not scouting the approaches.

This gave Simcoe another idea. "Sarjeant Wright being near the same size and appearance of Mr. Farley, was directed to exchange clothes with him, to mount his horse, and lead the advance guard." Before the situation could devolve any further into a Shakespearean comedy, however, Fairlie assured Simcoe that all the American troops were now on the south side of the river, an assurance that some wagon drivers, who had also been taken (but allowed to retain their clothing), confirmed.

"The cavalry immediately advanced," Simcoe wrote, "and the enemy being plainly seen on the opposite side, nothing remained but to stop some boats, which were putting off from the extreme point." The boats were filled with the remains of the unfortunate rear guard, about thirty men in all, who were taken prisoner by Simcoe.

Having missed the chance to capture Steuben and the arms and supplies at Point of Fork, Simcoe now tried to frighten the Americans into a hasty retreat by leading Steuben to believe that he faced Cornwallis's entire army, and not just Simcoe's detachment. Again he called on theatrics, sending the 71st Regiment "clothed in red" to the banks of the river, while the rest of the men (and, incredibly, women) were drawn up in the woods on high ground to give "the appearance of a numerous corps." His hope was that the Prussian would abandon the supplies in panicked flight.

Steuben did not fall for it but remained encamped on high ground across the river, about three-quarters of a mile from the banks. Simcoe set a guard around his camp to keep a wary eye out for surprise attack. As he explained in his diary, the military abilities of amateur American officers, "whom accident had placed at the head of armies . . . ," did not concern him, but in this case "the enemy were led by a Prussian officer. . . . [T]he Baron Steuben had shown himself an able officer, and that he well knew how to adapt the science of war to the people whom he was to instruct, and to the country in which he was to act." Simcoe would not underestimate an officer of Frederick the Great.

This was high praise, but, ironically, it was Steuben's behavior at Point of Fork, more than any other decision he made while commanding in the field, for which he would be most criticized. In public correspondence, Lafayette was noncommittal about the baron's decision to abandon the place without a fight, but in private letters he was scathing in his appraisal. To Washington, he wrote,

> The Conduct of the Baron, my dear general, is to me Unintelligible. Every man woman and Child in Virginia is Roused Against Him. They dispute even on His Courage But I Cannot Believe their assertions.

Lafayette knew that Steuben had more than five hundred "New levies" as well as Lawson's militia, giving him a two-to-one advantage over Simcoe. He also believed that Steuben's position at Point of Fork was "unattackable" due to the depth of the river, though Steuben had said that the Rivanna was easily fordable and offered no protection.

According to Lafayette, militia members and new levies had been demoralized by the retreat and were now abandoning Steuben. "I do not know where to employ Him," Lafayette wrote in confidence to Washington, "without Giving offense."

It is hard to imagine, however, that Lafayette really thought new recruits and militia, many of whom were sick and all of whom were ill-equipped, would stand up to Simcoe's mounted veterans, even given their numerical advantage. Nor would the advantage of numbers last long, as Steuben knew that Tarleton was also on his way to Point of Fork. And Lafayette himself had pointed out that Simcoe and Tarleton were the terror of the Virginia militia.

The marquis had no personal knowledge of how difficult it might be to ford the Rivanna River, only the word of Steuben and his detractors. Simcoe, in his detailed journal, makes no mention of the river crossing as he moved his men to the abandoned Point of Fork, suggesting that it posed no obstacle. In fact, Simcoe, like Steuben, considered Point of Fork difficult to defend and had second thoughts about spending the night there. He "would have quitted his camp . . . to search for a more favourable position" had he not judged his men too tired.

Lafayette was getting most of his information secondhand, from people who almost universally loathed the baron. Indeed, Lafayette's negative reaction paled next to the outcry from the Virginia assembly. Speaker of the lower house and militia lieutenant Benjamin Harrison (who would become Virginia's governor the following year, and whose son would, in 1840, become the ninth president of the United States) called Steuben the worst officer in the Continental Army and tried to get him cashiered. Point of Fork was the first thing that could be called a military failure for Steuben, and his many detractors piled on for all it was worth. The only surprise was Lafayette's willingness to join them.

The argument over the retreat at Point of Fork would echo for months, but Steuben and Simcoe had more immediate concerns. Steuben had managed to transport the bulk of the stores across the river, and what was left—some ordnance and broken muskets, some clothing, a few barrels of rum, and sundry other items—was not worth fighting for. He gave orders for his ragtag army to march off before daylight could give Simcoe the opportunity to strike again.

In the dark, from across the water, Simcoe could hear the sound of the Americans destroying the boats they had secured on the south side of the river. The rebels built up their campfires to fool the British into thinking they were staying, but that ruse had become so well known that, instead, it tipped off Simcoe to the fact that they were moving out.

Later that night, a canoe crossed the river from the American camp with two deserters on board, one a drummer boy. As it happened, the drummer boy had been attached to the British 71st Regiment, a part of which was now with Simcoe, and taken prisoner at the Battle of Cowpens. Rather than suffer as a prisoner of war, the boy had enlisted in the American army. Now, seeing a chance to escape the rebels, he crossed the river and surrendered to British pickets. The commander of the detail to whom he surrendered was his father.

The morning revealed that the Americans had indeed marched off in the night. Simcoe had a man swim across the river to fetch a large canoe left on the opposite bank, and with that and a few smaller canoes they found, Simcoe sent a few men across the Fluvanna to reconnoiter the enemy and see what had been left behind. Meanwhile, he set more of his men to constructing a raft so that they could float the troops and captured goods down the river to Cornwallis rather than marching back to the ford over which they had come.

Steuben had been forced to leave behind a fair amount of ordnance, including a 13-inch mortar, five brass 18-inch howitzers, and four long brass 9-pounders, all of which would soon be firing at American troops from the British redoubts at Yorktown. He also abandoned more than a thousand broken muskets, which had been sent to Point of Fork for repair. While Simcoe was loading what he wanted and burning the rest, Tarleton's troops continued south and Cornwallis pushed west for Jefferson's Plantation near Point of Fork. There, the two detachments would link again with the main army. Steuben, meanwhile, began moving his troops as far as he could from that dangerous neighborhood.

CHAPTER *18* The Promise of a Fleet

FRANÇOIS-JOSEPH PAUL de Grasse-Rouville, Comte de Grasse, Marquis de Tilly, was a big man, like George Washington. He stood six foot two, broad and strong, and made an impressive sight in the deep blue and scarlet uniform of a French admiral, the red sash of the Order of St. Louis across his chest.

Like Washington, he came from one of his country's oldest and most respected families, and lineage mattered even more—substantially more—in Bourbon France than in Virginia, where aristocratic outlooks were tempered with republican aspirations. He had fixed on a career as a naval officer while still a boy, but the French navy being then in a poor state, his father had sent him to serve on the ships of the Knights of Malta. He was twelve years old when he sailed with the knights, and at age eighteen he joined the French navy, rising through the ranks in a distinguished career that had extended thirty-eight years by the time he took part in the American Revolution.

De Grasse had fought in the Battle of Ushant in 1778 and had sailed as a *chef d'escadre*, or commodore, to the West Indies in 1779. Serving under the Comte d'Estaing, he had participated in the disastrous attempt to capture Savannah, Georgia, that same year. He had returned with d'Estaing's fleet to France in the beginning of 1781, just as the French ministry was casting around for a new commander for the squadron being assembled for the West Indies. After two others declined it, de Grasse was selected for the post. He was fifty-eight years old.

The ships for the upcoming season, both men-of-war and merchant-men, gathered in Brest in February and March. These included ships destined not only for the West Indies but also for Africa, India, South America, and North America—all the places touched by the world war. On March 22, the wind came fair and the massive fleet stood out to sea—26 ships of the line, 8 smaller men-of-war, and 157 merchant vessels and transports. Among them were merchantmen transporting the supplies promised to the Comte de Rochambeau, with the 57-gun *Sagittaire* as escort, and the 20 ships of the line and the convoy that de Grasse was taking to the West Indies. It was an enormous failure of British strategy and initiative that such a fleet, well known in London, was allowed to sail with not the least bit of interference.

Before parting company with *Sagittaire*, de Grasse sent aboard a letter more specifically outlining his orders and intentions for the coming year. *Sagittaire* carried this letter toward Rochambeau while de Grasse shaped his course for the West Indies, where Admirals Rodney and Hood were waiting for him.

Four days after de Grasse put to sea, the *Concorde* sailed from Brest, bound for Boston with Admiral de Barras and Rochambeau's son on board. The fast frigate quickly outpaced the merchant ships that had sailed ahead of her, arriving in Boston well in advance of them and their escort *Sagittaire*. Aboard the *Concorde* was the first hint of a possible French naval superiority off the coast of North America.

When Washington and Rochambeau met at Wethersfield on May 21, the *Sagittaire* and its convoy were still at sea. The two generals did not, therefore, have the benefit of de Grasse's letter to Rochambeau with its detailed plans and instructions. Concluding their conference, they returned to their respective headquarters and began the laborious process of uprooting their settled armies and getting them on the road for New York. One of their decisions had been that Barras would move his fleet to Boston, but now the admiral, who had not been at the conference, hesitated. At a council of the French command held aboard the flagship *Duc de Bourgogne*, it was decided that the fleet would remain in Newport instead. With de Grasse in the West Indies and possibly available for operations along the American coast in the summer, Barras would be in a much better position to cooperate if he kept his fleet south of Cape Cod.

Washington still felt that Boston was the better choice, but he did not fight the change, realizing, perhaps, that Barras could do as he pleased. Washington conceded that such a decision "partly depends upon a knowledge of Marine Affairs of which I candidly confess my ignorance"— the caveat he habitually appended to his many mentions of naval strategy. The only direct impact of the decision on Washington, and the chief reason he preferred to have the fleet in Boston, was that more militia would be required to protect the ships at anchor in Newport.

Of greater importance to Washington was the speed with which French troops could get underway so that joint operations against New York could commence. "At any rate I could wish that the march of the troops might now be hurried as much as possible," he wrote to Rochambeau. Increasingly bleak reports were arriving from the Marquis de Lafayette, and Washington's long-standing desire to take on Sir Henry Clinton in New York was reinforced by a growing conviction that such an offensive would be the best way to relieve Virginia. With his base threatened, Clinton would withdraw troops from the South for his own defense—or so Washington suspected, and he was reading his old adversary exactly right.

Rochambeau had been making arrangements to begin moving his troops to New York since his return from Wethersfield. On June 7, Claude Blanchard reported,

> I was invited to a great farewell dinner on board the Duc de Bourgogne. There were sixty persons present, several of whom were ladies of Newport and the vicinity. The quarter-deck had been arranged with sails, which made a very handsome hall.

If Rochambeau's army was going to leave Newport, they were going to do it like Frenchmen.

On June 10, the French forces boarded boats that took them up the Narragansett Bay, the first time the army had stirred from Newport in almost a year save for the aborted attempt to trap Benedict Arnold. By the twelfth, they were in Providence preparing for the next leg of their march to link with Washington.

Rochambeau was still in Newport, however, awaiting the convoy that his son had said would be arriving with supplies, troops, and money. Finally, on June 12, thirty-six days after *Concorde*'s arrival, two-thirds of the convoy straggled into Boston Harbor with the escort *Sagittaire*, "the rest dispersed by a gail of wind." Aboard *Sagittaire* was de Grasse's letter to Rochambeau.

De Grasse's letter included the first explicit promise that a powerful French fleet would be coming to the coast of America, and soon. He informed Rochambeau that he would be at Cap François on Santa

Domingo (present-day Cap Haitien in Haiti) at the end of June, and he asked that information on "the naval forces that the British have in North America, of their different Stations and where they commonly cruise, in what number and in what manner they keep them . . ." be sent to him there. He asked also that pilots be sent with knowledge of the places the French fleet might go in North America and reminded Rochambeau that the French ships "differ very much from the British, in their deepness in the water," a likely allusion to New York and the difficulty of crossing the bar at Sandy Hook. De Grasse doubtless recalled d'Estaing's inability to get his ships into New York in 1778.

The French admiral told Rochambeau in a coded section of the letter that he would be off the coast of North America by July 15 at the earliest but warned him that his stay would not be long. He wanted to be back in the Caribbean by the end of October, the close of the hurricane season there and the time when rough autumnal weather would begin afflicting the North American coast. He suggested therefore that "all that can be useful for the success of your projects should be ready that a moment for action may not be lost."

Rochambeau forwarded the letter to Washington with one of his own, reminding Washington of "the importance of the Secret on this Letter [Rochambeau was unimpressed with Washington's ability to keep a secret, having seen so much information fall into Clinton's hands] and of the necessity we are under at the same time, to make our preparations in consequence." The Frenchman explained that he had advised de Grasse of their plans to march on New York and had provided him with intelligence regarding the troop strength in New York and the number of men Clinton had sent to Virginia. He had asked de Grasse to bring with him another five or six thousand troops.

Rochambeau had made another suggestion to de Grasse too, and now he confessed it to Washington. Despite what they had agreed to at Wethersfield, it had occurred to Rochambeau that, "by reason of the constant wind, it would be a great stroke [for de Grasse] to go to [Chesapeake Bay, in which] he can make great things against the naval force that will be there . . . ," after which he could sail to New York. The prevailing wind on America's eastern coast blows from southwest to northeast in the summer, so Rochambeau was right that the French fleet could easily detour to the Chesapeake on their way north.

Washington, of course, had made it more than clear that New York was their objective. Now Rochambeau had taken it upon himself to direct de Grasse to the Chesapeake first.

In fact, Rochambeau was pulling more strings behind Washington's back than the commander-in-chief realized. The French general has been rightly praised for his willingness to let Washington take the lead in military matters, and the two men generally got along. But Rochambeau could also be difficult. Many of his officers complained about the treatment they received from him, and Blanchard wrote, in an admitted fit of pique, "He mistrusts every one and always believes that he sees himself surrounded by rogues and idiots."

The French general clearly believed that Washington's single-minded focus on New York was a mistake. Washington was revered among the French officers in America, but Rochambeau might have looked on him as something of an amateur strategist. Rochambeau knew how long the British had had to dig in at New York, and he knew that no French fleet had yet been able to cross the bar into New York Harbor. He had his own ideas for the coming campaign, and events would prove him right.

In the meantime, while agreeing on the one hand with Washington's plan to attack New York, Rochambeau was writing privately to de Grasse with his other hand that an attack on Lord Cornwallis in the Chesapeake would be far more likely to succeed. The British would certainly know of Washington's plans to attack New York—spies would see to that if it were not obvious enough already—but they would not guess, with the season already advanced, that the army might move hundreds of miles south to strike in the Chesapeake. And the Chesapeake, unlike New York Harbor, would present no severe navigational challenges to de Grasse. In fact, though Rochambeau could not know it, Cornwallis would soon make the approach from sea easier by moving to the deepwater port of Yorktown.

Washington was happy to read of Rochambeau's request for an additional five or six thousand men. For some time, he had been obfuscating with Rochambeau regarding how many troops he might raise for the fighting in 1781, and now he admitted that he would probably be unable to assemble much of a force, at least not by the time de Grasse arrived off the coast. "You cannot," Washington wrote, "in my opinion, too strongly urge the necessity of bringing a *Body of Troops* with him." (Italicized words were written in cipher.)

The commander-in-chief was unhappy, however, to learn of Rochambeau's suggestion that de Grasse go to the Chesapeake. "Your Excellency will be pleased to recollect that *New York* was looked upon by us as the only practicable object under present circumstances," he reminded the count, though he admitted the possibility of finding other targets as well. Washington was afraid that de Grasse would get a mixed message, and he asked Rochambeau, if the frigate with his response to de Grasse had not yet sailed, to explain fully to the admiral that New York was their sole object.

Washington did offer an alternative suggestion for the Chesapeake. It occurred to him that the Comte de Barras's fleet was nearly equal in strength to Vice-Admiral Marriot Arbuthnot's and so could move to the Chesapeake and prevent any troops from sailing from there to New York and also stop any supplies from reaching Cornwallis. He assured Barras that it was simply an idea, not a move he would advise, "unacquainted as I am with naval affairs."

Barras was not terribly enthusiastic about Washington's idea. He agreed that it might be tried, but he would need four hundred men from the troops left in Newport to fill out his crews, and he could not be ready to sail until the middle of July. So the focus of the combined armies would be on Sir Henry Clinton's garrison in New York.

Spencer's Ordinary

After abandoning Point of Fork, the Baron de Steuben marched his men west along the southern shore of the Fluvanna River and then south and west to the Staunton River, about 60 miles away, all the while furiously sending out express letters "to 14 Counties on this side James River to call out every man that can possibly be armed."

Steuben was working in the dark. He had not had a letter from the Marquis de Lafayette in more than a week and did not know where the Frenchman was, what he was doing, or what he intended. And it had been almost two weeks since he had heard from Nathanael Greene, with whom he still believed he was going to rendezvous.

Since traveling south with Greene the previous year and finding himself waylaid in Virginia, Steuben had been trying to reach his original destination and join Greene's army, but that was not to be. On June 13, Lafayette wrote to Steuben from Mechum's Creek, north of Richmond on the Pamunkey River. Cornwallis was moving toward Richmond, and Anthony Wayne's Continentals had finally joined Lafayette's troops. "Our jonction with the Pennsylvanians is formed, and we Have Again got Betwen the Ennemy and our Stores," he wrote.

Lafayette wanted to bring all his disparate troops together. His army would still be no match for Cornwallis, but neither would it be a wholly insignificant force. "I Request, my dear Sir," he wrote to Steuben, "you will Immediately Return this Way and with the Continentals and Militia under your Command Hasten to form a jonction with us."

Lafayette wrote that unless Steuben had received orders from Greene directing him to march south (which he had not), he should plan on remaining in Virginia. "I Can assure you His [Greene's] desire is that we Should form a jonction." This was true. Greene now agreed that Steuben's men should remain with Lafayette.

Lafayette was still trying to guess Cornwallis's next move. If the earl crossed the James River, it would mean that he was heading back for the Carolinas, and in that case Lafayette requested of Steuben that "Every obstruction be given to them" until he and Wayne could arrive. Lafayette did not believe Cornwallis would do that, however, and happily for Steuben, he was correct.

It is hardly a surprise that Lafayette did not know what Cornwallis was planning, as Cornwallis did not, either. The best the Frenchman could do was to trail behind the British army, close enough to look interested in a battle but far enough away to make a battle unlikely. He wrote to the Chevalier de La Luzerne, "We make it seem we are pursuing him, and my riflemen, their faces smeared with charcoal, make the woods resound with their yells; I have made them an army of devils and have given them plenary absolution."

Lafayette kept his army about 20 miles from Cornwallis, staying between the British and Fredericksburg and moving when the enemy moved, hoping to give the impression of being more in command than he was. "[W]hen he moves from one place to another, I try to let my movements give his the appearance of a retreat. Would to God there were a way to give him the appearance of a defeat."

But that was not likely to happen. Cornwallis continued his slow movement east, which Lafayette was pleased to characterize as a retreat. Along the way, he scooped up any ordnance he found and wished to keep, destroying what he did not want along with thousands of hogsheads of tobacco. Lieutenant Colonels Simcoe and Tarleton maintained a rear guard, making sure that Lafayette did not swoop in unexpectedly.

On June 21, Cornwallis left Richmond and began a march for Williamsburg. Simcoe, with the Jaegers and the Queen's Rangers, was ordered to the rear to cover the army's movement and mask it from Lafayette, who was doing his best to threaten their right flank. Cornwallis camped at Bottoms Bridge on the Chickahominy that night, and on the twenty-second, he reached New Kent Courthouse.

The following afternoon, Simcoe and Captain Johann Ewald were summoned to Cornwallis's tent for new orders. That night, they were to move out from the main army in two detachments and head for the Chickahominy River. Cornwallis had learned of a foundry and boats in the river there, and he wanted those targets destroyed. Simcoe and Ewald were then to "round up all the slaughter cattle and drive them to the army, burn all the military and commercial storehouses, and then march to Williamsburg," where Cornwallis would arrive on the twenty-fifth. Tarleton would form the rear guard of Cornwallis's army and keep in contact with the detachments.

The two detachments moved out in the early hours of June 24, but according to Simcoe "found little or nothing to destroy on the Chickahominy." This was hardly surprising, since he and Ewald and been plundering that area for the past six months, first under Benedict Arnold, then Major General William Phillips, and now Cornwallis. They rested the remainder of the night and at first light headed out again.

With daylight, they had better luck. The two detachments followed roughly parallel routes about a half hour's march apart, finding ample stores to destroy. "We had rounded up many cattle, laid waste to various flour and tobacco storehouses, and burned several vessels in the river," Ewald wrote. That evening, they neared the bridge over the Diascund Creek, a branch of the Chickahominy, but militia had torn down the bridge and Simcoe's men were "much too fatigued with their march" to repair it that night.

An inspection of the bridge by the morning light of June 25 showed that it "had been carelessly destroyed." Using lumber from nearby demolished buildings, they soon had the bridge well-enough repaired that "the cattle as well as the cavalry and the ranger battalion crossed over it." Ewald's men formed the rear guard, with orders to burn the bridge after crossing it. Ewald was getting a bad feeling about being exposed in the countryside so far from the main army, and he was careful in his deployment. He sent his Jaegers across to cover the cavalry, the light infantry, and the grenadiers, then "set the bridge on fire with straw" and waited until it was completely burned before rejoining Simcoe.

The Americans were keeping a close eye on this activity. Anthony Wayne sent a hurried note to Lafayette saying that "Simcoe has also effected his escape" by repairing and then burning the Diascund bridge. But Wayne saw opportunity and advised Lafayette, "Colo. Butler will therefore Advance to the fork of the road leading to James Town & Williamsburg, as the only chance of falling in with this *Cattle Drove*, I shall advance to support him."

Lafayette was eager to strike a blow now that the chance presented itself. "I . . . much approve of your Endeavours to Relieve Clel. Simcoe of His Burthen," he wrote, and instructed Wayne to make an effort to stop Simcoe's marauding, draw Tarleton into an ambush, and harass Cornwallis's rear.

Simcoe was starting to share Ewald's unease and "felt his situation to be an anxious one." He knew that Lafayette and Wayne were out there somewhere, hanging on the rear of Cornwallis's army, ready "to take any little advantage which they could magnify in their newspapers." He had received no word from Cornwallis, and he and Ewald agreed that they could expect no help from the patrols Cornwallis sent out. The detachment was flapping in the breeze and hampered by the cattle they were driving along.

On the morning of June 26, they arrived at a tavern called Spencer's Ordinary, about 6 miles from Williamsburg at the intersection of the Williamsburg and Jamestown roads. While they waited for their drovers to bring up the cattle, Simcoe had the fences pulled down to open up a field of fire and deployed his infantry in a defensive line. The mounted troops were sent to a nearby farm to feed their horses.

Meanwhile, Wayne sent Butler's regiment forward to intercept the British before they could rejoin Cornwallis. Despite "a fatiguing march," the foot soldiers were unable to overtake Simcoe's fast-moving detachment, but fifty dragoons and fifty mounted infantry charged on ahead.

The morning was warm, promising another brutally hot day's march, when Ewald and his men arrived at the tavern and lay down on the grass for some much-needed sleep. "I had hardly closed my eyes," Ewald wrote, "when several shots were fired in front on the left." The Hessian leaped to his feet and was told that the rebels were shooting at the cattle drovers, but soon Simcoe arrived and told Ewald he could go back to sleep for the time being. Ewald did just that, only to be awakened again moments later by a more determined volley. He grabbed his horse, swung up into the saddle, and led his men toward the fighting.

The mounted American troops had surprised the British pickets, hit them hard, and driven them in. Soon after, some of Lafayette's riflemen arrived and "began a smart Action." Simcoe and Ewald's men rallied quickly, veterans that they were, and began to advance against the Americans, who had formed a line at a rail fence. "The enemy . . . ," Ewald wrote, "waited for us up to forty paces, fired a volley, killed two-thirds of the grenadiers, and withdrew from his position." Riflemen firing from cover were deadly, but the rifles were slow to reload, and the remaining German and British troops drove Butler's men back before they could inflict much more damage.

The fight at Spencer's Ordinary produced high casualties on both sides for so brief a skirmish. The British likely received the worst of it. Simcoe reportedly had three officers and thirty privates killed or wounded. Lafayette reported nine killed, fourteen wounded, and one prisoner, though Cornwallis later claimed that three American officers and twenty-eight privates had been made prisoner.

Simcoe and Ewald had driven off the attackers, but they still did not know where the rest of Lafayette's army lurked, and they guessed it was nearby. Leaving their wounded under a flag of truce at the tavern, they hurried off toward Williamsburg. They had marched less than 2 miles, however, when they ran into Cornwallis himself, who was rushing to the fight with the advance units of his army. Thus reinforced, Simcoe returned to Spencer's Ordinary to collect his wounded before resuming the slow march to Williamsburg.

"[W]e are threatened with a siege"

Soon after the Wethersfield conference, Washington wrote to Lafayette,

> Upon a full consideration of our affairs in every point of view - an attempt upon New York with its present Garrison . . . was deemed preferable to a Southern operation as we had not the Command of the Water. . . . The French Troops are to March this way as soon as certain circumstances will admit.

But it was not Lafayette who read these words first. The letter was intercepted on its way south (a circumstance that would not have surprised Rochambeau) and delivered to Sir Henry Clinton in New York, and it stirred the previously somnambulant general to action. Now he knew. Washington and the French were coming to New York.

Clinton had around ten thousand men fit for duty to defend the city, and he believed that Washington's Continental troops, the French, and militia units together "might form an army of 20,000 men." It was time to stop indulging Cornwallis in the South and think about protecting his own position.

It was by now clear to Clinton that he had made a mistake in allowing Cornwallis to correspond directly with George Germain, and he was frustrated by the fact that he received one letter from Cornwallis for every five or so he sent. On June 8, he wrote to his subordinate pointing out that, since Cornwallis was now much closer to New York than he had been, "it will be unnecessary for you to send your dispatches immediately to the Minister; you will therefore be so good as to send them to me in future." Physical proximity notwithstanding, communication was still problematic, and Cornwallis would not receive this letter for more than a month.

With it, Clinton enclosed copies of Washington's intercepted correspondence. "[B]y these your Lordship will see that we are threatened with a siege," he wrote. He reminded Cornwallis that the enemy he faced in Virginia consisted only of Lafayette's small corps; the Pennsylvania line, who had revolted twice; and a handful of militia. "Your Lordship can therefore certainly spare two thousand, and the sooner they come the better."

The commander-in-chief also pointed out that he still had no idea what Cornwallis intended to do. Had it been possible "for your Lordship to have let me know your views and intentions," he wrote, "I should not now be at a loss to judge of the force you might want for your operations."

Three days later, Clinton wrote again to Cornwallis, reminding the earl how many men had been dispatched to the South over the past six months and pointing out that the troops under Phillips alone "would be sufficient of itself to have carried on operations in any of the southern provinces of America." He reiterated that New York would soon be under siege and that Lafayette posed no real threat to the British army in Virginia.

By way of a command, he wrote, "I beg leave to recommend it to you . . ." that once regular operations were finished, Cornwallis should "take a defensive station, in any healthy situation you choose, (be it at Williamsburg or York-town)." Once Cornwallis had established a defensive post, Clinton wished him to send to New York two battalions of light infantry, the 43rd Regiment, the 76th or 80th Regiment, the two battalions of German troops from Anspach, Simcoe's Queen's Rangers, the remains of the 17th Light Dragoons, and whatever artillery could be spared. With his remaining men, Cornwallis could content himself with "desultory movements by water, for the purpose of annoying the enemy's communications."

Four days later, Clinton wrote again, having in the interim received Cornwallis's letter expressing his skepticism of an advance against Philadelphia. Since Cornwallis did not care to go to Pennsylvania, Clinton wrote, and since he was likely done with any operations he planned for Virginia, he should "immediately embark a part of the troops . . ." Clinton had requested.

Four days after that, on June 19, Clinton sent yet another letter to Cornwallis, this time pointing out that the French would soon be marching from Rhode Island to New York and that a superior French fleet might well be on its way. "In the hope that your Lordship will be able to

spare me three thousand men, I have sent two thousand tons of transports from hence," he wrote. He also requested that Cornwallis send the
twenty-four boats that Arnold had built in Portsmouth.

On June 25, Cornwallis's troops entered Williamsburg, the former
capital of Virginia, and occupied the town. Originally called Middle
Plantation, Williamsburg had been built on high ground on the Virginia
Peninsula midway between the York and James rivers. Its name change
had come upon its elevation to Virginia's capital in 1699, during the
reign of King William III. Fearing British attack, Thomas Jefferson (who
had become the state's second governor after Patrick Henry's 1775–1779
term) had moved the capital to Richmond in 1780. Subsequent events
had borne out Jefferson's fears, though Richmond had proved little
safer.

Cornwallis had been operating in Virginia more than a month, and
not once since May 24 had he written Clinton to let him know what he
was doing or planning. The earl, however, had a good sense for what
Clinton expected of him. The day after he arrived at Williamsburg, two
of Clinton's letters found him there, including the one of June 11
instructing him to take up a defensive post at Williamsburg or Yorktown.

Part of Clinton's plan for Virginia had always been the creation of a
naval base that could accommodate large ships of the line. Landlocked
Williamsburg seems an odd suggestion unless Clinton had become so
focused on having Cornwallis establish a post that could be defended by
the minimum number of troops that he no longer cared about a naval
base. According to Ewald, the marshy banks of Archer's Hope and
Queen creeks, between which Williamsburg was located, meant that the
town could only be approached over one of two bridges, making it "a
very good position for an army." As with so many places in the Virginia
tidewater, however, a successful defender of Williamsburg "must also be
master of the Chesapeake Bay, so that no one can land in its rear."
Phillips and Arnold's assault on the town two months before had demonstrated that clearly enough.

A few days after arriving in Williamsburg, Cornwallis rode out to investigate Yorktown as a possible base for his army. Ewald and three companies of rangers went ahead, driving off a party of militia they met on the
way and taking a post on the high ground around Yorktown. "The Americans who had several works at Gloucester on the left [north] bank of

the York River . . . ," he wrote, "saluted me with a number of heavy pieces, but did not injure me." It was Ewald's first chance to be shot at by American artillery while at Yorktown, but it would not be his last.

Later that morning, Cornwallis arrived, with Simcoe and his cavalry escorting him. Ewald felt that Yorktown would make an excellent defensive post, but he could see that Cornwallis felt differently. "It appeared to me that he did not like this place at all for such a purpose," he wrote. Cornwallis returned to Williamsburg, the Americans at Gloucester giving him the same salute they had given Ewald.

After this reconnaissance, Cornwallis finally wrote to Clinton with an account of everything that had taken place since his departure from Petersburg on May 24, including the raids on Charlottesville and Point of Fork and the subsequent march to Williamsburg. He reiterated his belief that "untill Virginia was to a degree subjected, we could not reduce North Carolina, or have any certain hold on the back Country of South Carolina." He also repeated his objections to going to Philadelphia.

Ewald had read Cornwallis's thoughts on Yorktown correctly. He was not impressed. "Upon viewing York," he told Clinton, "I was clearly of the opinion, that it far exceeds our power, consistent with your plans, to make safe defensive posts there & at Gloucester, both of which would be necessary for the protection of Shipping."

Responding to Clinton's request for troops, Cornwallis assured his commander-in-chief that once he crossed the James River to Portsmouth and reconnoitered that town as a possible defensive post, he would embark all the men the available transports could carry. He was not so willing, however, to fester away in Virginia carrying on "desultory" raids on rebel storehouses and disrupting the enemy's communications. Cornwallis claimed to have come to America "with no other view, than to endeavour to be usefull to my Country," which he did not feel he could do "in a defensive situation here." Lord Rawdon, still in command in the Carolinas, was in poor health and planning a return to England. That being the case, Cornwallis suggested yet another change of plans, writing, "I am willing to repair to Charlestown if you approve it."

Years later, Clinton would write a footnote to this offer: "[A]fter doing all the mischief he could, the good Earl is *willing* to leave me the responsibility."

CHAPTER *19* *The Battle of Green Springs*

With Lord Cornwallis's army in Williamsburg, the Marquis de Lafayette remained about 20 miles away, watching his lordship and begging anyone who might help for men and supplies. Desertion once again became a problem, particularly among the local militia, and the surrounding wooded countryside made it hard to prevent. "They Have no Reason to Complain," Lafayette wrote to Virginia's governor. "[T]hey Cannot Even Contrive Any, But Say they were only Engaged for Six weeks and the Harvest Time Recalls them Home."

It was certainly true that many of them had signed for short enlistments, an inherent problem with militia, and that as soon as their times were up, they would disappear. "You Might as well Stop the flood tide," Lafayette added, "as Stop Militia whose times are out." He was sure the governor would understand, because the governor was no longer Thomas Jefferson. The British raids through Virginia, the state's inability to mount an effective defense against them, and Jefferson's own ignominious though necessary flight from Monticello and Tarleton's dragoons had so damaged his reputation that he had declined to stand for a second term. Virginia had turned to General Thomas Nelson, founder of the Virginia militia and a signer of the Declaration of Independence, as its new governor.

Lafayette continued his pretense of taking the offensive. He never kept his army camped together but rather spread them over several camps to make their numbers look greater. He always maintained an appearance of wanting to fight, and, as he had demonstrated at Spencer's Ordinary, he was always ready to take advantage of any opportunity that presented itself. And Cornwallis knew it.

On July 4, 1781, the fifth anniversary of the signing of the Declaration of Independence, Cornwallis marched his army out of Williamsburg and 5 miles south to Jamestown, on James Island, from which he intended to cross the James River to Cobham on the south side and then march for Portsmouth. That evening, Lieutenant Colonel John Simcoe and the Queen's Rangers crossed the river along with Captain Johann Ewald and his Hessians, setting up posts on high ground to cover the crossing of the main army. As a result, those units missed one of the hardest fights in the six-month Virginia campaign.

After months of long patrols and sharp fighting, Simcoe and Ewald had become close. "I must say . . . that [Simcoe] is truly my friend," Ewald wrote in his journal, "that he strives to make me happy." While they were camped out at Cobham, Simcoe offered Ewald a position as major in the Queen's Rangers, an offer that tempted and flattered the German, though he did not really consider accepting it. "I am a Hessian, body and soul," he explained, "and it seems to me that I could not be happy outside this splendid corps in which I serve."

The next day, Cornwallis sent the wagons over, an operation that took all the daylight hours. The James River was 3 miles wide at that point, but happily for Cornwallis he had officers and seamen of the Royal Navy at his disposal. On July 6, he sent across the bat horses and the rest of the baggage, intending to move the remainder of the army across on the seventh. Meanwhile, Lieutenant Colonel Banastre Tarleton's dragoons made wide sweeps around the approaches to Jamestown, beating up various elements of Lafayette's army and then falling back toward the main army.

As baggage was moving across the wide, brown reaches of the river, foraging parties reported that enemy troops were approaching the lines. Tarleton gave "money and encouraging promises to a negroe and a dragoon, to communicate false intelligence, under the appearance of deserters." These two were supposed to inform the Americans that the bulk of the British army had already crossed and only a rear guard remained on the Jamestown shore. It was an invitation to attack.

It is unclear whether Tarleton's disinformation campaign had any effect, but the Americans were definitely probing the British lines, hoping to make life difficult for Cornwallis. "The 6th I detached an advanced Corps, under General Wayne, with a view of reconnoitering the Enemy's situation," Lafayette later wrote to General Nathanael Greene. Wayne was commonly known as "Mad" Anthony. Though various explanations exist for his sobriquet, its origin was probably his aggressive leadership style, a style he demonstrated once again in his push toward Cornwallis's camp.

As Wayne and his troops and riflemen advanced, the British pickets began to fall back as if in retreat. The wooded, swampy countryside left only a narrow approach to James Island. Tarleton moved up his cavalry to keep the advancing Americans in the woods and prevent them from seeing the rest of the British force.

When word was carried to Cornwallis of the approach of Wayne's troops, the earl guessed at the Americans' mistake. "Concluding that the Enemy would not bring a considerable Force within our reach," he later wrote, "unless they supposed that nothing was left but a rear-guard, I took every means to convince them of my Weakness, & suffered my picquets to be insulted & driven back." Cornwallis ordered the other regiments to remain quiet in camp and not give away their presence.

All through the afternoon, the Americans and British continued to skirmish without really engaging. Reconnoitering the British lines, Lafayette could see that Cornwallis had sent off his baggage and "posted his army in an open-field, fortified by the shipping." It was nearly sunset when he rejoined Wayne, only to find that Wayne's eight hundred troops were formed up in front of the British camp and locked in a sharp fight.

Once the American artillery began to fire, Cornwallis knew it was time to hit them with the full weight of his army. "I then put the Troops under Arms & ordered the Army to advance in two Lines," he wrote. The right wing of the British advance met only militia, who put up little resistance before making a fast retreat. But the left wing, composed of the 43rd, 76th, and 80th Regiments, ran directly into Wayne's Pennsylvania line, including some light infantry and three field pieces. Despite being outnumbered, the Americans pushed forward into the fight.

Only 50 yards separated the British and American lines as they exchanged small-arms fire and grapeshot from field artillery. "The conflict on the quarter was severe and well contested," Tarleton wrote. "[O]n the left of the British, the action was for some time gallantly maintained by the continental infantry, under General Wayne." The muzzle flashes of muskets and cannon flamed brilliant in the fading light and lit up roiling gray clouds of smoke from within.

The two sides kept up their fierce exchange for some time, but night was coming on and Lafayette could see that the British lines were extending around the American flanks and threatening to turn them. He sent orders to Wayne to fall back half a mile to where two battalions of light infantry had been sent up in support. With his artillery horses dead, Wayne was forced to abandon his cannon to the enemy as he retreated to Green Springs.

Darkness prevented Cornwallis from pursuing Lafayette and Wayne, and the next day he resumed his laborious crossing of the James River. Tarleton was desperately eager to go after the Americans and argued at some length—in his memoirs, at least—that doing so would not have slowed the river crossing and might have altered the outcome of the war. But Cornwallis did not pursue, nor did he offer any explanation for not doing so. His focus, apparently, was on getting to Portsmouth and embarking the troops that Sir Henry Clinton had requested.

Portsmouth

Two days after the Battle of Green Springs, Cornwallis had his entire army on the south side of the James River, but he had not lost sight of his initial objective of depriving Greene of supplies. Having ravaged the territory between Portsmouth and Charlottesville, he now sent Tarleton and his legion, along with eighty mounted infantry, on a long raid west toward Prince Edward Courthouse and Bedford County, 150 miles away in the foothills of the Allegheny Mountains.

Tarleton and his men rode out on July 9 in the nearly unbearable midsummer heat of Virginia. They traveled hard in the early morning hours, rested during the midday heat, and pushed hard again as evening came on. Along the way, they skirmished with American militia, each scrap taking its toll on the mounted troops.

Cornwallis believed that Tarleton would find a considerable stockpile of stores at Prince Edward Courthouse waiting to go south, but Tarleton reported that "The intelligence which occasioned this march was exceedingly imperfect." He found few stores along the way, and whatever had been stockpiled at Prince Edward Courthouse had been sent to Greene a month before. He led his troops back by a different route, covering a total of 400 miles "attended with many unfavorable circumstances to the corps." The mission had been a failure. As Tarleton summed it up, "The stores destroyed, either in a public or private nature, were not in quantity or value equivalent to the damage sustained in the skirmishes on the route, and the loss of men and horses from the excessive heat of the climate."

His men returned to find the army's situation largely unchanged. Lafayette remained on the north side of the James River with no practical way to cross. The trap Cornwallis had sprung on him at Green Springs had given the young marquis a new respect for the earl, who was twice his age. He wrote to a friend,

> This devil Cornwallis is much wiser than the other generals with whom I have dealt. He inspires me with a sincere fear, and his name has greatly troubled my sleep. This campaign is a good school for me. God grant that the public does not pay for my lessons.

Lafayette was still trying to figure out where Cornwallis was going. Tarleton had been seen riding off in the direction of Petersburg, and when Lafayette put this together with the British army's move across the James, he concluded that Cornwallis must be heading back to the Carolinas. "I shall either follow his Lordship in case he proceeds with his whole force," he wrote, "or form a junction with Gen. Greene."

But his conclusion, though perfectly reasonable, was wrong. Cornwallis was still the only general officer on either side who considered Virginia more than a sideshow or a secondary consideration in the war. Rather than turn west to follow Tarleton or south toward the Carolinas, Cornwallis turned east and continued his slow march to Portsmouth. Lafayette began to revise his thinking as more intelligence came in. "The Ennemy appear to Be Going up towards Petersburg," he wrote to Governor Thomas Nelson. "However part of them is destined to Carolina and an other part to Newyork."

He was still convinced that Tarleton, at least, was heading to the Carolinas to reinforce Lord Rawdon, so he sent Wayne and the Pennsylvania line, along with a newly raised Virginia regiment, to reinforce Greene. They marched on July 13, the day before the first of Cornwallis's troops reached Portsmouth. Soon, reports reached Lafayette that Tarleton was heading back toward Portsmouth. He sent word to Wayne and to Daniel Morgan, who had come out of retirement, to be careful of Tarleton but also to see if the mounted British column might be surprised in the area of Petersburg. The Americans, however, were unable to intercept Tarleton's fast-moving column.

While Tarleton was moving fast, Cornwallis was plodding along at his languid pace. It took the main army more than five days to move the 30 miles from Cobham to Portsmouth, as the heat and insects of the tidewater summer drove them to distraction. Their clothes (which soldiers of the eighteenth century wore in abundance) were always soaked through with perspiration. The heat, Ewald recalled, was "often so intense that one can hardly breathe, especially after a terrible thunderstorm, when all the air seems to vanish." Often the thunderstorms brought violent rains that lasted half the night.

Insects were another hardship. For some time, the troops were plagued by biting flies, and when those disappeared they were replaced by a tiny insect Ewald could not identify but which left small, itchy boils. The afflicted men looked as if they had smallpox and bled from excessive scratching. Ewald felt that "we were the most tormented people in the world." He knew he wasn't in Hesse-Cassel anymore.

Correspondence

The correspondence and miscommunications between Sir Henry Clinton and Lord Cornwallis continued as the two men worked at cross-purposes while their plans grew increasingly convoluted. Thrown into the mix were months-old letters from George Germain, which began arriving at the same time. In July of 1781, this three-way communications debacle reached a crescendo.

The day he crossed the James River, Cornwallis wrote a lengthy letter to Clinton describing the Battle of Green Springs and his current situation. He assured Clinton that the troops the commander-in-chief had requested were on their way to Portsmouth, where they would board the transports for New York.

Cornwallis once again pointed out how useless it was, in his opinion, to maintain a small defensive post in Virginia, "which cannot have the smallest influence on the War in Carolina, & which only gives us some Acres of an unhealthy swamp, & is forever liable to become a prey to a foreign Enemy, with a temporary superiority at Sea." The sort of "desultory operations" that Clinton prescribed, and which Cornwallis had no interest in pursuing, could, Cornwallis felt, just as easily be launched from New York as from a post in the Chesapeake.

General Alexander Leslie, who had begun the fortification of Portsmouth the year before, was once again with Cornwallis's army, having been sent south by Clinton with the reinforcements needed to execute Sir Henry's "experiment" of taking and holding Philadelphia. That plan had gone nowhere, but Cornwallis told Clinton that he would not send Leslie to New York, "as he will be the properest person to command [in Virginia], in case you should approve of my returning to Charles-town."

On the same day that Cornwallis was writing that, Clinton was writing to Cornwallis. He reminded his subordinate of the need for "a naval station for large ships as well as small" and that Yorktown was an important point to hold for securing such a base. Admiral Thomas Graves (who had replaced Vice-Admiral Arbuthnot in command of the North American fleet only a few days before, on July 4) had made it clear that he needed a deepwater port in a warm place to overwinter his ships. If he could not get one in the Chesapeake, he would have to take his squadron to the West Indies. "I cannot but be concerned," Clinton wrote, "that Your Lordship should so suddenly lose site of it, pass the James River, and retire with your army to the sickly post of Portsmouth."

Portsmouth had been fortified as a base for frigates and small ships, but it was not good for much else. Captain de Tilly's failure to get his single man-of-war close enough to attack Benedict Arnold demonstrated how inaccessible the Elizabeth River was for large ships. What's more, both Major General William Phillips and Arnold had felt that it was a poor defensive position. For all these reasons, Clinton deemed Portsmouth a less-than-ideal base of operations. In fact, he felt it could be abandoned altogether once a better location was taken and fortified.

Clinton, of course, was missing the point. Cornwallis was not thinking of Portsmouth as a naval base. He was thinking of it as the place to embark the troops for New York and himself for Charleston. His object in coming to Virginia had been the conquest of that state for the purpose of cutting off aid to the Carolinas. If he could not carry out major operations against the enemy, he did not care to remain.

But now that Cornwallis was in Virginia, Clinton wanted him to stay, and he was finally becoming more forceful in his instructions. Cornwallis had told Clinton that "it far exceeds our power" to hold Yorktown, but Clinton was skeptical. Even if Cornwallis sent back to New York the three thousand troops Clinton had requested, he would still have four thousand on hand. "I confess I could not conceive you would require above four thousand in a station wherein General Arnold had represented to me (upon report of Colonel Simcoe) that two thousand would be amply sufficient."

Sir Henry was sure that Lafayette would immediately occupy Yorktown and fortify it once he heard that Cornwallis had crossed the James, which meant that the British would then have to go to the trouble of retaking it. "I therefore flatter myself, that even although your Lordship may have quitted York and detached troops to me, that you will have a sufficiency to re-occupy it, or that you will at least hold Old Point Comfort, if it is possible to do it without York."

As the correspondence made its way up and down the coast, carried aboard the vessels of the Royal Navy and by express messengers, Cornwallis continued to ready the embarkation of troops for New York. On July 14, Simcoe's Rangers along with the light infantry and the 43rd and 76th Regiments marched from Suffolk to Portsmouth. On the twentieth, with full packs on their backs and muskets in hand, they clambered aboard the ships and settled into the uncomfortable but mercifully short routine of life on board troop transports.

When Phillips and Arnold had begun fortifying Portsmouth half a year earlier, taking up where Leslie had earlier left off, they had never clearly understood what Clinton expected. This had been thanks to Clinton's opaque orders, and now Cornwallis, reading the old correspondence between Phillips and Clinton, was likewise confused. Phillips had interpreted the orders to mean that fortifying Portsmouth as a naval base was the chief priority, but Cornwallis, reading the same orders, did not divine from them that a naval base was a priority at all.

To be fair to Clinton, his former priority had been for the troops in Virginia to act in support of Cornwallis. Now that Cornwallis was in Virginia, the naval base became the priority. He and Graves, with whom he had been consulting on the point, were leaning toward Old Point Comfort (in present-day Newport News), the point of land on the northern side of the James River entrance and the terminus of the Virginia Peninsula between the York and James rivers. If that was fortified, they believed, it would command the approaches to Hampton Roads and render that a protected anchorage. Clinton also suggested fortifying Yorktown and Gloucester by way of protecting the back door to Old Point Comfort and denying the enemy access to the York River as well.

Clinton and Graves had other ideas brewing, too. With the three thousand men Cornwallis was sending north, they began to formulate plans for an attack on the military stores in Philadelphia, the French fleet in Newport, and the French artillery stored at Providence. After all, the troops would already be underway. It would simply be a matter of rendezvousing with them at sea and diverting them from New York. It was the type of bold plan that Clinton was good at formulating but for one reason or another never pulled off. This time, the reason came from London.

In the early weeks of July, Clinton finally received the scathing letter Lord George Germain, Secretary of State for American affairs, had written on May 2, the one in which Germain expressed his "great Mortification" that Clinton intended to withdraw troops from the Chesapeake. Germain wrote that his concern over Clinton's plans had forced him to ask the opinions of the king and his ministers, who, unsurprisingly, concurred with Germain's vision for prosecuting the war and condemned Clinton's.

The letter was a slap to Clinton's face and further confirmation that it was Cornwallis who had Germain's ear. And the insult Clinton read into the words was intended. "I expect little exertion from that quarter," Germain wrote to a confidant. "When we are to act with such a man as Clinton we must be cautious not to give him an opportunity of doing a rash action under the sanction of what he may call a positive order."

Germain's words, Clinton wrote, "seem to insinuate that there was a possibility of my doing more than I have done." He also took the letter to mean that he was not to demand any of Cornwallis's troops for the defense of New York. Years later, Clinton would write that Germain had actually forbidden him from removing a single man from Virginia until the state was conquered, even reproducing as evidence a passage from Germain's letter stating as much. But the passage Clinton reproduced does not appear in the original letter and was apparently fabricated by

Clinton to justify his actions. Be that as it may, the commander-in-chief no longer felt that he had the authority to order men away from the Chesapeake.

From that point forward, the correspondence shifted from politely formal to nasty. Anyone who questioned Clinton's motives or actions could expect a wildly prolix and acid response, and both Germain and Cornwallis were so punished. Clinton wrote a screed to Germain justifying his actions point by point and taking Germain to task for his relentless and unwarranted optimism, an attitude that could come only from someone with no firsthand knowledge of the war. "I can say little more to Your Lordship's sanguine hopes of the speedy reduction of the southern provinces," he wrote, "than to lament that the present state of the war does not altogether promise so flattering an event."

He also wrote to Cornwallis, whom he had just learned was moving toward Portsmouth. He suggested that Cornwallis might have "waited for a line from me . . . before you finally determined upon so serious and mortifying a move as the re-passing of the James river, and retiring with your army to Portsmouth."

He went on to counter each of Cornwallis's arguments regarding the pointlessness of a defensive post on the Chesapeake, making it clear that he intended for Cornwallis to hold the defensive post only until more positive operations could commence. He said that he did not approve of Cornwallis going to Charleston.

Finally, he made an about-face with regard to Cornwallis sending troops to New York. Whereas before he had been adamant that Cornwallis send him at least three thousand men, he now told his subordinate that he was "at full liberty to employ all the troops under your immediate command in the Chesapeake, if you are of opinion they may be wanted for the defense of the stations you shall think proper to occupy." That said, he still hoped his lordship would send any men he did not need to New York.

Germain did not insist that Clinton leave Cornwallis's army intact, as Clinton would later suggest, but Sir Henry took the letter to mean that he had better not demand any of Cornwallis's men. He sent a ship to intercept the transports coming from Portsmouth with orders for them to return to Virginia "and follow such further directions as you may receive from His Lordship."

To add to the mounting tension, in the second week of June, Cornwallis had finally received Clinton's letter of May 29 in which Sir Henry said that if he had known Cornwallis was moving toward Virginia, he would "certainly have endeavored to have stopped you." This, incredibly, was the first Cornwallis had heard of Clinton's disapproval of his leaving the Carolinas, and he was not happy about it. In his reply, Cornwallis repeated the reasons he had given for the move: that he could never have reached Rawdon in time to help him fight Greene; that the rivers were all but impassable; and that provisions were not to be had.

Clinton had suggested in the May 29 letter that Phillips was seriously threatened by American forces while waiting for Cornwallis—but this arrived on the heels of a series of letters in which Clinton had assured Cornwallis that Lafayette's army was no threat at all. Cornwallis wrote, "I cannot help observing, that in this instance your Excellency seems to think the force in Virginia more formidable than you have done on some other occasions."

Cornwallis also received at that time Clinton's more recent letters, and he did not care for the tone of those, either. They were, he wrote, "to me as unexpected as, I trust, they were undeserved." He took Clinton to task for issuing conflicting and vague orders, pointing out that he could not find in any of the correspondence with Phillips "any trace of the extreme earnestness that now appears to secure a harbor for ships of the line." Clinton expected him to send troops to New York *and* to fortify Williamsburg or Yorktown, but Cornwallis explained once again that he did not have enough men to do both.

Cornwallis argued, quite correctly, that he had crossed the James in order to get to Portsmouth and comply with Clinton's order to embark troops for New York as quickly as possible. "I must acknowledge," he wrote, "I was not prepared to receive, in the next dispatch from your Excellency, a severe censure for my conduct."

Despite the now-open animosity between the two men, Cornwallis continued to follow his commander-in-chief's instructions. He sent an engineer to Old Point Comfort to survey the land and sound the approaching channels. He visited the proposed site of the fortification himself, with the captains of the navy ships then at Portsmouth, to get their opinion on its suitability. The captains agreed unanimously that "a work on Point Comfort would neither command the entrance, nor secure his Majesty's ships at anchor in Hampton Road."

Cornwallis went on to write:

> This being the case, I shall in obedience to the spirit of your Excellency's orders, take measures with as much dispatch as possible, to seize and fortify York and Gloucester, being the only harbour in which we can hope to be able to give effectual protection to line of battle ships. I shall likewise use all the expedition in my power to evacuate Portsmouth and the posts belonging to it, but until that is accomplished it will be impossible for me to spare troops. For York and Gloucester, from their situation, command no country; and a superiority in the field will not only be necessary to enable us to draw forage and other supplies from the country, but likewise to carry on our works without interruption.

Lord Cornwallis was keeping his entire army in Virginia, and he was moving it to Yorktown.

CHAPTER *20* *The March on New York*

IT WAS LATE June before George Washington's troops were ready to march from New Windsor on the first leg of their move against Sir Henry Clinton. They would move out in three columns, the first of which, under the command of Major General Samuel Holden Parsons, got underway on June 21.

The British made no attempt to interfere as the army crossed to the east side of the Hudson and made their new camp at Peekskill, about 50 miles north of New York City. Like the French, the Americans had been sedentary for a long time, and many were delighted by the change. Surgeon James Thacher wrote, "A splendid world is now open to our view, all nature is in animation - the fields and meadows display the beauties of spring." Thacher enjoyed the "music of the feathered tribe," but, having been with the army since the beginning of the war, he felt that even birdsong "could not compare with that martial band, the drum and fife."

The men did not know where they were going or what they would be doing. According to Thacher, most thought "the object of the campaign is to besiege New York." Perhaps none of them thought Washington would even consider an assault on that fortified city. They were ordered to have four days' provisions cooked and to march with no baggage beyond a single blanket. "It is remarkable," the doctor recorded, "that we have so much as four days' provisions on hand."

A few days before Washington's men moved out from New Windsor, the Comte de Rochambeau's troops left Providence. They were organized into four regiments with staggered departures, the Bourbonnais leaving on June 18, the Deux-Ponts on the nineteenth, the Soissonnais on the twentieth, and the Saintonge on the twenty-first. The French had a long way to go, nearly 200 miles, to meet up with their allies. The summer heat was so brutal that the men had to break camp in the predawn hours to finish each day's march, generally around 18 miles, by noon.

"The roads are badly laid out and very difficult," wrote one French officer. Artillery and heavy wagons were hard to move over the steep and broken roads, and the baggage often showed up hours after the army had quit marching for the day.

The rough going was somewhat relieved by the lovely country through which they were marching, what one officer called "the beautiful, rich Connecticut valley." Wherever the French made their camps, the locals turned out for the sight, so unlike any they had seen before. "We furnished the music and they danced," Captain Louis-Alexandre Berthier wrote. "Every day there was a new party."

By June 28, although the French were still just west of Hartford, in the middle of Connecticut, Washington was ready to strike his first blow. Two detachments were sent against "the Enemys Posts at the No. end of Yk. [York, i.e., Manhattan] Island," Washington wrote in his diary. Both failed, and Washington decided to reevaluate his approach before trying anything else. He "did not care to fatigue the Troops any more . . . ," electing to let them rest with muskets ready while he reconnoitered the enemy's works.

On the fourth of July, Washington's troops marched south along the Hudson River to the town of Dobbs Ferry, where they marked out a camp for the French troops. This part of the country, ravaged by the fighting that had played back and forth along the Hudson in earlier years, was not nearly as charming as Connecticut. Half-burned Tory homes were scattered like corpses after a battle, untended grass growing several feet high around them.

The first of the French troops marched into camp on July 6. Though the French force had been in America nearly a year, this was the first time that most of Washington's troops had seen them, and they were impressed. One Connecticut soldier wrote that the French were "as good locking soldiers as can be. They look much better than our lousey army who have Neither money nor close [clothes] God Bless the State of Connecticut you noes what I mean."

The French, however, were less impressed with their hosts. Claude Blanchard's opinion was typical: "The soldiers marched pretty well, but they handled their arms badly. There were some fine looking men; also many who were small and thin, and even some children twelve or thirteen years old. They have no uniforms and in general are badly clad."

A series of inspections and drills followed, and officers of each army invited their counterparts to dine. These congenial overtures led Thacher to speculate that this joint venture "must have a happy tendency to eradicate from the minds of the Americans their ancient prejudices against the French people." But despite the warmth between the two armies, there was a certain standoffishness as well, with each keeping pretty much to their own. Language, of course, was a barrier. Even among the officers, few Frenchmen spoke English and few Americans spoke French. Still, French fascination with America and American gratitude for French aid helped maintain good relations between the armies over the next four months of joint operations in the field. Things might have gone otherwise. Seventeen years before, the Americans and French had been fighting one another in a vicious frontier war, and many senior officers on both sides were veterans of that conflict.

Soon after the juncture of the two armies, Washington wrote to the Marquis de Lafayette in Virginia hinting at big things to come, specifically the promised arrival of the French fleet. "I shall shortly have occasion to communicate matters of very great importance to you," he wrote. He instructed Lafayette to establish a chain of express riders so that word might travel safely and quickly between them.

Lafayette, meanwhile, was pining for New York and headquarters. "Virginian Operations Being for the Present in a State of languor, I have more time to think of My Solitude," he complained to his commander-in-chief. From his headquarters at Malvern Hill, about 20 miles southeast of Richmond, he continued to watch Lord Charles Cornwallis in Portsmouth and to try to divine what he was up to. In Hampton Roads, thirty transport ships filled with British troops were swinging at their anchors with no apparent intention of going anywhere. "They Had Excellent winds and Yet they Are not Gone," Lafayette reported.

Cornwallis had spent more than two weeks in Portsmouth, pursuing his epistolary back-and-forth with Clinton and trying to decide his next move. Finally, on July 29, he loaded the 80th Regiment into boats, and he himself boarded the ship *Richmond*. The little fleet moved down the James River, past Old Point Comfort to the north and Willoughby's Point to the south. They then turned north into the mouth of the York River and stood on to Yorktown and Gloucester. High winds made the going treacherous, and it took them four days to cover that short distance, but at least they did not have Lafayette sniping at them the whole way.

The troops landed at Gloucester on August 1 and immediately set in to fortify the point. Over the next two weeks, Cornwallis moved most of his men by water from Portsmouth to Gloucester and Yorktown, where they went to work on the earthworks that would secure the port for the navy. By August 12, he could report to Clinton that "The works on the Gloucester side are in some forwardness, and I hope in a situation to resist a sudden attack." He assured Clinton that once the evacuation of Portsmouth had been completed, he would "send to New York every man that I can spare, consistent with the safety and subsistence of the force in this country."

In the end, the number of men he could send turned out to be none.

The West Indies Fleets

The previous year, in March of 1780, Admiral Thomas Graves in England had received instructions from the Lords Commissioners of the Admiralty "to proceed, with His Majesty's ships under your command, without a moment's Loss of time, to No. America, in order to join and re-enforce the squadron under the comand of Vice Admiral Arbuthnot." Graves was fifty-five years old, the son of an admiral by the same name. At sixteen, he had accompanied his father on an expedition against Cartagena. Two years later, he gained his lieutenancy, and at the age of thirty he was made post captain. Two years after that, while captain of a 20-gun sloop-of-war, he was court-martialed for avoiding battle with what he took to be a French seventy-four but what the court believed had been an Indiaman, a merchant vessel. Graves was found guilty of an "error of judgement," which was not a career-ending sentence. (His sentence was rendered on the same day as that of Admiral Byng, who was found guilty of negligence and shot, a definite career-ender.)

The thirty years that Graves had spent in naval service before the outbreak of the American Revolution was, like Rear-Admiral Sir Samuel Hood's, for the most part honorable and competent but not outstanding. Graves was certainly no fire-eater of the Admiral George Brydges Rodney mold, nor would he, like Hood, prove to be a skilled fleet commander, but he seemed to have functioned well enough as Vice-Admiral Marriot Arbuthnot's second.

As the campaigning season of 1781 opened, one question was foremost on everyone's mind, American, British, and French: Where was the Comte de Grasse and what would he do? It was pretty well agreed, both by those who had inside knowledge of the situation and those who did not, that de Grasse would be heading for the coast of America during the hurricane season in the West Indies. But where on the coast he would go, and when, were the crucial questions.

Clinton wrote to Rodney on the subject in late June. Sir Henry had enjoyed his brief respite from Arbuthnot during Rodney's appearance in New York the previous fall, and he certainly did not want the doddering old admiral in charge of the fleet if a powerful French squadron should arrive on his doorstep. Intercepted rebel correspondence strongly suggested that de Grasse would be sailing for New York during the hurricane season of August through October. "Let me hope, my dear Sir George," he wrote, "that, if de Grasse comes here or even detaches in great force (which authentic intelligence confirms he will), you will come here if possible in person."

On July 4, as Cornwallis was marching his men out of Williamsburg for Jamestown, Arbuthnot, to Clinton's undoubted delight, finally resigned his command. Rear-Admiral Robert Digby had been assigned to replace Arbuthnot, but the Admiralty had decided that Arbuthnot need not await Digby's arrival in New York to step down. Given Arbuthnot's many complaints of ill health and Clinton's frequent threats to quit if Arbuthnot was not replaced, the Lords Commissioners of the Admiralty acquiesced to the admiral's "desire to resign the Command of the Squadron of his Majesty's Ships in North America, to any officer immediately on the spot." Thomas Graves was the man on the spot.

The new naval chief in New York was already losing sleep over the French. Just a few days before Arbuthnot's resignation, Graves had written to Rodney with the latest intelligence from North America, some of which was obtained from George Washington's intercepted correspondence, copies of which Clinton sent with his letter. The correspondence "will shew you the apprehension of the considerable force, expected from the French Commander in Chief in the West Indies, in concert with whom M. de Barras seems to act."

The British squadron was weaker by one ship, the *Royal Oak* being then in Halifax, Nova Scotia, "heaving down"—that is, having her guns, stores, and masts removed and the ship itself rolled on its side between tides so that its bottom could be cleaned and repaired. With de Grasse likely to appear on the coast of North America, Graves and Clinton were looking to Rodney to provide naval support. "[T]he fate of this country," Graves warned Rodney, "must depend upon the early intelligence, and detachments which may be sent by you hither, upon the first movements of the enemy."

A few weeks later, Graves received word from London that a convoy of supplies—consisting of money, clothing, and military stores—was already underway from France for North America under the protection of just one ship of the line and two frigates. These were the supplies promised in the dispatches delivered to the Comte de Rochambeau by his son, who had crossed aboard the *Concorde*, and the note from London suggested that this was the most important convoy ever sent from the French to their allies and the only thing that would keep the war effort afloat.

Accordingly, on July 21, Graves "proceeded with the Squadron into Boston Bay, to be in the way of intercepting the Supplies from France." It was a dangerous time to be gone from New York, with de Grasse expected at any time and no one certain what the Comte de Barras in Newport would do. It was also a futile endeavor. "The intence fog which prevailed without intermission as we approached St. Georges Bank," Graves wrote, "deprived us of all possibility of seeing."

Clinton was not pleased by Graves's departure. He was still the only member of the British command who seemed to understand the existential threat a powerful French fleet posed to the army in North America. Writing to Lord George Germain, he said, "I must beg leave to repeat to your lordship that if the enemy remained only a few weeks superior at sea our insular and detached situation will become very critical." Despite his tendency to cry wolf, Clinton's assessment was spot on, as future events would prove.

Germain was aware of the threat, but he treated it with the same absurd optimism with which he seemed to view all military operations. When the campaigning season in the West Indies was over, he wrote to Clinton, "I have every reason to believe the French fleet will push for

North America and Sir George Rodney will certainly follow them to prevent them from giving you any interruption in your operations."

While the British command in New York worried about de Grasse and his fleet, Rodney and Hood were already tangling with them in the Caribbean. In February, as Rodney was still tallying up the take from St. Eustatius, reports arrived that a French squadron of about nine or ten ships of the line was at sea and apparently bound for the West Indies.

The reports were premature, given that de Grasse's fleet did not clear Brest until March 21, but they were credible—a smaller squadron did indeed depart France in February. Still, like a dragon perched on his treasure, Rodney was unwilling to leave St. Eustatius. "The Lares [domestic gods of the Romans] of St. Eustatius," Hood wrote to George Jackson, Second Secretary of the Admiralty, "were so bewitching as not to be withstood by flesh and bone." Instead, after a two-week delay, Rodney sent Hood to intercept the French. For a month and a half, Hood cruised the approaches to Fort Royal on Martinique, keeping an eye out for the squadron. Finally, on April 28, he sighted an enemy fleet, but, rather than the reported ten ships of the line, he counted twenty. It was not the smaller squadron that had been reported but de Grasse's fleet.

Though de Grasse was more powerful, he was apparently not interested in engaging, despite Hood's heaving to and practically inviting the French to attack. Instead, the two sides exchanged shots at long range. Later in the day, four of Hood's ships managed to get out ahead of their squadron and were mauled by twice their number from de Grasse's fleet. Two of the ships could not maintain station "from their leaks, occasioned by a number of shot under the water." Three had their lower masts badly damaged.

That was the closest the two fleets came to a real sea fight, and the next day Hood broke off the contact. Hood wrote, "I believe never was more powder and shot thrown away in one day before."

De Grasse would later claim that it was Hood who had avoided action by taking advantage of the superior speed of his coppered ships. Whatever the case, de Grasse quickly moved on to better things. On May 9, the French launched two simultaneous attacks, one under the command of de Grasse himself against the island of St. Lucia and one under Lieutenant Colonel M. Philibert de Blanchelande against Tobago. De Grasse's forces were repulsed and his attack failed, but Tobago fell to the French.

By the end of May, Rodney was at sea again, directing the actions of the fleet under his command. Thinking he might still save Tobago, he steered his ships for the island, only to find out en route that he was too late. On June 5, the two fleets closed within sight of one another between Granada and the Grenadines, but this time, with night coming on, it was Rodney who declined action, not wanting darkness to catch his fleet in the tricky interisland currents and navigation. Once again, de Grasse elected not to force a battle, and, on June 18, the French fleet anchored in Fort Royal, Martinique.

In the first week in July, a patrolling British frigate sighted a fleet from Fort Royal standing out to sea. From a captured British schooner, they learned that it was de Grasse's fleet escorting a homeward-bound convoy of nearly two hundred merchant vessels. Once again, the French fleet was on the move, and once again no one knew where they were bound.

On July 7, Rodney wrote to Arbuthnot, unaware of the recent change in command in New York, with a warning that de Grasse's fleet was underway. "As the enemy has at this time a fleet of twenty-eight sail of the line at Martinique," he wrote, "a part of which is reported to be destined for North America, I have dispatched His Majesty's sloop *Swallow* to acquaint you therewith." Rodney assured the admiral that he would keep a good eye on de Grasse and that the British fleet would be ready to counter whatever move the French might make. The French squadron, Rodney said, "will sail, I am informed, in a short time . . . ," but he did not know if they would stop first at Cap François (now known as Cap Haitien, on the northern coast of Haiti). Either way, he assured the admiral, "[Y]ou may depend on the squadron in America being reinforced should the enemy bend their force that way."

The *Swallow* made for New York but did not find Graves there. The senior captain on the station read the dispatches and sent the *Swallow* off to the Gulf of Maine to find Graves—who was then patrolling for the French convoy rumored for Boston—and deliver this important news. But the *Swallow*'s captain, Wills, was distracted by an American privateer brig of fourteen guns, which he captured not long after clearing New York. Postponing his mission so he could return to New York with his prize, he fell in with four more privateers, which forced the *Swallow* ashore on Long Island. Wills destroyed the dispatches so that they would not fall into rebel hands, and, as a result, they did not fall into Graves's hands, either.

Happily for Graves, who was still ignorant of the possible French appearance, de Grasse did not sail directly for America but rather made for Cap François. On July 16, the French fleet worked its way without mishap through the treacherous approaches, which were strewn with "the vestiges of several wrecked vessels," and came to anchor in the wide harbor.

The town itself was lovely, "the most agreeable town in the West Indies," wrote one visitor. "It is the Paris of the Islands." And riding at anchor there, having arrived a little more than a week before, was the frigate *Concorde* with the pilots de Grasse had requested and letters for the admiral from his many correspondents in the United States. As long as he had the biggest fleet in the Americas, Admiral de Grasse would never be lonely.

Cornwallis's army was approaching Portsmouth and the first of his troops were preparing to board transports for New York as the French men-of-war dropped their hooks in Cap François. In New York, Clinton was furthering his plans for an attack on Rhode Island and Philadelphia and writing Cornwallis to remind him of the need for a "proper harbor for line-of-battle ships." And in London, Germain, having again changed his opinion, was writing to Clinton expressing his and the king's "appro-bation of the plan you have adopted for the prosecuting the war." Germain assured Clinton that "The purpose of the enemy was long known here, and Sir George Rodney has been appraised of it and will certainly not lose sight of Monsieur de Grasse."

In New York, the armies of Washington and Rochambeau were taking the field in preparation for Washington's long-anticipated siege of New York. And in Cap François, de Grasse began plowing through his stack of correspondence. The letters were filled with news, intelligence, plans, and entreaties, often contradictory, but one message was consistent: his fleet was needed on the coast of America, desperately and soon.

The Admiral's Decision

There were letters from Rochambeau, Washington, and the Chevalier de La Luzerne, the French minister in Philadelphia. De Grasse must have read them with mixed emotions and more than a little confusion. For all the harmony between the French and American command, there did not seem to be a lot of agreement. What's more, things were looking rather bleak.

Rochambeau had written on May 28, one week after the Wethersfield conference and more than two weeks before his receipt of de Grasse's letter by the *Sagittaire*. Distressed as Washington was to learn in mid-June that Rochambeau was writing to de Grasse to suggest a diversion to the Chesapeake en route to New York, he would have been furious to learn that Rochambeau had first made that suggestion in the letter of May 28. "The enemy is making the most vigorous efforts in Virginia," he wrote, and went on to detail Cornwallis's movements up to that point and how he "ravages in small armed boats all the rivers of Virginia."

The count then assessed the state of Washington's army—"no more than 8500 regulars and 3000 militia for carrying on the campaign against New York." (Gloomy though that assessment was, the actual number was much lower.) He provided de Grasse with intelligence on the movement of the British fleet and Washington's thoughts on what could be done against New York.

"There are two points at which an offensive may be made against the enemy," Rochambeau concluded, "Chesapeake Bay and New York. The southwesterly winds and the state of distress in Virginia will probably make you prefer Chesapeake Bay, and it will be there where we think you may be able to render the greatest service." Just seven days earlier, he had agreed with Washington that New York would be the objective.

Five days before Rochambeau wrote those words, Washington, still at Wethersfield, had written a letter to Luzerne that he hoped the minister would pass along to de Grasse. After explaining that New York would be the focus of the coming campaign, he had reiterated all the objections raised at Wethersfield against making an attack on Cornwallis. "For this I have a stronger plea when I assure you," he wrote, "that General Rochambeau's opinion and wishes concur with mine and that it is at his instance principally I make you this address."

Latter-day access to Rochambeau's complete correspondence makes clear that the French general played a double game. Even while agreeing with Washington at Wethersfield that New York should be their focus, he intended to engineer events toward the Chesapeake. The comte felt compelled to follow Washington, but not blindly, and he would sacrifice French lives for the American cause, but not foolishly. If

Washington's army fell apart, Rochambeau's orders were to preserve his own force and move it to the West Indies.

Whatever one thinks of Rochambeau's duplicity toward his ally, it is clear through the crystal lens of hindsight that his strategic understanding was sound. British resources were concentrating in the Chesapeake. Cornwallis was vulnerable from land and sea in ways that Clinton, given the difficult bar at Sandy Hook and the massive defenses built up in New York over nearly five years, was not. Cornwallis's army was no longer the insignificant sixteen-hundred-man force with which he had marched into Virginia. The juncture with Major General William Phillips and Brigadier General Benedict Arnold's men and the reinforcements sent from Clinton under General Alexander Leslie had given Cornwallis around seven thousand troops, only three thousand less than Clinton retained in New York. The loss of that army would be a significant blow to the British.

The idea of attacking Cornwallis was not without flaws, starting with the possibility that his army would not even be there when de Grasse arrived. The Marquis de Lafayette seemed certain that Cornwallis was abandoning the Chesapeake and had communicated as much to Washington. Nor could Lafayette hold Cornwallis at Yorktown until the fleet arrived. His army was so outnumbered and outclassed that Cornwallis could brush him aside and head back to the Carolinas anytime he chose. But those possibilities notwithstanding, Rochambeau felt that the Chesapeake was the best place to strike, and he was not reticent about persuading de Grasse to his way of thinking.

On June 6, still one week prior to receiving de Grasse's letter from the *Sagittaire*, Rochambeau wrote the admiral again with a new wrinkle. The French army had money enough to last only through August 20. More was coming on the convoy announced by Rochambeau's son, but even that would extend the army's solvency only another two months. Rochambeau asked de Grasse to use "the influence of his credit" to borrow "up to the amount of 1,200,000 livres in specie."

The letters de Grasse read on July 16 had been written over the course of months as events in America unfolded, but the effect of reading one right after another must have thrown the issues into dramatic relief for the admiral. Luzerne had also written, and he, too, emphasized that the

Chesapeake was their most promising theater for successful operations. The last letter from Rochambeau was the bleakest yet:

> I must not conceal from you, Monsieur, that the Americans are at the end of their resources, that Washington will not have half of the troops he reckoned to have, and that I believe, though he is silent on that, that at present he does not have 6000 men; that M. de La Fayette does not have 1000 regulars with militia to defend Virginia.

Rochambeau urged de Grasse to bring as many troops with him as he could: "4000 or 5000 men will not be too many."

Before sending that letter, Rochambeau had read Washington's letter to de Grasse, in which Washington made clear that their target was New York. "I yield, as is fitting, my opinion to his," Rochambeau wrote, though certainly that weak concurrence would not undo all his forgoing arguments in favor of the Chesapeake.

De Grasse considered his options while the fleet resupplied itself and mended the various wounds inflicted by battle and the sea. On the morning of July 23, his entire squadron was threatened by an unfortunate accident aboard the 74-gun *Intrepide*. All French naval vessels on the American station served either brandy or taffia, a drink like brandy but stronger, for breakfast. (Wine was served with midday dinner and with supper.) That morning, the clerk of the *Intrepide* went below to draw taffia for the crew. When only a trickle came out of the barrel, he held his candle closer to the tap to see what was wrong. The flame jumped over to the liquor, and the cask burst into flames.

At 7:30 A.M., "the *Intrepide* made a signal of distress," wrote an officer of the fleet, "but no one could imagine what the matter was." No flames or smoke could be seen, but down below the men were frantically fighting the fire. At first, the clerk had tried to put it out himself; by the time he called for help, it was too late.

To prevent the fire from spreading through the fleet, the officers of the *Intrepide* ordered the anchor cable cut. The big ship drifted ashore and ran up on the mud, clear of the other vessels. On board, the frantic crew began to throw barrels of gunpowder over the side for fear of the explosion that would otherwise be inevitable when the fire reached the magazine. The cannons had been left loaded, as was likely the practice, and now "The gun carriages were broken so as to point the cannons up." In that way, when the powder cooked off and the guns fired, the shot would, with luck, fly harmlessly skyward.

As the men of the seventy-four flung everything they could reach over the side, the boats of the other men-of-war and the merchant ships in the harbor swarmed around, fishing things out of the water or towing them away. With no flames showing outside the hull, there seemed little danger, but down below the fire was spreading fast. Finally, someone shouted "Sauve qui peut!" (liberally translated, "Run for your lives!"), and the hundreds of men on the ship dropped what they were doing and fled to the boats.

Black, thick smoke roiled up from below, blotting out the sun, and flames poured out of the open gunports. One by one, the guns went off, until "the roadstead, the town, and the shore, received her whole broadside." Moments later, the fire reached the remaining powder, and the man-of-war's stern blew apart, blasting splinters in every direction, "wounding many and killing some." Just over four hours after the clerk had gone for the breakfast taffia, the massive ship of the line was gone.

Incredibly, two days later, word arrived that the 40-gun frigate *Inconstante*, sailing off the coast, had caught fire in exactly the same way. Without the aid of a nearby fleet, the disaster had been much worse. More than two hundred men had been killed.

These accidents were unwanted distractions for de Grasse, who continued to wrestle with his options. By the end of the month, he had made his decision. On July 28, he sent a letter back aboard the *Concorde* to Rochambeau saying he would embark troops on board "25 or 26 ships of war which will leave this place on August 3 and reach as soon as possible Chesapeake Bay, the place which seems to me to have been indicated by Rochambeau, Washington, Luzerne, and Barras as the surest to operate best as you propose."

De Grasse had more than Rochambeau's request to consider. The admiral was under orders to support France's other ally, Spain, with their operations in the region. Thus, the senior Spanish military commander in the Americas, Bernardo de Gálvez, essentially held veto power over de Grasse's decision to go to America. Gálvez was planning an attack on Florida but did not intend to launch it until the winter, so he was willing to let de Grasse do as he wished at least until the end of October.

About thirty-four hundred French troops under the command of the Marquis de Saint-Simon had been lent to Gálvez, and Gálvez now lent them to de Grasse on the condition that they be back by November. These were not the five or six thousand that Rochambeau and Washington had hoped for, but they were a significant force.

Gálvez sent his aide Francisco de Saavedra to Cap François to coordinate plans with de Grasse, and the two men laid out a strategy for mutual cooperation over the next nine months. The ideas agreed upon at this conference would have profound effects on the outcome of the American Revolution. A decision was made not to divide de Grasse's forces, but rather to fall with a full hammer blow on one target after another. Thus, the entire French fleet, not just a portion of it, would be sailing for the Chesapeake.

This was the one thing the British did not expect. The convoy of merchant ships bound back to France with the year's trade from the West Indies had sailed with de Grasse to Cap François and remained under his protection. British observers assumed that part of de Grasse's fleet would be held back to escort those ships to Europe and that another part would be retained in the West Indies. Thus, when Rodney sent a warning to Arbuthnot on August 13, he wrote, "The French fleet under Monsieur de Grasse, when they left the Grenades to collect their convoy, consisted of 26 sail of the line and two large ships armed en-flûte; and I imagine, at least 12 of those ships . . . will be in America." Had de Grasse taken only a dozen ships to America, as Rodney guessed, Graves's fleet would have been nearly equal in strength to the French and, thanks to copper bottoms, superior in speed and maneuverability.

Instead, de Grasse left only one 64-gun ship of the line to escort the convoy, which arrived safely in France months later. He left none of his fleet in the West Indies, where it was agreed "that a Spanish squadron should protect the coasts and commerce." Even without the addition of Barras's squadron, that decision would give de Grasse overwhelming strength off the American coast.

The admiral's last concern was the money Rochambeau had asked that he secure for maintaining the army. He approached local French merchants, who agreed to make a loan on two conditions. One was that de Grasse detach more men-of-war to escort the convoy to Europe, and the other was for collateral to secure the loan. De Grasse refused the first request, as he did not want to weaken the force he would send to America, but he pledged his plantation on the island for collateral, as did the captain of the *Bourgogne*. The merchants accepted this counteroffer, probably hoping that the money would not be repaid, for the plantations were worth considerably more. But they were unable to raise the cash, so de Grasse appealed instead to a Spanish official in Cap François. The official wrote the Spanish governor in Havana, who was able to raise the sum in the course of a day through public and private funds. The women of Havana reportedly offered their diamonds for the cause. The frigate *Aigrette* was sent to collect the money.

On August 5, the order passed through the fleet to unmoor—that is, to come to a single anchor and prepare to get underway. Then, at 4:00 A.M. on August 6, the order came to loosen sail. One by one, the ponderous ships, twenty-six in all, hauled their anchors dripping from the warm Caribbean water and gathered way, working slowly out of the narrow channel through which they had entered the harbor almost three weeks before.

De Grasse did not head directly for America but instead sailed toward Cuba to collect *Aigrette* and her valuable cargo. The fleet picked its way through the Old Channel between Cuba and the Bahamas, what one officer called "the famous dreaded channel, where no French fleet had ever passed." That route would get them to the environs of Havana more quickly than the more easily navigated but longer route through the Yucatan Channel, and the diversion toward Cuba would help disguise their destination from the British. The fleet spent anxious days in the tricky passage, challenged by reefs and shifty winds.

Many of the French sailors hoped for shore leave in Havana, "the richest and strongest place in America," but that was not to be. On August 18, 9 miles off the coast of Cuba, the fleet hove to and the pilots who had guided them through the Old Channel were sent ashore. Two ships of the line that had not sailed with them from Cap François now joined them, raising the French strength to twenty-eight of the line. With *Aigrette* in company, they turned north toward the twin capes of the Chesapeake.

CHAPTER **21** *An Operation to the Southward*

THROUGH THE FIRST few weeks of July, the French and American troops remained in camp at Dobbs Ferry, north of New York, doing little more than get accustomed to one another. Admiral Graves sent frigates up the Hudson River past the encampment and as far as Tarrytown, causing consternation but resulting in nothing more than a long-range exchange of gunfire and the capture by the British of a boatload of French bread, fifty uniform coats, and some other supplies.

On July 13, George Washington sent a request to the Comte de Rochambeau for more than two thousand men and artillery for a march to King's Bridge, which spanned the Harlem River at the northern tip of Manhattan Island. At the same time, around two thousand Americans, "consisting of the most active and soldierly young men and officers," were also made ready to move out. These men, nearly four thousand in all, were "to cover and secure a reconnoitre of the Enemys Works on the No. end of York Island." A driving rain prevented them from marching on the fourteenth, and it was not until July 21 that they moved.

Meanwhile, Washington and Rochambeau decided to see what they were up against. On July 18, the two generals, along with a few of their senior officers and an escort of 150 dragoons, crossed the Hudson River to New Jersey, then rode along the western shore of the river observing Sir Henry Clinton's defenses across the water. What they saw was not encouraging.

A few days later, Rochambeau called on Washington "in the name of Count de Barras, for a definitive plan of the Campaign," as Washington recorded in his diary. Ostensibly, the questions posed by Rochambeau were designed to clarify the plan for the Comte de Barras and "make it known to the Compe de Grasse on his arrival in these seas." In actuality, however, the questions, which rehashed many of the issues supposedly settled at the Wethersfield conference, represented another attempt to persuade Washington to turn his attention to the Chesapeake.

"Let us suppose that the Count de Grasse does not look on it as practicable to force Sandy Hook," the first hypothetical read, "and that he does not bring with him any Land Troops." Rochambeau reminded Washington that such a scenario was likely, as "the Seamen look on Sandy Hook Bar as impossible to force," and the letters from the ministry in France made no mention of de Grasse's bringing more soldiers. With no additional troops, the French and American armies together would not be much larger than the British army defending New York. Did Washington then think "that it will be possible to undertake with success something against that place"?

And if not, the questions continued, "could not the operations be directed against Virginia, M^r De Grasse be sent to Chesapeake Bay . . ."? Still phrasing his suggestions as questions, Rochambeau laid out how troops could be marched to Head of Elk and transported by water to Virginia. "Would not we then be in a condition to undertake with success on Lord Cornwallis and force him to evacuate Virginia?" (It is interesting to note that even in this imagined scenario, Rochambeau does not envision actually capturing Cornwallis's army.)

Washington admitted in his answer that "It is next to impossible at this moment, circumstanced as we are, and laboring under uncertainties to fix a definitive plan for the Campaign." Any plan would have to depend on the situation at the time of the Comte de Grasse's arrival. He did allow that if the admiral could not get his ships over the bar in outer New York Harbor and did not bring troops, then "we ought to throw a sufficient garrison into West Point, leave some Continental Troops and Militia to cover the country contiguous to New York, and transport the remainder (both French and American) to Virginia."

He could hardly have answered otherwise, given how Rochambeau had posed the questions, but he nevertheless concluded that in the right circumstances, "New York and its dependencies should be our primary object." Again, he urged Barras to go to the Chesapeake to prevent Cornwallis from reinforcing Clinton.

Though still focused on New York, Washington began thinking more about Virginia. The reconnaissance of New York may have made it clearer to him that taking the city would be a formidable task, one that was perhaps beyond the means at his disposal. The day after receiving Rochambeau's questions, he wrote a letter to de Grasse that was to be delivered to the admiral upon his arrival on the American coast. After outlining the strengths and locations of American, French, and British forces, he warned de Grasse that "The American [army] is at this time but *small*, but expected to be *considerably augmented*. In this however we may be disappointed." Using the same language he had used with Rochambeau, he reiterated that New York was the primary object.

Toward the end of the letter, however, he wrote that "The second object, in case we should find our force and means incompetent to the first, is the relief of Virginia." The extent to which he was starting to lean in that direction was clear from his revelation to de Grasse that "preparations are making to facilitate such a movement." To that end, Washington had ordered the Marquis de Lafayette to establish magazines in Virginia, to increase the number of his mounted troops as much as possible, and to establish a safe and reliable express between his headquarters and New York. "But of this I hope there will be no occasion . . . ," Washington concluded.

A little more than a week later, Washington wrote to Lafayette addressing the young Frenchman's desire to return to New York. Washington seemed to take for granted that Cornwallis would be sending troops to Clinton or perhaps already had. Lafayette, Washington wrote, would likely be happy that he was in Virginia, "especially when I tell you, that, from the change of circumstances with which the removal of part of the Enemy's force from Virginia to New York will be attended, it is more than probable that we shall also intirely change our plan of operations." He hinted at the likelihood of a superior French fleet arriving on the coast but did not dare write anything too specific, given how many of his letters seemed to end up on Clinton's desk. He told Lafayette that he wished he could send "a confidential person to you to explain at large what I have so distantly hinted . . . ," but he did not know anyone apart from his own staff whom he trusted enough to send, and his staff were too busy to go.

On July 21, the four-thousand-man reconnaissance force moved down to Morrisania at the southern end of what is today the Bronx, where the Harlem River meets Long Island Sound, but the British had abandoned their posts there and retreated into New York. The American and French troops marched back toward King's Bridge, where they remained until the twenty-third, then returned to Dobbs Ferry, having accomplished nothing.

The British in New York were aware of their enemy's movements but did not feel particularly threatened. Before the French and Americans fell back from King's Bridge, Clinton rode out to the north end of Manhattan Island to observe their lines. He ordered a few cannon fired at the allied troops to flush them out, which "enabled him to form a good judgment of their numbers." His observations caused him little concern. After observing the French and Americans for a few hours and from several vantage points, "he returned to his house at the 4 mile stone to Dinner."

During the few skirmishes that the French and Americans fought with the British during this reconnaissance, the French troops got a better sense for what the Continental Line was made of. Baron Ludwig von Closen wrote in his diary, "I admire the American troops tremendously! It is incredible that soldiers composed of men of every age, even children of fifteen, of white and blacks, almost naked, unpaid and rather poorly fed, can march so well and withstand fire so steadfastly." The American army may have been more ragtag than ever, but years of campaigning had given them a steady professionalism that even a European soldier could respect. The Baron de Steuben, who was then in Charlottesville sick with exhaustion, deserved a good measure of credit for that transformation.

The allied troops remained in their camp north of Manhattan Island as preparations continued for a move against New York. More than two hundred boats had been built, repaired, or collected. Heavy ordnance and stores had been moved into position. All Washington lacked was sufficient men.

Immediately after the Wethersfield conference, the commander-in-chief had sent letters to the northern states asking that they enroll men in the army and forward them to camp. But after six years of fighting, war-weariness and apathy made recruiting nearly impossible even when the states tried hard, which they often did not. Of the sixty-two hundred men Washington had "pointedly and continually called for . . . ," only 176 had arrived from Connecticut and 80 from New York. To make matters worse, Clinton received a reinforcement of nearly three thousand German recruits around this time.

With so inadequate a force, Washington wrote in his diary, "I could scarce see a ground upon wch. to continue my preparations against New York . . . and therefore I turned my views more seriously (than I had before done) to an operation to the Southward." He began to inquire after the availability of transports to shift men and supplies to Virginia, and he ordered artillery chief Henry Knox to start thinking about how heavy guns might be moved south.

Washington was slowly turning his sights to a campaign in the Chesapeake, unaware that the decision had already been made for him. Then, on August 14, he received a letter from Barras in Newport that changed everything. Six days earlier, Barras reported, the well-traveled *Concorde* had arrived at Newport with the letter de Grasse had written at Cap François detailing his intended operations in the Chesapeake and his desire "to have every thing in the most perfect readiness to commence our operations in the moment of his arrival."

It is hard to imagine what Washington thought as he read Barras's letter. He understood immediately that he must give up, at least for the foreseeable future, his idea of moving against New York, a plan that had been central to his thinking for nearly three years. Fortunately, his thoughts had already been turning toward Virginia. He certainly appreciated how significant a blow to the British a defeat of Cornwallis would represent. He probably did not think it would end the war, as the taking of New York would certainly have done. Even Rochambeau, who had campaigned both overtly and covertly for a campaign in Virginia, was thinking only of driving Cornwallis from the state.

What's more, the entire operation hinged on French naval supremacy. For more than three years, Washington had wished for that, and time and again he had been disappointed. He certainly must have been buoyed by Barras's report that de Grasse would be coming "with between 25 and 29 Sail of the line and 3200 land Troops . . . ," but, at the same time, he likely harbored a healthy skepticism toward French projections and promises.

The scenario taking shape in the Chesapeake would be nearly identical—though on a larger scale—to that which had played out earlier in the year when Washington had hoped to trap Arnold in Virginia.

Arnold's force had had its back to the water, pinned in place by a swelling American army, with control of the sea the deciding factor. The French navy had let him down on that occasion, just as they had every time before that.

All these considerations must have played out in his mind as he considered shifting his and Rochambeau's armies, and the entire focus of the war, to the Chesapeake. But he did not hesitate to make his move.

Yorktown and Gloucester

In Virginia, Lord Cornwallis was still digging in, pushing his men twelve hours a day through killing heat to complete the works on both sides of the York River. "[W]e have bestowed our whole labour on the Gloucester Side," he wrote to Clinton in response to yet another request that troops be sent to New York, "but I do not think the Works there, (after great fatigue to the Troops) are at present or will be for some time to come, safe against a Coup de Main with less than one thousand men."

While Gloucester Point was being fortified, engineers began to lay out the defenses in Yorktown. Portsmouth was still being evacuated. Observing British movements from his headquarters at Malvern Hill and pondering the reports of spies and deserters, Lafayette had been struggling to comprehend Cornwallis's plans. Thinking at first that the British might be making a waterborne push up the York and Pamunkey rivers, Lafayette moved his troops to Newcastle on the Pamunkey, only to learn that the British had stopped at Yorktown. The Frenchman wrote to Anthony Wayne that when a general "is to Guess at Every Possible Whim of an Army that flies with the Wind and is not within the Reach of Spies or Reconnoiters He Must forcibly Walk in the dark."

One thing became clear to Lafayette, however, and that was how vulnerable Cornwallis had made himself. In a very timely letter to Washington, he wrote, "Should a french fleet Now Come in Hampton Road the British army would, I think, Be ours."

By the second week in August, it was clear that Cornwallis was going no farther than Yorktown. Lafayette had earlier apologized to Washington for the fluctuating intelligence he was sending north. By way of explanation, he wrote, "I am positive the British Councils Have also Been fluctuating."

Now he was able to report that "Lord Cornwallis is Entrenching at York and Gloucester. The Sooner we Disturb Him the Better." Lafayette had received Washington's cryptic letter hinting at the possibility of moving operations to Virginia. The Frenchman assured Washington that he understood and begged for more details.

Lafayette also reported that Cornwallis's army was sickly, which was the case. Lieutenant Colonel John Simcoe and his men were so sick that Simcoe wrote to Clinton asking that the Queen's Rangers be returned to New York, as a sea voyage might be the only thing that would get them well.

By August 22, Cornwallis reported that the defenses at Gloucester were well along and that Portsmouth had been completely evacuated. The work at Yorktown, however, was only just beginning, and in that climate "all the labour that the troops here will be capable of, without ruining their health, will be required at least for six weeks to put the intended works at this place in a tolerable state of defense." Cornwallis warned Clinton that he had only five heavy cannon and six hundred stand of spare arms. What's more, provisions were being consumed at an alarming rate by the troops, by a number of Loyalists who had sought refuge in the British camp, and by the many freed and escaped slaves he had hired on for the work.

By this time, Clinton had plenty of evidence that Washington might be heading south. The American and French troops had marched 18 miles north from Dobbs Ferry, crossed the Hudson at King's Ferry to the town of Stony Point, and then marched 40 miles south to camp near Chatham, New Jersey, 7 miles southeast of Morristown. Clinton wrote to Cornwallis warning him that Washington might be planning to "suspend his offensive operations against this post and to take a defensive station at the old post of Morristown, from whence he may detach to the southward." Having just received his reinforcement of German troops, Clinton requested that Cornwallis "keep with you all the troops you have there." He was even willing to send Cornwallis "such recruits, convalescents, etc. . . . which are all that I can at present spare."

Washington was now fully committed to the Chesapeake, but Clinton was not yet certain of that. He warned that the movement might be a feint and that Washington might move north again, which he "certainly will do if de Grasse arrives." Should de Grasse not show up in New York, Clinton offered to send more troops to reinforce Cornwallis. Not once in the letter, however, did he raise the possibility of de Grasse going to the Chesapeake.

By the third week in August, Lafayette had moved downriver from Newcastle to the fork where the Pamunkey and Mattaponi join to form the York, about 27 miles above Yorktown. It was then that he received a letter from Washington informing him that his previously moribund campaign was about to become the chief theater of action for the war. "Count de Grasse . . . ," Washington wrote, "was to leave St. Domingo the 3d. of this month with a Fleet of between 25 and 29 sail of the line, and a considerable Body of Land forces. His destination is immediately for the Chesapeak."

Washington instructed the Frenchman to position his troops to prevent Cornwallis from slipping away into the Carolinas. If Wayne's troops, who were preparing to march south and join Nathanael Greene, had not yet left (they had not) or had not gone too far, he was to stop them. Lafayette was not to call out a large body of militia for fear of raising Cornwallis's suspicions. Like any good hunter, Washington did not want to spook his prey.

Lafayette was just weeks shy of his twenty-fourth birthday when the responsibility for overseeing the most crucial part of the war was temporarily dumped in his lap. It would be a tricky job to hem in Cornwallis, whom he had come to respect and fear, without letting on what he was doing. He likely did not fully appreciate that Clinton's orders, more than any threat from his motley army, were responsible for Cornwallis having stayed put thus far.

On reading Washington's letter, Lafayette flew into action. He sent a letter to Governor Nelson requesting a call-up of six hundred militia, enough to help but not enough to alert the British. He called for all boats on the Roanoke to be destroyed so as to hinder any possible movement of the British army southward into North Carolina. He ordered Wayne to prepare to cross the James River at Westover, and he moved his own troops south toward Jamestown and James Island, which he thought might make a good spot to join the Pennsylvanians.

This, Lafayette understood, could well be the first scene of the final act of the six-year-old War for Independence. The young Frenchman could not end his letter to his beloved Washington on a businesslike note. "Adieu, My dear General," he wrote. "I Heartly thank You for Having ordered me to Remain in Virginia and to Your goodness to me I am owing the Most Beautifull prospect that I May Ever Behold."

After all the blood and suffering, after all the years in which it seemed impossible that the Americans could even hold an army together, much less defeat a powerful, well-trained, well-equipped enemy—and worse, an enemy with an overwhelming command of the sea—now, finally, all the stars were aligning, all the elements coalescing to make a final victory possible. It had not happened through any grand plan, any coordinated effort. Many factors, each operating independently of the others, had conspired to let things fall into place. If one wished to see the hand of Divine Providence in such a circumstance, a good case could be made. Provided, that is, the French fleet could take control of the seas.

As August drew to an end, all of Cornwallis's forces were in Yorktown and Gloucester. Lafayette's troops were leveling the defenses at Portsmouth that General Leslie, Brigadier General Arnold, and Major General Phillips had put such effort into constructing. The thirty ships of Cornwallis's squadron, mostly transports but also the 44-gun *Charon* and two frigates, were crowded together in the York River.

The defenses at Yorktown were laid out, but construction was just beginning by August 31, starting with a fort and battery that would command the river and give Clinton his protected anchorage. That morning, Cornwallis awoke to a sight that could not have pleased him. A French ship of the line and two frigates lay at anchor at the mouth of the York River, and with them was the armed vessel *Loyalist*, once part of Cornwallis's squadron but now a prize.

Cornwallis sent a lieutenant from the *Charon* with a squad of dragoons down to Old Point Comfort to see what was going on. Upon his return, the lieutenant reported to Cornwallis, and Cornwallis in turn wrote a terse note to Clinton: "[T]here are between 30 and 40 Sail within the Capes, mostly Ships of War, & some of them very large."

The Comte de Grasse had arrived.

"I immediately determined to proceed"

More than a month earlier, when de Grasse's fleet was coming to anchor at Cap François, Admiral George Brydges Rodney had still been in command of the British fleet in the West Indies. It was clear to Rodney that naval operations would be shifting to the coast of North America, but he was unsure whether he himself could be part of it. His health, which had never been great, had suffered considerably in the tropical climate. For some time, he vacillated between going to New York with the bulk of his fleet or returning to London.

Rear-Admiral Samuel Hood, who would take over if Rodney left, was driven to distraction by his superior's indecision. Hood had long been writing nasty letters about Rodney behind his commander's back. Now he wrote to George Jackson, Second Secretary of the Admiralty, "It is quite impossible from the unsteadiness of the Commander-in-Chief to know what he means three days together."

There was probably more on Rodney's mind than just his health. After months of sparring with de Grasse, he had nothing to show for it. Tobago had been lost, and he was already hearing repercussions about his actions at St. Eustatius. Some of the British merchants whose goods he had confiscated and sold as prizes of war had been engaged in practices that were unethical but not actually illegal, and now they wanted compensation for their losses. It would only get worse.

Against that backdrop, Rodney dearly would have liked to chalk up a major victory before sailing home, but in the end his poor health won out. On August 1, he sailed for England, leaving Sir Samuel Hood in command in the West Indies.

Hood was unsure where de Grasse was or what his next move would be, so he did not know with any certainty what he himself should do. On August 3, while still in the West Indies, he "spoke with an armed brig from New York with dispatches from Sir Henry Clinton and Rear-Admiral Graves addressed to Sir G. Rodney." Since Hood had supplanted Rodney, he took it upon himself to read the correspondence. Clinton's letter to Rodney was the one in which he asked the admiral to come in person to New York and enclosed intelligence suggesting that de Grasse was on his way.

The information from New York convinced Hood that de Grasse was, indeed, heading that way. After the armed brig had taken fresh water on board, he sent her back with word to Clinton that he would sail immediately for the coast of America. He would follow Rodney's original plan of going first to Cape Henry to see if the French were in the Chesapeake. "From thence I shall proceed to the Capes of Delaware;

and not seeing, or hearing anything of De Grasse, or any detachment of ships he might have sent upon this coast, shall then make the best of my way off Sandy Hook."

Hood took on board the 49th Regiment, whom he would deliver to Clinton, and, at first light on August 10, his heavy first- and second-rate ships of the line won their anchors, let fall their massive topsails, and stood out to sea with the steady easterly trade wind off their quarters. He had hoped to link up with four other ships of the line under the command of another of the admirals on the West Indies station, Rear-Admiral Francis Drake, a descendant, though indirectly, of the famous sixteenth-century circumnavigator. Drake had not returned from a scouting mission to Fort Royal, so Hood proceeded without the additional ships, but as his squadron was standing out to sea, Drake appeared and joined them. Hood's fleet—fourteen ships of the line, four frigates, one sloop, and a fireship—shaped a course for America.

Hood was off Cape Henry on August 25, with de Grasse six days behind and making for the same spot. Seeing no French squadron inside the bay, Hood headed north, his fleet lifted along by the prevailing southwesterly winds of the temperate-latitude summer. He found the Delaware Bay equally free of French ships, and on August 28, his squadron rounded up and dropped anchor on the seaward side of Sandy Hook. Hood, "foreseeing great delay and inconvenience might arise from going within the Hook," did not attempt to cross the bar. Getting in and out of New York Harbor was a tricky business for deep ships of the line, requiring the right combination of wind and tide. This, he knew, was not a time to get trapped in harbor.

Neither Admiral Graves nor General Clinton was in the city, Clinton having traveled to Long Island to discuss with Graves the plans they had been laying for an offensive against Newport. With most of Rochambeau's army gone from that town, and only a handful of French regulars and American militia protecting Newport Harbor, Barras's squadron made a tempting target, and they were considering how they might exploit it. For all of Clinton's former fears for the safety of New York, he did not seem overly worried now that the campaign by the combined French and American armies was underway. "[T]he enemy's menaces of attacking New York had not induced any very great apprehensions for my posts in that district," he later wrote.

Hood had his boat swayed over the side, went ashore, and located the two senior officers. Graves felt that Hood should move his ships into the harbor, but Hood, though junior to Graves, demurred. Instead, the aggressive Hood "humbly submitted the necessity which struck me very forcibly, of such of Rear Admiral Graves's squadron as were ready coming without the Bar immediately." Upon hearing Hood's report from the West Indies, Graves realized that he might indeed have to get to sea quickly, so he ordered his ships to join Hood's on the seaward side. As it happened, light winds held Graves's ships in the harbor for four days, a God-given *I told you so* for Hood.

As Clinton, Graves, and Hood continued their conference on Long Island, they received startling news—Barras had sailed with his entire squadron three days before. It is unclear why that news took three days to travel from Newport to New York, but that, coupled with Hood's warning that de Grasse was underway, spurred Graves to action. "I immediately determined to proceed with both squadrons in hopes to intercept one or both if possible," he reported to Philip Stephens, Secretary of the Admiralty.

On August 31, the last of Graves's ships crossed the bar. Hood's squadron, which had arrived from the Caribbean only three days before, heaved up their anchors, catted and fished them, and set sail to a moderate breeze from the west northwest. The 90-gun *Barfleur*, flagship of Sir Samuel Hood, made a salute to Graves's flagship, the 98-gun *London*, which returned the salute with thirteen guns. Their course, as recorded in the *London*'s log, was simply "South."

Rodney had sent two more ships of the line, the *Torbay* and *Prince William*, to Jamaica to escort a convoy, with positive orders to join Graves after their mission was completed. The commanding officer there, however, chose to keep the ships with him, and they did not arrive at New York until October 11. Even without those vessels, however, Graves was likely feeling confident as he made his way south. Barras had eight sail of the line, and Graves's fleet now consisted of a formidable nineteen, including the two three-deck flagships of ninety or more guns. What strength de Grasse might bring to bear Graves could not know, but he did not imagine it would be overwhelming.

The admiral had no idea what he was sailing into.

CHAPTER **22** *The Arrival of de Grasse*

THE FRENCH FLEET took twelve days to make the thousand-mile passage from Cuba to the Virginia capes. Their average speed of about 80 miles per day was pitiful given the northward lift of the Gulf Stream and the favorable prevailing winds. The Comte de Grasse claimed to have been "hindered by calms as much as one could be . . . ," but many of the French ships were not coppered, and the fleet could only sail as fast as the slowest vessel, which was slow indeed.

Despite their glacial progress, they managed to scoop up a number of British vessels along the way. This helped keep the fleet's approach a secret from Cornwallis, as those ships might otherwise have alerted the British in Virginia. On board one of the captured vessels was the ailing and terribly unlucky Francis, Lord Rawdon, who was on his way home to England to convalesce. The young nobleman, just twenty-six years old, had distinguished himself in the Battle of Bunker Hill at age twenty, had served as Sir Henry Clinton's aide-de-camp (before becoming one of many young British officers to fall out with Clinton), had seen action at the Battle of Monmouth, and had shown himself a brilliant tactician in his victory over Nathanael Greene's larger army at the Battle of Hobkirk's Hill just the previous April. Now he would have the chance to witness even more history unfold. Over the next month and a half, from the deck of a French man-of-war, he would see the English defeated by land and sea.

By August 29, the day after Rear-Admiral Samuel Hood's squadron anchored outside Sandy Hook, de Grasse's fleet was approaching the Virginia capes in light and variable winds, with men in the chains heaving the leads as they came into soundings. Tallow smeared on the bases of the leads picked up samples from the sea bottom, from which an experienced pilot could tell a great deal. "Lead showed fourteen fathoms," recorded the log of the *Citoyon*, "sand grey-yellow and fine, with pieces of shell."

The wind was dropping and the sunlight fading, and the pilots on board the deep-keeled men-of-war suggested that the fleet come to anchor. Thick hawsers rumbled out of hawsepipes as the massive best bower anchors of the ships of the line dropped into the "grey-yellow" sand of the seabed and the fleet came to rest with Cape Henry 6 leagues, or 18 miles, to the west.

A frigate was dispatched through the fleet with orders from de Grasse for the ships to be ready to weigh anchor at four o'clock the following morning. In the predawn hour, the hawsers were heaved aboard again, anchors were catted, and the fleet got underway for the final run between Cape Henry and Cape Charles and into the Chesapeake Bay.

The wind began to pick up, blowing brisk and fair out of the east southeast as the French ships stood into the Chesapeake and prepared to anchor in Lynnhaven Bay, tucked inside Cape Henry about 25 miles southeast of the York River mouth. De Grasse had divided his fleet into three squadrons, and now he ordered them to anchor in columns by squadron, with "the squadron commanders each at the head of their column." It was in this array that the startled lieutenant of the *Charon*, sent to Old Point Comfort, first saw the overwhelming naval force across the water.

No sooner had de Grasse's flagship, *Ville de Paris*, come to anchor than an aide-de-camp from the Marquis de Lafayette boarded with a letter to the admiral outlining the positions of the American and British troops. Lafayette suggested that de Grasse send ships up the James River to prevent the English from crossing and making their escape into the Carolinas. De Grasse agreed to do so, adding that the ships would also cover the landing of the Marquis de Saint-Simon and the thirty-four hundred men under his command. Additionally, de Grasse would send "three or four vessels up York River to force General Cornwallis to decide whether to hold the right or the left side of the river."

De Grasse was eager to move. "For several reasons the combined troops must then be ready to go into action immediately . . . ," he wrote to Lafayette. He was concerned that sending so many men and boats ashore would leave him in a poor position to fight Admiral Thomas

Graves if the combined British fleet should arrive. A swift stroke against the enemy would also prevent Lord Cornwallis from placing further obstacles in the way of the attackers and give him a healthy fear of his enemy. But primarily, de Grasse knew he could only stay until the middle of October; knowing how operations could drag out, he did not want to risk having to withdraw his troops midsiege.

Lafayette did not think an immediate assault was a good idea. The allied forces would be outnumbered even after being augmented by Saint-Simon's troops, particularly as Cornwallis had stripped the vessels in his squadron of sailors who were now helping to build the defenses at Yorktown. The marquis told George Washington that "unless I am greatly deceived their will be madness in attacking them now with our force." He was reasonably confident of beating Cornwallis if he sallied, but not while he was behind his works.

Before de Grasse could insist further, he received a letter written jointly by General Washington and the Comte de Rochambeau on August 17 outlining their plans "to shift the whole of the French Army and as large a detachment of the American as can be spared, to Chesapeak, to meet Your Excellency there." Thus reassured that the allied armies were on their way, the admiral was placated for the time being. He contented himself with deploying Saint-Simon's troops and waiting for the second shoe to drop on Cornwallis.

"I am distressed beyond expression"

That second shoe was dropping fast. As in the final act of a Shakespearean drama, all the players were assembling on stage. Lafayette and Cornwallis had been chasing one another around Virginia for months. De Grasse and Saint-Simon had arrived. Now Washington, Rochambeau, Graves, and Hood were on their way.

According to his diary, Washington made the decision to move his army and the entire focus of the war from New York to Virginia on August 14, the day he received word that de Grasse was bound for the Chesapeake. He had, however, been contemplating the idea for some time—perhaps since his July 18 reconnaissance of Clinton's defenses in New York—and the arguments for abandoning New York had been crystallizing in his mind with active prompting from Rochambeau. From his entry of August 14, it is clear how much thought he had already put into the relative merits of a northern or southern campaign:

> Matters having now come to a crisis and a decisive plan to be determined on, I was obliged, by the shortness of Count de Grasses' promised stay on the Coast, the apparent disinclination of their Naval Officers to force the harbour of New York and the feeble compliance of the States to my requisitions for Men, hitherto, and little prospect of greater exertions in the future, to give up all idea of attacking New York; and instead thereof to remove the French Troops and a detachment for the American Army to the Head of Elk to be transported to Virginia for the purpose of cooperating with the force from the West Indies against the Troops in that State.

He put aside his earlier objections to moving the army south—the impossibility of transporting troops by sea, the devastation the heat would wreak on troops on a long march—in light of the very real possibility of trapping Cornwallis's entire army at Yorktown.

On August 19, just five days after learning that de Grasse intended to sail to the Chesapeake, and with no certainty that he would actually do so, Washington watched the American and French troops begin their epic march for Virginia in a driving rain. Clinton may have had the upper hand in men, supplies, and naval superiority, but Washington possessed a decisiveness and a willingness to gamble that the British general could not touch, and it would cost Sir Henry the war.

As the French army was transported across the Hudson River at Stony Point, Washington made his headquarters 10 miles upriver at the house opposite West Point where Benedict Arnold and Major John André had plotted Arnold's treason. The initial troop movement was disguised as an advance toward Staten Island and the prelude to an attack on New York. Thirty cumbersome flatboats were mounted on carriages to give the impression of a pending amphibious assault. The French built ovens within sight of the city as an indication that their army would not be moving for a while.

The deception worked to the extent that Clinton was never certain, right through the end of August, whether Washington and Rochambeau were staying put or marching for the Chesapeake. Even the French and American troops had no idea what was in store. After crossing the Hudson and marching south along the river, Sergeant Joseph Plumb Martin recalled, "We then expected we were to attack New-York in that quarter, but after staying here a day or two, we again moved off and arrived at Trenton by rapid marches." Doctor James Thacher wrote, "Our situation reminds me of some theatrical exhibition, where the interest and expectations of the spectators are continually increased, and where curiosity is wrought to the highest point. Our destination has been for some time [a] matter of perplexing doubt and uncertainty."

That uncertainty was put to rest for the American and French soldiers when the army began filing off in three columns south through New Jersey. By the third week in August, all the British posts in New York had been left behind, and the troops were marching for Philadelphia. Thacher wrote, "wagons have been prepared to carry the soldiers' packs, that they may press forward with greater facility. Our destination can no longer be a secret. The British Army, under Lord Cornwallis, is unquestionably the object of our present expedition."

By the end of August, Washington and Rochambeau were in Philadelphia, having traveled ahead of the armies so that they might see to the massive logistical arrangements needed to move men, horses, supplies, and heavy siege artillery by land and sea to Yorktown. The march south, the part of the plan under Washington's immediate control, was proceeding smoothly. But the naval component of the plan, over which Washington had no control at all, was causing him considerable anxiety.

Reports from observers monitoring the waters off New York were coming in, and they were not what Washington wanted to hear. During the march south, the commander-in-chief received word that eighteen large men-of-war, thought to be Admiral Rodney's fleet, had arrived off Sandy Hook. Combined with the ships under Graves's command, that would make a British fleet of twenty-three ships of the line, a near match for de Grasse.

Those numbers were exaggerated, of course. Hood had arrived with fourteen ships of the line, and subsequent expresses reported the numbers more accurately. On September 1, an express from New York indicated that the combined fleets of Graves and Hood had disappeared over the horizon, heading south. Washington guessed, correctly, that they were hunting for Barras's squadron, but where the Comte de Barras was or what he was doing, Washington did not know.

Barras had been senior to de Grasse prior to the latter's promotion, and he did not care to serve under de Grasse now. Nor had de Grasse insisted that he do so, giving Barras the option of joining him in the Chesapeake or continuing to operate in the North Atlantic. To the mutual horror of Washington and Rochambeau, Barras had decided to carry out an attack on Newfoundland. Both generals wrote to suggest in no uncertain terms that this was no time to divide the French naval force on the American coast. Barras had relented grudgingly and, after enumerating the reasons that he should not do so, had agreed to sail for the Chesapeake with the siege artillery the French had stored at Providence and the troops remaining in Newport.

Now all the fleets—those of Graves, Hood, Barras, and de Grasse—were at sea, and how it all might play out was anyone's guess. If the combined British squadrons met Barras alone, they would likely take his squadron apart. But if Barras and de Grasse met up first and then encountered the combined British fleet, de Grasse's already superior numbers would be overwhelming. Or then again, if the British made it to the Chesapeake before any of the French ships did, the current effort to capture Cornwallis might be as great a failure as the earlier effort to capture Arnold had been.

Any of these scenarios was as likely as any other. There was palpable anxiety in Washington's words when he wrote to Lafayette from Philadelphia on September 2:

> But my dear Marquis, I am distressed beyond expression, to know what has become of the Count de Grasse, and for fear the English Fleet is occupying the Chesapeake (towards which my last accounts say they were steering) should frustrate all our flattering prospects in that quarter. I am not a little solicitous for the Count de Barras, who was to have sailed from Rhode Island on the 23d Ulto. & from whom I have heard nothing since that time. Of many contingencies we will hope for the most propitious events.

There were not many men to whom Washington would have written such a frank expression of his fears, but Lafayette was one of them. There was no turning back, and the commander-in-chief made it clear that, worries notwithstanding, he was letting his chips ride:

You See, how critically important the present Moment is. For my own part I am determined still to persist, with unremitting ardor my present Plan, unless some inevitable & insuperable obstacles are thrown in our way. Adieu my Dear Marquis! If you get any thing New from any Quarter, send it, I pray you, *on the Spur of Speed*; for I am all impatience & anxiety, at the same time, that I am With sentiments of the warmest affection & personal regard Your Most Obedt. Servt.

Washington would have been much more at ease, at least for the moment, if he could have known what was happening on the high seas and in the Chesapeake. Lafayette had written to him just the day before to say, "From the Bottom of My Heart I Congratulate You upon the Arrival of the french fleet." Lafayette's letter went on to provide a rundown of troop deployments around Yorktown and an inventory of wagons, supplies, and all the other issues relevant to the upcoming campaign. "It Appears Count de Grasse is in a Great Hurry to Return [to the West Indies]," he warned his commander-in-chief.

De Grasse also wrote to Washington at this time. Washington had asked the admiral in his letter of August 17 to send small vessels, transports, and frigates up the bay to Head of Elk so as to carry the combined armies down to Yorktown, but de Grasse replied that he had few small vessels, only his ships of the line, which were too big for the purpose, and four frigates that were needed to blockade the James River. The British were pretty well bottled up at Yorktown and Gloucester, however, and the French fleet was anchored inside Cape Henry, ready to meet any force coming to relieve Cornwallis, "whom I regard as blockaded until the arrival of Your Excellency."

The admiral explained to Washington that he had "resolved to attack York with the Marquis de la Fayette's troops and those which I brought in my ships," but on reading Washington's letter had decided instead to await the arrival of the generals and their men. He told Washington that, if needed, he could supply eighteen hundred men from the fleet as well as siege guns. These, he warned Washington, would be mounted on gun carriages designed for shipboard use, not field carriages, "but their bullets create quite as much disturbance as if they were mounted on gun carriages used on land." Understanding that Washington would be eager for word of the fleet's arrival, de Grasse gave the packet of correspondence to the captain of a cutter from his fleet with instructions to sail for Baltimore and see that the letters were delivered as quickly as possible to the commander-in-chief.

As word of the fleet traveled north, Washington traveled south. By September 5, the rear of the French army was arriving in Philadelphia, the American army having marched through that city three days before. The citizens of the capital, along with the Continental Congress, turned out to watch and cheer as the 2-mile-long train of tough, ragged American veterans marched past in the great cloud of dust raised by their battered shoes and bare feet. The people turned out to witness the French army as well, presenting a very different sight in their immaculate white uniforms, so elegant that one French aide-de-camp was mistaken for the general he served.

As the French rear proceeded through the city, Washington rode for Head of Elk to oversee the embarkation of the artillery on what few vessels his aides had managed to gather. As he passed through the town of Chester, an express rider hurried up, driving his horse hard. His instructions from Brigadier General Mordecai Gist in Baltimore had been to ride day and night to find the general. Now he handed over the packet of letters from the Chesapeake, within which was the news Washington wanted more than any other to hear.

"I have received with infinite satisfaction, My Dear Marquis, the information of the Arrival of the Count de Grasse," Washington wrote to Lafayette. What he did not know as he read those welcome words was that 250 miles south, even as he was breaking the seals on the letters, de Grasse's fleet was slipping their anchor cables and sheeting home topsails. On the long swells of the Atlantic Ocean, with not one American taking part, the fate of the nation was about to be decided.

Graves and de Grasse

On Saturday, September 1, Admiral Thomas Graves's squadron left Sandy Hook astern and headed southward in pursuit of the French; Barras or de Grasse, they did not know who they might find. The cryptic entry in the flagship *London*'s journal records the first day's sailing: "at 7 Bore away & M[ade] Sail Standing to y Suthward in all 19 Sail of y Line a fi[f]ty Gun Ship & Some Frigts with a Fier [Fire] Ship. Saw Strang Sails in Diferant Points of y Compass which we Chaced. But Did Not Com up with."

The fleet enjoyed an easy run down the coast in light to fresh breezes that veered from northeast to southwest and back again. The weather began to turn nasty as they approached the Virginia capes in the predawn hours of September 5, with heavy downpours and lightning illuminating the fleet in flashes of yellow. The men turned out from hammocks to swarm aloft in the dark and wet. Perched on footropes a hundred or more feet above the rolling deck, they sent down the topgallant yards and close-reefed the canvas topsails, which could weigh upwards of a ton when wet. It was, for them, the most unremarkable of jobs.

As the sun came up, the weather began to moderate. Topgallant yards and sails went up again as reefs were shaken out of topsails. "Mod[erate] & Clear at 6 AM," the *London*'s log reported. The fleet was plowing along at five or six knots in the fresh breeze, about as well as those heavy, bluff-bowed vessels could hope to do even with their coppered bottoms. In the forechannels, seamen stood strapped to the rigging and cast their conical leads into the ocean ahead, letting the marked lines run out to measure the depth. The leadsmen found consistent depths between 16 and 24 fathoms, comfortable for the big ships, and a fine white sand stuck to the tallow.

Their course was southwest, and Cape Henry, forming the southern boundary of the Chesapeake Bay entrance, lay a few hours' sailing time ahead when Graves ordered the signal made for the frigates *Richmond* and *Solebay* to come within hailing distance. Faster and much nimbler than a lumbering line-of-battle ship, frigates were the scouts, messengers, and mounted cavalry of an eighteenth-century fleet. When the *Richmond* and *Solebay* ranged alongside, Graves ordered them to "Look Into Chesepeek for y Enmiens Fleet."

This was familiar territory for Graves. He had sailed that way six months before looking for a French fleet, but then there had been only nine ships of the line in the British fleet, not nineteen, and the prize for which they had contended was Arnold's small division, not Cornwallis's army, the loss of which could influence the course of the war. And in March, of course, Graves had not been in command.

By nine thirty, the frigates had taken their look into the Chesapeake and were racing back to the fleet. "[A]bout 10 A.M.," Hood later wrote, "one of the look-out frigates made the signal for a fleet, and at eleven we plainly discovered twenty-four sail of French ships of the line and two frigates at anchor about Cape Henry." This was clearly not just Barras's squadron. The daunting sight of all those masts arrayed across the mouth of the Chesapeake told Graves that de Grasse had arrived. Though he never recorded as much, the admiral likely guessed that he was seeing the combined fleets of Barras and de Grasse. He would have been even less sanguine had he known that all those ships were de Grasse's squadron alone, and that Barras, whose ships he had passed after leaving New York without either fleet seeing the other, was still on his way.

But even if he had known that, it would have made no difference. His next move had been decided for him. He would have to fight. Signals were made "to Call In all Cruzers"—that is, for the outlying ships to close with the fleet—and for the ships to clear for action.

With the command "clear for action," the otherwise orderly operation of a man-of-war turned instantly into a frenzy of activity. A ship the size of *London* carried a full complement of more than seven hundred men, and every one of them had a job to do and a place to be during action. The temporary bulkheads that screened off the officers' quarters came down so that the gun decks were completely open fore and aft. Guns were made ready, and netting was rigged over the upper deck to catch shattered rigging falling from aloft. The ship's boys, now designated "powder monkeys," took up the long leather cylinders with which they would carry gunpowder cartridges to the guns. Sailors were issued sidearms to use in (or against) boarding parties, officers took command of their divisions, and the ships' captains, swords buckled on, uniforms in good order, stood on the windward side of their quarterdecks.

Graves's fleet had been sailing in a haphazard manner, but now it was time to fall into line of battle, that orderly line of ships that was the standard arrangement for a sea battle in the eighteenth century, as it had been for centuries before and would continue to be until the middle of the nineteenth century when rifled, exploding ordnance made wooden ships and broadsides obsolete. The log of Hood's flagship, *Barfleur*, records that sometime around eleven o'clock that morning, Graves made "the Sigl. for the Line ahead at two Cables length asunder"—that is, the fleet would form one line with two cable lengths, or about 480 yards, separating the stern of one ship from the end of the jibboom (an extension of the bowsprit) of the ship behind it. At those intervals, Graves's fleet stretched out over four and a half nautical miles.

The British fleet was arranged in three divisions, each led by one of the three admirals. Hood's division was in the van, or lead, with the 74-gun *Alfred* at the head of the line. Following was the sixty-four *Belliqueux*, the seventy-four *Invincible*, and then Hood's powerful three-decker, the 90-gun *Barfleur*. Two more seventy-fours completed the first division.

Admiral Thomas Graves commanded the second division as well as the fleet as a whole. His flagship was the *London*, a 98-gun second-rate and the largest ship in the British fleet. (A first-rate carried 100 to 120 guns.) Preceding *London* were the sixty-four *America*, the seventy-four *Resolution*, and the seventy-four *Bedford*, whose masts had been cut away the previous winter to save her from being driven ashore on Long Island.

The rear division, commanded by Sir Francis Drake, consisted of the two seventy-fours *Terrible* and *Ajax*, followed by Drake's flagship, the 70-gun *Princessa*, then the seventy-four *Alcide*, the sixty-four *Intrepid*, and the seventy-four *Shrewsbury*. In all, Graves had nineteen ships of the line and seven frigates mounting 1,408 guns and manned by 11,511 men. This was far more guns and men than Cornwallis had under his command, but not more than de Grasse.

The French saw the British fleet at about the same time the British saw the French. The Comte d'Éthy, captain of the 74-gun *Citoyon*, wrote in his journal, "The vessels that were moored farther ahead in the Bay Signaled 25 sails toward the East. The Admiral answered immediately to that signal. The look-outs on top of the masts counted 24 at 10:15." Like Graves, de Grasse had frigates patrolling his fleet's perimeter, and these, too, came racing into the bay with signal flags flying. Also like Graves, the French admiral had initially hoped this newly discovered fleet was Barras's squadron but quickly realized it was not.

The British had arrived at an awkward time. The French fleet was still in the process of disembarking Saint-Simon's thirty-four hundred men and artillery and replenishing their water supply. These demanding jobs required most of the boats of the fleet and around ninety officers and twelve hundred sailors, all of whom were currently engaged in that work. Worse, it was not the landsmen or ordinary seamen who had been given the job of manning the boats, but the most skilled and experienced hands.

De Grasse might have stayed where he was. It would have been a tricky job for Graves to attack the fleet at anchor, working in through the shallows around the mouth of the Chesapeake. But the French admiral had reason to believe that Barras was on his way, and if Barras stumbled into Graves's superior force, he might be annihilated before the anchored fleet could come to his aid, particularly if the tide or wind was against them.

These thoughts likely occurred to de Grasse, but he did not record any sort of debate, internal or otherwise, about his course of action. The admiral immediately gave the signal for the French fleet to prepare for battle and to get their men and boats back on board. D'Éthy ordered his ensign hoisted with a weft (tied in a long bundle), the signal for the boats to return, but to no avail. The fleet was at anchor in Lynnhaven Bay, while the boats were as much as 30 miles away up the James River. While some were close enough to see the signals and return, many were not, and many prime seamen would have to be left behind.

Nor was there time for the laborious task of raising the anchors, which could take an hour or more. "At half past eleven," wrote one officer, "orders were given to slip our cables, and leave the buoy." Rather than hauling the anchors up, the huge cables were allowed to slip overboard—or, in some cases, were cut away—with a buoy on the end to mark them for later retrieval. Admiral Hood noted that the French ships had "their topsail yards hoisted aloft as a signal for getting under sail."

Three ships of the line had worked their way up the York River to keep close tabs on Cornwallis, and de Grasse left them there, reducing to twenty-four the number of ships he could take into battle. One by one, the big men-of-war hoisted in their boats, buoyed and slipped their cables, and slowly gathered way under topsails and staysails. Around noon, the tide began to ebb, and with that lift and a light wind from the north northeast, the fleet stood out to sea. De Grasse signaled for the vessels to clear the bay in no particular order, just as fast as they could. The Battle of the Capes, perhaps the most significant naval battle in American history, was underway.

THE FRENCH FLEET getting underway from Lynnhaven Bay resembled chaos more than the orderly execution of a naval evolution. The entrance to the Chesapeake between Cape Henry to the south and Cape Charles to the north is more than 12 miles across, but the northern half of the opening is laced with shoals covered by 2 to 4 fathoms at low water, and eighteenth-century ships of war were liable to run aground in less than 4 fathoms (24 feet) of water. (HMS *Victory*, Lord Nelson's flagship at the Battle of Trafalgar in 1805, was built in 1765 and drew 28 feet 9 inches.) Charts of the time suggest that these waters were even less navigable two centuries ago than today. Then, as now, Middle Ground Shoal squatted like a loose stopper in the neck of a bottle just north of the halfway point between the capes. To further complicate navigation, Horseshoe Shoal extended 12 miles east southeast from the Hampton shore north of Old Point Comfort, bounding Lynnhaven Bay to the north and leaving a gap less than 2¼ miles wide between its eastern terminus and Cape Henry, effectively extending the confines of the James River almost to the Atlantic Ocean. These shoals to the north and northeast greatly limited the fleet's maneuvering room, and twenty-four cumbersome ships of the line needed a lot of room to maneuver.

The wind was light and shifting between northeast and east northeast, which forced the fleet to tack several times to clear Cape Henry. Only the ebb tide, running strong and all but sweeping the French fleet out of the bay, allowed the Comte de Grasse's ships to put to sea. For all the hurry and confusion, they were underway in remarkable time. As one observer wrote, "The maneuver was accomplished with such speed that, although 90 officers and 1,200 sailors were absent at the debarkation, nevertheless the fleet was arranged within three quarters of an hour."

The Comte d'Éthy, captain of the *Citoyon*, recorded that de Grasse's orders called for "the fleet to form into line of battle very quickly, even if not in their proper post." The *Citoyon* was part of the *arriére-garde*, or third division. Rather than slip her cable, the sailors managed to get the secondary anchor, the small bower, up before getting underway. The seventy-four gathered speed under topsails and staysails, standing east on a larboard (port) tack.

The *Citoyon*'s first officer was one of those who had been left behind, and the acting first officer was on the forecastle getting the cat tackle rigged to haul up the anchor the rest of the way. The big ship headed for sea, keeping close to the Cape Henry shore and clear of the other vessels gathering way but making right for an invisible, barely submerged sandbar.

Then the frigate *Aigrette*, which had tacked over to starboard and was standing north into the bay, passed close ahead of *Citoyon*'s bow. An officer on board the frigate shouted a warning to the *Citoyon*'s first officer that if the seventy-four did not alter course, she would run aground on Cape Henry. The first officer raced aft to warn d'Éthy, but the captain was not so sure and did not care to make a quick and unexpected change of course amid the crowd of ships. He called over to *Aigrette* to confirm and was told, he later recorded, that "her pilot was positive that if I continued this way, I would be on a sand bar."

Now fully convinced, d'Éthy gave the command for the men to go to stations to tack the ship. With little canvas spread and the wind light and fluky, the heavy *Citoyon* must have been agonizingly slow to turn from port to starboard tack. Finally, she settled onto her new course, sailing away from Cape Henry and ducking behind the stern of the massive *Ville de Paris*, de Grasse's flagship. At last, "being free of all the vessels sailing out of the bay," d'Éthy wrote, "I tacked again to port to get out too."

The hurried departure of the French fleet prevented the ships from assuming their proper line of battle. Indeed, they were hardly organized at all. "The fleet formed in very bad order," one participant wrote, "for, to tell the truth, there were only four vessels in line, the *Pluto*, the *Bourgogne*, the *Marseillais*, and the *Diadème*." These four vessels, all seventy-fours, were pretty much on their own, having cleared the capes much sooner than the rest. About a mile astern of them and to leeward were the seventy-fours *Réfléche* and *Caton*. Command of this first division fell to Admiral Louis Antoine de Bougainville in the 80-gun *Auguste*, which, like most of the fleet, cleared the capes well astern of the four lead ships.

De Grasse's 104-gun flagship, the first-rate *Ville de Paris*, sailed out between the seventy-fours *Destin* and *Victoire*, in the middle of the line, the proper place for the admiral in command. Just ahead of this cluster was the 80-gun *Languedoc*, carrying Admiral Baron de Monteil. With Bougainville commanding the *avante-garde* and de Grasse and Monteil in the center, or *corps de bataille*, there was no flag officer in command of the *arriére-garde*, so de Grasse signaled Monteil to fall back and take command there.

The *Citoyon* was feeling the absence of so many of the ship's company, as were all the other vessels in the French fleet. Accounts varied, but between twelve hundred and eighteen hundred sailors had been left ashore. "Missing from *Citoyon*," d'Éthy wrote, "counting absents, the dead, the sick, [were] about two hundred men and five officers," more than a third of the usual complement. D'Éthy ordered the acting first officer to see that the great guns were manned, but there were too few hands to work them all. So he ordered "all the marines as well as the officers, to replace those missing, but it was still not enough." Finally, he had to strip the crews from the smaller upper-deck guns and send most of the sail handlers below to man the ship's main batteries. It was an inauspicious beginning to what promised to be a major sea fight.

As the French emerged from the Chesapeake, they could see the English fleet about 12 miles to the northeast, a distance the converging fleets could close in about ninety minutes if the breeze continued light. The English were upwind, meaning, in the naval parlance of the day, that they held the weather gauge. Gliding toward the French with the wind almost directly from astern, the English were blessed with maximum maneuverability.

The French fleet, in contrast, was close-hauled with their larboard tacks aboard, meaning that they were sailing as close to the wind as they could with the wind coming over their left, or larboard, sides. With the wind wafting in from the northeast, the best the French could manage was a southeasterly heading. They could not get up to the British, but the British could run down on them. The choice of how to attack belonged to Admiral Graves.

Line of Battle

Unlike de Grasse, Graves had had ample time to get his ships into formation, and he had them under tight control. One French officer wrote, "the English were in the best possible order, bowsprit to stern, bearing down on us, and consequently to our windward." Another French officer observed that the British "made an immense number of signals to each other before engaging us." From the *London*'s gaff, mastheads, and yardarms, Graves flew signal flags calling for the rear division to make more sail; for the *Alfred* to lead more to starboard; for the rear division to make still more sail; for the *Centaur* to keep her station; for the lead ships to increase their lead; for the *Resolution, America,* and *Bedford* to get into their stations; and so on. Graves would maintain this stream of signals until nightfall put an end to it.

Around 12:45 P.M., as the first French vessels were clearing the capes, Graves decided to tighten his line of battle. The wind began to freshen, but the weather continued fair. *Royal Oak*'s journal recorded that "at 40 Minutes past 12 the Admiral m^d. the Sign^l to form the Line of Battle ahead at one Cables length asunder." Graves was cutting the distance between ships from two cable lengths to one, shortening his line from more than 4¼ to a little over 2¼ nautical miles.

By deploying haphazardly as he did, de Grasse had presented Graves with a rare opportunity to destroy his enemy's fleet piecemeal, pouncing on the lead French ships and crushing them with overwhelming force before the rest of de Grasse's fleet could get into the fight, but Graves failed to exploit the opening. Rear-Admiral Samuel Hood would later complain to his friend George Jackson, Second Secretary of the Admiralty, that the French "began to come out in a line of battle ahead, but by no means regular and connected, which afforded the British fleet a most glorious opening for making a close attack to manifest advantage, but it was not embraced."

Other contemporaries joined Hood in condemning the failure, and historians, too, have found fault with it. Graves's inclination to maintain a proper line of battle seems to have outweighed all other considerations. British admirals of the day operated under a set of fighting instructions issued by the Admiralty, which treated the line of battle as sacrosanct and discouraged individual initiative. It was likely the influence of these instructions combined with his own conservative outlook on naval tactics that led Graves to make the choices he did.

At one o'clock, still closing on Cape Henry and the French fleet, Graves hauled down the signal for line ahead and ran up the signal for the fleet to form an east-west line while maintaining the cable-length's separation between ships. The fleet slowly turned more westerly to sail roughly parallel with the French fleet, but in the opposite direction. Had the fleets been able to close with one another on their respective headings, the result would have been a classic line-of-battle evolution, the two lines passing one another on opposite tacks while exchanging broadsides, but they were still too far apart for this.

For forty-five minutes, Graves's fleet ran west by south (i.e., a little south of due west) as the admiral hoisted signal after signal and the French fleet cleared Cape Henry for the open sea. *Citoyon*, the lead ship in the last division of the French fleet, cleared Cape Henry at 1:45 with seven ships following astern of her. Only then could Graves see with certainty what he was up against. *London*'s log recorded, "At 2 found the Enemy's fleet to consist of 24 Ships of the Line and 2 frigates their Van bearing So. 3 miles standing to the Eastward with their Larboard Tacks on board. in a Line ahead."

The fine weather began to deteriorate, turning squally, and the ships shortened sail, taking the first reef in their topsails. By then, it was clear to Graves that he would not converge with the French line of battle on that tack. In his report to Secretary of the Admiralty Philip Stephens, he wrote, "when I found that our van was advanced as far as the shoal of the middle ground would admit of, I wore the fleet and brought them upon the same tack with the enemy, and nearly parallel with them." By this, Graves meant that he ordered the fleet to turn simultaneously from a westerly heading to an easterly heading, roughly the same course that the French were sailing.

All together, like dancers in an eighteenth-century minuet spread over miles of ocean, each of Graves's two- and three-decked ships turned in place, changing from a west-by-south heading to a course that was south of east and nearly parallel with the French line still slowly forming to leeward. Now the line of battle was reversed. Whereas before, Rear-Admiral Hood had commanded in the van, or the lead, and Sir Francis Drake the rear, now Drake had the van and Hood the rear, with Graves still maintaining the center. The seventy-four *Shrewsbury*, which had been last in line, now led, with the sixty-four *Intrepid* astern of her and the seventy-four *Alcide* next. Fourth in line was Drake's flagship, the *Princessa.*

Both fleets were now running east by south on a larboard tack, but the French were still struggling to form their line of battle. More ominously for de Grasse, the lead ships in the French van were "greatly extended beyond the centre and rear, and might have been attacked with the whole force of the British fleet." Graves still had a chance to exploit the lack of cohesion in the French line by swooping down on the four lead ships with his entire lead division and likely destroying them before the rest came up, then taking on each cluster of French vessels as they closed. Had he done so, at least by Hood's estimation, "several of the enemy's ships must have been inevitably demolished in half an hour's action, and there was a full hour and half to have engaged it before any of the rear could have come up."

Instead, soon after the English fleet came around to their easterly heading, Graves ordered his ships to heave to—effectively to stop in place by turning the sails set from the mainmast in such a way that they countered the drive of the other sails—"in Order to let the Center of the Enemy's Ships come abreast of us." Incredibly, Graves was giving the enemy a chance to get organized before attacking them. Sixteen ships back, fourth from the end of the line, Sir Samuel Hood aboard his flagship *Barfleur* must have torn his hair out upon hearing his signal officer relay that order.

Graves might have feared losing control of his line of battle if the fight devolved into a general melee. His actions seemed to be those of a man who valued complete control over opportunistic advantage, as indicated by the constant stream of signals flying from his flagship.

De Grasse was happy to use the time Graves provided to get his line of battle in order. He signaled for the fleet to make more sail and to tighten its line, and he ordered "all vessels to follow the movements of the lead vessels." But the French admiral, like Hood, could see the danger his van was standing into, getting so far ahead and to windward of the rest of the fleet. Around three o'clock, he ordered them to alter course to leeward, making their heading more southerly so as to angle away from the British line. This would give the rest of the fleet a greater opportunity to catch up, "in order that the entire fleet with combined power might be able to produce so much stronger fire."

The afternoon was wearing on, the hours of daylight dwindling, and still the guns of the two fleets were silent. The British fleet remained partially hove to, their speed checked to allow the French line to draw more nearly abreast. "So soon as I judged that our van would be able to operate," Graves wrote, "I made the signal [for the van] to bear away and approach, and soon after to engage the Enemy close." It was time for the maneuvering to end and the fighting to begin.

"[T]he action was begun at 4 o'clock"

Graves's flagship *London* kept her main topsail aback, the wind pressing the sail from the wrong side and slowing the ship to a crawl, as the admiral directed his fleet. At 3:17 P.M., he repeated his signal for the ships in the van—the *Shrewsbury, Intrepid,* and *Alcide*—to "keep to Starbd." The French fleet was sailing roughly in line ahead, to leeward and south of the British fleet. By ordering the lead ships to bear off to starboard, Graves was angling his line down on the enemy. But the fleet was still sailing in line ahead, arrayed along an imaginary line that extended from the lead ship through the flagship and back through Hood's rear division. In that line, they were approaching the French at an angle—the two fleets resembling a chevron of geese—which meant that the *Shrewsbury* would reach the enemy first and would find herself momentarily alone as the other ships followed behind, not an ideal way to go up against a superior fleet.

Around three thirty, Graves ordered "the Ships A Stern to Make more Sail." He had already narrowed the separation between ships from two cable lengths to one, then increased it back to two. Now he once again signaled for the ships to form up one cable length apart. The *London*'s log read, "the Enemys Ships advancing very Slow and evening approaching the Adml. judging this to be the Moment to attack made the Sigl. for the Ships to bear down and Engage their Opponents, filld. the Main Topsail & bore down to the Enemy."

Cape Charles

Wind shifting

Middle Ground Shoal (submerged)

Cape Henry

British Admiral Thomas Graves has his fleet in a tight line-of-battle formation and has been on a westerly heading for roughly an hour when, a little after 2:00 P.M., he judges that his ships are getting too close to Middle Ground Shoal. He signals his fleet to wear around to an easterly heading while, to the south, French Admiral Comte de Grasse's fleet is still struggling to get out of the bay and form a line of battle.

After heaving-to long enough to allow the French fleet to emerge from the bay, Graves orders his fleet to "bear away and approach" a little after three o'clock. In line-ahead formation, the British van (the leading ships) sail down on the French. Meanwhile, de Grasse orders his van ships to bear off on a more southerly course to allow the rearmost ships to get in line.

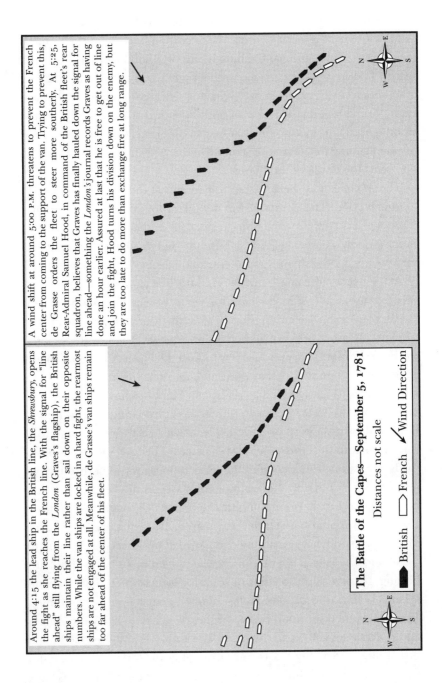

Around 4:15 the lead ship in the British line, the *Shrewsbury*, opens the fight as she reaches the French line. With the signal for "line ahead" still flying from the *London* (Graves's flagship), the British ships maintain their line rather than sail down on their opposite numbers. While the van ships are locked in a hard fight, the rearmost ships are not engaged at all. Meanwhile, de Grasse's van ships remain too far ahead of the center of his fleet.

A wind shift at around 5:00 P.M. threatens to prevent the French center from coming to the support of the van. Trying to prevent this, de Grasse orders the fleet to steer more southerly. At 5:25, Rear-Admiral Samuel Hood, in command of the British fleet's rear squadron, believes that Graves has finally hauled down the signal for line ahead—something the *London*'s journal records Graves as having done an hour earlier. Assured at last that he is free to get out of line and join the fight, Hood turns his division down on the enemy; but they are too late to do more than exchange fire at long range.

The Battle of the Capes—September 5, 1781

Distances not scale

◆ British ▢ French ↙ Wind Direction

With their topsails full and the black muzzles of their great guns run out from tiers of gunports, white water curling back from their cutwaters, massive bows rising and falling in the swells of the open ocean, the British fleet bore down at an oblique angle toward the French. Every man aboard every ship—more than thirty thousand men in all, more than the combined land forces of both sides in the American theater—stood tensed and waiting for that first smoldering slow match to touch off the priming in the first vent and fire the first shot in what would be known as the Battle of the Capes.

The *Montagu* was the first ship to fire, but at too great a distance to do much good. The *Royal Oak* was next. Her log recorded seeing "at 4 o'Clock the Signal for each Ship to steer for and engage his opponent in the Enemy's Line. . . . [A]t 12 Min's the Sigl. for Battle, immediately we were engaged with our Opponent, all the Fleet were soon in Action."

At the head of the line, *Shrewsbury* was the first to engage at close quarters, her broadside of more than thirty-seven 18- and 32-pounder guns roaring out as she drew alongside *Réfléche*, the fourth ship in the French van, just ahead of Bougainville's flagship *Auguste*. The two ships closed to about a musket shot apart—a few hundred feet, less than point-blank range for a 32-pounder—battering one another mercilessly. The captain of the *Réfléche* was killed, and Captain Mark Robinson of the *Shrewsbury* lost his leg. *Shrewsbury*'s first officer was killed along with twenty-five men, and forty-six were wounded. The *Shrewsbury*'s foremast and foreyard were both shot through in three places. The fore and main topsail yards were shot clean away, and the main topmast was shot through just above the cap, with only the straining topmast shrouds keeping the mass of rigging and spars from going by the board. "[T]otally disabled very early from keeping her station," the ship drifted, shattered and barely under command, her remaining company led by the second lieutenant.

Behind *Shrewsbury*, the 74-gun *Intrepid* ranged up into the fight, guns blazing, "exposed to two ships of superior force, which the noble and spirited behavior of Captain Molloy obliged to turn their sterns to him." *Intrepid* was then set upon by two of the French van, likely the *Auguste* and *Diadème*, and she paid the price. Her topsails were shredded in the broadsides, and all her masts and yards below the topgallants were shot through. Gaps in the smoke revealed that her fore topsail yard was hanging broken, and her main topmast had been shot through in two places and was threatening to come down. Her rudder, too, was severely damaged, as well as "five side timbers, each of them cut in two—the upper quarter-gallery shot to pieces, and the stern-gallery much damaged." The carpenter reported sixty-five shot holes in the starboard side, including "nineteen between wind and water," or near her waterline.

One by one, the British ships converged with the French line, their bows exposed to the enemy's broadsides as they approached. At 4:11, according to the *London*'s log, Graves "hauld down the Sigl. for the Line ahead that it might not interfere with the Sigl. to Engage close."

This hardly mattered for Drake's division in the van, who were getting into the fight as quickly as they could. But with the British fleet approaching the French at an angle, Hood's squadron in the rear was still beyond even extreme cannon range. And Hood believed, as he afterward wrote, that "the *London* had the signal for close action flying, as well as the signal for the line ahead." Others, too, would claim that Graves never hauled down the signal for line ahead.

It was nearly a repeat of Vice-Admiral Marriot Arbuthnot's debacle at the Battle of Cape Henry, the difference being that Arbuthnot had failed to replace the signal for line ahead with the signal for close action, whereas Graves apparently flew both at the same time. The result was the same—the rear division failed to engage in any effective way.

The question of what flags were flying during the Battle of the Capes would be fiercely debated for years to come. The *Royal Oak*, which was stationed just astern of the flagship, does not record in her log the signal for line ahead being hauled down, nor does the log of Hood's *Barfleur*. The *London*'s log, however, is quite specific about when the signal was down and when up. The day after the battle, Graves wrote a memorandum to his captains explaining, "When the signal for the line of battle ahead is out at the same time as the signal for battle, it is not to be understood that the latter signal shall be rendered ineffectual by too strict an adherence to the former." In other words, Graves explained—when it was too late—that he meant the signal for close action to take precedence over the signal for line ahead.

His captains had not seen it that way, and they knew from precedent that a commander left the line of battle at his own peril. If things went poorly, either the enemy or a subsequent court martial would likely end his career. Admiral Hood penned a scathing rebuttal, apparently for his own satisfaction, on the back of his copy of Graves's memorandum. Had the signal for line ahead been hauled down, or had the captains understood that the signal for close action took precedence, the ships would have turned out of line and fallen on their opposite numbers in de Grasse's disorderly grouping with one sudden hammer blow. With de Grasse's rear struggling to get into the fight, they might have inflicted real damage against an even number of vessels.

Instead, the British captains maintained their line ahead, approaching the French at an oblique angle, because it was their understanding that the line of battle was always to be maintained if that signal was flying. "Now, had the centre gone to the support of the van," Hood later complained to Jackson, "and the signal for the line been hauled down, or the commander-in-chief had set an example of close action, even with the signal for the line flying, the van of the enemy must have been cut to pieces," and the rest of the British line would have been brought into the fight.

It was an important point for Hood to make. His rear division did not participate in the battle, and it was later suggested that Hood had not tried as hard as he might to join the action. This was an ugly accusation, implying an unwillingness to support his commanding officer—or worse, though it was never overtly stated, cowardice.

Thanks to this confusion, Drake's division doled out and received the majority of the punishment. *Alcide*, Drake's flagship *Princessa*, *Ajax*, and *Terrible* each in turn took their place in the line. While *Shrewsbury* and *Intrepid* had taken a pounding, the French were also mauled, with Drake's ships nearly overwhelming Bougainville's. A French officer wrote, "The four ships in the [French] van found themselves, consequently, entirely cut off from the rest of the fleet, and constantly engaged with seven or eight vessels at close quarters."

Around that time, de Grasse, still trying to connect his van to the center, made the signal for the ships to turn more southerly and bear away even more. The lead ships did not comply, finding the order "impracticable, as they were fighting within gun-shot distance, and would have got a severe handling, had they presented the stern."

Diadème, sixth in the French line, was locked in battle with several vessels, including Drake's *Princessa*, which was firing from so close that the wadding from the *Princessa*'s guns kept flying aboard the French ship and setting her on fire. In short order, *Diadème* was so battered she could hold out no longer. Her crew prepared to board *Princessa* in hopes of carrying the flagship by fighting hand to hand on her deck, but *Princessa* pushed on ahead. *Diadème* had only four 36-pounders and nine 18-pounders left in her battery that were still serviceable, but these she turned on *Terrible*, which was joining the fight astern of *Ajax*.

Behind *Diadème* was the 80-gun *Saint-Esprit*, which had also engaged with *Princessa*, her captain, M. de Chabert, having been wounded in the exchange. Seeing how hard pressed *Diadème* was, Chabert "hoisted sail and was soon in her wake; then he opened a terrible fire, that the gentlemen of Albion could not stand, and had to haul their wind."

Princessa, too, took extensive damage in the exchange. "Main topmast shot thro' in three places Maintopsail Yard shot away 12 feet from the arm—a shot through the middle of the fore-mast 10 feet under the hounds—foretop gallant mast shot thro'." The list went on at length. It does not seem to have been the practice at the time to tow a ship's boats astern during battle, and it's clear from the action reports why that practice was later adopted. All the ships that were closely engaged reported "All the boats damaged," "boats much hurt," and the like.

Graves continued to manage his line as they headed into the swirl of smoke and flames at the point of convergence. Less than ten minutes after the action had commenced, he once again hoisted the signal for line ahead. The British ships were starting to bunch up as they raced to get down to the French, and Graves wanted them to maintain their proper spacing.

The flagship was still about a mile from the enemy, extreme range for a 32-pounder, when she began firing at what Hood would later dismiss as "a most *improper* distance," while the other ships in the center also opened up on the enemy. D'Éthy, aboard *Citoyon*, was unimpressed. "The enemy to windward were firing from a distance so that they could say that they fought," he wrote in his journal. "It was quite different at the head of the two fleets. We could only see fire and smoke from both sides."

For half an hour, the two fleets continued on their courses, sailing roughly southeast with the wind a little forward of the beam. The breeze, which had earlier been strong, lightened again in the late afternoon. Those ships still able to hold their places in line continued to trade fire with heavy guns as more and more ships got into the fight. The weak and variable winds made it difficult for the *arriére-garde*, or rear of the French line, to get up with the center, and Hood's division continued to follow in the wake of the *London*, obeying the signal for line ahead that Hood believed was flying but which the *London*'s log would claim was hauled down a second time at 4:27.

"At 5 o'clock," wrote Karl Tornquist, a Swedish observer with de Grasse's fleet, "when the wind had veered 4 points [to our disfavor], our *avant-gardie* was too much to windward." A veer, or shift, of four points, or 45 degrees, would have resulted in the wind blowing more or less from the east, leaving the French van almost dead to windward of the rest of the fleet, which was still struggling to catch up, and in even greater danger of being cut off. De Grasse again ordered the ships in the van to turn more southerly so that they would be running downwind to get in line with the rest. According to Tornquist, de Grasse, "who with much eagerness desired a general engagement," made that signal "in order to invite Admiral [Graves] to follow."

Graves reported that "The van of the enemy bore away to enable the center to support them, or they would have been cut up." (When Admiral George Brydges Rodney read Graves's report sometime later, he was apoplectic about the whole thing, but that line in particular stuck in his craw. "His letter I cannot understand," Rodney fumed, "and his terms, particularly his cut up, a term neither military or seamanlike; it must have been a mistake in printing; he meant cut off the vans from the centre.") But Graves showed little inclination to follow the French line to leeward.

The first eight ships in the British line did the bulk of the fighting and took the brunt of the punishment. Hood complained that "our centre division did the enemy but little damage, and our rear ships being barely within random shot, three only fired a few shot." According to Hood, Graves finally hauled down the signal for line ahead at 5:25, nearly a full hour after the time recorded in the *London*'s journal. The *London*'s journal, meanwhile, recorded that Graves "Repd. y Sigl. for a Closer Action," around 5:25 and says nothing about the signal for line ahead. Whatever the truth, Hood took this as his cue to get into the fighting at last.

Hood's rear division peeled off from Graves's division in the center and ran off to leeward to catch the French fleet, finally putting an end to Graves's line-ahead formation. Soon they were about half a mile to leeward of the center division, bearing down as fast as they could, but they were too late. Even as they descended on the French van, the French were running off to leeward in accordance with de Grasse's orders.

The French *corps de bataille* and *arriére-garde* were just straggling into the line of battle as Hood's division swept down. *Citoyon* was the lead ship in the rear division. "At 5:45," d'Éthy wrote, "the three-deck vessel at the rear of the enemy, came close, as well as two other vessels ahead of her, to the *Palmier* and *Solitaire*," a seventy-four and a sixty-four that formed the end of the center division. The three-deck vessel must have been Hood's *Barfleur*, which hove to and tried a few shots at the French ships opposite them. "He fired a few shots, as did the other two vessels that were hove to like him. . . . [F]ire became general all the way to us, but it did not last long." *Citoyon* was hit a few times in the hull and masts, and a few shots passed through her sails. *Barfleur* reported no damage at all.

The sun was approaching the western horizon as *Barfleur* and *Citoyon* exchanged their long-range shots, and Graves was thinking about his formation for the night and what he would do when the sun came up the next day. Around six o'clock, the *London* "Made the *Solebay*'s & *Fortunee*'s signal to come within Hail." When the two frigates ranged alongside the three-deck flagship, Graves issued their orders. "After night I sent the frigates to the van and rear to push forward the line and keep it extended with the enemy, with a full intention to renew the engagement in the morning."

The *London*'s log recorded that at 6:23 P.M., Graves made "the Sigl for the Line 1 Cable length and haul'd down the Sigl for Close Action," one of the few instances where her log and that of *Barfleur* agreed. "¼ past, the fire ceased on both Sides," the log continued.

Six months of shuffling fleets around the Atlantic, of planning and worrying, orders, speculation, and recrimination had come down to ninety bloody minutes off the capes of the Chesapeake Bay. And still the fate of Lord Cornwallis and his army was undecided.

CHAPTER *24* *"The signal was not understood"*

As THE SUN set over Virginia to the west, the gunfire died away and the great pall of smoke that had enveloped the head of the fleet was pulled apart and swirled away by the evening breeze. The fighting was over for that day. The British fleet had 90 men killed and 246 wounded, the French about the same.

Admiral Graves sent the frigates *Solebay* and *Fortunee* to relay instructions for the disposition of the fleet through the night hours. It was Graves's intention to have Sir Francis Drake's squadron, in the van, match the course and speed of the French fleet and to extend the rest of his line so it was parallel with the Comte de Grasse's, putting them in a proper line of battle to resume the fight at dawn.

Around seven o'clock that evening, the *London* ran up the night signal for line ahead at two cable lengths asunder. Soon after, the *Fortunee* ranged up out of the twilight, close-hauled, having passed Graves's instructions to the van. The word she brought back was that "several of the ships had suffered so much that they were in no condition to renew the action until they had secured their masts." The four that had suffered the most damage—*Shrewsbury, Intrepid, Montagu,* and *Princessa*—were so holed and torn up aloft that they could not maintain their places in the line. Aboard *Princessa,* the main topmast was expected to come down at any moment.

The 74-gun *Terrible,* rearmost in Drake's division, was also in rough shape. She had gone into the action with her foremast badly cracked and her hull leaking so much that she required near constant pumping, and the fight with the French had not helped matters. Now she had two shots clean through her already-damaged foremast and two more buried in it. Her topsails were torn up, and she had several holes between wind and water (i.e., in the side of her hull close to the waterline). "The pumps blown, and only kept together by tarr'd canvas, lead and would-ings [tight wrappings of line]," she reported, ". . . makes two inches water in 25 minutes."

The Battle of the Capes was an epoch-making event, yet there had been nothing extraordinary in the performance of either fleet. The French had fought well given their handicaps: the surprise appearance of Graves, the fact that so many of their men had been left ashore, and the fact that only half the fleet was copper bottomed, which meant that in the light air prevailing they had not been able to form a line of bat-tle as efficiently as they would have wished. Lacking the weather gauge, they had not been in a position to act offensively and thus could only react to their enemy's tactical decisions.

Some historians have criticized de Grasse for giving battle at all. Cer-tainly, his prime directive was to support the Comte de Rochambeau and General Washington in their operations, and abandoning the Chesa-peake even temporarily put those operations at risk. But de Grasse knew that the Comte de Barras was likely at sea and making for the Chesa-peake and that he might fall victim to Graves if he did not fight Graves first.

De Grasse, though, has suffered much less criticism than Admiral Thomas Graves. Rear-Admiral Samuel Hood and Graves's ostensible friend Admiral George Brydges Rodney began heaping abuse on him shortly after the battle, and the criticism was taken up by other contem-poraries and later by historians. Some of it was deserved, but much was not.

Hood made three complaints against Graves's conduct of the battle. First, he faulted Graves for not falling on the French fleet as quickly as possible, while the disorganized ships were haphazardly clearing the bay. It is certainly possible that the British might have wreaked havoc at that vulnerable time, but it is also possible that they could have run into trou-ble among the tricky tidal currents and sandbars at the bay entrance. Graves would certainly have lost tactical control of his fleet if they had swept down in no particular order, and the battle would have devolved into a series of ship-to-ship duels.

The second fault Hood found was that Graves heaved to and gave the enemy time to form a line of battle rather than falling on the separated ships of the van and destroying them. Of all the chances missed, this seems the most obvious. Hood thought it a huge mistake, "when the enemy's van was greatly extended beyond the centre and rear, that it was not attacked by the whole force of the British line."

Graves, however, did attack de Grasse's van. As he explained to the Earl of Sandwich, First Lord of the Admiralty, after wearing the fleet around and putting it on the same tack as the French, he "lay with the main topsail to the mast dressing the line and pressing toward the enemy, until I thought the enemy's van were so much advanced as to offer the moment of successful attack. . . . The enemy's centre and rear at this time were too far behind to succour their own van."

When Graves finally did give the order for the ships "to bear down and Engage their Opponents," the French van was still far ahead of its center, and de Grasse kept trying to close that gap throughout the course of the battle. Perhaps Hood felt that Graves should have moved in for the attack earlier, rather than allowing more of the French fleet to exit the bay. But perhaps Graves was afraid that the French would return to the shelter of the capes before he could get at them. Unfortunately, Graves made no record of his thoughts or intentions for that day, leaving only speculation in his wake.

The one point that is indisputably true is that at least half of Graves's fleet took no effective part in the battle. Many did not even fire a gun. Had those powerful ships, including the three-deckers *London* and *Barfleur*, come into the fight, the result might have been different. But why did so many of the British fleet not close with the enemy? That has been the most intriguing, debated, and unanswerable question in the entire affair.

Hood believed that the signal for line ahead flew continuously throughout the battle, alongside the signal for close action, and that the line-ahead signal took precedence. This he stated unambiguously, both to George Jackson and apparently to Graves. Hood was either sincere in this statement or lying to cover his own inaction, but the log of the *Barfleur* does not record the signal for line ahead coming down until 5:25 P.M.

Graves claimed, and the *London*'s log seems to confirm, that the signal for line ahead was up only at a few specific times and was hauled down specifically so as not to interfere with the signal for close action.

On the other hand, it seems unfair to accuse Hood of not wishing to engage the French, since once Hood believed that the signal for line ahead had been hauled down, he appears to have wasted little time going after the enemy, though by then it was too late. Graves seemed satisfied with Hood's explanation, at least in the immediate aftermath of the battle. He wrote to Sandwich while still at sea off the Chesapeake, "I think had our efforts been made together, some of their van, four or five sail, must have been cut to pieces. The signal was not understood. I do not mean to blame anyone, my Lord. I hope we all did our part."

Graves's letter was certainly more charitable than the vituperative Hood was willing to be. Hood never admitted even the possibility that he might have been wrong about the signal for line ahead or that he might have misunderstood Graves's intentions.

An interesting quirk in the *Barfleur*'s log, however, suggests some possible confusion. The log records that at 4:00 P.M., "the Admiral Made a Sigl. with a Blue & Yellow Checquer'd flag with a White pandant [pendant] over it." Later, the log reads "20 Minutes past 4. haul'd down the White pendant & keept the Blue & Yellow Checquer'd flag flying."

It is unusual for a ship's log to describe a flag rather than simply stating its meaning, nor does the log indicate what the officers on *Barfleur* took those flags to mean, suggesting that perhaps they did not know. Certainly a great deal of the blame for the outcome of the Battle of the Capes lies in a failure to communicate.

One reason for this failure was a lack of familiarity. Hood and Drake were fresh from the West Indies and had operated under Graves's command for all of five days. At the time of the American Revolution, there was a standard set of shipboard signals issued by the Admiralty, but admirals could and did edit and augment those signals to fit their ideas of how a battle should be waged. Graves had his own signals, and he must have provided them to Hood prior to their sailing, but Hood and his officers could not have been intimately familiar with Graves's system by the time they met de Grasse's fleet.

More to the point, Hood could not have had a sense for what Graves expected in the context of a battle—whether, for example, Graves considered maintaining the line to be of paramount importance. Graves would write on September 6 that his captains were not to consider that the signal for close action "shall be rendered ineffectual by too strict an adherence" to the signal for line ahead. That he wrote those words on the day following the battle would suggest that he had not made the point explicit beforehand.

Ironically, Rodney had included in his fighting instructions language that specifically addressed that issue, writing, "every ship in the squadron is to steer for the Enemy which, from the disposition of the two squadrons must be her lot to engage, not withstanding the signal for the Line ahead will be kept flying." Hood had operated under those fighting instructions in the West Indies, but he did not know whether Graves had the same imperative in mind.

Whether the signal for line ahead was kept flying during the entire battle is a question that will never be answered. Hood raised another interesting question when he pointed out to Jackson that Graves might have "set the example of close action even with the signal for the line out." Had Graves wanted the fleet to close quickly with the French rather than maintain its line ahead and come into the fight one ship at a time, he could have turned *London* out of line and made right for the enemy. Between that and the signal for close action, it seems likely that the others would have understood his intent and followed suit. Instead, the *London* stayed in line, and Graves never explained why, though it seems likely that he was concerned about maintaining order in a fleet consisting largely of captains whom he did not know. The end result was that the already outnumbered British fleet never brought their full weight of metal to bear on the French and thus lost their one hope for victory.

"Handsomely in a Pudding Bag"

Washington left Rochambeau in Philadelphia on September 4 or 5 and pressed on for Head of Elk to oversee the embarkation of the artillery. From the capital, the French troops marched south toward the town of Chester on the Delaware River, but Rochambeau and his entourage decided to make the passage in a small vessel. The French were using the opportunity presented by the march south to visit various battlefields of the Revolution, as tourists would continue to do from then on. At Trenton and Princeton they had been treated to a review of the scenes of action by Washington himself. On September 5, drifting down the Delaware in lovely late summer weather, they were able to observe various sites of the American defense in 1777 against the advancing British and Hessian troops.

Baron Ludwig von Closen was with Rochambeau's party on the river, and he wrote that "it would be difficult to have a more beautiful view than that of Philadelphia as one leaves it by water." As they moved downstream, they took note of the various fortifications and the locations of the *chevaux-de-frise*, the underwater obstructions that had slowed but not stopped the British fleet four years earlier.

On Mud Island, the Frenchmen could see Fort Mifflin, one of the chief defensive posts in the series. "They are really trying to finish this fortification," von Closen noted, "but God only knows when it will be done, since it appears to be the American principal *to work only on threatened places* (by and by the American motto)." Baron de Steuben and the Marquis de Lafayette in Virginia would certainly have agreed with that sentiment, though they might have argued further that even an immediate threat by the enemy was not enough to motivate most Americans.

As Rochambeau and his aides approached Chester, they saw a sight few had seen before or would ever see again. Von Closen wrote, "We discerned in the distance General Washington, standing on the shore and waving his hat and a white handkerchief joyfully." The Frenchmen likely guessed what news might make the stoic Washington behave in such a manner, and, as they disembarked, the commander-in-chief told them that de Grasse was in the Chesapeake with twenty-eight sail of the line and three thousand troops.

A deep-felt and universal joy swept over the party. "MM. de Rochambeau and Washington embraced *warmly* on the shore," von Closen observed, and his words hint at the occasional tension that existed between the two generals. Von Closen had no doubt of who was responsible for things falling neatly into place. He wrote that Rochambeau "must indeed have felt deep satisfaction in having the time draw near when his long-considered plans would be executed and in winning the approval of General Washington, who originally had been bent on a campaign against New York."

The news and concomitant excitement whipped through the army. The troops spoke of Lord Cornwallis as if he had already been captured. Von Closen warned that "one must not count his chickens before they are hatched." But then he added, "It is true that he will be taken soon."

In Williamsburg and in the lines surrounding Yorktown, the excitement ran even higher. St. George Tucker, who had stood in the second line at the Battle of Guilford Courthouse before being overrun by Cornwallis's men, and who was now a colonel of the Virginia Militia, was barely able to contain himself as he wrote the "torrent of good news" to his wife, Fanny. He recounted the arrival of de Grasse's fleet, "with four thousand land forces sent to our assistance by Louis the Great." The French troops, he reported, were ashore and marching for Williamsburg.

Tucker had heard a rumor, not true, that de Grasse had promised the commodore of Cornwallis's small fleet that he would put every man to the sword if that fleet was destroyed before the ships became French prizes. He heard another rumor, this one true, that Lord Rawdon was a prisoner on board the French fleet. The troops in Virginia were not generally aware that Washington was marching to join them, however. Only just that morning, September 5, had Tucker learned "to my great surprise and pleasure" that Washington was at Head of Elk.

Heaping good news upon good news, Tucker wrote to Fanny that the Comte de Barras's squadron was on the way from Rhode Island and expected at any time. Tucker did not know if Rochambeau and his men were on board Barras's ships, but, in a clear sign of how confident the Americans were feeling, he did not think it mattered very much.

There was only one thing Tucker wished he could add to the letter, and that was word that Cornwallis's army was already in their possession. But that news, he hoped, "in that providence to which I prostrate myself with grateful adoration for the present happy aspect of our affairs, will be the subject of some future letter."

That same day, General George Weedon wrote to Nathanael Greene from Fredericksburg, "The business with his Lordship in this State will very soon be at an end, for suppose you know e're this that we have him very handsomely in a pudding bag with 5000 land forces and about 60 ships including transports." Weedon went on to congratulate Greene for not swallowing Cornwallis's bait and following him to Virginia, a decision that events had proved correct.

While it was clear to everyone that taking Cornwallis would be a significant turning point in the war, it was not yet clear that it would be the final turning point. Weedon looked forward to shifting operations to South Carolina "the moment we do the business here." Nonetheless, there was a sense in the American camp that the end was near. Tucker intimated to Fanny that he would be seeing her again soon. Weedon wrote, "I am all on fire. By the Great God of War, I think we may all hand up our swords by the last of the year in perfect peace and security!"

All the Americans who had heard of the arrival of de Grasse's fleet were jubilant. What they failed to appreciate was that the fleet's arrival did not necessarily make them master of the seas. Washington received the news on September 5, the same day that both Tucker and Weedon penned their letters and the same day that de Grasse's fleet left the Chesapeake to do battle with Graves. Even as the Americans were celebrating a victory in the offing, the contest for control of the seas was playing out.

Battle's End

Diadème was the most heavily damaged ship in the Comte de Grasse's fleet. A French officer wrote that "she had lost 120 men and had no sails or rigging, having received 125 balls in her hull and 12 under the water line. We should have had to abandon her, had the sea run high."

Calm seas and light winds prevailed through the night after the battle, a blessing for both fleets as they were "Employ'd Knotting and Splicing the Rigging, Carpenters Stopping the Shot holes &ᶜᵉ." Despite the damage his fleet had suffered, Admiral Graves managed to get his ships into some semblance of a line with signal lanterns burning in the rigging to help each vessel keep her station. *Europe* and *Montagu*, the lead ships in the center division, were in bad shape. At nine o'clock that evening, the *Montagu* hailed the flagship to say she was too shot up to keep her station. Her rudder was split and her masts were in danger of coming down, particularly as the standing rigging that supported them was hanging in shreds, with "Nineteen lower shrouds, ten topmast shrouds, six backstays . . . the running rigging and sails very much cut."

London and the ships farther astern had also taken hits, but those seemed more in the manner of lucky shots from the French than the destruction wrought by ship-to-ship action, though some of those lucky shots did real damage. *London* had three guns dismounted, two men killed, eighteen wounded, and her "Main & Fore Mast Dangerously Wounded."

The two fleets sailed on through the night, parallel to one another, maintaining a roughly southeasterly course away from the Chesapeake. The wind was light, shifting from northeast to east as the fleets maintained a larboard tack. At dawn, Cape Henry was about 20 miles astern.

As the sun came up, Graves could see de Grasse's fleet about 3 miles to the south and to leeward of the British line. He wrote that "they had not the appearance of near so much damage as we had sustained, though the whole of their van must have experienced a good deal of loss."

Graves still retained the weather gauge, which meant that de Grasse could not bring him to battle. That must have been a relief to Graves, despite his determination of the night before to resume the fight. "We continued all day the 6h. in sight of each other repairing our damages," he wrote. Sir Francis Drake shifted his flag to the seventy-four *Alcide*, while the crew of *Princessa* sent up a new main topmast. Graves sent Captain Colpoys of the frigate *Orpheus* to take command of the *Shrewsbury*, whose captain had lost his leg and whose first officer had been killed in the opening moments of the battle.

Terrible was in a shape befitting her name. She had six hand pumps augmenting her chain pumps, which were falling apart even as the men furiously cranked them up and down to keep the water from gaining. Captain William Finch was informed by the carpenter that if the hand pumps were abandoned, the water in the hold would be 6 feet deep within an hour. *Terrible*'s foremast, cracked before the battle, was threatening to go over the side.

To the south, from the quarterdeck of *Citoyon*, the Comte d'Éthy could see the furious activity in the British fleet. One of the British ships was repairing damage to her mainmast. Five were replacing their topmasts, no small task on a vessel as big as a ship of the line. Before the topmast could be got down, the topgallant mast, yard, and sail had to be lowered to the deck. Then the topsail yard and sail, along with its attendant rigging, easily a ton or more of gear, had to be lowered as well. Topmast shrouds, stays, and backstays had to be loosened, and finally the entire topmast was lowered through the top and eased down to the deck. Then the entire process had to be reversed as the new topmast was sent up. Now the rigging had to be put on and set up—that is, tightened and adjusted—a more difficult process than casting it off.

All of September 6 was taken up with repairs to the British and French fleets. In the late morning, Graves sent word to Rear-Admiral Hood "desiring his opinion whether the action should be renewed." For some reason, Hood seems to have taken offense at having his opinion solicited through a third party. His petulant reply to Graves read, "I dare say Mr. Graves will do what is right; I can *send* no opinion, but whenever he, Mr. Graves, wishes to see me, I will wait upon him with great pleasure."

No attempt was made to renew the action, though the ships were just a few miles apart, sailing slowly in the light breeze with their larboard tacks aboard. That evening, Graves sent for Hood and Drake, and the three admirals met in the great cabin of the *London*. There, Graves related intelligence he had received concerning the French ships left in the Chesapeake, and a letter from Clinton to Cornwallis, which he was sending to Cornwallis aboard the frigates *Richmond* and *Iris* (the former American frigate *Hancock*). Hood was of the opinion that the entire British fleet, not just the frigates, should make for the Chesapeake, but that advice was not followed.

At daybreak on September 7, the fleets remained in largely the same situation, with the Chesapeake even farther to the west. The breeze was almost nonexistent, and Graves's ships were unable to hold a proper line. Then, around ten thirty, the wind began to fill in, this time from the southwest. Suddenly, for the first time, de Grasse held the weather gauge.

"The admiral signaled the fleet to form a battle line," d'Éthy wrote. The French fleet trimmed their sails to a starboard tack and began to work their way toward the British fleet. De Grasse arranged his ships in *échiquier*, or checkerboard fashion—that is, with the ships in a staggered line—as he cautiously approached the enemy.

Graves formed his fleet into a line of battle, but the entire day was consumed by maneuvers as de Grasse adjusted his line to make certain the French retained the weather gauge. "We had not speed enough in so mutilated a state to attack them had it been prudent," Graves wrote, "and they shewed no inclination to renew the attack, for they generally maintained the wind of us, and had it often in their power."

The following day, the wind swung into the northeast again, blowing strong. During the night, the *London* close-reefed her topsails and later sent her topgallant yards down to the deck to reduce weight and windage aloft. "Squally with Thunder & Lightning & Rain," her log recorded.

Dawn revealed the French fleet still to the south and about 12 miles off. De Grasse was becoming concerned about the distance he was putting between himself and the Chesapeake, and he continued to worry about the possibility of Graves intercepting Barras. One French officer wrote, "The English held the north, and it was precisely from this direction that the French expected M. de Barras from Newport. It was essential to gain the weather gage of the enemy, to prevent his revenging himself upon that squadron."

Accordingly, de Grasse tacked his fleet to starboard and stood off toward the north, his ships again arranged in checkerboard fashion. Graves's squadron was still sailing roughly southeast in line ahead, and according to French sources was "in a line badly formed, and appeared inclined, notwithstanding their bad order, to dispute the wind."

The two fleets were converging on opposite tacks, the French close-hauled, the British with the wind astern. De Grasse made the signal for his foremost ship "to pass within the distance of a pistol shot of the enemy." On that heading, the two fleets would pass and exchange broadsides, but once having passed, the British would be left to leeward, giving the French the weather gauge.

Not wanting to give up his windward position, Graves ordered his fleet to tack in succession. One by one, the big ships turned into the gusting wind, their heavy sails flogging as they came around on the new heading, settling on the same tack as the approaching French. But Graves was too late. He did not have enough time to tack the entire fleet before the French were up with them, and he did not want to get caught under French guns in the middle of the evolution. When only three ships had come about, Graves ordered the rest to form a rear guard and run off before the wind, yielding the weather gauge to de Grasse. The

French fleet continued on without firing on the British. Now they were between Graves and the Chesapeake and, perhaps, Barras.

Graves had other things to worry about. *Terrible* had been taking on water fast even in moderate seas, and now, with the wind and seas rising and the man-of-war's hull working more, things became much worse. Her captain made a signal of distress, and Graves sent the frigates *Fortunee* and *Orpheus* to assist.

Later that night, the British fleet wore around so that they too were sailing roughly north by west, beginning to retrace the track they had been sailing since wearing off to port tack at Middle Ground Shoal more than three days before. Soon after, *Intrepid* signaled that she wished to speak to the admiral. The fleet hove to, and Graves was informed that *Intrepid*'s main topmast had gone over the side and they feared their fore yard would go at any moment. "These repeated misfortunes in sight of a superior enemy, who kept us all extended and in motion," Graves wrote to Secretary Philip Stephens, "filled the mind with anxiety and put us in a situation not to be envied."

The following day was September 9, four days since the two fleets had met off the capes, and they were still within sight of one another though upward of 10 miles apart. The weather was overcast, and occasionally the fleets disappeared from each other's view. They were nearly 100 miles from the Chesapeake.

The Comte de Grasse, meanwhile, was rethinking his situation. It was clear that bringing Graves to action would not be easy as long as the British were reluctant to engage. The farther he got from the Chesapeake, the more likely it became that a shift of wind would make it impossible for him to return. He had around thirteen hundred of his men ashore, not to mention the boats and the thirty-four hundred troops under the Marquis de Saint-Simon whom he was responsible for returning to the Spanish in the Caribbean. It was time to head back to the capes.

De Grasse's intentions were clear to Hood, if not to Graves. "On the 9th, the French fleet carried a press of sail," Hood wrote to George Jackson, "which proved to me beyond a doubt that De Grasse had other views than fighting." Hood was eager for Graves to order the British fleet to set sail as well and make for the Chesapeake to cut off de Grasse, but

Graves did not. Rather, at nightfall, Graves put the fleet about on the opposite tack and soon after ordered them to heave to. In the morning, the French fleet was nowhere to be seen.

"This alarmed me exceedingly," Hood wrote, "and I debated with myself some little time whether I should venture to write Mr. Graves a few lines or not." Hood did not think it proper for a subordinate officer to send advice unsolicited to a senior (though he thought nothing of writing incendiary comments behind his commanding officer's back), but, in the end, he decided to throw discretion to the wind. He wrote to Graves, saying, "I flatter myself you will forgive the liberty I take in asking whether you have any knowledge where the French fleet is, as we can see nothing of it from the *Barfleur*." Hood went on to suggest that the French were likely making for the Chesapeake, and he asked rhetorically if the frigates Graves had sent to reconnoiter might not be cut off, and if de Grasse would not "succeed in giving most effectual succour to the rebels?"

The note was passed to Hood's repeating frigate, the vessel used to repeat signals that might not be visible to ships in a line of battle, or to relay messages. The frigate raced to the *London* to deliver it to Graves. Soon after, Graves summoned Hood, along with Drake, to another council of war aboard the flagship. Hood was astonished to find that the senior admiral was as ignorant as Hood was of the whereabouts of the French fleet and, more incredibly, had not sent any of the fleet's several frigates to shadow them. De Grasse had been allowed to disappear over the horizon.

Graves asked the others for their opinions as to what should be done. Hood said that his letter had explained his views, but if Graves wished him to say more, it was simply that they "should get into the Chesapeake to the succour of Lord Cornwallis and his brave troops if possible . . . ," but he believed it was too late. De Grasse, he had no doubt, had already blocked the way into the Chesapeake, "which human prudence suggested we *ought* to have done against him."

There was another matter for the admirals to consider. *Terrible* was increasingly in danger of sinking. Her captain, Finch, had thrown overboard five of the lower-deck guns and had asked permission to jettison the guns from the forecastle and quarterdeck. He also wished to take off the stores and distribute them to the fleet, as they "may be of Service to some other Ship, and in our present Situation we should be as well without them."

The following day, Finch sent another letter to Graves informing him that the pumps could not keep up and that he had divided the crew for distribution to other ships, if need be. He included certificates signed by the ship's five lieutenants, the master, the boatswain, the gunner, and the carpenter testifying that they did not believe *Terrible* could make it into port and that no additional number of men sent on board would help. The council of war reviewed these and the earlier notes from Finch and concluded that they should "take out her People and sink her." September 10 was taken up with getting out what supplies they could and redistributing her crew around the fleet. On the following day, "H[is] M[ajesty's] Ship *Terrible* was Sett on fier."

De Grasse had indeed set out for the Chesapeake, just as Hood had feared. Two strange sails were sighted en route, and the fleet gave chase, but they turned out to be the *Glorieux* and the *Diligente* rejoining the fleet after having remained behind in the bay. The fleet stood on toward the Chesapeake with the frigates *Aigrette* and *Diligente* leading the way.

As they approached the capes, they encountered *Richmond* and *Iris*, whom Graves had sent to reconnoiter, making for open water with all the sail they could carry. The British frigates had decided to venture into the bay and cut away the buoys marking the anchors the French had left behind in their hurry to get to sea, a stroke that would amount to little more than an annoyance to the French. After a sharp fight that nearly the entire French fleet tried to join, the two frigates were taken. As one French officer wrote, "They paid dearly for the petty advantage of cutting the buoys which the fleet had left at the anchorage."

On September 11, as Admiral Graves was burning the sinking *Terrible*, the Comte de Grasse's entire fleet dropped anchor in Lynnhaven Bay. The Comte de Barras was already there, having anchored the night before. In the holds of Barras's ships were the siege artillery that would batter Cornwallis's defenses into dust.

Graves was still far at sea, having lost sight of de Grasse on the tenth. Once the poor *Terrible* had burned down to her waterline, Graves put the fleet on a heading for the Chesapeake, though he must have strongly suspected that he was too late. He sent the frigate *Medea* racing ahead to look into the bay and report back.

On the morning of September 13, *Medea* returned with the unhappy news that "the French fleet are at anchor above the Horse Shoe in Chesapeake." Graves forwarded this news to Hood with a request for Hood's opinion on how to proceed. Graves must have known he would get an unpleasant reply, and Hood did not disappoint. He sent a note back to the admiral expressing his extreme concern about the disposition of the French fleet, but "it is no more than what he expected." Hood went on to write, in the third person, "Sir Samuel would be very glad to send an opinion, but he really knows not what to say in the truly lamentable state we have brought ourselves."

For the third time since the battle, the three admirals met in the spacious great cabin of *London* to discuss the intelligence brought by *Medea*. They considered "the position of the Enemy, the present condition of the British Fleet, the season of the year so near the Equinox, and the impracticality of giving any effectual succour to General Earl Cornwallis in the Chesapeake."

With all that in mind, "It was resolved, that the British Squadron . . . should proceed with all dispatch to New York, and there use every possible means of putting the Squadron into the best state for service." For the time being, Cornwallis would be abandoned. There was nothing else they could do.

CHAPTER 25 *The Siege of Yorktown*

LIEUTENANT COLONEL BANASTRE Tarleton wanted Lord Cornwallis to fight his way out. He thought the army had a good chance. And he was convinced that it was their only chance.

British spirits had been lifted briefly by the appearance of Admiral Graves's fleet and the Comte de Grasse's immediate departure from the Chesapeake. The heavy gunfire from the fighting at sea could be heard clearly from Yorktown, some 50 or 60 miles away. For days, as the two fleets ran southeast out to sea and then turned to retrace their outward journeys, Cornwallis's army waited to learn the outcome of the battle. Many American soldiers, meanwhile, were not even aware that de Grasse had left or that a naval battle was being fought.

Then, on the evening of September 10, as Tarleton later recalled, "This state of hope was interrupted by the arrival of Count de Barras's division in the Chesapeake from Rhode island." Soon after, word reached Yorktown of de Grasse's victory and the British fleet's return to New York. Things were growing bleaker by the day. The British, better informed than many Americans, were already aware that General George Washington and the Comte de Rochambeau were on their way south with their armies.

Cornwallis sent out Tarleton with a handful of dragoons to reconnoiter the American lines. Tarleton's intelligence, combined with a report brought in by a Loyalist woman regarding the allied troop strength, led Cornwallis to believe that a night march followed by a predawn attack could succeed in breaking out the army and allowing them to march for the Carolinas.

Before he could try this roll of the dice, however, word arrived from Sir Henry Clinton. The commander-in-chief acknowledged receiving Cornwallis's letter reporting the arrival of de Grasse's fleet, and he informed Cornwallis that he had "no doubt that Washington is moving with at least six thousand French and rebel troops against you." Clinton went on to say, "I think the best way to relieve you is to join you, as soon as possible, with all the force that can be spared from hence, which is about four thousand men." The troops were already embarked on transports, and Clinton was only waiting for word that it was safe to sail. Additionally, Rear-Admiral Robert Digby, en route to relieve Graves of his temporary command, was expected to arrive any day with more ships to reinforce the New York fleet.

Clinton's letter had been written on September 6, while the fleets were still at sea repairing their battle damage, and Cornwallis received it on September 16 after it was somehow smuggled through the American lines. The problem with Clinton's plan, as Tarleton would later point out, was that Clinton had no idea what he was talking about.

When the commander-in-chief wrote the letter, he did not know the outcome of the Battle of the Capes. But by the time Cornwallis received the letter, de Grasse and Barras were anchored nearby with an overwhelming force, Washington and Rochambeau's armies were at Head of Elk, and the defenses at Yorktown were "in too unfinished a state to resist a formidable attack." With de Grasse's fleet in the Chesapeake, Clinton had no reasonable way to land the troops he proposed to send. Worse, though Clinton could not know this for certain, the addition of four thousand men would still have left the garrison at Yorktown badly outnumbered.

Tarleton made all those points in his memoirs, but it is not clear that he made them to Cornwallis. Even if he did not, Cornwallis was perfectly aware of the situation. But, rather than attempt his contemplated breakout, he was willing to dig in and wait for Clinton to come. "If I had no hopes of relief," he wrote Clinton, "I would rather risk an action than defend my half finished works; but as you say Digby is hourly expected, and promise every exertion to assist me, I do not think myself justified in putting the fate of the war on so desperate an attempt."

Tarleton thought this was ridiculous, but even writing after the war, he could not find fault with his beloved Cornwallis. "England must lament the inactivity of the King's troops," he wrote, "whether it proceeded from the noble Earl's misconception, or from the suggestions of confidential attendants, who construed the commander in chief's letters into a definitive promise of relief."

Cornwallis felt that he could find provisions for six weeks "[b]y examining the transports with care, and turning out useless mouths." The cavalry horses could not be kept alive. And, despite agreeing with Clinton's plan, Cornwallis did not seem terribly optimistic. Writing to Clinton on September 16, he said, "This place is in no state of defense. If you cannot relieve me very soon, you must be prepared to hear the worst."

A little more than a month later, Clinton heard just that.

The Siege of Yorktown was won at the Battle of the Capes. All the strategy and maneuvering that followed on the American side were simply the steps prescribed to reach an inevitable end, and the subsequent plans made by Clinton and Graves were little more than wishful thinking, largely divorced from reality. That fact is clear in hindsight and was clear enough at the time, as evidenced by the outpouring of joy upon de Grasse's arrival and the extent to which even those Americans jaded by years of disappointment soon looked on Cornwallis's capture as a foregone conclusion. The French and American troops moving toward Yorktown numbered around sixteen thousand men. With the addition of the men from the blockaded ship, Cornwallis had about eighty-three hundred, many of whom were sick. Even the cautious Washington was willing to write in his general orders of September 6, "Nothing but the want of exertion can possibly blast the pleasing prospect before us."

After hearing the news of de Grasse's arrival on September 5, Washington moved on ahead of the army to Head of Elk, from where he hoped to send the troops by water down the Chesapeake Bay to Williamsburg. Despite having sent orders for vessels to be collected, he found there "a great deficiency of Transports." He remained at Head of Elk for a couple of days, "writing many letters to Gentn. of Influence of the Eastern Shore, beseeching them to exert themselves in drawing forth every kind of Vessel which would answer."

He and Rochambeau and a company of guards then continued on to Baltimore, where there was "Great joy in town, illuminations, address, &c." The next day, Washington left for Mount Vernon, about 60 miles away, riding hard to get there as soon as possible. It was the first time in six years that he had been home. With him was Colonel Jonathan Trumbull, the future painter, then secretary to the commander-in-chief. Rochambeau and his entourage followed at a more leisurely pace.

Trumbull, the young Connecticut Yankee, was taken with the trappings of southern aristocracy, noting Mount Vernon's "elegant seat and situation, great appearance of opulence and real exhibitions of hospitality & princely entertainment." Rochambeau arrived a day later, and the two generals and their "families" spent a few days at Mount Vernon before heading south toward Jamestown. Washington must have felt mixed emotions indeed, the pangs of regret over having to leave his beloved Mount Vernon jumbled together with joy at the very real possibility of capturing Cornwallis's entire army, a thing that just a month earlier he had not even dared to consider.

Washington was about 20 miles south of Mount Vernon when another express rider caught up with him. The letters the rider carried contained "an account of an action between the two Fleets, & that the French were gone out from the Bay in pursuit of the English. The event not known."

This was the first that Washington had heard of the Battle of the Capes, and he was distressed to read that de Grasse had left the Chesapeake and that no one knew where he was or what the outcome of the battle had been. Suddenly, there loomed the real possibility that the whole debacle of the previous spring involving Benedict Arnold, the Marquis de Lafayette, Vice-Admiral Arbuthnot, and Chevalier Destouches was playing itself out again.

The news was old, of course, and the outcome had been decided days before, but Washington did not know that, and he feared the ruination of all his plans. With so many resources shifted south, with such spiraling optimism at the news of de Grasse's arrival, failure now would have vastly greater consequences than the disappointment he had suffered in the spring from the failure to capture Arnold. Failure now might finally break the spirit of a war-weary nation. No one had been more ecstatic over the possibility of a pending victory than Washington, and the letters must have been a terrible blow.

"Much agitated," Trumbull wrote.

The company rode grimly on, and the following day, word of the naval battle's outcome began to filter back to them. "Rumours of the return of the French Fleet, with some advantage," Trumbull wrote, "which relieved our fears."

On September 15, Washington and Rochambeau rode unannounced into Williamsburg. The Virginia militia, caught unaware on the outskirts of the encampments around the town, did not have time to parade for Virginia's favorite son. St. George Tucker was surprised and delighted when Washington recognized him and addressed him by name. Soon after, the Marquis de Lafayette, Thomas Nelson, and the other senior officers in Williamsburg rode up to greet their arriving commander-in-chief.

"Never was more joy painted in any countenance than theirs," Tucker wrote. One might expect no less, as the leader they so loved and admired had arrived at what seemed likely to be the scene of his greatest triumph. Lafayette, in keeping with his youth and national character, "rode up with precipitation, clasped the General in his arms and embraced him with an ardor not easily described."

As word spread of Washington and Rochambeau's arrival, troops and civilians alike turned out to greet them. The Marquis de Saint-Simon persuaded the officers to ride through the French lines. "The troops were paraded for the purpose and cut a most splendid figure," drawn up in perfect lines, their white uniforms glowing in the late afternoon sun. Cannons boomed out a salute as the generals rode into the camp of the Continental Line. By then, a great parade of people were following behind, and "men, women and children seemed to vie with each other in demonstrations of joy and eagerness to see their beloved countryman."

It was a spontaneous outpouring of joy. Nearly all the American troops at Williamsburg, and those who were on their way, were veterans of the years of suffering and deprivation that had characterized the War for Independence. Veterans of one defeat after another, they had clung stoically to the cause when so many others—including one of their most respected general officers, the traitorous Arnold—had given up on it. Now, in the fine, cool days of mid-September in Virginia, their moment had come at last. "We are all alive and so sanguine in our hopes," Tucker told his wife. Though the work of capturing Cornwallis had scarcely begun, Tucker assured his wife that the British general "may now tremble for his fate, for nothing but some extraordinary interposition of his guardian angels seems capable of saving him and his whole army from captivity."

"[M]on cher petit général!"

Among Washington's first priorities was a meeting with the Comte de Grasse. On the day of his arrival in Williamsburg, the commander-in-chief wrote to de Grasse "to express the Pleasure, which I have in congratulating your Excellency on your Return to your former station in the Bay." One can imagine the relief Washington felt on learning with certainty that both de Grasse and Barras were safely at anchor and that the Battle of the Capes had been a victory for the French fleet.

Washington made a few immediate requests of the admiral. One was that de Grasse send as many transports as he could to Head of Elk. The second was that he send "some fastsailg Cutter" to take him and Rochambeau out to the flagship. And the last was that he furnish Rochambeau's aide-de-camp with some means of returning to Head of Elk "to hurry down the Troops embarking on the Bay."

De Grasse was happy to comply. In fact, he had anticipated the first two requests and had already set his vessels in motion. "[A]ll the transports which M. du Barras had brought with him . . ." had been dispatched to Head of Elk, and, to add insult to British injury, he had also sent the 44-gun *Romulus*, which Captain de Tilly had captured on the first French foray to the Chesapeake the previous February, as well as some of Cornwallis's vessels that his fleet had taken on their arrival.

To convey Washington and Rochambeau to the *Ville de Paris*, the admiral sent his personal launch, which carried them down College Creek in Williamsburg to the James River. There they boarded the *Queen Charlotte*, a former British 18-gun ship and the vessel that had been carrying Lord Rawdon when de Grasse scooped her up as a prize on his way to the Chesapeake.

Accompanying the commander-in-chief and Rochambeau were the Marquis de Chastellux, one of Rochambeau's subordinate generals and the officer who had first leaked to Washington the plan for de Grasse's arrival on the American coast; French engineer General Louis Duportail, who had served under Washington since Valley Forge; General

Henry Knox, head of American artillery and one of Washington's most trusted officers; and Colonel Jonathan Trumbull. A fair wind carried them down the James River, but the turn of the tide forced them to lie overnight in the river's lower reaches. The next morning they completed the 60-mile trip to Lynnhaven Bay and the *Ville de Paris*.

De Grasse's fleet made an awesome sight, stretched out across the mouth of the Chesapeake Bay. As Sergeant Joseph Plumb Martin described it, the more than one hundred masts with sails furled "resembled a swamp of dried pine trees." James Thacher called it "the most noble and majestic spectacle I ever witnessed, and we viewed it with inexpressible pleasure." It was undoubtedly the largest collection of men-of-war that Washington had ever seen. One can imagine that he was awed by the size of the powerful flagship as his boat drew alongside the towering three-decker. It is likely that *Ville de Paris* was only the second ship of the line Washington had ever been aboard, after the *Duc de Bourgogne* in Newport. She was certainly the largest ship he had been aboard, as few in the world were larger.

The generals and their entourages were "received with great ceremony and military naval parade and most cordial welcome," as befitted the occasion. Jonathan Trumbull, for one, was much taken with de Grasse. "The Admiral is a remarkable man for his size, appearance and plainness of dress," he wrote. De Grasse was a big man, bigger even than Washington. There is a story that upon meeting Washington, de Grasse threw his arms around him in the Gallic manner and shouted *"mon cher petit général!"* (my dear little general!). If true, that was another first for Washington.

When the greetings and ceremony ended, the officers got to work. Washington had written out six questions that he wished to address with the admiral. In a preamble, he had written, "The Peace & Independence of this Country, & the general Tranquility of Europe will, it is more than probable, result from our Complete success." Complete success, he suggested, could only be achieved if the French fleet remained in the Chesapeake as long as was necessary. Disgrace and the ruin of the American cause would be the probable result if they did not.

The first two questions had to do with how long de Grasse could remain and whether he could leave any of his ships behind when it came time to convey Saint-Simon's men back to the West Indies. De Grasse answered that his instructions called for him to depart on October 15, but, given the stakes and the enormity of the arrangements that had been made, he agreed to remain until the end of October. He could stay no longer, and on November 1, his fleet and Saint-Simon's men would be heading for warmer climes.

Washington asked next if de Grasse could push ships up the York River above Yorktown to facilitate communications between the east and west banks. De Grasse did not think that necessary, but he agreed to try. Question four was how many men de Grasse could spare to aid the land forces. The admiral said he could "offer 1800 or 2000 men from my Ships; But I wish that these troops may not be employed but in a Coup de Main."

Next, Washington asked if de Grasse might spare some ships to blockade Wilmington, North Carolina, and capture the harbor of Charleston. To that, de Grasse replied simply, "The form of my Vessels do not admit of the enterprise," by which he might have meant that they were too deep of draft for those waters. But what he really meant, though he did not say it, was that he was not about to start splitting up his fleet and sending them to other ports when he had no idea where Graves might be.

Finally, Washington asked whether de Grasse could spare any cannons and powder. De Grasse replied that he could provide both, but after his sparring with Admiral Rodney in the West Indies and with Admiral Graves off the capes, he could spare "but a small quantity of the latter."

Trumbull recorded that the business was "soon dispatched to great satisfaction." This was largely true, though Washington was disappointed that de Grasse would stay no longer than November 1 and had not agreed with any certainty to send ships up the York River above Yorktown. The land forces would have six weeks to dislodge Cornwallis before the British would once again command the seas. Siege-craft was time consuming, and there was not much time.

"After this, dinner is served," Trumbull wrote, "and then we view the ship, her batteries, accommodations, &c, - a noble prospect, - the world in miniature." Nearly all the captains in the French fleet had come aboard the *Ville de Paris* to meet the famous George Washington. Around sunset, Washington, Rochambeau, and their party climbed down the steep sides of the flagship and into the boat that ferried them back to the *Queen Charlotte*. Sailors cheered them from the yards, tops, and shrouds of surrounding ships, and the guns of the *Ville de Paris* roared out a salute. The *Queen Charlotte*'s anchor came up, and the little ship got underway, moving slowly toward Hampton Roads in the light air.

All through the night and into the following day, the ship drifted in the lower James River with barely enough wind to give her steerage. In the afternoon, the wind piped up, and the *Queen Charlotte* was finally making decent way upriver when she ran hard aground. Washington and the others spent their second frustrating night aboard.

The next morning, the ship was still lodged in the unforgiving mud of the river, so the army men left her and took to the ship's boat instead. With the mast stepped and the sail set they made good time, while the *Queen Charlotte*, free of the bottom at last, followed astern. Trumbull wrote, "we sail fast in our boat, as the wind freshens up, but not very comfortably. We are wet with the sprays. Our little ship comes up with us, and we return to her."

The wind continued to rise, and soon the *Queen Charlotte* was forced to come to anchor in the lee of the land to ride out the blow. The officers spent their third night on board, and in the morning the ship weighed anchor and beat upriver against a headwind, making slow progress. Darkness fell, and Washington and his comrades spent a fourth night on the ship. In the morning, with the wind still on the bow, they once more took to the boat and, hugging the shoreline, arrived in Williamsburg around noon, nearly four days after leaving the flagship at anchor 60 miles away. They could have walked that distance in half the time.

Washington's irritation can be imagined. He had been allotted six weeks by the admiral in which to force Cornwallis's surrender, and he had used almost a tenth of that allotment just getting back to camp. He was somewhat mollified, however, when he discovered that most of the troops he had left at Head of Elk had arrived. About a week earlier, Joseph Plumb Martin had reached Head of Elk with his regiment to find "a *large* fleet of *small* vessels, waiting to convey us and other troops, stores, &c. down the bay." Despite the number of vessels, there were not enough for all the men. Most of the troops continued on by land, while the small ships were crammed beyond capacity with all the men and gear they could carry, which made for crowded and uncomfortable conditions.

"We passed down the bay," Martin wrote, "making a grand appearance with our mosquito fleet." The ships dropped anchor in Annapolis around September 12. The next day they continued on, but they were soon recalled. Rumors of a naval battle were reaching inland, and no one knew what the outcome had been. If the French had lost, this was the end of the line. A French cutter was sent down the bay to gather intelligence while the fleet remained at anchor.

On September 15, the day Washington arrived at Williamsburg, Dr. James Thacher aboard the schooner *Glasco* in Annapolis heard the good news that "the naval engagement between the two fleets has resulted in the defeat of the British." The same storm that lashed Washington's company aboard the *Queen Charlotte* slowed the mosquito fleet as well, but most of the vessels arrived near Jamestown by September 22, the day before Washington made it back to camp.

Around the same time, Admiral de Grasse sent three ships of the line and a frigate up the York River, close to Yorktown. Until then, Cornwallis had enjoyed fairly easy communication with New York, correspondence from Clinton having either made its way into the British lines at Gloucester on the east side of the river and then by boat across to Yorktown, or been carried by small sailing craft right through the French fleet and up the York River. Now the French squadron threatened to cut even that tenuous lifeline.

Commodore Thomas Symonds, captain of the *Charon* and commander of the naval detachment under Cornwallis, had among his fleet the fire ship *Vulcan*, though, indeed, any wooden vessel could serve as a fire ship. A few days earlier, in an attempt to block the French from sending ships above the town, Symonds had sunk ten transport ships between Yorktown and Gloucester, a common but generally futile tactic. But there were still plenty of transports left. When Symonds's guard boats reported that the three French men-of-war were "not keeping that look out, which might be expected from advanced Ships . . . ," he ordered four of the remaining transports "to be fitted out as Fire Vessels, with the utmost expedition."

Around midnight on the night of September 22, the five ships got underway and headed unseen downriver toward the French men-of-war. The night was dark, the wind and tide just right for the attack, but the men who manned the ships were not quite up to the perilous mission. "[T]he impatience, or want of resolution of the officers and sailors of the transports, soon rendered all advantages useless," Tarleton wrote. As so often happened in fire ship attacks, the crews set off the combustibles too early. Suddenly presented with the sight of blazing ships bearing down on them, the French men-of-war opened up with their broadsides.

Captain Palmer of the *Vulcan* showed more resolution than the others and held his ship on course, but the gunfire was too much for his men. They took to the boat and were ready to abandon him when he finally set the ship on fire, though she was still too far from the French to do any good.

The fire ships at least put a scare into the French, which was as much as fire ships generally did. The men-of-war cut their cables to get away, and in the process two of them ran into each other and went aground, though they soon got off. In one of the last bold strokes Cornwallis would make in the war, he had managed to do little more than annoy the enemy.

De Grasse had a scare of a different sort in store for Washington. In Williamsburg, Washington received intelligence that Admiral Digby had arrived in New York, though the number of vessels with him was unknown. Naturally, Washington forwarded what information he had to the admiral, who did not react as Washington had imagined he would.

"The enemy are beginning to be almost equal to us," de Grasse wrote back, "and it would be imprudent of me to put myself in a position where I could not engage them in battle." Earlier intelligence had suggested to de Grasse that Digby would bring six ships of the line. This still left de Grasse with a significant superiority, but not enough to suit him, particularly if the British fleet should again catch him at anchor.

De Grasse suggested that he leave two ships of the line and all the sloops and frigates in the bay and put to sea with the rest of his fleet so as to meet the enemy on equal footing if they were to arrive and try to force their way into the Chesapeake. The admiral was no doubt recalling what a close thing it had been when he had to send his fleet out to meet Graves in a broken and straggling line. He suggested that he might even sail to New York, "where, perhaps, I could do more for the common cause, than by remaining here, an idle spectator."

Washington was horrified. "Sir," he replied, "I cannot conceal from your Excellency the painful anxiety under which I have labored since the receipt of the letter which you have honored me." The commander-in-chief went on for several pages reiterating how close the allies were to capturing Cornwallis—"as certain as any military operation can be rendered by a decisive superiority of strength"—and how much Cornwallis's defeat would do to bring the war to a close.

Washington laid out every argument he could think of in his letter to de Grasse, but it turned out that he might have saved himself some ink. Even as he was composing his cri de coeur, de Grasse assembled his officers in a council of war to consider his proposal, and they did not like it, either. The admiral wrote to Washington that even though "the plans I had suggested for getting under way while the most brilliant and glorious did not appear to fulfill the aims we had in view." Instead, de Grasse would shift the major part of his fleet into the mouth of the York River and station four or five ships in the James.

Three days later, the American and French troops in Williamsburg moved against Cornwallis's defenses at Yorktown.

"[T]he epoch which will decide American Independence"

In the early morning hours of September 28, the American and French armies began the 11-mile march from Williamsburg to the outskirts of Yorktown. They set out in a single column with Continental troops leading the way, but en route they split, with the Americans marching off to the right and the French to the left. The British put up virtually no resistance. The pickets that Cornwallis had positioned out beyond his defenses were driven in. Tarleton's dragoons, protecting the British left, were dissuaded from attacking when a few field pieces were brought up and fired in their direction. That night, Washington and his staff slept in the open with just the limbs of a tree for shelter. Trumbull, already thinking of posterity, suggested that the tree "will probably be rendered venerable from this circumstance for a length of time to come."

Cornwallis's main defensive works were backed up close to Yorktown, known alternately as York, which had been a thriving tobacco port, its commercial activity peaking around 1750. The town consisted of around two hundred and fifty buildings on a bluff about 30 or 40 feet above the York River. Some two thousand people had lived in Yorktown prior to Cornwallis's arrival, but preparations for the siege had lowered those numbers considerably. Until then, Yorktown had been largely spared from the ravages of war that had swept through much of the tidewater region of Virginia. Now its turn had come.

The British defenses consisted of a line of earthworks a little over a mile long, forming a rough semicircle around the town. The works were punctuated by eight redoubts, out from which Cornwallis's largest guns faced in every direction. Those guns, however, were neither very large nor very numerous. There were sixty-five cannon in all, none larger than 18-pounders, puny compared with the many 32-pounders the French had brought to the party. To get what guns he had, Cornwallis had had to strip the *Charon* of her main battery.

Along with the eight redoubts built into the inner perimeter of earthworks, two more, known as Numbers 9 and 10, had been built free standing, not connected to the earthworks, which provided additional coverage against an attack from that direction. About a half-mile out from the inner defenses, Cornwallis had constructed another line of redoubts and entrenchments. The lay of the land made the British left most vulnerable to attack, so it was there that Cornwallis concentrated this second perimeter.

As Washington and Rochambeau reconnoitered the British works, Cornwallis took the measure of his enemy. Most of the British troops were positioned in the outer defenses, and Cornwallis, putting a bold face on things, wrote to Clinton that there was "one wish throughout the whole army, which was that the enemy would advance." But Washington gave no indication that he was going to throw lives away with an unnecessary frontal assault.

That night, a boat snuck through the French fleet with word from Clinton. The commander-in-chief informed Cornwallis that a council of war of the general officers and admirals had determined that "above five thousand men, rank and file, shall be embarked on board the King's ships, and the joint exertions of the navy and army made in a few days to relieve you, and afterwards co-operate with you." The fleet would consist of twenty-three sail of the line which, it was hoped, would be underway by October 5.

Clinton's letter addressed none of the obvious problems inherent in this plan, including the fact that the British land and naval forces would still be vastly outnumbered. But it was enough for Cornwallis, who wrote that the plans gave him "the greatest satisfaction." Believing that reinforcements were on the way, Cornwallis decided to abandon the outer works and pull his forces back to the inner line of defenses around Yorktown, hunker down, and wait for relief.

Around that time in London, American Secretary George Germain wrote to Clinton, displaying yet more of the thoughtless optimism and utter denial that had characterized so much of the British approach to the war in North America and that had led directly to the hopeless position they were now in. "I trust before the end of that Month [August] Sir Samuel Hood will have been with you, and that after his junction with Admiral Graves, Our Superiority at Sea will be preserved," he wrote. That being the case, Germain was confident that Washington would not attack New York, and he looked forward to hearing of Clinton's successful move against Philadelphia.

The first day of October opened with a surprise for the allied forces. "In the morning it is discovered that the Enemy have evacuated all their exterior works, and retired to their interior defense near the town," Trumbull wrote in his journal. The Americans and French were pleased to get that real estate for free. As Washington wrote in his diary, "Immediately . . . we possessed them, and made those on our left (with very little alteration) very serviceable to us."

Cornwallis may have hoped the allies would launch a frontal assault, a coup de main, but they did not. Instead, they elected to dig. Following the method formalized by Marshal Sébastien Le Prestre de Vauban during the reign of Louis XIV, the allied plan was to dig trenches parallel to the British defenses, initially out of cannon range but getting progressively closer to the enemy's works. Smaller trenches called saps would connect the "parallels," which would be dug in a zigzag pattern that prevented the enemy from enfilading them. The dirt excavated from the parallels would build redoubts and earthworks.

As the allies prepared to begin digging, Washington wrote words of inspiration to the troops. Earlier, he had seen the capture of Cornwallis as something that would be of great benefit to the war. By the time he was standing on the abandoned British redoubts, looking over the expanse of green and open ground to the brown earthworks around Yorktown, he had come to fully appreciate the significance of what they were doing. "The present moment offers, in prospect," he wrote, "the epoch which will decide American Independence."

The first week of October was taken up with transporting heavy field artillery from its landing place on the James River to the artillery park established south of Yorktown, a job supervised by Henry Knox; with preparing the material needed for the trenches; and with building the first of the American redoubts facing the enemy. Finally, on the evening of October 6, forty-three hundred French and American troops turned out to begin work on the first parallel. Of those, fifteen hundred would do the actual digging while the rest stood guard in case the British sallied from their works. Before the digging began in earnest, Washington hefted a pickax and struck a few blows in the ground. It was "a mere ceremony," Joseph Plumb Martin wrote, "that it might be said Gen. Washington with his own hands first broke ground at the siege of Yorktown."

From that evening on, the siege-work continued unabated, with all the methodical inevitability of a properly engineered approach. Cornwallis's guns roared incessantly, but though they managed to inflict a few casualties, they did not slow the work. By October 10, the French and American guns were in place. Trumbull wrote:

> All our batteries open early this morning with a terrible roar. . . . 60 cannon and mortars, exceedingly well served and judiciously thrown. Continue till 10 o'clock and slacken. The enemies fire silenced & they driven from their lines, which can make no opposition to ours.

Like the first bit of earth to be turned, it was left to Washington to fire the first shot from an American battery. A few hours before that, Captain Johann Ewald had crossed the York River from Gloucester to Yorktown to speak with Cornwallis. He found the earl at dinner with some of his officers when the first shot was fired from the American lines. The ball crashed through the wall of the home in which they were sitting at table, took a leg from a lieutenant of the 76th Regiment, and killed the commissary general, a man named Perkins. Perkins's wife had been sitting between the two men but escaped unharmed.

Once begun, the barrage was unrelenting. Two days after the first shot was fired, Ewald wrote, "The greater part of the town lies in ashes." Heated shot from the French batteries set the *Charon* and three of the transports on fire, and they burned to the waterline while swinging at their anchors.

On the night of October 11, the second parallel was begun. The commander of the American forces working on that approach was Baron de Steuben, who had rejoined the army after convalescing in Charlottesville. As the only American officer with experience in this type of warfare, Steuben resumed his earlier role of military instructor, issuing orders on how the troops were to position themselves in the trenches in readiness for a British attack.

From the Battle of Bunker Hill onward, American troops had shown a particular skill with the shovel, and that had not changed. In one night, the sappers managed to open up a trench 7 feet wide, 3½ feet deep, and nearly half a mile long.

The opening of the second parallel rendered the British redoubts in advance of the works surrounding Yorktown, known as Numbers 9 and 10, a threat to the American lines. The two redoubts were part of the inner line of defense but not connected to those works; rather they were a few hundred yards in advance. From that position the men in Redoubts 9 and 10 would have been able to fire down the length of the new parallel. Baron de Vioménil was given command of the French division that would assault Number 9, with Colonel Guillaume, Comte de Deux-Ponts, his second. The Marquis de Lafayette's light infantry was responsible for taking Number 10, and Lieutenant Colonel Alexander Hamilton would lead the attack.

Inside the British works, Ewald, wracked with fever but absent the delusion that seemed to have struck many of his fellows, could see that the redoubts were essential to holding back the siege. "I have told everyone that as soon as one of these redoubts is taken the business is at an end, and Washington has us in his pocket," he wrote. "Yet still one hears, 'But our fleet will come before that time and raise the siege.'" By the morning of October 15, both redoubts were in the hands of the allies, and, as Ewald had understood, almost nothing remained between Washington and victory.

The previous day, Clinton had written a letter to Cornwallis updating him on the status of his relief effort and the glacial progress of the fleet. For the better part of a month, Graves's ships had been repairing the damage suffered in the Battle of the Capes and trying to resupply for a return to the Chesapeake. That same day, Hood wrote to George Jackson, telling him that "the repairs of the squadron have gone on unaccountably tedious, which has filled me with apprehension that we shall be too late to give relief to Lord Cornwallis."

Clinton's letter outlined three potential spots in the Chesapeake where the British fleet might land the five thousand troops being sent to relieve the Yorktown garrison. He made no mention of how they would get past the thirty-three ships of the line and the more than twelve thousand American and French troops that stood between them and Cornwallis. Hood had earlier proposed "to have three or four fire ships immediately prepared . . . ," his thought being that "the enemy's fleet may possibly be deranged and thrown into some confusion, and thereby give a favorable opening for pushing through." The idea was insane.

Nor did it matter. On October 15, the Americans completed the second parallel, connecting it to the newly acquired redoubts Numbers 9 and 10. Cornwallis wrote to Clinton:

> My situation now becomes very critical; we dare not shew a gun to their old batteries, and I expect that their new ones will open to-morrow morning; experience has shewn that our fresh earthen works do not resist their powerful artillery, so that we shall soon be exposed to an assault in ruined works, in a bad position, and with weakened numbers. The safety of this place is, therefore, so precarious, that I cannot recommend that the fleet and army should run great risque in endeavouring to save us.

The next morning, an hour before dawn, Cornwallis sent out the one and only sortie he would make against the American lines. Three hundred fifty men stormed out, took two of the American batteries, and spiked the guns before returning to their lines. But the effort was wasted. By ten o'clock that morning, the spiked guns had been repaired and were firing once again on the British works.

Cornwallis felt he had only two options left. One was to evacuate the troops at Yorktown across the river to Gloucester, which would buy them a little more time. The other was to surrender. Cornwallis chose the former.

On the night of October 16, he prepared sixteen large boats and, after nightfall, moved part of his army across the York River. Before any more could join them, however, a storm blew up with violent winds and driving rain. The boats, some with troops still aboard, were swept downriver. Cornwallis's remaining options were now cut in half.

By the following morning, the American batteries were fully established. "The whole of our works are now mounted with cannon and mortars," Dr. Thacher wrote, "not less than one hundred pieces of heavy ordnance have been in continual operation during the last twenty-four hours. The whole peninsula trembles under the incessant thunderings of our infernal machines." The hail of iron tore into the charred ruins of the town of York and the remains of Cornwallis's earthworks. Off to the American left, French batteries were pounding away. Then, between the intermittent salvos of the guns, there came the brisk tattoo of a drum beating "parlay." Beside the drummer stood a red-coated officer waving a white handkerchief. Jonathan Trumbull wrote, "Expect to begin our new roar of cannon, mortars, &c. but are prevented by the appearance of a flag from his Lordship, which bears a letter proposing a sessation of hostilities & a conference of commissioners to consider on terms for the surrender of the ports of York & Glocester."

The Siege of Yorktown was over.

EPILOGUE: *"A most glorious day"*

"I HAVE THE mortification to inform your Excellency that I have been forced to give up the posts of York and Gloucester, and to surrender the troops under my command."

Lord Charles Cornwallis wrote those words to Sir Henry Clinton on October 20, 1781, the day after his army had officially surrendered. Negotiations, begun on October 17, continued through the following day. Cornwallis first proposed that the British and German troops be surrendered as prisoners and then returned to their respective countries "under engagement not to serve against France, America or their allies, until released or regularly exchanged." That idea George Washington deemed "inadmissable."

Washington saw no need to negotiate, rather informing Cornwallis that he, Washington, would "declare the general Basis upon which a Definitive Treaty and Capitulation must take place." When Charleston had fallen to the British siege seventeen months earlier, Clinton had humiliated the surrendering garrison by ordering them to march out with their colors cased—that is, with their flags rolled and covered, not flying. Sir Henry had also rejected a second traditional token of a victor's respect for the surrendering army, forbidding the Americans from playing a British march as they paraded from their works. Now Washington informed Cornwallis that his army would receive the same terms. The troops from Yorktown and the sailors of Cornwallis's squadron would then be marched to some part of the country where they could be held prisoners of war.

Dr. James Thacher's journal entry of October 19 begins, "This is to us a most glorious day; but to the English, one of bitter chagrin and disappointment." Around noon, the victorious armies, American and French, were drawn up on either side of the Yorktown road in a double line that stretched over a mile long. As usual, the French presented the more impressive sight in their immaculate white uniforms, while the Americans "were clad in small jackets of white cloth, dirty and ragged, and a number of them were almost barefoot."

At the head of the French line stood the Comte de Rochambeau and his aides, with Washington and his "family"—his core group of officers—at the head of the Americans. Thacher reported as many spectators as soldiers but noted that complete silence was maintained by the thousands present.

Around two o'clock, the British and German troops marched out from the defenses surrounding Yorktown, their drums beating a British march. It is unclear whether fifes played as well, nor is it known what march the defeated soldiers chose, but centuries-old legend notwithstanding, it was almost certainly not a tune called "The World Turned Upside Down." There is, in fact, no evidence that a march of that name even existed then.

At the head of the British army was Brigadier General Charles O'Hara, second in command, Lord Cornwallis having sent word that he was ill and could not attend. It was almost universally assumed that he was simply avoiding the humiliation of the surrender ceremony. The Comte de Grasse, however, was genuinely sick and sent the Comte de Barras to stand in for him.

Cornwallis had sent his sword with O'Hara to be presented to Washington, but Washington would not accept the sword from the second in command, instructing O'Hara rather to give it to *his* second, General Benjamin Lincoln. It was Lincoln who had been forced to surrender Charleston to Clinton and Cornwallis, and he now had the satisfaction of receiving Cornwallis's surrender in return. He took the sword from O'Hara as a gesture of accepting the surrender, then immediately returned it.

The British troops were dejected and angry as they marched down the road between the French and American lines. The Germans, hired mercenaries who had little interest in the outcome of the war and could blame their loss on the British command, were more serene. At the spot designated for the troops to ground their arms, the British, according to Thacher, "manifested a *sullen temper,* throwing their arms on a pile with violence, as if determined to render them useless." Lincoln, overseeing the procedure, quickly put a stop to that.

Cornwallis's letter to Clinton announcing the surrender was sent by the sloop of war *Bonetta*, which, as one of the terms of capitulation, had been left for Cornwallis to use as he wished. Soon after the British and Germans laid down their arms, *Bonetta* put to sea and made her way to New York. On her arrival there, however, she failed to find General Clinton, Admiral Graves, or the British fleet.

As *Bonetta* had sailed north, the fleet, with Clinton and five thousand troops aboard, was sailing south to rescue Cornwallis. The admirals and captains had spent more than a month repairing and outfitting their ships, and by the middle of October, the fleet was finally ready to get underway. They weighed anchor and stood out to sea on October 19, the same day that Cornwallis's army marched out from their works and surrendered, and a full two weeks after the date Clinton had promised to Cornwallis. *Bonetta* and the fleet managed to pass each other at sea.

Around October 24, the British fleet was nearing Cape Charles when a small schooner sailed toward them, a tiny, insubstantial craft among the behemoth men-of-war. On board the schooner were three men, two of them black, the other white. One of the black men, James Robinson, was the former pilot of the *Charon*, the flagship of Commodore Thomas Symonds's little fleet at Yorktown. Robinson and the two others had made their escape before Cornwallis had officially capitulated, and now they delivered to Graves and Clinton the news those two men least wanted to hear.

After further confirmation of Cornwallis's surrender, Graves detached the ship *Rattlesnake* to carry his and Clinton's dispatches to London "that Government might be prepared to receive the particulars of so sad a catastrophe." Graves added that he hoped the Lords of the Admiralty would not think that any part of the disaster had "proceeded from the want of attention or exertion on my particular part." With that, the fleet put about and returned to New York.

The Lords of the Admiralty might not have been inclined to fault Graves or themselves, but Clinton certainly did. In fact, Clinton gave the Royal Navy nearly all the credit for the military disaster at Yorktown, pointing out to American Secretary Lord George Germain that Cornwallis could likely have been saved if the fleet had "been able to sail at, or within a few days of, the time we first expected." Clinton, more than anyone else in the British command, had always appreciated the centrality of sea power to the war in North America, and he rightly blamed the loss of Cornwallis's army on the loss of control of the sea.

For the tardiness of the relief operation, he blamed Graves and the other admirals—Samuel Hood, Francis Drake, and the recently arrived Robert Digby—while the admirals in their turn blamed the paucity of naval stores in New York for their inability to get the fleet back to sea more quickly. While that was valid to a point, it is also likely that the admirals were in no hurry to embark on what they had to realize was a dangerous and probably futile endeavor, one that carried the potential for genuine disaster. None of them expressed such misgivings in any surviving record, but that is not surprising. Expressing doubt was not always the best career move in the Royal Navy. Sometimes it was better to drag your feet while protesting that you were moving as fast as you could given the Admiralty's inability to keep the shipyards stocked.

For the overall failure in the Chesapeake, Clinton correctly blamed the inferiority of the British fleet. "To this inferiority, then," he wrote to Germain, "I may with confidence assert, and to that alone, is our present misfortune to be imputed." Clinton never even mentioned the operations of the land forces. The defeat at Yorktown, he knew, was at its heart a naval defeat.

If there was one constant in Sir Henry's writing, it was that he himself was to blame for none of it. He reminded Germain that he, Germain, had led Clinton to believe "that our fleet here would not only have been augmented at least in proportion to that of the enemy, but that our naval reinforcements would have arrived on this coast even before theirs." Despite his ongoing feud with Cornwallis, Clinton did not blame the failure on his subordinate—not, that is, until he read Cornwallis's letter of October 20.

Clinton did not receive the letter sent aboard the *Bonetta* until he returned to New York, but when he did read it he must have been livid. In addition to relating the events that led to the surrender, Cornwallis reiterated, forcefully and often, that he had never liked Yorktown as a post to fortify, that the selection of Yorktown had been Clinton's idea, and that he, Cornwallis, would have made an effort to break out and make a forced march for New York, or at least fought Washington on open ground, if he had not been assured by Clinton that help was on the way. The American Revolution may have effectively ended with Yorktown, but the war between these two men, which had been kindled even before Cornwallis's march into Virginia, would rage on until both of them were dead.

Echoes of Yorktown

By the beginning of November, rumors reached Europe that Cornwallis's army was in a tenuous position at Yorktown, though ministers in London and Paris did not know how seriously threatened the earl might be. It was clear, however, that the loss of Cornwallis would be a significant blow to British prospects in America. The Earl of Sandwich's letter of November 9 to Hood, written in response to Hood's report on the Battle of the Capes, reflected the British ministry's thinking:

> If you are not more successful in your present enterprise, the fate of which is probably determined long before this time, there is, I fear, an end to all our expectations of a favourable conclusion of the American war, and consequently that all hopes of a peace in which the power and riches of this country are not to be annihilated have no longer any existence.

Like the ministers in London, Benjamin Franklin and his fellow diplomats in Paris were aware of the developing situation in the Chesapeake, at least in its broad strokes, and had been speculating about the ramifications of the British army falling into Washington's hands, or, conversely, a victory by Cornwallis and Clinton over the allies. Of one thing they felt certain: the outcome of the fighting in Virginia would likely determine the outcome of the war one way or the other.

The news of Cornwallis's capitulation finally reached Paris on November 20, five days before it reached London. Around midnight, a courier to Franklin's home delivered a note from the Comte de Vergennes, the French foreign minister, throwing Franklin, as one observer put it, into "an ecstasy of joy." With help from Franklin, who knew a thing or two about public relations, word spread quickly throughout France. The country was immediately swept up in the old philosopher's delirium, and the victory was celebrated in the streets of every French city and town.

Clinton's letter from the Virginia capes arrived in London aboard the *Rattlesnake* on November 25, and the reaction there was more sober if no less intense. Lord Frederick North, the prime minister, on hearing the news, exclaimed, "Oh God! it is all over!"

The news came at a bad time for the North government and indeed for anyone advocating a continuation of the war effort. In what had grown from a colonial insurrection to a world war, the British had suffered losses in India, Minorca, the West Indies, and Florida, and the combined French and Spanish fleets were again threatening the English homeland. Perhaps of greater importance, the "country gentlemen" of England, whose taxes had largely financed the war, were growing ever more recalcitrant about pouring money down the American drain.

By the spring of 1782, the North ministry was gone, swept from office in the rising tide of discontent over the conduct of the American war, a tide that finally spilled its banks with the receipt of the news from Yorktown. North's government was replaced by that of Charles Watson-Wentworth, Lord Rockingham, a former prime minister and a supporter of American independence. King George III disliked Rockingham intensely, just as he disliked the thought of American independence, but in the end he had no choice but to accept first the one and eventually the other.

Despite war weariness on both sides of the ocean in the wake of Yorktown, the conflict did not end there but continued another two years. De Grasse sailed from the Chesapeake on November 4 as the end of the hurricane season and his commitments to the Spaniards shifted his theater of operations back to the West Indies. "I consider myself infinitely happy," he wrote to Washington, "to have been of some service to the United States."

De Grasse had initially agreed to escort troops under the command of the Marquis de Lafayette to Wilmington, North Carolina, for an attack on the British there, but ultimately decided he did not have enough time for that. He and Washington discussed objectives they might pursue the following year. General Washington hoped, perhaps even expected, that the defeat of Cornwallis would end America's war, but that was by no means certain in October and November 1781.

The war with England was definitely not over for de Grasse, who continued to operate in the West Indies through the end of 1781 and the first part of 1782. In April 1782, the admiral once again collided with Rodney and Hood, but this time the British possessed the superior numbers, with thirty-six ships of the line to de Grasse's thirty. The Battle of the Saints was a disaster for the French. Six French ships were captured, including the massive flagship *Ville de Paris*, taken by Hood's *Barfleur* and the *Russell.*

De Grasse found himself a prisoner of war, and upon his return to Paris, he was court-martialed. Although acquitted on most counts, he fell into disfavor with the king and retired to his family home in Tilly. He eventually regained favor at court, but he never again served in the navy of France. The Comte de Grasse died in Paris in 1788 at the age of sixty-six.

The tall and burly de Grasse, one of the few men with an even more imposing physical presence than Washington, was the only French admiral to fulfill Washington's vision of naval superiority, and in so doing proved Washington's thoughts on the subject correct. He and Washington met only twice, both times aboard the *Ville de Paris.* Today, below the bluffs of Yorktown, near where the York River flows into the Chesapeake Bay, there stands a pair of statues showing the American commander-in-chief and the French admiral conferring on the flagship's deck, a tribute to this brief and unlikely partnership that was so instrumental in the winning of the American Revolution.

For Clinton and Cornwallis, the war was certainly over. Clinton remained in New York until replaced by Sir Guy Carleton in the spring of 1782, then returned to England, where he wrote his memoirs of the war and resumed his seat in Parliament. In 1794, he was appointed governor of Gibraltar, but he died before he could take that post.

Cornwallis was held as a prisoner of war before being exchanged for the American congressman Henry Laurens, who had been captured at sea by the Royal Navy and held in the Tower of London. Cornwallis then resumed his military career, and he served as governor-general of India and later as Lord Lieutenant of Ireland, where he put down a rebellion in 1798. He was then reappointed governor-general of India and died there in 1805. His grave overlooks the Ganges River.

Lieutenant Colonel Banastre Tarleton, also taken prisoner, later returned to England on parole, where he was received as a hero. He served in the House of Commons until 1812, and, though he saw no more active military service, he retained his commission and was ultimately promoted to general. He died in 1833 at the age of seventy-eight.

Lieutenant Colonel John Graves Simcoe also returned to England on parole and was introduced to the king by George Germain. He, too, served in Parliament briefly before being appointed lieutenant governor of Upper Canada. He was an excellent administrator, helping to settle the region—often by convincing his former cavalry soldiers to move there—establishing a system of public education, and taking steps to abolish the slave trade. (His old friend Tarleton, as MP from Liverpool, was meanwhile actively working in support of slavery.) Simcoe is looked upon as one of the founding fathers of Toronto and London, Ontario. He also served briefly as commandant of St. Domingo (Haiti) and was sent to replace the deceased Cornwallis in India, but he took ill en route and returned to England, where he died in 1806.

The Rockingham government assumed office with its policy of ending the American war already accepted, and the new government wasted little time in implementing it. Plans were made for the evacuation of New York and Charleston, with troops from those posts to be sent to the Caribbean to reinforce the garrisons there. Though America was to be abandoned, the new government was not ready to give up on all fronts, particularly not in the valuable West Indies.

Sir Guy Carleton, the former governor of Quebec, replaced Clinton in command of the army in North America in the spring of 1782. Carleton had fought Benedict Arnold in the Battle of Valcour Island on Lake Champlain in the autumn of 1776. Arnold's ragtag fleet had been demolished, but Arnold succeeded in postponing the British advance from Canada into New York until 1777, and that set the stage for the American victory at the Battle of Saratoga. There, General John Burgoyne surrendered the only other British army to be given up during the war on October 17, 1777, four years to the day before Cornwallis sent his drummer to the top of the earthworks at Yorktown to begin talks with Washington. Now Carleton arrived in New York expecting to negotiate a peace as well as to oversee the evacuation of the garrison there, but after his arrival he discovered that negotiations had already begun in Paris.

The surrender at Yorktown effectively ended America's War for Independence. Like sparks in the embers, a few inconsequential skirmishes followed, but there was no major fighting in the former colonies from that point forward. From an American point of view, the war had been a simple fight between Continental troops and British and German soldiers for possession of the thirteen former colonies, and the peace that concluded it might likewise have been expected to be straightforward.

But the war was anything but simple for its other participants. It was an enormously complicated, multinational affair, and the peace negotiations were equally complex. The talks included not just the Americans and British but France, Spain, and the various interests of the Bourbons as well as the Netherlands. At issue were the many places worldwide in which the European powers had territorial claims, including the West Indies, the Mediterranean, Gibraltar, India, and, of course, North America.

The complexity of the negotiations and the slowness of communications caused more than two years to elapse before the American war was officially over. The Treaty of Paris was signed on September 3, 1783, and the British departure from New York—long delayed by logistical issues, a dearth of shipping, and the flooding of the city by Loyalist refugees and freed slaves—was finally completed in the months following. The last British ships set sail from the harbor on November 25, and they were barely out of view when General Washington led his Continental troops down Broadway to The Battery. The hour of his triumphant return, which he had longed for and fought for ever since the disastrous Battle of Long Island more than seven years earlier, had arrived at last. This was the hour that he had thought might be within his grasp in the summer of 1781. Instead, he had gambled everything on Yorktown. The route had been more indirect, but it had led him here at last.

On January 14, 1784, the Congress of the United States heard a resolution calling for King George III and the United States "to forget all past misunderstandings and differences that have unhappily interrupted the good correspondence and friendship which they mutually wish to restore." The first article stipulated that "His Britannic majesty acknowledges said United States . . . to be free, sovereign and independent states." The vote in Congress was unanimous. The war was won. The Paris Peace Treaty was ratified. The United States was born.

George Washington and the Importance of Naval Power

George Washington had not been qualified to take command of the army in 1775. His last military experience had been seventeen years earlier, and he had never led anything larger than a regiment. But he was the most qualified American-born military officer available at the time—and certainly the most famous. As it turned out, he was also exactly the leader the nascent United States needed in command of its armed forces. Of all the men and women who contributed to the success of the American Revolution, Washington is arguably the one individual without whom it could not have been won. He was the indispensable man.

When he rode into Cambridge on July 2, 1775, Washington could number among his shortcomings a lack of familiarity with the European-style warfare that was to take place on the eastern seaboard. Most of his campaigning during the French and Indian War, the early proving ground of so many officers on both sides of the War for Independence, had been done on the frontier. He was more familiar with woodland fighting than with maneuvering regiments on an open field of battle. And he knew almost nothing about ships and the sea.

Washington found a stalemate when he took command of the army. Boston at that time was virtually an island, connected to the mainland only by a narrow neck, and the Americans had the British garrison completely cut off by land. But as long as the sea lanes were open, there would be no starving the enemy out, as the British were able to resupply using the tens of thousands of tons of merchant shipping available to them and sailing under the watchful eye of the Royal Navy.

This was Washington's first lesson in the importance of sea power, and he thought initially there was nothing he could do. The rebellious colonies had no naval power to match that of the Royal Navy and no means to acquire it. When it was suggested to him, likely by John Glover of Marblehead, that armed schooners would suffice to capture unarmed merchant vessels, Washington saw the wisdom in this and embraced the idea. Soon he had seven vessels armed and fitted out and hunting the ships carrying supplies into Boston. Washington had built himself a navy, tiny though it was, and had introduced himself to the idea of contesting the seas.

He saw the possibilities of naval power again in 1776, when Benedict Arnold was able to challenge the British for control of Lake Champlain. Still, Washington believed that America lacked the resources to build, outfit, and man a navy to challenge that of Great Britain. Trying, he felt, was a waste of time and money. He was probably right.

As the Revolution wore on, Washington could only watch as the British navy transported troops up and down the coast—to New York, Charleston, Philadelphia, Virginia—allowing them to strike at will and depart with the same ease. He came to understand that sea power was the key to the war and that the Americans could never win unless they possessed it, however briefly. And for that, he knew he had to look to the French.

From the day in 1778 when France pledged its help in America's fight for independence, Washington hoped that they would provide the naval superiority he wished for, and time and again they let him down. By July 1780, when the Comte de Rochambeau and the Chevalier de Ternay arrived with a French fleet in Newport, Washington thoroughly understood the strategic challenges he faced. He wrote to the French commanders that "In any operations, and under all circumstances, a decisive naval superiority is to be considered as a fundamental principle, and the basis upon which every hope of success must ultimately depend."

Still, Washington would have to wait more than a year for all the stars to align over Yorktown. And making them align would take an enormous gamble on his part. Had he marched his army to the Chesapeake only to find that the French fleet had gone elsewhere or been repulsed by the British—as had happened earlier in the year in the abortive attempt to take Arnold—the Continental Army would quite likely have simply fallen apart and disbanded. Washington warned de Grasse of that very thing, and if past performance had told him anything, it was that the French navy was not to be counted on.

But de Grasse came through, and even as Washington and Rochambeau were marching their men south, Cornwallis's downfall was decided, not on the green fields of Virginia but on the gray and heaving waters of the Atlantic off the Virginia capes. A decisive naval superiority was indeed the basis upon which every hope of success ultimately depended. And when, for that brief and shining moment, de Grasse gave that superiority to the United States, he gave that nation its freedom as well.

Time Line

1778

July 10: Encouraged by the American victory in the Battle of Saratoga, France declares war on Great Britain, enlarging the American rebellion into a world war.

December 29: The British capture Savannah, Georgia. The failure of a combined French/American force to retake the city the following year convinces the British of the wisdom of their new plan to subdue the former colonies from south to north.

1780

May 12: British generals Sir Henry Clinton and Lord Charles Cornwallis force the surrender of Charleston, South Carolina. General Benjamin Lincoln, commander of America's southern army, is captured. Cornwallis begins to move his army north through the Carolinas, while Clinton returns to New York, which is surrounded but not immediately threatened by George Washington's northern army.

June 13: George Washington recommends Nathanael Greene to replace General Lincoln in the south, but Congress instead gives command of the southern army to Major General Horatio Gates, the nominal but undeserving hero of Saratoga.

July 11: French troops under the command of the Comte de Rochambeau land at Newport, Rhode Island. General Washington welcomes the arrival of the troops but is even more excited about the fleet that accompanies them. Five years of war have convinced Washington that America has no chance of winning as long as England maintains unchallenged naval superiority.

August 16: Gates is badly beaten at the Battle of Camden, South Carolina, and abandons the battle on horseback, riding 180 miles north in three days.

September 23: Benedict Arnold's treason—his plan to give the fort at West Point, which he commands, and with it control of the Hudson River to the British—is discovered. Arnold flees to the British.

October 14: Yielding at last to rising criticism, Congress removes Gates from the southern command. Washington appoints Nathanael Greene—an inspired choice—to command what remains of the southern army.

1781

Late 1780 through January 17: Greene divides the already-weak southern army in the face of Cornwallis's stronger army—a highly unorthodox move. He sends Brigadier General Daniel Morgan with six hundred men into the Carolina backcountry west of Charlotte, guessing correctly that Cornwallis will divide his own army in response. Cornwallis sends Lieutenant Colonel Banastre Tarleton after Morgan's wing, and Morgan, making brilliant tactical use of his regular troops and militia, defeats Tarleton at the Battle of Cowpens, South Carolina, on January 17.

January 4–January 20: Benedict Arnold, now a British general, is sent to Virginia by Sir Henry Clinton to destroy rebel supplies flowing south to Greene's army and to establish a British base on the Chesapeake Bay. Arnold leads a raiding party up the James River to Richmond, burning and looting, then retires to Portsmouth to start fortifications for a base.

February 20: Washington sends the Marquis de Lafayette to Virginia with twelve hundred men in hopes of capturing Benedict Arnold's troops. The French fleet is to assault Arnold's position from the water, forming the other half of the pincer. The fleet heads south from Newport, and the British fleet leaves Long Island in pursuit.

March 15: Lord Cornwallis defeats Nathanael Greene at the Battle of Guilford Courthouse, North Carolina, but at such a heavy cost to his army that, after initially marching his army to Wilmington, he decides to abandon the Carolinas and march for Virginia.

March 16: The French and British fleets meet outside the Chesapeake for the Battle of Cape Henry. The British are mauled but win a tactical victory when the French abandon their attempt to get to Virginia.

Lacking control of the bay, the Americans are forced to abandon their assault on Arnold.

April 28: A French fleet under Admiral de Grasse arrives in the West Indies.

May 19: Cornwallis crosses into Virginia and links his army with that of Benedict Arnold. The combined army moves at will through tidewater Virginia during the summer, scarcely hindered by Lafayette's inferior force.

August 1: In execution of ambiguous orders from Clinton, with whom he is now feuding, Cornwallis begins to fortify Gloucester and Yorktown, Virginia.

August 14: Washington gets word that de Grasse will shift his fleet from the West Indies to the Chesapeake, and he and Rochambeau begin to move their armies south to meet the French fleet in the hope of trapping Cornwallis. It is a virtual replay of the move against Arnold the previous spring, only this time against Cornwallis's entire army. Washington gambles everything on the effort, marching south with most of his army.

August 30: De Grasse arrives in the Chesapeake with a powerful fleet and three thousand additional French troops.

September 1: The British fleet under the command of Admiral Thomas Graves leaves New York to pursue the French fleet and to relieve Cornwallis.

September 5: The British fleet arrives off the Chesapeake. The Battle of the Capes ensues, and de Grasse's superior fleet drives the British off. The sailors in this battle outnumber all the soldiers on both sides of the war in North America. When the victorious French fleet returns to the Chesapeake, Cornwallis's capture is all but assured.

October 14: French and American troops storm two of Cornwallis's redoubts and capture them. This is the only significant fighting during the Siege of Yorktown.

October 17: Cornwallis sends word that he would like to discuss terms of surrender.

October 19: The British army marches out from the works at Yorktown and formally surrenders. It is the end of significant combat in the American Revolution. The following spring, peace negotiations begin.

ACKNOWLEDGMENTS

FOR ALL THE time a writer spends alone in his or her office, staring at a
screen or thumbing through fragile old books, there are many people
in the outside world whose efforts are essential on the long journey from
idea to published volume. Here, then, are some of the many people to
whom I owe thanks. To Myonne Lee, for her heroic efforts in translat-
ing eighteenth-century French naval documents. Thanks to William Far-
raro and Philander Chase for their invaluable help to me with the Papers
of George Washington and the important work they do for all historians of the Revolution. Thanks to Jim Martin for his help and insights
and to Paul Lockhart for his help with Steuben questions and his fine
book *Drillmaster of Valley Forge*.

My thanks to Chris Page and Iain MacKenzie of the Portsmouth Naval
Shipyard in England for tracking down ships' logs for me and enter-
taining an interesting discussion of signal flags. Another interesting and
insightful discussion was had with Glenn Williams of the National
Museum of the U.S. Army Project Office and Bob Selig concerning siege
operations at the Battle of Yorktown.

My old friend Charley Sealey, librarian extraordinaire, provided
invaluable service locating online sources unavailable to the civilian
researcher. And once again, I owe a debt of gratitude to the people who
run the two great libraries in my midcoast Maine neighborhood. I could
not live and work where I do without them. My thanks to the people at
Bowdoin College library in Brunswick, Maine, for running a top-notch
institution and for their patience with the less-than-timely way that I
return books. And thanks to all the research staff at the Curtis Memo-
rial Library in Maine, for their efforts on my behalf and in behalf of all
the people in this area who rely on them. They are Janet Fullerton,
Linda Oliver, Carol Lestock, Paul Dostie, and Marian Dalton.

Again, my thanks to Dr. Charles "Pip" Pippinger for his friendship,
support, and the many and timely books that he has sent me, and to

Ernest Haas, the other half of the Burlington Militia. None of this would be possible were it not for the support of my friend and agent Nat Sobel and all the fine people at Sobel Weber Associates, Inc., in particular, Adia Wright, who stands on the front lines. My thanks to all the folks at McGraw-Hill, in particular, Lisa Stracks, Molly Mulhern, and Marisa L'Heureux. Jon Eaton, my editor, is the finest I have ever worked with, and I remain thoroughly grateful for his support, patience, and hard work on behalf of this and the other books we have done together.

And, of course, my love and gratitude to my wife, Lisa, who holds it together in the twenty-first century while I am off in the eighteenth.

Endnotes

Abbreviations

CIV: Stevens, *The Campaign in Virginia*
DAR: Davis, *Documents of the American Revolution*
JP: Jefferson, *The Papers of Thomas Jefferson*
LAAR: Idzerda, *Lafayette in the Age of the American Revolution, Selected Letters and Papers, 1776–1790*
SP: Zemenszky, *The Papers of General Friedrich von Steuben*
WGW: Washington, *Writings of George Washington*
WP LC: Washington Papers, Library of Congress

Prologue

Yorktown

x The description of the attacks on Redoubts Numbers 9 and 10 are taken primarily from Joseph Plumb Martin's *Memoir of a Revolutionary Soldier*, perhaps the best primary source description of the fight. Additional sources are Hamilton's Report and Lafayette to Luzerne in Idzerda, *Lafayette in the Age of the American Revolution*; von Closen's account in *Revolutionary Journal*; Thacher, *Eyewitness to the Revolution*; and Guillaume, *My Campaigns in America*, along with other primary and secondary sources. Some liberties have been taken in this Prologue with regard to assigning thoughts and words to the participants. This was done for the sheer fun of it. The action, however, is based upon the written record.

xi *You will understand:* Lafayette to Luzerne, *LAAR,* 4:421.

Chapter 1 Washington and Rochambeau

France in the War

4 *fifty-one hundred soldiers: LAAR,* 3:83.
4 *on the Arrival of a large Land and Naval Armament:* General Orders, July 20, 1780, *WGW,* Vol. 19.
5 *gave additional animation to the spirit of rebellion:* in Ketchum, *Victory at Yorktown,* 27.

Expédition Particulière

6 *Expédition Particulière:* Kennett, *French Forces,* 10.

6 *a very rough and obstinate man:* Lafayette, *Memoirs,* 384.

7 *Send us troops:* quoted in Mackesy, *War for America,* 350.

8 *relinquish the idea:* Washington to Lafayette, July 16, 1780, *WGW,* Vol. 19.

9 *day for the re-embarkation:* Washington to Rochambeau, *LAAR,* 3:88.

War at Home and Abroad

10 *combined fleet:* Quoted in James, *British Navy in Adversity,* 179.

10 Importance of West Indies and the ministry's reaction: Mackesy, *War for America,* 184–85.

11 *The object of the war:* Ibid., 186.

12 *And I am of the opinion:* Wright to Clinton, *DAR,* 18:46.

12 Capture of Charleston: Middlekauff, *Glorious Cause,* 448–51; Miller, *Sea of Glory,* 420–22.

13 *Their destination:* Germain to Clinton, *DAR,* 18:84.

14 *I am apprehensive:* Clinton to Cornwallis, *CIV,* 1:212.

"[R]ather too indecent to be suffered"

14 *seemed to look upon my proposals:* Clinton, *The American Rebellion,* 198.

15 *So many letters Came* and following: Lafayette to Washington, *LAAR,* 3:109.

15 *the object of it:* Washington to Rochambeau, July 21, 1780, *WGW,* Vol. 19.

15 *it is extraordinary:* Washington to Rochambeau, July 27, 1780, ibid.

16 *a very considerable force:* Clinton, *The American Rebellion,* 203.

16 *120 miles in the most inclement and sickly season:* Ibid., 205.

16 *[T]his last extraordinary treatment:* Ibid., 205.

16 *in the commander of the fleet:* Clinton to Germain, ibid., 454.

CHAPTER 2 SEA POWER FOR THE GENERAL

19 *If a foreign aid of money:* WP LC.

19 *Next to a loan of money:* Washington to Laurens, quoted in Allen, *Naval History,* 547.

19 *In any operation: LAAR,* 3:88.

Stalemate and Treason

20 *From the commencement:* Thacher, *Eyewitness,* 216.

22 *thrown into some degree:* Washington to Congress, September 26, 1780, *WGW,* Vol. 20.

22 *The French have not moved:* Clinton to Germain, *CIV,* 1:283.

23 *[De Ternay] was not popular:* Berthier, "Journal," in Rice and Brown, *Campaigns of Rochambeau's Army,* 1:237.

23 *The French squadron has remained:* Lafayette, *Memoirs,* 384.

"[A]nother Expedition into the Chesapeak"

23 *I have always thought:* Clinton to Cornwallis, *CIV*, 1:269.

24 *that Sir Henry Clinton and Vice-Admiral Arbuthnot:* Germain to Cornwallis, ibid., 293.

24 *to make a diversion* and following: Clinton to Leslie, ibid., 271.

25 *My Instructions to General Leslie* and following: Clinton to Cornwallis, ibid., 310.

CHAPTER 3 "THE PARRICIDE ARNOLD"

26 *very bad, infamously provided:* Simcoe, *Operations of the Queen's Rangers*, 168.

26 *the very high estimation:* Clinton, *The American Rebellion*, 235.

26 *objects of this expedition:* Clinton to Germain, *DAR*, 17:256.

27 *make known your intention* and following: Clinton to Arnold, ibid.

29 *kept up a brisk fire:* Arnold to Clinton, *DAR*, 20:40.

29 *their pockets filled:* Ewald, *Hessian Journal*, 266.

29 *who immediately reprimanded them* and following: Simcoe, *Operations of the Queen's Rangers*, 161.

29 *greatly superior in numbers:* Ibid., 162.

29 *a large quantity of tobacco* and following: Arnold to Clinton, *DAR*, 20:41.

30 *detestable:* Ewald, *Hessian Journal*, 268.

30 *daring courage:* Simcoe, *Operations of the Queen's Rangers*, 180.

30 *set fire to all the magazines:* Ewald, *Hessian Journal*, 268.

30 *the expedition greatly resembled:* Ibid.

31 *Within less than 48 hours* and following: Jefferson to Washington, *JP*, 4:334.

"The Divine Providence manifests itself"

32 *Light Infantry and Grenadiers* and following: Washington to Jefferson, January 2, 1781, *WGW*, Vol. 20.

32 *If the advantages:* Clinton to Arbuthnot, Clinton, *The American Rebellion*, 481.

32 *a secure port in the Chesapeake:* Germain to Clinton, ibid., 483.

33 *squadron shall remain:* Arbuthnot to Clinton, ibid., 481.

35 *Recent letters from Virginia* and following: Washington to Rochambeau, January 29, 1781, *WGW*, Vol. 20.

35 *The Divine Providence manifests itself:* Rochambeau to Washington, January 29, 1781, *WP LC*.

35 *the confirmation will have enabled:* Washington to Rochambeau, February 7, 1781, *WGW*, Vol. 20.

36 *Why are we not ready:* Berthier, "Journal," in Rice and Brown, *Campaigns of Rochambeau's Army*, 1:238.

36 *If Mr Des touches should have acquired:* Washington to Rochambeau, February 7, 1781, *WGW*, Vol. 20.

CHAPTER 4 COPPER BOTTOMS

38 *a very late invention:* Falconer, *Dictionary,* 261.

38 *For God's sake, and our country's:* Quoted in James, *British Navy in Adversity,* 8.

38 *It is impossible for me:* In Chadwick, *Graves Papers,* xxiii.

38 *Chevalier Destouches waits:* Rochambeau to Washington, February 8, 1781, *WP LC.*

39 *divine naval superiority:* Lafayette to Luzerne, *LAAR,* 3:317.

39 *as many pieces:* Washington to Rochambeau, February 15, 1781, *WGW,* Vol. 21.

39 *The general must be very convinced: LAAR,* 3:332.

39 *to give the enterprise:* Washington to Rochambeau, February 17, 1781, *WGW,* Vol. 21.

39 *The destruction of the detachmt.* and following: Washington to Rochambeau, February 19, 1781, *WGW,* Vol. 21.

"Three french Ships of War"

40 *Repairing Barracks, foraging:* Arnold to Clinton, *CIV,* 1:324.

40 *Three french Ships of War* and following: Arnold to Clinton, ibid., 326.

41 *to frustrate the designs* and following: Clinton to Arbuthnot, Clinton, *The American Rebellion,* 488.

42 *a general press:* Arbuthnot to Russell, ibid., 488.

42 *reason to suppose that the ships:* Clinton to Arnold, *CIV,* 1:326.

42 *under no Apprehensions* and following: Arnold to Clinton, ibid.

42 *the elite of my army:* Clinton to Phillips, ibid., 403.

Lafayette

43 *open a correspondence* and following: Instructions to Lafayette, February 20, 1781, *WGW,* Vol. 21.

44 *It is amusing:* Lafayette to Luzerne, *LAAR,* 3:332.

44 *that Consistent with prudence* and following: Lafayette to Steuben, ibid., 342.

44 *fast sailing vessels* and following: Washington to Lafayette, ibid., 347.

44 *Convinced that a naval operation:* Washington to Steuben, February 20, 1781, *WGW,* Vol. 21.

45 *On Monsr Tillys arrival:* Steuben to Washington, March 1, 1781, *SP.*

45 *Seven or eight Merchant Vessells:* Ibid.

45 *There are a variety of positions:* Washington to Rochambeau, February 15, 1781, *WGW,* Vol. 21.

46 *On the 24th:* Blanchard, *Journal,* 90.

46 *marches but very slowly:* Rochambeau to Washington, February 22, 1781, *WGW,* Vol. 21.

47 *The Letters, found on board* and following: Ibid.

Chapter 5 Head of Elk

48 *the States of Boston and Rhode-Island* and following: Rochambeau to Washington, February 22, 1781, *WGW*, Vol. 21.

48 *to operate in Chesapeak* and following: Washington to Lafayette, *LAAR*, 3:357.

49 *he says that he cannot answer:* Rochambeau to Washington, February 22, 1781, *WGW*, Vol. 21.

49 *seems to make a difficulty:* Washington to Lafayette, *LAAR*, 3:357.

49 *Depth of the Mud* and following: Lafayette to Washington, ibid., 359.

50 *The Commanding Officer* and following: Lafayette to the Commanding Officer in Virginia, ibid., 363.

50 *This delay may prove fatal:* Lafayette to Gist, ibid., 365.

50 *I have it therefore in my Power:* Steuben to Washington, March 1, 1871, *SP*.

51 *You need not, my Dear General:* Ibid.

51 *a number of Cruisers out up the Bay:* James Maxwell to Jefferson, March 5, 1781, *SP*.

"[A] sufficient force to clear the Chesapeake Bay"

51 *rest assured every attention:* Clinton to Arnold, *CIV*, 1:326.

51 *There being indications:* Simcoe, *Operations of the Queen's Rangers*, 178.

52 *upwards of three Thousand Men* and following: Arnold to Clinton, *CIV*, 1:340.

52 *We are however all in high Spirits:* Ibid.

52 *in an uninhabited country:* Arbuthnot to Sandwich, Barnes and Owen, *Private Papers of John, Earl of Sandwich*, 4:167.

53 *I have lost almost totally:* Arbuthnot to Sandwich, ibid., 3:267.

53 *I flatter myself:* Clinton, *The American Rebellion*, 490.

53 *proceed instantly with the squadron:* Ibid., 253.

54 *to send them under two frigates:* Ibid., 491.

The French Move

54 *Everyone was vying:* Berthier, "Journal," in Rice and Brown, *Campaigns of Rochambeau's Army*, 1:241.

54 *I set out in the morning for Rhode Island:* Washington to Lafayette, *LAAR*, 3:358.

55 *I mark, as a fortunate day:* Blanchard, *Journal*, 93.

55 *The firing from the French ships:* Daniel Updike, quoted in Stone, *French Allies*, 363.

55 *forming a great parade:* Berthier, "Journal," in Rice and Brown, *Campaigns of Rochambeau's Army*, 1:241.

55 *The nobility of his bearing:* Ibid.

56 *a light norther:* Ibid., 242.

CHAPTER 6 THE BATTLE OF CAPE HENRY

58   *part of the squadron was caught:* Berthier, "Journal," in Rice and Brown, *Campaigns of Rochambeau's Army*, 1:242.

58   *This separation was alarming:* Blanchard, *Journal*, 94.

59   *The* Bedford *was rather in confusion* and following: Arbuthnot to Sandwich, Barnes and Owen, *Private Papers of John, Earl of Sandwich*, 4:167.

60   *to the great satisfaction of all:* Blanchard, *Journal*, 95.

"[A] more pleasing prospect"

61   *with their larboard tacks aboard:* Relation de la sortie de l'Escadre Française.

61   *At first the Admiral gave the signal* and following: Ibid.

61   *signaled the squadron:* Berthier, "Journal," in Rice and Brown, *Campaigns of Rochambeau's Army*, 1:242.

61   *neither avoided nor sought battle:* Ibid., 243.

61   *He realized the impossibility:* Relation de la sortie de l'Escadre Française.

62   *give the boastful English:* Ibid.

62   *[I]t favoured our operations:* Arbuthnot to Sandwich, Barnes and Owen, *Private Papers of John, Earl of Sandwich*, 4:168.

63   *so as to allow* and following: Berthier, "Journal," in Rice and Brown, *Campaigns of Rochambeau's Army*, 1:243.

66   *[T]he enemy* and following: Arbuthnot to Sandwich, Barnes and Owen, *Private Papers of John, Earl of Sandwich*, 4:168.

67   *hailed Captain Cosby:* Ibid.

67   *to give his ships a better chance:* Berthier, "Journal," in Rice and Brown, *Campaigns of Rochambeau's Army*, 1:243.

67   *At one o'clock:* Ibid.

Fleet Action

67   *which obliged me to form:* Arbuthnot to Sandwich, Barnes and Owen, *Private Papers of John, Earl of Sandwich*, 4:169.

68   *the van was by this means* and following: Ibid.

68   *[N]othing can exceed the gallant behaviour* and following: Ibid.

68   *One of their ships was so disabled* and following: Blanchard, *Journal*, 97.

69   *had, for its part, to sustain the attack* and following: Ibid.

70   *the English three-decker* and following: Berthier, "Journal," in Rice and Brown, *Campaigns of Rochambeau's Army*, 1:243.

70   *After a very short show:* Arbuthnot to Sandwich, Barnes and Owen, *Private Papers of John, Earl of Sandwich*, 4:169.

70   *to close up the battle line* and following: Berthier, "Journal," in Rice and Brown, *Campaigns of Rochambeau's Army*, 1:243.

71   *M. des Touches, whose object was purely offensive:* Quoted in James, *British Navy in Adversity*, 274.

CHAPTER 7 "AN ATTEMPT TO CONQUER VIRGINIA"

72 *We arrived here on the 18ᵗʰ:* Arbuthnot to Sandwich, Barnes and Owen, *Private Papers of John, Earl of Sandwich,* 4:169.

72 *I was much hurt:* George III to Sandwich, in ibid., 170.

72 *gave orders for every person:* Simcoe, *Operations of the Queen's Rangers,* 185.

72 *a squadron with French colours:* Ibid., 186.

72 *a fleet should appear:* Clinton to Arnold, *CIV,* 1:330.

72 *he had the pleasure:* Simcoe, *Operations of the Queen's Rangers,* 185.

73 *put to sea immediately:* Arbuthnot to Arnold, *CIV,* 1:372.

73 *The troops under Phillips:* Clinton to Cornwallis, ibid., 345.

73 *I will frankly own:* Ibid., 111.

74 *It is probable, whenever the objects:* Clinton to Phillips, ibid., 350.

74 *the very agreeable and important intelligence* and following: Germain to Clinton, *DAR,* 20:131.

Best-Laid Plans

75 *Contrary Winds, Heavy Rains:* Lafayette to Washington, March 7, 1781, *SP.*

75 *Comte de Rochambeau thinks His troops Equal* and following: Lafayette to Washington, *LAAR,* 3:386.

76 *We can only be answerable:* Jefferson to Steuben, March 10, 1781, *SP.*

76 *The Number of Small frigats:* Lafayette to Washington, *LAAR,* 3:397.

77 *[I]t is to be feared* and following: Steuben to Washington, March 15, 1781, *SP.*

77 *thought it More polite:* Lafayette to Washington, *LAAR,* 3:397.

77 *To My Great disappointment:* Lafayette to Jefferson, ibid., 401.

77 *From the information we have just received:* Meade to Steuben, March 20, 1781, *SP.*

78 *We are full of anxiety here:* Walker to Steuben, March 20, 1781, *SP.*

78 *Nothing Could Equal My Surprise* and following: Lafayette to Washington, *LAAR,* 3:409.

78 *A circumstance in which the Winds and Weather:* Washington to Destouches, March 31, 1781, *WP LC.*

CHAPTER 8 THE BEGINNING OF THE END

83 *a Wilderness, with a few cleared fields:* Greene, *Papers,* 7:434.

83 *green plaid pants:* Hatch, *Battle of Guilford Courthouse,* 138.

83 *Cornwallis's pedigree was as good as they came:* Fischer, *Washington's Crossing,* 119.

The Battle of New Garden

85 *Immediately between the head of the Column:* Cornwallis to Germain, *CIV,* 1:364.

85 *As the front of the British column approached:* Tarleton, *Campaigns,* 272.

86 *to arms at four in the morning:* Lee, *Memoirs,* 273.

86 *the column to retire by troops:* Ibid.

86 *still in a walk* and following: Ibid.

87 *the dragoons came instantly to the right about:* Ibid.

87 *he should trample his enemy:* Ibid.

87 *the fire of the Americans was heavy:* Tarleton, *Campaigns,* 271.

87 *frightened Lee's horse:* Lee, *Memoirs,* 274.

87 *came running up with trailed arms:* Ibid.

88 *Lee . . . behaved himself:* Lamb, *British Soldier's Story,* 84.

88 *retreated with precipitation:* Tarleton, *Campaigns,* 271.

88 *between twenty and thirty of the guards:* Ibid.

88 *attacked with his usual good conduct:* Cornwallis to Germain, *CIV,* 1:364.

88 *An engagement:* Tarleton, *Campaigns,* 271.

88 *the long avoided:* Lee, *Memoirs,* 275.

CHAPTER 9 THE AMERICAN COMMAND

89 *9 or 10,000 men:* Cornwallis to Germain, *CIV,* 1:364.

89 *standing drawn up in perfect battle order: Journal of Von Bose,* S.48.

91 *Major General Gates immediately repair:* Ford, *Journals of the Continental Congress,* 17:508.

91 *Grand Army:* Middlekauff, *Glorious Cause,* 454.

91 *Was there ever an instance:* quoted in Maass, "Complete Victory."

91 *gave great satisfaction to every one* and following: Moultrie, *Memoirs,* 249.

92 *if it deserves the name of one:* Greene to Washington, Greene, *Papers,* 6:542.

The Road to Guilford Courthouse

93 *camp of repose* and following: Greene to unidentified person, Greene, *Papers,* 7:175.

93 *give protection to that part of the country:* Greene to Morgan, Greene, *Papers,* 6:589.

93 *could be brought to stand* and following: Moultrie, *Memoirs,* 245.

94 *continentals and backwoodsmen gave ground:* Tarleton, *Campaigns,* 217.

94 *unaccountable panic extended itself:* Ibid.

94 *impossible to forsee* and following: Cornwallis to Clinton, *CIV,* 1:364.

95 *1426 Infantry Men:* Council of War, Greene, *Papers,* 6:596.

95 *The Corps had now a great number of sick: Journal of Von Bose,* S.45.

95 *In this campaign:* Lamb, *British Soldier's Story,* 90.

96 *force was much more respectable:* Greene to Huntington, Greene, *Papers,* 7:433.

"We waited the approach of the Enemy"

96 *ciatick pain* and following: Morgan to Greene, Greene, *Papers*, 7:191.

96 *[P]ut the remainder of the Militia:* Morgan to Greene, ibid., 324.

96 Disposition of troops and battle: Greene, *Papers*; Hatch, *Battle of Guilford Courthouse*; *Journal of Von Bose*; Lamb, *British Soldier's Story*; Lee, *Memoirs*; Stevens, *CIV*; Seymour, *Journal of the Southern Expedition*; Tarleton, *Campaigns*.

97 *Corps of observation:* Greene to Huntington, Greene, *Papers*, 7:434.

98 *The greater part of the County:* Ibid.

98 *I posted in my rear:* Stevens to Lee, quoted in Hatch, *Battle of Guilford Courthouse*, 37.

98 *two Brigades:* Greene to Huntington, Greene, *Papers*, 7:434.

99 *not be afraid of the British:* Lee, quoted in Hatch, *Battle of Guilford Courthouse*, 37.

99 *they should obtain his free permission:* Quoted in ibid., 37.

99 *In this position:* Greene to Huntington, Greene, *Papers*, 7:434.

CHAPTER 10 THE BATTLE OF GUILFORD COURTHOUSE

100 *calm, and illuminated with a cloudless sun:* Lee, *Memoirs*, 283.

100 *bring forward the Guns:* Cornwallis to Germain, *CIV*, 1:364.

100 *The three British 6-pounders:* Greene, *Papers*, 7:436n.

100 *The Prisoners taken by Lieut Colonel Tarleton:* Cornwallis to Germain, *CIV*, 1:364.

100 *impracticable for cannon:* Ibid.

101 *Lieutenant O'Hara, a spirited young officer:* Tarleton, *Campaigns*, 273.

101 *a most tremendous fire:* Tucker to his wife, quoted in Hatch, *Battle of Guilford Courthouse*, 44.

102 *The order and coolness:* Tarleton, *Campaigns*, 273.

102 *raked by their fire:* Lee, *Memoirs*, 277.

103 *the movement was made* and following: Lamb, *British Soldier's Story*, 89.

103 *with more than even his usual commanding voice:* Ibid.

103 *To our infinite distress:* Lee, *Memoirs*, 277.

103 *without firing at all:* Greene to Huntington, Greene, *Papers*, 7:435.

104 *base desertion:* Lee, *Memoirs*, 278.

104 *warmly engaged:* Cornwallis to Germain, *CIV*, 1:366.

104 *the regiments became somewhat more separated:* Journal of Von Bose, S.49.

104 *[O]n finding that the left of the 33rd* and following: Cornwallis to Germain, *CIV*, 1:364.

The Second Line

105 *keep his Cavalry compact:* Cornwallis to Germain, *CIV*, 1:365.

106 *our brigade major came:* Houston, *Journal*, in *Key Original Source Outline*.

106 *The excessive thickness of the woods:* Cornwallis to Germain, *CIV*, 1:364.

106 *stood their ground:* Greene to Washington, quoted in Hatch, *Battle of Guilford Courthouse*, 57.

106 *the conflict became still more fierce* and following: Lamb, *British Soldier's Story*, 89.

106 *Virginia Militia gave the Enemy:* Greene to Huntington, Greene, *Papers*, 7:435.

107 *This threw the militia into such confusion* and following: Tucker to his wife, in Commager and Morris, *Spirit of 'Seventy-Six*, 1166.

108 *the broken enemy to make frequent stands:* Cornwallis to Germain, *CIV*, 1:364.

108 *Some corps meeting with less opposition:* Tarleton, *Campaigns*, 274.

108 *more ardour than prudence:* Lee, quoted in Hatch, *Battle of Guilford Courthouse*, 66.

108 *When Webster advanced upon our third line:* Howard, in *Key Original Source Outline.*

109 *At this period the event of the action was doubtful:* Tarleton, *Campaigns*, 274.

CHAPTER 11 A PYRRHIC VICTORY

110 *Glowing with impatience:* Cornwallis to Germain, *CIV*, 1:366.

110 *premature, confused and scattering fire:* Colonel Edward Carrington, quoted in Greene, *Papers*, 7:440n.

111 *Leaping a ravine:* Lt. Holcomb, quoted in Hatch, *Battle of Guilford Courthouse*, 77.

111 *retook the cannon:* Tarleton, *Campaigns*, 274.

111 *One recounting, perhaps apocryphal:* In Hatch, *Battle of Guilford Courthouse*, 81.

112 *by a well-directed fire:* Cornwallis to Germain, *CIV*, 1:366.

112 *Cornwallis, seeing the vigorous advance:* Lee, *Memoirs*, 277.

113 *and got into the rear of the Virginia Brigade:* Greene to Huntington, Greene, *Papers*, 7:434.

113 *much dissatisfied:* Lee, *Memoirs*, 282n.

"[A] well-contested action"

113 *the enemy were soon put to flight* and following: Cornwallis to Germain, *CIV*, 1:366–67.

114 *General Hugar:* Greene to Huntington, Greene, *Papers*, 7:435.

114 *were retreating in good order:* Tarleton, *Campaigns*, 274.

114 *followed our army:* Lee, *Memoirs*, 282.

114 *had suffered but little:* Cornwallis to Germain, *CIV*, 1:367.

114 *close with the left of the Continental line:* Lee, *Memoirs*, 281.

114 *[T]he Remainder of the Cavalry:* Cornwallis to Germain, *CIV*, 1:367.

115 *the guards and the Hessians were directed:* Tarleton, *Campaigns*, 276.

115 *their light horse came on us:* Journal of Samuel Houston in *Key Original Source Outline.*

115 *Thus ended:* Tarleton, *Campaigns,* 276.

"[A] signal Victory"

115 *My Lord:* Cornwallis to Germain, *CIV,* 1:363.

116 *The night . . . was remarkable:* Stedman, in *Key Original Source Outline.*

116 Casualty figures from Hatch, *Battle of Guilford Courthouse.*

116 *leaving us in great numbers:* Greene to Joseph Reed, Greene, *Papers,* 7:450.

116 *were acquainted with wood and tree fighting:* Lee, *Memoirs,* 285n.

117 *Our army is in good spirits* and following: Greene to Reed, Greene, *Papers,* 7:450.

117 *wishing for an opportunity:* Greene to Thomas Sumpter, Ibid., 442.

117 *We have little to eat:* Greene to Reed, ibid., 450.

117 *so totally destitute of subsistence:* Cornwallis to Germain, *CIV,* 1:369.

117 *compleat victory obtained:* Cornwallis Proclamation, ibid., 371.

118 *the greatest number of our friends* and following: Cornwallis to Clinton, ibid., 397.

118 *the remainder without Shoes:* Ibid.

118 *Lord Cornwallis don't wish to fight us:* Lee, *Memoirs,* 290.

119 *the Americans insulted the yagers:* Tarleton, *Campaigns,* 279.

119 *so barren and thinly settled:* Lee, *Memoirs,* 290.

119 *determined to carry the War:* Greene to Washington, Greene, *Papers,* 7:452.

CHAPTER 12 REINFORCING THE CHESAPEAKE

121 *The very numerous important advantages* and following: Clinton, *The American Rebellion,* 275.

122 *If the Admiral, disapproving of Portsmouth:* Clinton to Phillips, *CIV,* 1:347.

122 *With regard to a station:* Clinton, *The American Rebellion,* 493.

122 *recognized in him:* Ewald, *Hessian Journal,* 296.

122 *I think the present situation:* Phillips to Clinton, *CIV,* 1:378.

123 *the principal object of your expedition:* Clinton to Phillips, ibid., 347.

123 *operation in favor of Lord Cornwallis:* Ibid.

123 *a station to protect the King's ships:* Clinton to Phillips, ibid., 404.

123 *It is unlucky for us:* Phillips to Clinton, ibid., 377.

124 *he may have bought it dear:* Phillips to Clinton, ibid., 409.

The Next Move

124 *described to me:* Cornwallis to Clinton, *CIV,* 1:397.

124 *Wilmington, which had been occupied specifically:* Mackesy, *War for America,* 404.

124 *the Inhabitants on each side:* Ibid.

124 *by blindly trusting:* Tarleton, *Campaigns*, 280.

124 *it was impossible to procure:* Cornwallis to Clinton, *CIV*, 1:397.

125 *retained great zeal:* Tarleton, *Campaigns*, 280.

125 *united all the virtues of civil life:* Ibid., 281.

125 *our military operations:* Cornwallis to Clinton, *CIV*, 1:396.

125 *I am very anxious* and following: Ibid., 399.

126 *the great rivers:* Cornwallis to Phillips, ibid., 428.

126 *with a considerable force:* Cornwallis to Germain, ibid., 420.

127 *My situation here:* Cornwallis to Phillips, ibid., 428.

127 *Now, my dear friend:* Cornwallis to Phillips, Cornwallis, *Correspondence*, 1:87.

127 *in hopes to withdraw Greene* and following: Cornwallis to Phillips, *CIV*, 1:428.

127 *it is my wish that you should continue:* Clinton to Cornwallis, ibid., 406.

127 *I take the liberty of giving:* Cornwallis to Germain, Cornwallis, *Correspondence*, 1:90.

128 *nothing to add to it* and following: Cornwallis to Clinton, *CIV*, 1:424.

128 *your Lordship's success in Carolina* and following: Clinton to Cornwallis, ibid., 443–44.

CHAPTER 13 "[T]HE ENEMY HAVE TURNED SO MUCH OF THEIR ATTENTION TO THE SOUTHERN STATES"

130 *Baron Stuben will join this Army:* Greene to Washington, May 1, 1781, *SP*.

130 *As soon as we were assured:* Steuben to Muhlenberg, April 1, 1781, *SP*.

131 *I was fearful our Scheme:* Weedon to Steuben, April 1, 1781, *SP*.

131 *no Extraordinary Movement:* Ibid.

131 *carry the greatest part of their force* and following: Steuben to Weedon, April 1, 1781, *SP*.

132 *I cannot think this will be advisable:* Greene to Lafayette, *LAAR*, 4:4.

132 *I wish the detachment* and following: Washington to Lafayette, ibid., 7.

133 *Appeared Ridiculous* and following: Lafayette to Washington, ibid., 10.

133 *Since the enemy:* Washington to Steuben, *WGW*, Vol. 20.

134 *Since my letter of yesterday* and following: Washington to Lafayette, *LAAR*, 4:8.

134 *I would Have Been allowed* and following: Lafayette to Washington, ibid., 13.

134 *Had no Monney:* Lafayette to Greene, ibid., 37.

135 *They will Certainly obey:* Lafayette to Washington, *LAAR*, 4:32.

135 *they like Better Hundred:* Ibid.

The British on Offense

135 *This Much is certain:* Muhlenberg to Weedon, April 6, 1781, *SP*.

136 *busied strenghening their works:* Steuben to Washington, April 15, 1781, *SP*.

136 *In endeavoring to guard:* Steuben to Weedon, April 11, 1781, *SP.*

136 *a Post of force:* Phillips and Arnold to Clinton, *CIV,* 1:410.

136 *so tolerably complete* and following: Phillips to Clinton, ibid., 408.

137 *the light infantry, part of the 76th:* Arnold to Clinton, *DAR,* 20:142.

137 *a plain Tale of many Difficulties* and following: Phillips to Clinton, *CIV,* 1:413.

138 *Gen. Phillips informed the officers:* Simcoe, *Operations of the Queen's Rangers,* 189.

138 *I have recd Intelligence:* Innes to Muhlenberg, April 18, 1781, *SP.*

139 *uncommonly dark and tempestuous* and following: Simcoe, *Operations of the Queen's Rangers,* 191.

139 *Colo. Simcoe has his Corps:* Steuben to Jefferson, *JP,* 5:526.

139 *Quartermaster M'Gill, with some of the huzzars:* Simcoe, *Operations of the Queen's Rangers,* 192.

139 *they destroyed the few articles:* Jameson to Madison, April 28, 1781, *SP.*

140 *they possessed themselves:* Innes to Jefferson, April 22, 1781, *SP.*

140 *destroyed several armed ships:* Arnold to Clinton, *DAR,* 20:142.

The Americans on Defense

140 *should the enemy Land:* Steuben to Innes, April 19, 1781, *SP.*

140 *by intense Fatigues* and following: Innes to Jefferson, April 22, 1781, *SP.*

141 *Halt one Day* and following: Lafayette to Greene, *LAAR,* 4:37.

141 *a few Hatts, Some Shoes* and following: Lafayette to Greene, ibid., 38–39.

142 *The Battery at Hoods:* Steuben to Lafayette, ibid., 51.

142 *to oppose the Enemy:* Steuben to Innes, April 23, 1781, *SP.*

142 *now Standing up James River:* Innes to Steuben, April 23, 1781, *SP.*

CHAPTER 14 THE BATTLE OF BLANDFORD

144 *[I]t was apparent:* Simcoe, *Operations of the Queen's Rangers,* 195.

144 *ordered General Muhlenberg* and following: Steuben to Greene, April 25, 1781, *SP.*

145 *Lieut. Col. Abercrombie* and following: Simcoe, *Operations of the Queen's Rangers,* 197.

145 *I have the pleasure to say* and following: Steuben to Greene, April 25, 1781, *SP.*

"[A] scene of singular confusion ensued"

146 *with the light infantry:* Arnold to Clinton, *DAR,* 20:143.

147 *of all the stores collected:* Steuben to Greene, May 5, 1781, *SP.*

147 *a very considerable force:* Arnold to Clinton, *DAR,* 20:143.

147 *expressed a desire* and following: *JP,* 5:558n.

148 *to the last extremity:* Arnold to Clinton, *DAR,* 20:143.

148 *With difficulty she brought:* Simcoe, *Operations of the Queen's Rangers,* 199.

148 *opened from an unexpected quarter:* Ibid.

149 *kept up a heavy fire:* Arnold to Clinton, *DAR,* 20:143.

149 *grape shot must inevitably:* Simcoe, *Operations of the Queen's Rangers,* 199.

149 *parlying with the boat's crew* and following: Ibid., 200.

150 *Want of boats:* Arnold to Clinton, *DAR,* 20:143.

150 *whom their many sea voyages:* Simcoe, *Operations of the Queen's Rangers,* 201.

151 *Two ships, three brigs:* Arnold to Clinton, *DAR,* 20:143.

Lafayette and Phillips

152 *Have Spoke with Surprise:* Lafayette to Weedon, *LAAR,* 4:78.

152 *authorized to inflict* and following: Phillips to Lafayette, Ibid., 69.

152 *where preparations are making* and following: Phillips to Lafayette, ibid., 72.

153 *Bombastic:* Lafayette to Greene, ibid., 79.

153 *your long absence* and following: Lafayette to Phillips, ibid., 73.

154 *proceeded up the river:* Arnold to Clinton, *DAR,* 20:144.

154 *determined to defend that Capital:* Lafayette to Steuben, *LAAR,* 4:81n.

154 *The Ennemy are advancing:* Ibid.

154 *spectators of the conflagration:* Arnold to Clinton, *DAR,* 20:144.

154 *being charged by a few Dragoons:* Lafayette to Greene, *LAAR,* 4:80.

154 *[W]hen he [Phillips] was going to give:* Lafayette to Washington, ibid., 83.

CHAPTER 15 THE BRITISH WAR AT SEA

169 *a decisive naval superiority:* Washington to Rochambeau, July 15, 1780, *WGW.*

170 *Naval operations from:* Chadwick, *Graves Papers;* Coggins, *Ships and Seamen;* James, *British Navy in Adversity;* Mackesy, *War for America;* Rodney, *Letter-Books.*

170 *we should not have taken:* Quoted in James, *British Navy in Adversity,* 192.

171 *His Majesty's Territories:* Rodney, *Letter-books,* 1:10.

172 *the best officer:* Nelson, *Graves' Dispatches,* 252.

172 *surprise and astonishment:* James, *British Navy in Adversity,* 255.

"I cannot venture to pass the Roanoke"

173 *seize as many boats as possible* and following: Tarleton, *Campaigns,* 285.

174 *honour and future happiness* and following: Cornwallis to Tarleton, Tarleton, *Campaigns,* 330.

175 *more fruitful:* Ibid.

175 *if it appears by your information:* Ibid.

175 *their efforts were baffled* and following: Tarleton, *Campaigns,* 287.

176 *I can learn no satisfactory accounts:* Cornwallis to Phillips, Tarleton, *Campaigns,* 332.

176 *I cannot describe my feelings:* Cornwallis, *Correspondence,* 2:98.

176 *several warehouses with 150 hogsheads:* Arnold to Clinton, *DAR*, 20:144.

177 *the last material order:* Simcoe, *Operations of the Queen's Rangers*, 204.

Wethersfield

178 *[I]nstead of having everything in readiness:* Washington, *Diaries*, 208.

178 *The Last engagement:* Rochambeau to Washington, March 28, 1781, *WP LC.*

178 *It is unfortunate:* Washington to Lund Washington, March 31, 1781, *WGW*, Vol. 21.

179 *I assure your Excellency:* Washington to Rochambeau, April 30, 1781, ibid.

179 *wrote only to have the means:* Rochambeau to Washington, May 5, 1781, *WP LC.*

179 *retard and injure:* Washington to Rochambeau, April 3, 1781, *WGW*, Vol. 21.

180 *the Militia service is preffered:* Washington to Rochambeau, April 7, 1781, ibid.

180 *such a force from your army:* Ibid.

181 *your Excellency may well think* and following: Rochambeau to Washington, May 8, 1781, *WP LC.*

183 *The great waste of Men* and following: May 23, 1781, *WGW*, Vol. 22.

Chapter 16 Juncture

184 *Sent to Annoy:* Lafayette to Weedon, *LAAR*, 4:78.

184 *It is not only on account:* Lafayette to Washington, ibid., 84.

185 *By letters from North Carolina* and following: Lafayette to Washington, ibid., 88.

185 *Every thing that Can do:* Lafayette to Steuben, ibid., 91.

185 *His Command of the water* and following: Lafayette to Washington, *LAAR*, 4:84.

185 *Here I am in the enemy's former camp:* Lafayette to Luzerne, *LAAR*, 4:90.

186 *hopes of being in time:* Simcoe, *Operations of the Queen's Rangers*, 207.

186 *had not quitted James river:* Tarleton, *Campaigns*, 289.

186 *I have just received yours:* Cornwallis to Tarleton, ibid., 332.

187 *The immediate infliction:* Tarleton, *Campaigns*, 290.

187 *the irrecoverable state:* Simcoe, *Operations of the Queen's Rangers*, 209.

187 *will look without pistol, sword:* Lafayette to Luzerne, *LAAR*, 4:90.

188 *You will conceive my distress:* Cornwallis to Rawdon, Cornwallis, *Correspondence*, 98.

188 *loss I cannot sufficiently lament:* Cornwallis to Clinton, ibid., 99.

188 *I cannot immediately say:* Cornwallis to Rawdon, Cornwallis, *Correspondence*, 98.

New Theaters and Old

188 *The security of the two Carolinas* and following: Clinton to Phillips, Clinton, *The American Rebellion*, 515.

189 *For, until they do:* Clinton to Phillips, ibid., 518.

190 *Nothing Can attract My Sight* and following: Lafayette to Washington, *LAAR*, 4:88.

190 *If the Chesapeake had become:* Quoted in Larrabee, *Decision at the Chesapeake*, 127.

190 *bear too great a resemblance:* Cornwallis to Clinton, Clinton, *The American Rebellion*, 523.

191 *I shall therefore only observe:* Germain to Clinton, ibid., 527.

191 *to push the war from south to north:* Germain to Cornwallis, *DAR*, 18:152.

191 *I should certainly have endeavored:* Clinton to Cornwallis, *CIV*, 1:497.

192 *But what is done:* Ibid.

192 *will have the advantage:* Ibid., 496.

192 *can be no longer secure* and following: Ibid., 497.

193 *I shall be constrained:* Clinton to Germain, Clinton, *The American Rebellion*, 507.

193 *in the civilest manner:* Clinton to Germain, *CIV*, 1:448.

193 *Admiral Arbuthnot is not recalled:* Ibid.

193 *it would be cruelty:* Sandwich to Arbuthnot, Barnes and Owen, *Private Papers of John, Earl of Sandwich*, 4:172.

CHAPTER 17 "I AM INCLINED TO THINK WELL OF YORK"

195 *proceeded to learn:* Tarleton, *Campaigns*, 292.

195 *about one thousand continental troops:* Cornwallis to Clinton, Cornwallis, *Correspondence*, 1:100.

195 *I will now proceed* and following: Ibid.

196 *health had benefitted by the sea air* and following: Tarleton, *Campaigns*, 292–95.

197 *The army appears similar* and following: Ewald, *Hessian Journal*, 305.

198 *I cannot understand what has become:* Lafayette to Luzerne, *LAAR*, 4:90.

198 *A Correspondence With Arnold:* Lafayette to Greene, ibid., 112.

198 *Moved Back:* Lafayette to Weedon, ibid., 137.

199 *It is Said Clel. Tarleton Has Mounted:* Lafayette to Greene, ibid., 112.

Charlottesville and Point of Fork

200 *if it pleases Lord Cornwallis:* Lafayette to Weedon, *LAAR*, 4:138.

200 *500 men under arms* and following: Steuben to Lafayette, ibid., 139.

201 *prevail upon the Gentlemen:* Lafayette to Weedon, ibid., 142.

201 *Here I am with 550 men* and following: Steuben to Lafayette, ibid., 166.

202 *without apprehension or difficulty:* Tarleton, *Campaigns*, 294.

202 *From what I could learn:* Cornwallis to Clinton, Cornwallis, *Correspondence,* 1:100.

202 *as most distant* and following: Tarleton, *Campaigns,* 295.

"[M]y situation became critical"

205 *Lt. Spencer completely imposed:* Simcoe, *Operations of the Queen's Rangers,* 215.

205 *I recev'd intelligence that the Enemy* and following: Steuben to Lafayette, *LAAR,* 4:170.

206 *The advanced men of the hawsers* and following: Simcoe, *Operations of the Queen's Rangers,* 217.

207 *whom accident had placed* and following: Ibid., 218.

207 *The Conduct of the Baron:* Lafayette to Washington, *LAAR,* 4:194.

208 *would have quitted his camp:* Simcoe, *Operations of the Queen's Rangers,* 220.

CHAPTER 18 THE PROMISE OF A FLEET

210 De Grasse: Dull, *French Navy;* Chadwick, *Graves Papers;* Lewis, *De Grasse.*

211 *partly depends upon:* Washington to Rochambeau, June 4, 1781, *WGW,* Vol. 22.

212 *At any rate I could wish:* Ibid.

212 *I was invited:* Blanchard, *Journal,* 106.

212 *the rest dispersed:* Rochambeau to Washington, June 12, 1781, *WP LC.*

213 *the naval forces that the British have* and following: De Grasse to Rochambeau, March 29, 1781, *WP LC.*

213 *the importance of the Secret* and following: Rochambeau to Washington, June 10, 1781, *WP LC.*

214 *He mistrusts every one:* Blanchard, *Journal,* 106.

214 *You cannot* and following: Washington to Rochambeau, June 13, 1781, *WGW,* Vol. 22.

215 *unacquainted as I am:* Ibid.

Spencer's Ordinary

215 *to 14 Counties on this side:* Steuben to Lafayette, *LAAR,* 4:182.

216 *Our jonction:* Lafayette to Steuben, *LAAR,* 4:179.

216 *I Request, my dear Sir* and following: Ibid.

216 *We make it seem we are pursuing him* and following: Lafayette to Luzerne, ibid., 186.

217 *round up all the slaughter cattle:* Ewald, *Hessian Journal,* 306.

217 *found little or nothing to destroy:* Simcoe, *Operations of the Queen's Rangers,* 225.

217 *We had rounded up many cattle:* Ewald, *Hessian Journal,* 306.

218 *much too fatigued* and following: Simcoe, *Operations of the Queen's Rangers,* 226.

218 *the cattle as well as the cavalry* and following: Ewald, *Hessian Journal*, 306.

218 *Simcoe has also effected* and following: Wayne to Lafayette, *LAAR*, 4:211.

218 *I . . . much approve:* Lafayette to Wayne, *LAAR*, 4:214.

218 *felt his situation* and following: Simcoe, *Operations of the Queen's Rangers*, 226.

219 *a fatiguing march:* Wayne to Lafayette, *LAAR*, 4:211.

219 *I had hardly closed my eyes:* Ewald, *Hessian Journal*, 308.

219 *began a smart Action:* Lafayette to Greene, *LAAR*, 4:216.

219 *The enemy:* Ewald, *Hessian Journal*, 309.

"[W]e are threatened with a siege"

220 *Upon a full consideration:* Washington to Lafayette, *LAAR*, 4:154.

220 *might form an army:* Clinton, *The American Rebellion*, 304.

220 *it will be unnecessary* and following: Clinton to Cornwallis, *CIV*, 2:16.

221 *would be sufficient of itself* and following: Clinton to Cornwallis, ibid., 19.

221 *immediately embark a part:* Ibid., 23.

221 *In the hope that your Lordship:* Ibid., 25.

222 *a very good position:* Ewald, *Hessian Journal*, 313.

222 *must also be master:* Ibid.

222 *The Americans who had several works* and following: Ibid.

223 *untill Virginia was to a degree subjected* and following: Cornwallis to Clinton, *CIV*, 2:33.

223 *[A]fter doing all the mischief:* Ibid.

CHAPTER 19 THE BATTLE OF GREEN SPRINGS

224 *They Have no Reason to Complain* and following: Lafayette to Nelson, *LAAR*, 4:228.

225 *I must say . . . that* and following: Ewald, *Hessian Journal*, 316.

225 *money and encouraging promises:* Tarleton, *Campaigns*, 353.

225 *The 6ᵗʰ I detached an advanced Corps:* Lafayette to Greene, *LAAR*, 4:236.

226 *Concluding that the Enemy would not:* Cornwallis to Clinton, *CIV*, 2:38.

226 *posted his army in an open-field:* Lafayette to Greene, *LAAR*, 4:236.

226 *I then put the Troops under Arms:* Cornwallis to Clinton, *CIV*, 2:38.

226 *The conflict on the quarter:* Tarleton, *Campaigns*, 353.

Portsmouth

227 *The intelligence which occasioned* and following: Tarleton, *Campaigns*, 358.

227 *This devil Cornwallis:* Lafayette to Vicomte de Noailles, *LAAR*, 4:241.

227 *I shall either follow his Lordship:* Ibid.

227 *The Ennemy appear to Be Going:* Lafayette to Nelson, ibid., 250.

229 *often so intense that one can hardly breathe* and following: Ewald, *Hessian Journal*, 318.

Correspondence

229 *which cannot have the smallest influence* and following: Cornwallis to Clinton, *CIV*, 2:57.

230 *a naval station for large ships* and following: Clinton, *The American Rebellion*, 541.

232 *I expect little exertion:* Germain to Knox, James, *British Navy in Adversity*, 240.

232 *seem to insinuate:* Clinton to Germain, *CIV*, 2:82.

233 *I can say little more:* Ibid.

233 *waited for a line from me* and following: Clinton to Cornwallis, *CIV*, 2:74.

234 *certainly have endeavored:* Clinton to Cornwallis, Clinton, *The American Rebellion*, 524.

234 *I cannot help observing:* Cornwallis to Clinton, *CIV*, 2:90.

234 *to me as unexpected* and following: Cornwallis to Clinton, ibid., 104.

CHAPTER 20 THE MARCH ON NEW YORK

236 *A splendid world* and following: Thacher, *Eyewitness*, 263.

237 *The roads are badly laid out:* Clermont-Crèvecoeur, "Journal," in Rice and Brown, *Campaigns of Rochambeau's Army*, 1:29.

237 *the beautiful, rich Connecticut valley* and following: Berthier, "Journal," in ibid., 249.

237 *the Enemys Posts* and following: Washington, *Diaries*, 231.

237 *as good locking soldiers as can be:* Rouse in Kennett, *French Forces*, 119.

237 *The soldiers marched pretty well:* Blanchard, *Journal*, 121.

238 *must have a happy tendency:* Thacher, *Eyewitness*, 263.

238 *I shall shortly have occasion:* Washington to Lafayette, *LAAR*, 4:247.

238 *Virginian Operations* and following: Lafayette to Washington, ibid., 286.

239 *The works on the Gloucester side* and following: Cornwallis to Clinton, *CIV*, 2:125.

The West Indies Fleets

239 *to proceed, with His Majesty's ships:* Admiralty to Graves, Chadwick, *Graves Papers*, 4.

240 *Let me hope:* Clinton to Rodney, Clinton, *The American Rebellion*, 533.

240 *desire to resign the Command:* Arbuthnot to Graves, Chadwick, *Graves Papers*, 21.

240 *will shew you the apprehension* and following: Graves to Rodney, ibid., 19.

241 *proceeded with the Squadron* and following: Graves to Stephens, ibid., 32.

241 *I must beg leave to repeat:* Clinton to Germain, *DAR*, 20:157.

241 *I have every reason to believe:* Germain to Clinton, ibid., 175.

242 *The Lares:* Hood to Jackson, Hood, *Letters*, 22.

242 *from their leaks:* Ibid., 12.

242 *I believe never:* Hood, quoted in James, *British Navy in Adversity,* 259.

243 *As the enemy has at this time* and following: Rodney to Arbuthnot, ibid., 539.

244 *the vestiges of several wrecked vessels* and following: Shea, *French Fleet,* 57.

244 *proper harbor for line-of-battle ships:* Clinton to Cornwallis, Clinton, *The American Rebellion,* 547.

244 *approbation of the plan:* Germain to Clinton, ibid., 546.

The Admiral's Decision

245 *The enemy is making* and following: Rochambeau to de Grasse, Lewis, *De Grasse,* 119.

245 *For this I have a stronger plea:* Washington to Luzerne, May 13, 1781, *WGW,* Vol. 21.

246 *the influence of his credit:* M. de Tarlé to de Grasse, in Lewis, *De Grasse,* 122.

247 *I must not conceal from you:* Rochambeau to de Grasse, ibid., 124.

247 *the* Intrepide *made a signal* and following: Shea, *French Fleet,* 59.

248 *25 or 26 ships of war:* De Grasse to Rochambeau, in Lewis, *De Grasse,* 124.

249 *The French fleet under Monsieur de Grasse:* Rodney to Arbuthnot, Chadwick, *Graves Papers,* 60.

249 *that a Spanish squadron:* Shea, *French Fleet,* 150.

250 *the famous dreaded channel:* Ibid.

250 *the richest and strongest:* Ibid., 63.

Chapter 21 An Operation to the Southward

251 *consisting of the most active:* Thacher, *Eyewitness,* 266.

251 *to cover and secure* and following: Washington, *Diaries,* 235.

251 *make it known* and following: Questions Posed by Rochambeau, *WP LC.*

253 *The American is at this time* and following: Washington to de Grasse, July 21, 1781, *WGW.*

253 *especially when I tell you:* Washington to Lafayette, July 30, 1781, *WGW,* Vol. 22.

254 *enabled him to form:* Mackenzie, *Diary,* 572.

254 *pointedly and continually* and following: Washington, *Diaries,* 248.

255 *with between 25 and 29 Sail:* Barras to Washington, August 14, 1781, *WP LC.*

Yorktown and Gloucester

256 *[W]e have bestowed:* Cornwallis to Clinton, *CIV,* 2:127.

256 *is to Guess:* Lafayette to Wayne, *LAAR,* 4:296.

256 *Should a french fleet Now Come:* Lafayette to Washington, *LAAR,* 4:312.

256 *I am positive the British Councils:* Ibid.

257 *Lord Cornwallis is Entrenching:* Ibid.

257 *all the labour that the troops here:* Cornwallis to Clinton, *CIV*, 2:138.

257 *suspend his offensive operations* and following: Clinton to Cornwallis, Clinton, *The American Rebellion*, 562.

258 *Count de Grasse:* Washington to Lafayette, *LAAR*, 4:330.

258 *Adieu, My dear General:* Lafayette to Washington, ibid., 339.

259 *[T]here are between:* Cornwallis to Clinton, *CIV*, 2:146.

"I immediately determined to proceed"

260 *It is quite impossible:* Hood to Jackson, James, *British Navy in Adversity*, 264.

260 *spoke with an armed brig:* Hood to Stephens, Chadwick, *Graves Papers*, 57.

260 *From thence I shall proceed:* Hood to Clinton, *CIV*, 2:141.

261 *foreseeing great delay:* Hood to Stephens, Chadwick, *Graves Papers*, 58.

261 *[T]he enemy's menaces:* Clinton, *The American Rebellion*, 320.

262 *humbly submitted the necessity:* Hood to Stephens, Chadwick, *Graves Papers*, 58.

262 *I immediately determined:* Graves to Stephens, ibid., 53.

262 *South: The* London*'s Log:* Ibid., 170.

CHAPTER 22 THE ARRIVAL OF DE GRASSE

263 *hindered by calms:* De Grasse to Washington, *LAAR*, 4:373.

263 *Lead showed fourteen fathoms:* Log of the *Citoyon*, Chadwick, *Graves Papers*, 222.

264 *the squadron commanders:* Ibid., 224.

264 *three or four vessels* and following: De Grasse to Lafayette, *LAAR*, 4:375.

265 *unless I am greatly deceived:* Lafayette to Washington, *LAAR*, 4:381.

265 *to shift the whole of the French Army:* Washington and Rochambeau to de Grasse, August 17, 1781, *WGW*, Vol. 23.

"I am distressed beyond expression"

266 *Matters having now come to a crisis:* Washington, *Diaries*, 254.

267 *We then expected we were to attack:* Martin, *Memoir*, 125.

267 *Our situation reminds me* and following: Thacher, *Eyewitness*, 269.

268 *But my dear Marquis, I am distressed* and following: Washington to Lafayette, *LAAR*, 4:385.

269 *From the Bottom of My Heart* and following: Lafayette to Washington, ibid., 380.

269 *whom I regard as blockaded* and following: De Grasse to Washington, Institut Français, *Correspondence of Washington and de Grasse*, 9.

270 *I have received with infinite satisfaction:* Washington to Lafayette, *LAAR*, 4:391.

Graves and de Grasse

270 *at 7 Bore away & M[ade] Sail* and following: Journal of the *London*, Chadwick, *Graves Papers*, 164.

271 *[A]bout 10 A.M.:* Hood to Jackson, Hood, *Letters*, 28.

272 *to Call In all Cruzers:* Journal of the *London*, ibid., 165.

272 *the Sigl. for the Line ahead:* Log of the *Barfleur*, ibid., 203.

273 *The vessels that were moored:* Log of the *Citoyon*, ibid., 224.

274 *At half past eleven:* Shea, *French Fleet*, 69.

274 *their topsail yards hoisted:* Hood to Jackson, Hood, *Letters*, 28.

CHAPTER 23 THE BATTLE OF THE CAPES

275 *The maneuver was accomplished:* Tornquist, *Naval Campaigns*, 58.

276 *the fleet to form* and following: Journal of the *Citoyon*, Chadwick, *Graves Papers*, 224.

276 *The fleet formed:* Shea, *French Fleet*, 69.

277 *Missing from Citoyon:* Journal of the *Citoyon*, Chadwick, *Graves Papers*, 229.

Line of Battle

278 *the English were in the best:* Shea, *French Fleet*, 69.

278 *made an immense number:* Ibid.

278 *at 40 Minutes past 12:* Journal of the *Royal Oak*, National Archives.

278 *began to come out:* Hood to Jackson, Chadwick, *Graves Papers*, 87.

279 *At 2 found the Enemy's fleet:* Log of the *London*, Chadwick, *Graves Papers*, 181.

279 *when I found that our van:* Graves to Stephens, ibid., 62.

280 *greatly extended beyond* and following: Hood to Jackson, Hood, *Letters*, 31.

280 *in Order to let the Center:* Log of the *London*, Chadwick, *Graves Papers*, 181.

280 *all vessels to follow:* Log of the fleet, ibid., 213.

281 *in order that the entire fleet:* Tornquist, *Naval Campaigns*, 59.

281 *So soon as I judged:* Graves to Stephens, Chadwick, *Graves Papers*, 62.

"[T]he action was begun at 4 o'clock"

281 *keep to Starbd* and following: Log of the *London*, Chadwick, *Graves Papers*, 181.

284 *at 4 o'Clock the Signal:* Journal of the *Royal Oak*, National Archives.

284 *[T]otally disabled very early:* Hood to Jackson, Hood, *Letters*, 32.

284 *exposed to two ships:* Ibid.

285 *five side timbers:* Report of the *Intrepid*, Chadwick, *Graves Papers*, 70.

285 *hauld down the Sigl.:* Log of the *London*, ibid., 183.

285 *the London had the signal:* Hood to Jackson, Hood, *Letters*, 29.

285 *When the signal for the line of battle:* James, *British Navy in Adversity*, 293.

286 *Now, had the centre gone:* Hood to Jackson, Hood, *Letters*, 32.

286 *The four ships in the van:* Shea, *French Fleet,* 71.

286 *impracticable, as they were fighting:* Ibid.

287 *hoisted sail and was soon in her wake:* Ibid.

287 *Main topmast shot thro':* Report of the *Princessa,* Chadwick, *Graves Papers,* 71.

287 *a most* improper *distance:* Hood to Jackson, Hood, *Letters,* 29.

287 *The enemy to windward:* Journal of the *Citoyon,* Chadwick, *Graves Papers,* 230.

288 *At 5 o'clock* and following: Tornquist, *Naval Campaigns,* 59.

288 *The van of the enemy:* Graves to Stephens, Chadwick, *Graves Papers,* 62.

288 *His letter I cannot understand:* Rodney to Stephens, ibid., 135.

288 *our centre division:* Hood to Jackson, Hood, *Letters,* 29.

288 *Repd. y Sigl. for a Closer Action:* Journal of the *London,* Chadwick, *Graves Papers,* 167.

289 *At 5:45* and following: Journal of the *Citoyon,* ibid., 231.

289 *Made the* Solebay's & Fortunee's: Log of the *London,* ibid., 183.

289 *After night I sent the frigates:* Graves to Stephens, ibid., 63.

289 *the Sigl for the Line:* Log of the *London,* ibid., 183.

Chapter 24 "The signal was not understood"

290 *several of the ships had suffered:* Graves to Stephens, Chadwick, *Graves Papers,* 63.

290 *The pumps blown:* Report of the *Terrible,* ibid., 72.

292 *when the enemy's van:* Hood to Sandwich, Barnes and Owen, *Private Papers of John, Earl of Sandwich,* 4:190.

292 *lay with the main topsail to the mast:* Graves to Sandwich, ibid., 182.

292 *to bear down and Engage:* Log of the *London,* Chadwick, *Graves Papers,* 183.

293 *I think had our efforts:* Graves to Sandwich, Barnes and Owen, *Private Papers of John, Earl of Sandwich,* 4:182

293 *the Admiral Made a Sigl:* Log of the *Barfleur,* Chadwick, *Graves Papers,* 204.

293 *shall be rendered ineffectual:* Graves, "Memorandum," in James, *British Navy in Adversity,* 293.

294 *every ship in the squadron:* quoted in Breen, *Graves and Hood,* 62.

294 *set the example of close action:* Hood to Jackson, Chadwick, *Graves Papers,* 91.

"Handsomely in a Pudding Bag"

295 *it would be difficult* and following: Von Closen, *Revolutionary Journal,* 121.

296 *torrent of good news:* Tucker to Fanny, Commager and Morris, *Spirit of 'Seventy-Six,* 1218.

296 *The business with his Lordship* and following: Weedon to Greene, ibid.

Battle's End

297 *she had lost 120 men:* Shea, *French Fleet,* 73.

297 *Employ'd Knotting and Splicing the Rigging:* Log of the *Royal Oak,* National Archives.

297 *Nineteen lower shrouds:* Report of the *Montagu,* Chadwick, *Graves Papers,* 73.

298 *Main & Fore Mast:* Log of the *London,* ibid., 183.

298 *they had not the appearance:* Graves to Stephens, ibid., 63.

298 *We continued all day:* Ibid.

299 *desiring his opinion* and following: Hood to Jackson, Hood, *Letters,* 29.

299 *The admiral signaled:* Journal of the *Citoyon,* Chadwick, *Graves Papers,* 230.

299 *We had not speed enough:* Graves to Stephens, ibid., 65.

300 *Squally with Thunder:* Log of the *London,* Chadwick, *Graves Papers,* 191.

300 *The English held the north:* Shea, *French Fleet,* 157.

300 *in a line badly formed:* French account of the actions, Chadwick, *Graves Papers,* 254.

300 *to pass within the distance:* Tornquist, *Naval Campaigns,* 60.

301 *These repeated misfortunes:* Graves to Stephens, Chadwick, *Graves Papers,* 64.

301 *On the 9th* and following: Hood to Jackson, ibid., 88.

302 *I flatter myself* and following: Hood to Graves, ibid., 92.

302 *should get into the Chesapeake* and following: Hood to Jackson, ibid., 89.

302 *may be of Service to some other Ship:* Finch to Graves, ibid., 78.

303 *take out her People:* Council of War, ibid., 80.

303 *H[is] M[ajesty's] Ship Terrible:* Log of the *London,* Chadwick, *Graves Papers,* 197.

303 *They paid dearly:* Shea, *French Fleet,* 73.

304 *the French fleet are at anchor:* Graves to Hood, Chadwick, *Graves Papers,* 93.

304 *it is no more than what* and following: Hood to Graves, ibid., 93.

304 *the position of the Enemy* and following: Council of War, ibid., 83.

CHAPTER 25 THE SIEGE OF YORKTOWN

305 *This state of hope:* Tarleton, *Campaigns,* 365.

306 *no doubt that Washington is moving:* Clinton to Cornwallis, ibid., 418.

306 *in too unfinished a state:* Ibid., 368.

306 *If I had no hopes of relief:* Cornwallis to Clinton, ibid., 419.

306 *England must lament the inactivity:* Ibid., 365.

307 *[b]y examining the transports:* Cornwallis to Clinton, ibid., 419.

307 *This place is in no state:* Ibid.

307   *Nothing but the want:* General Orders, in Johnston, *Yorktown Campaign,* 95.

307   *a great deficiency:* Washington, *Diaries,* 259.

307   *Great joy in town* and following: Trumbull, "Minutes," 333.

308   *an account of an action:* Ibid.

308   *Much agitated* and following: Ibid.

309   *Never was more joy painted* and following: Tucker to Fanny, Commager and Morris, *Spirit of 'Seventy-Six,* 1224.

"[M]on cher petit général!"

310   *to express the Pleasure* and following: Washington to de Grasse, Institut Français, *Correspondence of Washington and de Grasse,* 31.

310   *all the transports which M. du Barras:* De Grasse to Washington, ibid., 33.

311   *resembled a swamp:* Martin, *Memoir,* 127.

311   *the most noble and majestic spectacle:* Thacher, *Eyewitness,* 278.

311   *received with great ceremony* and following: Trumbull, "Minutes," 333.

311   *The Peace & Independence:* Questions, Institut Français, *Correspondence of Washington and de Grasse,* 36.

312   *soon dispatched to great satisfaction* and following: Trumbull, "Minutes," 333.

313   *we sail fast in our boat* and following: Ibid.

313   *a large fleet* and following: Martin, *Memoir,* 126.

314   *the naval engagement:* Thacher, *Eyewitness,* 277.

314   *not keeping that look out:* Symonds to Graves, Chadwick, *Graves Papers,* 128.

315   *[T]he impatience, or want of resolution:* Tarleton, *Campaigns,* 366.

315   *The enemy are beginning:* De Grasse to Washington, Institut Français, *Correspondence of Washington and de Grasse,* 45.

316   *Sir, I cannot conceal from your Excellency:* Washington to de Grasse, ibid., 48.

316   *the plans I had suggested:* De Grasse to Washington, ibid., 51.

"[T]he epoch which will decide American Independence"

316   *will probably be rendered:* Trumbull, "Minutes," 334.

317   *one wish throughout:* Cornwallis to Clinton, Clinton, *The American Rebellion,* 577.

317   *above five thousand men:* Clinton to Cornwallis, *CIV,* 2:160.

318   *the greatest satisfaction:* Cornwallis to Clinton, ibid., 164.

318   *I trust before the end of that Month:* Germain to Clinton, ibid., 167.

318   *In the morning it is discovered:* Trumbull, "Minutes," 336.

318   *Immediately . . . we possessed them:* Washington, *Diaries,* 263.

319   *The present moment offers:* quoted in Johnston, *Yorktown Campaign,* 122.

319   *a mere ceremony:* Martin, *Memoir,* 130.

319 *All our batteries open* and following: Trumbull, "Minutes," 336.

320 *The greater part of the town:* Ewald, *Hessian Journal,* 334.

320 *I have told everyone:* Ibid., 335.

321 *the repairs of the squadron:* Hood to Jackson, Chadwick, *Graves Papers,* 117.

321 *to have three or four fire ships:* Ibid.

321 *the enemy's fleet may possibly:* Ibid.

321 *My situation now becomes very critical:* Cornwallis to Clinton, Tarleton, *Campaigns,* 369.

322 *The whole of our works:* Thacher, *Eyewitness,* 286.

322 *Expect to begin our new roar:* Trumbull, "Minutes," 337.

EPILOGUE: "A MOST GLORIOUS DAY"

323 *I have the mortification:* Cornwallis to Clinton, Tarleton, *Campaigns,* 340.

323 *under engagement not to serve:* Cornwallis to Washington, Commager and Morris, *Spirit of 'Seventy-Six,* 1240.

323 *inadmissable:* Ibid.

323 *declare the general Basis:* Ibid.

323 *This is to us a most glorious day:* Thacher, *Eyewitness,* 289.

324 *were clad in small jackets:* Von Closen, *Revolutionary Journal,* 153.

324 *manifested a* sullen temper: Thacher, *Eyewitness,* 290.

325 *that Government might be prepared* and following: Graves to Stephens,z Chadwick, *Graves Papers,* 138.

325 *been able to sail at:* Clinton to Germain, Clinton, *The American Rebellion,* 586.

326 *To this inferiority, then* and following: Ibid.

Echoes of Yorktown

327 *If you are not more successful:* Sandwich to Hood, Barnes and Owen, *Private Papers of John, Earl of Sandwich,* 4:201.

327 *an ecstacy of joy:* quoted in Schiff, *Great Improvisation,* 289.

327 *Oh God! it is all over!:* North, quoted in Mackesy, *War for America,* 435.

328 *I consider myself:* De Grasse to Washington, Institut Français, *Correspondence of Washington and de Grasse,* 153.

331 *to forget all past misunderstandings:* Ford, *Journal of the Continental Congress,* 26:23.

George Washington and the Importance of Naval Power

333 *In any operations:* quoted in Knox, *Naval Genius,* 62.

Bibliography

Primary Sources

Barnes, G. R., and J. H. Owen, eds. *The Private Papers of John, Earl of Sandwich, First Lord of the Admiralty, 1771–1782*. London: Naval Records Society, 1936.

Blanchard, Claude. *The Journal of Claude Blanchard, Commissary of the French Auxiliary Army Sent to the United States During the American Revolution, 1780–1783*, edited by Thomas Balch. Translated by William Duane. Albany, NY: J. Munsell, 1876.

Chadwick, French Ensor, ed. *The Graves Papers and Other Documents Relating to the Naval Operations of the Yorktown Campaign*. New York: Naval History Society, 1916.

Clinton, Sir Henry. *The American Rebellion: Sir Henry Clinton's Narrative of His Campaigns, 1775–1782, with an Appendix of Original Documents*, edited by William Willcox. New Haven, CT: Yale University Press, 1954.

Closen, Ludwig, Baron von. *Revolutionary Journal, 1780–1783*. Translated by Evelyn M. Acomb. Chapel Hill, NC: University of North Carolina Press, 1958.

Commager, Henry Steele, and Richard B. Morris. *The Spirit of 'Seventy-Six: The Story of the American Revolution as Told by Its Participants*. 1967. Reprint, New York: Castle Books, 2002.

Cornwallis, Charles, First Marquis. *Correspondence*, edited by Charles Ross, Esq. London: John Murray, Albemarle Street, 1859.

Davis, K. G., ed. *Documents of the American Revolution*. Vol. 17; Vol. 20, *Transcripts, 1781*. Dublin: Irish University Press, 1979.

Ewald, Captain Johann. *Diary of the American War: A Hessian Journal*. Translated by Joseph P. Tustin. New Haven, CT, and London: Yale University Press, 1979.

Falconer, William. *An Universal Dictionary of the Marine*. 1780. Reprint, Devon, UK: David and Charles (Publishers) Limited, 1970.

Ford, Worthington Chauncey, ed. *Journals of the Continental Congress, 1774–1789*, Washington, DC: Government Printing Office, 1905 (online version).

Graves, Thomas. *The Graves Papers and Other Documents Related to the Naval Operations of the Yorktown Campaign*, edited by French Ensor Chadwick, New York: Printed for the Naval History Society, 1916.

Greene, Nathanael. *The Papers of Nathanael Greene*, edited by Richard Showman. Vol. 6, 7, 8. Chapel Hill and London: The University of North Carolina Press, 1991.

Guillaume, comte de Deux-Ponts. *My Campaigns in America: A Journal Kept By Count William de Deux-Ponts, 1780–81*, edited and translated by Samuel Abbot Green. Boston: J. K. Wiggin and W. P. Lunt, 1868.

Henri, Doniol. *Histoire de la Participation de la France à l'Establissement des États-Unis d'Amérique: Correspondance Diplomatique et Documents*. Library Resources, 1970, microfiche, LAC 21022.

Hood, Sir Samuel. *Letters Written by Sir Samuel Hood in 1781–2–3*, edited by David Hannay. London: Printed for the Naval Records Society, 1895.

Idzerda, Stanley J., et al., eds. *Lafayette in the Age of the American Revolution, Selected Letters and Papers, 1776–1790*. Vol. 3 and 4. Ithaca, NY: Cornell University Press, 1981.

The Institut Français de Washington, ed. *Correspondence of General Washington and Comte de Grasse, 1781, August 1–November 4*. Washington, DC: United States Government Printing Office, 1931.

Jefferson, Thomas. *The Papers of Thomas Jefferson*, edited by Julian P. Boyd. Princeton, NJ: Princeton University Press, 1950.

Journal of the Honorable Regiment Von Bose, 1776–1783. Courtesy of Guilford Courthouse National Military Park, Greensboro, NC.

A Journal of the Proceedings of His Majesty's Ship the London. National Archives, Public Records Office, Kew, England, Admiralty Records ADM 51/552.

Key Original Source Outline for the Battle of Guilford Courthouse. Courtesy of Guilford Court House National Military Park, Greensboro, NC, 2005.

Kirkwood, Robert. *The Journal and Order Book of Captain Robert Kirkwood of the Delaware Regiment of the Continental Line*, edited by Rev. Joseph Brown Turner. 1910. Reprint, Port Washington, NY: Kennikat Press, 1970.

Lafayette, Marquis de (Marie-Joseph-Paul-Yves-Roch-Gilbert du Motier). *Memoirs Correspondence and Manuscripts of General Lafayette, Published by his Family*. New York: Saunders and Otley, 1837.

Lamb, Roger. *A British Soldier's Story: Roger Lamb's Narrative of the American Revolution*, edited by Don N. Hagist. Baraboo, WI: Ballindalloch Press, 2004.

Lee, Henry. *Memoirs of the War in the Southern Department of the United States*. 1812. Reprint, New York: Arno Press, 1969.

Mackenzie, Frederick. *The Diary of Frederick Mackenzie*. Vol. 2. Cambridge, MA: Harvard University Press, 1930.

Martin, Joseph Plumb. *Memoir of a Revolutionary Soldier*. 1830. Reprint, New York: Dover Publications, 2006.

Moultrie, William. *Memoirs of the American Revolution so Far as it Relates to the States of North and South Carolina, and Georgia.* 1802. Reprint, New York: The New York Times and Arno Press, 1968.

Newsome, A.R., ed. "A British Orderly Book, 1780–1781." *North Carolina Historical Review* 9, no. 1 (1932).

Relation de la sortie de l'Escadre Française, aux ordres du Ch^{er}. Destouches, & de l'affaire qui a eue lieu le 16 Mars 1781, entre cette Escadre & celle des Anglais, commandée par l'Admiral Arbuthnot. Copy in the American Antiquarian Society, Worchester, MA.

Rice, Howard C., Jr., and Anne S. K. Brown, eds. *The American Campaigns of Rochambeau's Army, 1780, 1781, 1782, 1783.* Vol. 1 and 2. Princeton, NJ: Princeton University Press, and Providence, RI: Brown University Press, 1972.

Rochambeau, Marshal Count de. *Memoirs of the Marshal Count de Rochambeau Relative to the War of Independence of the United States.* Translated by M. W. E. Wright. 1838. Reprint, New York: The New York Times and Arno Press, 1971.

Rodney, George, Lord. *Letter-Books and Order-Books of George, Lord Rodney, Admiral of the White Squadron, 1780–1782.* New York: Naval History Society, 1932.

Royal Oak's Journal. National Archives, Public Records Office, Kew, England, Admiralty Records, ADM 51/815.

Seymour, William. "A Journal of the Southern Expedition, 1780–1783." *Pennsylvania Magazine of History and Biography* 7 (1883).

Shea, John Dawson Gilmary, ed. *The Operations of the French Fleet under the Count de Grasse in 1781–2 as Described in Two Contemporaneous Journals.* 1864. Chicago: Library Resources, 1970, microfiche, LAC 16843.

Simcoe, Lieutenant Colonel John G. *A Journal of the Operations of the Queen's Rangers.* 1844. Reprint, New York: Arno Press, 1968.

Stevens, Benjamin Franklin, ed. *The Campaign in Virginia, 1781.* Vol. 1 and 2. London: Benjamin Franklin Stevens, 1888.

Tarleton, Lieutenant-Colonel Banastre. *A History of the Campaigns of 1780 and 1781 in the Southern Provinces of North America.* 1787. Reprint, Chapel Hill, NC: University of North Carolina, 1967.

Thacher, James, M.D. *Eyewitness to the American Revolution: The Battles and Generals as Seen by an Army Surgeon.* 1862. Reprint, Stamford, CT: Longmeadow Press, 1994.

Tornquist, Karl Gustaf. *The Naval Campaigns of Count de Grasse During the American Revolution, 1781–1783.* Translated by Amandus Johnson. Philadelphia: Swedish Colonial Society, 1942.

Trumbull, Jonathan. "Minutes of Occurrences Respecting the Siege and Capture of Yorktown." *Massachusetts Historical Society Proceedings* XIV (1875–1876), 331–38.

Washington, George. *The Writings of George Washington*, edited by John C. Fitzpatrick. Charlottesville, VA: University of Virginia Library, 1931–1944.
http://etext.virginia.edu/washington/fitzpatrick.
———. *The Diaries of George Washington, 1748–1799*, edited by John C. Fitzpatrick. Vol. 2. Boston: Houghton Mifflin, 1925.
———. *The Papers of George Washington*. Library of Congress,
http://memory.loc.gov/ammem/gwhtml/gwseries.html.
Zemenszky, Edith, von, ed. *The Papers of General Friedrich von Steuben*. Mill-
wood, NY: 1976–84, microfilm.

SECONDARY SOURCES

Allen, Gardner. *A Naval History of the American Revolution*. 1913. Reprint,
Williamstown, MA: Corner House Publishers, 1970.
Babits, Lawrence E., and Joshua B. Howard. *Long, Obstinate, and Bloody: The
Battle of Guilford Courthouse*. Chapel Hill, NC: The University of North Car-
olina Press, 2009.
Boyd, Thomas. *Mad Anthony Wayne*. New York: Charles Scribner's Sons, 1929.
Breen, Kenneth. "Graves and Hood at the Chesapeake." *Mariner's Mirror* 66
(1980).
Coggins, Jack. *Ships and Seamen of the American Revolution*. Harrisburg, PA:
Promontory Press, 1969.
Davis, Burt. *The Cowpens-Guilford Courthouse Campaign*. Philadelphia and New
York: J. B. Lippincott Company, 1962.
Drake, Francis S. *Dictionary of American Biography*. Boston: Houghton, Osgood
& Company, 1879.
Dull, Jonathan R. *The French Navy and American Independence: A Study of Arms
and Diplomacy, 1774–1787*. Princeton, NJ: Princeton University Press,
1975.
Elting, John, ed. *Military Uniforms in America: The Era of the American Revolu-
tion, 1755–1795*. San Rafael, CA: Presidio Press, 1974.
Fischer, David Hackett. *Washington's Crossing*. Oxford: Oxford University
Press, 2004.
Fleming, Thomas. *Liberty!: The American Revolution*. New York: Viking, 1997.
Hatch, Charles E., Jr. *The Battle of Guilford Courthouse*. Washington, DC: Office
of History and Historic Architecture, Eastern Service Center, 1971.
James, Captain W. M., C.B., R.N. *The British Navy in Adversity: A Study of the
War of American Independence*. London: Longmans, Green and Co., Ltd.,
1926.
Johnston, Henry P. *The Yorktown Campaign and the Surrender of Cornwallis,
1781*. New York: Harper & Brothers, 1881.
Kennett, Lee. *The French Forces in America, 1780–1783*. Westport, CT: Green-
wood Press, 1977.

Ketchum, Richard M. *Victory at Yorktown: The Campaign that Won the American Revolution.* New York: Henry Holt and Company, 2004.

Knox, Dudley W. *The Naval Genius of George Washington.* Boston: Houghton Mifflin Company, 1932.

Larrabee, Harold Atkins. *Decision at the Chesapeake.* New York: C.N. Potter, 1964.

Lee, Henry. *The Campaign of 1781 in the Carolinas With remarks Historical and Critical on Johnson's Life of Greene.* 1824. Reprint, Chicago: Quadrangle Books, 1962.

Lewis, Charles Lee. *Admiral De Grasse and American Independence.* Annapolis, MD: United States Naval Institute, 1945.

Lockhart, Paul. *The Drillmaster of Valley Forge: The Baron de Steuben and the Making of the American Army.* New York: Harper Collins, 2008.

Maass, John. "There Never Was a More Compleat Victory: Gates, Cornwallis, and the Battle of Camden, August 16, 1780." 2000. www.battleofcamden.org.

Macintyre, Captain Donald, R.N. *Admiral Rodney.* New York: W. W. Norton and Company, 1962.

Mackesy, Piers. *The War for America, 1775–1783.* 1964. Reprint, Lincoln, NE, and London: University of Nebraska Press, 1992.

Mahan, A. T. *The Influence of Seapower Upon History, 1660–1783.* 1890. Reprint, New York: Hill and Wang, 1957.

Martin, James Kirby. *Benedict Arnold, Revolutionary Hero: An American Warrior Reconsidered.* New York: New York University Press, 1997.

Middlekauff, Robert. *The Glorious Cause: The American Revolution, 1763–1789.* New York and Oxford: Oxford University Press, 1982.

Millar, John Fitzhugh. *Early American Ships.* Williamsburg, VA: Thirteen Colonies Press, 1986.

Miller, Nathan. *Sea of Glory.* Annapolis, MD: Naval Institute Press, 1974.

Schiff, Stacy. *A Great Improvisation: Franklin, France, and the Birth of America.* New York: Henry Holt and Company, 2005.

Stone, Edwin. *Our French Allies.* Providence, RI: The Providence Press Company, 1884.

Ward, Christopher. *The War of the Revolution.* New York: The Macmillan Company, 1952.

White, Thomas. *Naval Researches; Or a Candid Inquiry into the Conduct of Admirals Byron, Graves, Hood and Rodney, in the action off Grenada, Chesapeake, St. Christophers, and of the Ninth and Twelfth of April, 1782.* 1830. Reprint, Boston: Greg Press, 1972.

Willcox, William B. "Rhode Island in British Strategy, 1780–1781." *Journal of Modern History* 17: 318–21.

Wright, Robert K. *The Continental Army.* Washington, DC: Center of Military History, United States Army, 1983.

INDEX